COLLABORATIVE CAPITAL:
CREATING INTANGIBLE VALUE

ADVANCES IN INTERDISCIPLINARY STUDIES OF WORK TEAMS

Series Editor: Michael M. Beyerlein

Volume 1:   Theories of Self-Managing Work Teams
Volume 2:   Knowledge Work in Teams
Volume 3:   Team Leadership
Volume 4:   Team Implementation Issues
Volume 5:   Product Development Teams
Volume 6:   Team Performance Management
Volume 7:   Team Development
Volume 8:   Virtual Teams
Volume 9:   Team-Based Organizing
Volume 10: Complex Collaboration

COLLABORATIVE CAPITAL: CREATING INTANGIBLE VALUE

EDITED BY

MICHAEL M. BEYERLEIN
Department of Psychology, University of North Texas, USA

SUSAN T. BEYERLEIN
Department of Psychology, University of North Texas, USA

FRANCES A. KENNEDY
School of Accountancy and Legal Studies, Clemson University, South Carolina, USA

2005

ELSEVIER
JAI

Amsterdam – Boston – Heidelberg – London – New York – Oxford
Paris – San Diego – San Francisco – Singapore – Sydney – Tokyo

ELSEVIER B.V.	ELSEVIER Inc.	**ELSEVIER Ltd**	ELSEVIER Ltd
Radarweg 29	525 B Street, Suite 1900	**The Boulevard, Langford**	84 Theobalds Road
P.O. Box 211	San Diego	**Lane, Kidlington**	London
1000 AE Amsterdam	CA 92101-4495	**Oxford OX5 1GB**	WC1X 8RR
The Netherlands	USA	**UK**	UK

First edition 2005

British Library Cataloguing in Publication Data
A catalogue record is available from the British Library.

ISBN: 0-7623-1222-X
ISSN: 1572-0977 (Series)

∞ The paper used in this publication meets the requirements of ANSI/NISO Z39.48-1992 (Permanence of Paper).
Printed in The Netherlands.

Working together to grow
libraries in developing countries

www.elsevier.com | www.bookaid.org | www.sabre.org

ELSEVIER   BOOK AID
             International   Sabre Foundation

CONTENTS

LIST OF CONTRIBUTORS   *vii*

ACKNOWLEDGEMENTS   *ix*

ABOUT THE EDITORS   *xi*

INTRODUCTION
    Michael M. Beyerlein, Susan T. Beyerlein and   *xiii*
    Frances A. Kennedy

RESEARCH TEAMS IN AN AUSTRALIAN
BIOTECHNOLOGY FIELD: HOW INTELLECTUAL
PROPERTY INFLUENCES COLLABORATION
    Melissa Marot, John W. Selsky, William Hart and   *1*
    Prasuna Reddy

CREATING CULTURES OF COLLABORATION THAT
THRIVE ON DIVERSITY: A TRANSFORMATIONAL
PERSPECTIVE ON BUILDING COLLABORATIVE
CAPITAL
    Nancy L. Southern   *33*

EXPLOITING INTELLECTUAL AND
COLLABORATIVE CAPITAL FOR INNOVATION IN
KNOWLEDGE-INTENSIVE INDUSTRIES
    Anne H. Koch   *73*

CONNECTING ACROSS MILES AND WIRES:
EXAMINING COLLABORATIVE CAPITAL
DEVELOPMENT IN VIRTUAL SPACES
    Lindsey Godwin and Julie Rennecker   *91*

STRIVING FOR A NEW IDEAL: A WORK
ENVIRONMENT TO ENERGIZE COLLABORATIVE
CAPACITY ACROSS EAST AND WEST BOUNDARIES
    Jill Nemiro, Stefanus Hanifah and Jing Wang   *115*

TEAM-MEMBER EXCHANGE AND INDIVIDUAL
CONTRIBUTIONS TO COLLABORATIVE CAPITAL IN
ORGANIZATIONS
    Melvin L. Smith   *161*

LEADING TOGETHER, WORKING TOGETHER: THE
ROLE OF TEAM SHARED LEADERSHIP IN
BUILDING COLLABORATIVE CAPITAL IN VIRTUAL
TEAMS
    N. Sharon Hill   *183*

LEADERSHIP, COLLABORATIVE CAPITAL, AND
INNOVATION
    Xiaomeng Zhang and Henry P. Sims, Jr.   *211*

MINIMIZING THE IMPACT OF ORGANIZATIONAL
DISTRESS ON INTELLECTUAL AND SOCIAL
CAPITAL THROUGH DEVELOPMENT OF
COLLABORATIVE CAPITAL
    Michael F. Kennedy and Michael M. Beyerlein   *237*

MANAGING SOCIAL ENTROPY IN THE URBAN
DEVELOPMENT OF A CITY AND THE ROLE OF
SOCIO-ENGINEERING
    Claudia Bettiol   *285*

KNOTWORKING TO CREATE COLLABORATIVE
INTENTIONALITY CAPITAL IN FLUID
ORGANIZATIONAL FIELDS
    Yrjö Engeström   *307*

LIST OF CONTRIBUTORS

Claudia Bettiol	Via Fontana dell'Oste snc, Colleferro, Rome, Italy
Michael M. Beyerlein	Center for Collaborative Organizations, Denton, TX, USA
Yrjo Engestrom	Center for Activity Theory and Developmental Work Research, University of Helsinki, Helsinki, Finland
Lindsey Godwin	Weatherhead School of Management, Case Western Reserve University, Cleveland, OH, USA
Stefanus Hanifah	California State Polytechnic University, Pomona, W. Temple Ave., Pomana, CA, USA
William Hart	Department of Psychology, University of Melbourne, Parkville, Victoria, Australia
Michael F. Kennedy	Center for Collaborative Organizations, Denton, TX, USA
Anne Koch	Haas School of Business, University of California, Berkeley, CA, USA
Melissa Marot	Department of Psychology, University of Melbourne, Parkville, Victoria, Australia
Jill Nemiro	California State Polytechnic University, Pomona, W. Temple Ave., Pomona, CA, USA
Prasuna Reddy	Department of Psychology, University of Melbourne, Parkville, Victoria, Australia
Julie Rennecker	Weatherhead School of Management, Case Western Reserve University, Cleveland, OH, USA

John W. Selsky   Department of Psychology, University of
                          Melbourne, Parkville, Victoria, Australia

N. Sharon Hill   University of Maryland, College Park,
                          MD, USA

Henry P. Sims, Jr.   (Americanized: Alice) University of
                          Maryland, College Park, MD, USA

Melvin L. Smith   Weatherhead School of Management, Case
                          Western Reserve University, Cleveland,
                          OH, USA

Nancy Southern   Saybrook Graduate School and Research
                          Center, Danville, CA, USA

Jing Wang   California State Polytechnic University,
                          Pomona, W. Temple Ave., Pomana, CA,
                          USA

Xiaomeng Zhang   (Americanized: Alice) University of
                          Maryland, College Park, MD, USA

ACKNOWLEDGEMENTS

This work was partially supported by the Center for Collaborative Organizations, which was formerly The Center for the Study of Work Teams, at The University of North Texas. The change in name reflects our recognition that collaboration occurs at many levels of organization besides the team level. The Center has always considered bridging of the gap between the worlds of research and practice as a primary mission. The success of that bridging is critical for understanding practice and for basing practice on tested theory. The chapters in this book reflect this kind of bridging partnership.

We want to acknowledge the help and support of Nancy Gorman. For five of the 11 volumes in this series, Nancy has been responsible for communicating with authors, editors, and the publisher, arranging for flow of manuscripts back and forth among these people, educating all of us on manuscript format, arranging for proofing, catching the errors the editors miss and bringing the chapters, introduction, and preface together in a final assembly to complete a whole for the publisher. Nancy has done an outstanding job under significant time pressure to pull the pieces together into a carefully prepared manuscript. She has consistently taken the initiative to look for new ways to contribute – modeling the attitudes and skills that collaboration depends on. Much of the quality in appearance for this volume is due to her thoughtful work.

ABOUT THE EDITORS

Michael M. Beyerlein is Director of the Center for Collaborative Organizations (www.workteams.unt.edu) and Professor of Industrial/Organizational Psychology at the University of North Texas. His research interests include all aspects of collaborative work systems, organization transformation, work stress, creativity/innovation, intangible capital, knowledge management and the learning organization, and complex adaptive systems. He has published in a number of journals and has been a member of the editorial boards for *TEAM Magazine, Team Performance Management Journal*, and *Quality Management Journal*. Currently, he is senior editor of the Elsevier annual series of books *Advances in Interdisciplinary Studies of Work Teams* and the Jossey-Bass/Pfeiffer *Collaborative Work Systems Series*. He has authored or edited 15 books. His most recent are *Guiding the Journey to Collaborative Work Systems: A Strategic Design Workbook* (2003) and *Complex Collaboration* (2004). He has been involved in projects at the Center for Collaborative Organizations (formerly, The Center for the Study of Work Teams) with such companies as Boeing, Shell, NCH, AMD, Raytheon, First American Financial, Westinghouse, and Xerox and with government agencies such as Veterans Affairs, DCMAO, EPA, and the City of Denton.

Susan Tull Beyerlein holds a Ph.D. in organization theory and policy with a minor in education research from the University of North Texas. Since 1995, she has been an instructor of business and psychology at Our Lady of the Lake University in Irving, Texas. Susan has served as a research scientist/project manager with the Center for Collaborative Organizations at the University of North Texas, and has been a recipient of research grant awards from the Association for Quality and Participation, the National Science Foundation, and corporate donors. Since 1995, she has co-edited the Elsevier/JAI Imprint annual book series entitled, Advances in Interdisciplinary Studies of Work Teams, and has served as an *ad hoc* reviewer for The Academy of Management Review. She has been an editor of the Jossey-Bass/Pfeiffer Collaborative Work Systems series since its inception. Susan has published book reviews on contemporary business offerings in Business and the Contemporary World, and her work has also appeared in Structural Equation Modeling: A Multidisciplinary Journal, Journal of Management Education, Empirical Studies of the Arts, and Multiple Linear Regression Viewpoints. She is a member of the Academy of Management, Beta Gamma Sigma – the honor society for collegiate schools of business, and Phi Kappa Phi National Honor Society.

Frances A. Kennedy is an Assistant Professor at Clemson University. Her interest in teaming organizations comes after thirteen years of experience of industry and public accounting experience, including eight years with Rubbermaid, Inc., where she was extensively involved with the team pilot facility. She has published in the area of intellectual capital and conducts research in lean manufacturing, teams, performance measurement, and decision making. Recent articles are found *Advances in Interdisciplinary Studies of Work Teams* and *The Collaborative Work Systems Fieldbook*. Dr. Kennedy has also presented papers on team strategies and lean manufacturing at numerous international and national conferences. She continues research projects with several Fortune 500 companies.

INTRODUCTION

Attention focusing on intangible forms of capital is increasing in both research and practice. Lev and Zambon (2003) write in the introduction of a special issue of the *European Accounting Review*, "We strongly believe that intangibles are the major drivers of company growth" (p. 597). Intellectual capital seems to have led the way in the conceptual development of intangible values. However, other forms of intangible capital are being defined, including: organizational, human, relationship, social, political, innovation, and collaborative. This volume consists of papers that focus on the latter. We broadly define collaborative capital as the organizational assets that enable people to work together well. It is manifested in such outcomes as increased innovation and creativity, commitment and involvement, flexibility and adaptability, leveraging knowledge, and enhancing learning.

Collaborative capital may be categorized as a core competency, that is, a strategic resource. However, since it is seldom developed in a deliberate and systematic way, it is usually an incidental outcome of formal and informal organizational change. It may be increased by both formal and informal change in organizational systems, practices, design, learning, and culture.

Organizations may be viewed as networks of conversations and relationships where shared mental models enable the group to invest jointly to achieve challenging goals. The social technology and knowledge of soft infrastructure necessary for designing organizations that excel as such networks has been growing rapidly in a number of disciplines in the past decade. That knowledge captures the experiments managers are conducting with their business designs and codifies guidelines others can follow to increase the viability of their own organizations in the turbulent business environment. Effective collaboration is one of the cornerstones of viable organizations but limited conceptual and accounting tools for making the value of collaboration visible has limited the ability of strategic decision makers and change agents in developing collaboration as a core competency.

Since both research and practice are in early stages of development and evolving rapidly, a number of important basic and applied questions arise around the importance of collaboration such as: How is the value of collaboration...:

- captured by performance measurement systems,
- affected by accounting and finance functions,
- used by strategic decision makers,
- treated as a strategic goal,
- recognized as an avenue for generating other forms of capital including intellectual and financial.

Furthermore, the term collaborative capital has seldom been used in research literature dealing with how people work together. Consequently, the meaning, measurement, and impact of collaborative capital in practice have not been explored to any significant extent. As this is a relatively new topic, investigations are beginning to address some of the issues listed below that will aid our understanding of the nature of the collaborative capital construct, its behavior in various organizational settings under specific conditions, and its role in improving organizational performance. Specific inquiry efforts generally involve building the case implicitly or explicitly that collaborative capital is a useful concept for research and practice, and that it represents an organizational asset that adds significant value and contributes to competitive advantage. Potential areas of research include:

- Examining the ways collaborative capital impacts executive performance;
- Articulating the role of collaborative capital as a core competency;
- Reviewing principles of collaboration in light of their ability to contribute to collaborative capital;
- Linking collaborative capital to other forms of intangible capital, such as social, intellectual, organizational, relationship, and human capital;
- Building collaborative capital across boundaries, whether functional, geographic, or line of business, that allows the partners to find broader solutions to business challenges;
- Clarifying the process and context that enhances and extends individual expertise through collaboration to build collaborative capital;
- Identifying the circumstances where collaboration pays the largest dividends, such as with increased complexity of products;
- Specifying the outcomes of collaborative capital such as the ability to cross technical boundaries to find multidisciplinary solutions, enhance learning at organizational and individual levels, and generate solutions that are more innovative and integrated;

- Modeling the processes, conditions, support, success factors, and best practices that intentionally build collaborative capital;
- Analyzing company cases to reveal exemplary processes for building and capitalizing on collaborative capital;
- Demonstrating the role of collaborative capital in enabling effectiveness in supply chains, value chains, and value webs;
- Using of collaborative capital as a criterion for merger and acquisition choices;
- Linking trust with collaborative capital as the core process for building collaborative advantage;
- Articulating ways collaborative capital contributes to organizational alignment;
- Articulating ways collaborative capital contributes to organizational adaptability;
- Specifying the role of collaborative capital in specific organizational settings, such as research, R&D, new product development, and virtual organization;
- Identifying the ways collaborative capital contributes to strategy implementation and its coordination with organizational structure, management systems, and managerial behavior, with special focus on alternative ways to improve management and corporate performance;
- Finding solutions to the problems identified in the implementation of the balanced scorecard in capturing intangible forms of capital with an emphasis on collaborative capital;
- Linking performance metrics to strategy through new means, i.e., not confined to systems employing balanced scorecard and shareholder value analysis, with an emphasis on collaborative capital;
- Examining the ways collaborative capital contributes to and benefits from the drivers of corporate performance and the linkages between them;
- Analyzing the conditions under which selected performance measurement and management control systems are more or less effective in building collaborative capital;
- Evaluating non-financial performance metrics in decision making by various stakeholders with a focus on collaborative capital;
- Examining cross-border and cross-culture differences in the use of management control and performance measurement systems that suggest variation in methods for building collaborative capital;
- Framing the link between organizational culture and collaborative capital;

- Contributing to evolution in the use of management accounting research paradigms that use collaborative capital in management decision making.

Collaborative capital is a relatively new concept. Consequently, the meaning of the concept is obviously still being developed and clarified by researchers. In this volume, definitions of collaborative capital include: consensual social capital, empowerment within the team and empowered team members, soft infrastructure that enables collaborative work, and simply the capacity to work together well.

The context for collaborative capital in these chapters ranges from the team and the virtual team to the consortium and the city. Collaborative context that enables teaming exists in a variety of settings – an array of teaming structures ranging from alliances and partnerships, to cross-national teams and cross-disciplinary teams. Investing collaborative capital is assumed to raise the quality of work in those settings from mediocre to peak levels.

A number of theories act as lenses for the contributors to this volume. It may tempt the reader to look for the "right way to view collaborative capital," but we suggest the development of this field will result in a combination of lenses – nothing less can capture the complex nature of the construct.

The volume opens with a chapter by Melissa Marot, John Selsky, William Hart, and Prasuna Reddy on research teams in biotechnology in Australia. They examine the relationship of intellectual property (IP) and collaboration. IP is the key in aligning the behavior of various stakeholders and leverages both collaborative and entrepreneurial activity. The differences in meaning of IP across stakeholders creates challenges for effective collaboration. Intellectual property has different meanings for the two main stakeholder groups, that is, private sector actors such as pharmaceutical companies, biotechnology companies and venture capital firms, and public research sector actors such as academic scientists and administrators in public research institutes and universities. Forming a consortium has helped bridge those differences and established an infrastructure to enable communication, support research and promote learning.

Nancy Southern discusses the personal and organizational risk factors of collaboration in Chapter 2 and shows the necessity of creating organizational cultures that support collaborative action. The creation of collaborative capital is viewed as a transformative process requiring a shift in individual and collective beliefs and assumptions and new patterns of action and supporting structures that encourage communicative competence and risk taking. Collaboration is viewed through a relational lens incorporating hermeneutic concepts. A process is offered that begins a cultural change by strengthening communicative relationships among senior leaders. A city government and public utility in a major city in the United States provide examples of actions taken by senior leaders committed to the endeavor of creating cultures of collaboration.

In Chapter 3, Anne Koch examines the ways intellectual and collaborative capital are exploited for the purpose of innovation in knowledge-intensive industries. This joint exploitation is especially critical in the continuous generation of radical innovations. Koch presents a model introducing the interactions of human, intellectual and structural capital and develops a view of the exploitation of implicit knowledge and the dynamic capabilities of a firm. She concludes that empowered team-based organizational forms are the most appropriate collaboration pattern for knowledge-intensive industries and recommends that companies build collaborative capital to perpetuate further product innovations.

Virtual collaboration has become the dominant work context for most knowledge workers. Electronic communication overcomes the barrier of distance, so expertise can be pulled together from any location. In Chapter 4, Lindsey Godwin and Julie Rennecker examine the development of collaborative capital virtual spaces. They use an on-line conference of more than 600 participants in 50 countries to illustrate how virtual technology can influence the development and persistence of virtual information exchange. Using Himmelman's (1996, 1997) schema for interactions and Erikson and Kellogg's (2000) theory of translucence (visibility, awareness and accountability), the authors model the necessary characteristics of technology-based interchanges. Their proposed model suggests several lines for future research.

According to Jill Nemiro, Stefanus Hanifah, and Jing Wang in Chapter 5, collaborative capacity is an underpinning of collaborative capital and represents the extent to which collaboration is fostered both internally and externally to the organization. Through a cross-sectional exploratory study in five countries (South Korea, Malaysia, Singapore, Taiwan and the United States), Nemiro et al. examine environmental factors that affect collaboration in the various cultures. Surprisingly, they find that there are few differences between the East and West, but within the Eastern cultures, there are divergent effects across countries. Finally, they consolidate their findings into a model influencing collaborative capacity that may be used to spark future research in these areas.

In Chapter 6, drawing on social exchange theory and the norm of reciprocity, Melvin Smith examines how an individual's perceived social exchange relationship quality with the members of their team might impact their contributions to the communal social capital or collaborative capital of the organization. He also examines how engaging in such behavior affects individual job satisfaction and affective commitment, as well as leader- and peer-rated performance. Through the collection and analysis of sociometric data, communal social capital has been operationalized as the extent to which individuals share information, behave in a trustworthy manner, and engage in helping behavior toward others in the organization, all of which are suggested to contribute to the collaborative nature of the environment and to thus facilitate collective action.

N. Sharon Hill links collaborative capital to shared leadership in Chapter 7. Due to geographic dispersion and reliance on technology-mediated communication, development of collaborative capital can be a challenge in a virtual team. Knowledge sharing is one form of collaborative capital that has been identified as critical to virtual team success. Hill develops a theoretical model that proposes that shared leadership in virtual teams is positively related to knowledge sharing between team members, and that this relationship will be partially mediated by trust. The model also shows that a team's degree of reliance on technology-mediated communication will moderate the relationships in the model.

In Chapter 8, leadership, collaborative capital and innovation are linked. Xiaomeng Zhang and Henry Sims, Jr. explore how transformational leadership and empowerment leadership influence innovation through the creation of collaborative capital. According to Zhang and Sims, collaborative capital is manifested as empowerment within the team, and empowered team members who work together toward the shared goal represent collaborative capital. They describe four alternative models predicting innovation that depict empowerment as having potentially mediating and moderating effects, as well as suggest areas for future research to investigate the mechanisms through which collaborative capital and innovation are achieved.

Intellectual capital (IC) and social capital (SC) as forms of intangible value in organizations are crucial assets in today's volatile business environment. In Chapter 9, Michael Kennedy and Michael Beyerlein explore how IC is enhanced by SC, and how distress undermines both. Collaborative capital is presented as an asset that can be used to enhance both IC and SC and to mitigate the impact of distress. Knowledge from research and practice is accumulating to help organizations account for the costs of organizational distress, translate the importance of intangible value into tangible terms, and garner support for developing IC and SC to achieve business objectives. Deliberate and disciplined effort to build collaborative capital can facilitate the growth of IC and SC and minimize damage of organizational distress.

In Chapter 10, Claudia Bettiol's work examines a fourth kind of intangible capital which is the capability to transform a heterogeneous aggregate of people into a group, and then into a team. This is useful both on a macro and micro level. The transformation is illustrated through a case concerning a group of people involved in urban transformation with its many internal and external complexities. People assume various important roles in this process, for example, connector–mediator, translator and negotiator – and of necessity possess both human and technical skills within their respective areas. The connector creates links for people with external society, whereas the mediator helps us navigate our cultural differences. The translator helps individuals make sense of different social and technical languages, and the negotiator assists us in reaching common ground among our various organizational memberships and their different aims. Bettiol suggests that in this increasingly tightly interrelated socio–technical world, communication happens only at the borders of these various arenas, through both technical and relational means, thus making high-level skill in the connector–mediator, translator, and negotiator roles essential.

Yrjö Engeström in Chapter 11 makes an attempt at hybridization between three relatively separate fields of inquiry. These fields are: (a) theories and studies of collective intentionality and distributed agency, (b) theories and studies of social capital in organizations, and (c) cultural–historical activity theory. He argues that employees' collective capacity to create organizational transformations and innovations is becoming a crucially important asset that gives a new, dynamic content to notions of social and collaborative capital. In philosophy, sociology, anthropology and cognitive science, such capacity is conceptualized as distributed agency or collective intentionality (e.g., Barnes, 2000; Meggle, 2002).

Intellectual capital seems to be the cornerstone for creating sustainable competitive advantage in industry. Innovation depends on it. The question is: What conditions optimize the development and value of intellectual capital? Most of the chapters in this volume argue that it depends on social capital and that is built through collaborative capital. In other words, create the conditions where people can work well together and they will generate intellectual capital. Disciplined, systematic, and systemic investment in the hard and soft infrastructure that supports collaboration creates those conditions and so leads to competitive advantage. In the future, we need to examine this concept in much greater depth, including the financial and accounting perspectives, its role in strategic decision making and strategic change, and its value in guiding organization redesign. Our hope is that the chapters in this volume will engage your interest around these issues, and provide a strong platform for continuing the dialogue of inquiry into the value and role of collaborative capital as an enabler and context for creating sustainable innovation processes in 21st century organizations.

REFERENCES

Barnes, B. (2000). *Understanding agency: Social theory and responsible action*. London: Sage.

Erickson, T., & Kellogg, W. A. (2000). Social translucence: An approach to designing systems that mesh with social processes. In *ACM Transactions on computer-human interaction.* 7(1), (pp. 59–83). New York: ACM Press.

Himmelman, A. T. (1996). On the theory and practice of transformational collaboration: from social service to social justice. In: C. Huxham (Ed.), *Creating collaborative advantage* (pp. 19–43). London: Sage Publishers.

Himmelman, A. T. (1997). Devolution as an Experiment in Citizen Governance: Multi-Organizational Partnerships and Democratic Revolutions. A Working Paper for the *4th international conference on multi-organizational partnerships and cooperative strategy.* Oxford University, 8–10 July.

Lev, B., & Zambon, S. (2003). Intangibles and intellectual capital: An introduction to a special issue. *European Accounting Review, 12*(4), 597–603.

Meggle, G. (Ed.) (2002). *Social facts and collective intentionality.* London: Fouque London Publishing.

Michael M. Beyerlein
Susan T. Beyerlein
Frances A. Kennedy
Editors

RESEARCH TEAMS IN AN AUSTRALIAN BIOTECHNOLOGY FIELD: HOW INTELLECTUAL PROPERTY INFLUENCES COLLABORATION

Melissa Marot, John W. Selsky, William Hart and Prasuna Reddy

ABSTRACT

The purpose of this paper is to examine how research teams serve as building blocks for collaboration at a field level, and how these building blocks are assembled by a network of interacting organizations. The field setting is a medical sciences consortium in Australia established to encourage collaborative and entrepreneurial research among government, industry, research centers and university units. This consortium is examined as a case study. The analysis demonstrates how collaboration evolved at three interacting levels: research team, organization and interorganizational field.

The main findings are: (1) Intellectual property (IP) acts as the key orienting agent in this field to align the behavior of various stakeholders and leverage collaborative and entrepreneurial activity. (2) Tensions

Collaborative Capital: Creating Intangible Value
Advances in Interdisciplinary Studies of Work Teams, Volume 11, 1–31
Copyright © 2005 by Elsevier Ltd.
ISSN: 1572-0977/doi:10.1016/S1572-0977(05)11001-2

between the different ways that the commercial and public sector actors value IP serve to structure the interfaces among the consortium, the member organizations and the research teams. (3) The consortium is a key infrastructural element in the creation of collaborative capital in the Australian biotechnology field studied. The main contribution of the study is to highlight the nature of collaborative capital at a field level and begin to explore its implications.

INTRODUCTION

The Australian biotechnology sector is small by international standards but is robust, growing and targeted by the government as a strategic priority. Universities, research institutes, government agencies, non-profit organizations, leading hospitals, start-up firms and established companies have played key roles in either conducting and/or funding research. Increasingly complex research questions and widely dispersed expertise and resources have called for multi-disciplinary and multi-institutional approaches, as the needed skills and capabilities frequently are not housed in one organization. As a result, collaboration between teams and between institutions has become necessary, and a complex web of collaborations has proliferated in this field at multiple levels (multi-disciplinary, multi-institutional and multi-sectorial) in recent decades. These events in the Australian biotechnology sector appear to mirror what is happening at the global level.

Globally, knowledge in biotechnology is advancing rapidly. The sources of knowledge are widely dispersed, and the diverse players in this field develop various arrangements, often networks and alliances, to produce and access crucial knowledge and key competencies (Levin, 2004; Powell, Koput, & Smith-Doerr, 1996). The science, the technology, the organizational routines, and the institutional and inter-institutional practices are co-evolving (Nelson, 1994; Powell, Koput, Smith-Doerr, & Owen-Smith, 1999). However, variation among organizations in their ability to access external knowledge – and in their skills, funding and status – have stimulated the emergence of different profiles of collaboration (Powell et al., 1999).

The purpose of this chapter is to examine how inter-organizational collaboration emerged and evolved over 4 years in one Australian biotechnology field, and to distill lessons from that case for developing our understanding of "collaborative capital." While much literature has focused on research and development (R&D) collaborations and consortia in the private sector (see, for example, Contractor & Lorange, 1988), little research has focused on consortia initiated by the public sector and/or developed primarily by scientists in academia (but see some of the contributions in Faulkner & De Rond, 2000). In this chapter, we focus on one such group in Australia, a consortium of research centers and university units established in 2000. The consortium was established to enhance collaboration among government, industry and academia to encourage large-scale collaborative research programs and entrepreneurial research activities, and to assist players in the sector to form effective multi-institutional research teams. We examine how collaboration became necessary in this field because of certain structural factors, such as changes in federal policies and the restructuring of funding streams. By examining the development of the consortium, we demonstrate how collaboration evolved at three interacting levels: research team, organization and inter-organizational field. In making the connections among these three levels we are able to explore more fully how and why collaboration was structured and implemented in such a distinctive way in the Australian setting. In doing so, we also contribute to the evolving understanding of collaboration, including the recently introduced notion of collaborative capital.

Conceptually we draw on several areas of literature: innovation and networks in biotechnology (for example, Powell et al., 1996; Smith-Doerr, Owen-Smith, Koput, & Powell, 1998), inter-organizational fields and processes of collaboration within them (for example, Doz & Baburoglu, 2000; Phillips, Lawrence, & Hardy, 2000; Trist, 1983), research teams as boundary spanning units of multi-organizational and multi-sectorial collaboration (for example, Beyerlein, 2000; Hackman, 2002; Sundstrom, DeMeuse, & Futrell, 1990), and learning, knowledge management and intellectual property (IP). These conceptual anchors help us to navigate this complex terrain and are the foundation for two key notions: (1) that research teams serve as building blocks for collaborative capital in biotechnology fields and (2) that these building blocks are assembled in distinctive ways in each such field by a network of interacting organizations.

We use case study method in this chapter. The object of analysis is an Australian biotechnology consortium in the life sciences. The data consists of in-depth interviews with 18 major stakeholders of the consortium conducted in 2003–2004, discussions with the consortium's managers and document reviews, all conducted by the first author. All stakeholders were considered senior scientists and/or senior administrators by their peers and defined themselves as having multiple roles. Multiple roles encompassed conducting high-level science, directing and managing public research

organizations, leading research teams and/or programs as chief investiga-
tors, directing or managing spin-off or start-up companies, and acting as
scientific advisors to industry and/or government. Four of them were
founding members of the consortium. Interviews generally lasted 60–90 min
and were conducted in the offices of the interviewees. Numerous follow-up
sessions were conducted with some interviewees, and there has been ongoing
communication between the researchers and management staff of the
consortium. By agreement, the name of the consortium will remain
confidential.

LITERATURE THEMES

The Global and Australian Biotechnology Industries: Interactions in Networks

Since the early 1990s the biotechnology sector in Australia has experienced
significant changes in operating environments and funding patterns (Wills,
1998) driven by a number of factors. First, as in other centers of
biotechnology, public–private collaborations have become more common.
For example, multinational firms operating in Australia, as well as firms in
Australia's fledgling venture-capital sector, have increased their investments
in biotechnology research. Such initiatives have come at upstream and
downstream points in the value chain, ranging from contract research and
proof-of-concept research to the support of "blue sky" research. These
initiatives often entail collaborative project work.

Second, federal policies and macro- and microeconomic reforms have
opened the Australian economy to global competitive forces. In turn,
certain public incentives for R&D, and commercialization, have stimulated
a series of investment decisions by the private sector favorable to the
country's biotechnology industry (Gans & Porter, 2003). Those incentives
were intended to lift the nation's innovative capacity; that is, its ability to
develop and commercialize technologies.

Third, Australian industry is subject to the same pressures as global
industry. The pressures include intense global competition and hyper-
competition driven by high-velocity product and process innovation,
strategic search for access to complementary technologies and scientific
capabilities, increasing expense to address complex research questions, the
introduction of professional visibility and reputation as competitive

elements, and the need to rapidly and continually shift the basic science and innovation frontier (Gans & Porter, 2003; Powell et al., 1996).

The above factors – high rates of change, uncertainty and complexity in relationships – constitute problems of turbulence. They present significant challenges for managers and scientists in biotechnology organizations, as the ground rules for managing and strategizing may shift in uncertain ways (Meyer, Goes, & Brooks, 1993; Selsky & Smith, 1994). Further, the problem lies not with any individual organization but in the structural and normative relationships among organizations and in the wider institutional context (Selsky & Smith, 1994; Trist, 1983). Turbulence tends to unsettle pre-existing institutional arrangements and open up events to different interpretations and manipulations. Thus, turbulent conditions severely challenge the capacities of organizations – and networked fields of organizations – to adapt (Emery & Trist, 1965; McCann & Selsky, 1984).

Effective adaptation requires responding to the new possibilities opened up. For example, well-positioned or powerful actors may engage in "novel enactments" (Selsky & Smith, 1994; see also Phillips et al., 2000); that is, they may develop new arrangements in the field, such as new ways of cooperating, new bases for competing or new roles for public institutions. Lawrence, Hardy, and Phillips (2000) point to such new arrangements as indicators that a "proto-institution" has emerged in a field. In Australia the founding, development and ongoing evolution of the biotechnology consortium is an example; new forms of collaboration have changed the functional relationships among the field's actors and have evolved the field itself in important ways, that we document in this chapter.

Emergence and Evolution of Collaboration

Although the global biotechnology sector is regarded as intensely competitive and even hyper-competitive, successful collaborative endeavors occur in this sector on a large scale. How and why does this occur?

Collaboration is "a cooperative relationship among organizations that relies on neither market nor hierarchical mechanisms of control" (Phillips et al., 2000). This definition implies that collaborative activity can involve a wide range of functional relationships between organizations and the voluntary negotiation of roles and responsibilities among participants. Institutional fields influence collaboration by providing a foundation of rules and resources that actors use in their collaborative endeavors; conversely, collaboration helps to evolve institutional fields in certain ways (*ibid.*). Over time, collaborative interactions drive the process of institutional definition and shape ongoing interactions (DiMaggio & Powell, 1983). In a specific setting the outcome of this process is a structured field composed of a number of organizations which share institutionalized rules and resources, and provide the context for actual collaboration (Phillips et al., 2000). In such a field either existing practices get reproduced or new practices get invented, or some combination of both (Holm, 1995). Moreover, practices and resources may migrate across contexts (*ibid.*), for example from the academic biosciences sector to the private biotechnology sector. The possibility of such migration is relevant in the biotechnology industry where multi-sectorial collaborations are becoming more common. Through this process, inter-organizational collaboration can restructure entire fields (for example, Powell et al., 1996).

Indeed, collaboration has become a familiar response in biotechnology and other turbulent high-technology industries where networks and formal alliances often encompass universities and other specialized knowledge-oriented institutions (Freeman, Sharp, & Walker, 1991). Collaboration not only can provide competitive advantage for individual organizations but can also enhance the maintenance and development of the field itself. Powell et al. (1996) note that the biotechnology industry is organized around inter-organizational networks and that the technology, the knowledge base and the research institutions are all co-evolving in ways that tend to develop and deepen patterns of inter-organizational and inter-sectorial collaboration.

Interestingly, such network interactions occur in the context of intense competition, driven largely by innovation not price. As the intense network character of the industry, competition occurs largely between and among networks, and not between single organizations (Moore, 1996). In their study of biotechnology networks, Powell et al. (1996) provide evidence that the locus of competitive innovation lies in dynamic and evolving networks of learning. If this is a general feature of biotechnology fields, then learning at the level of the organization *and the field* is a function of participation in the right networks (Dodgson, 1993; Levinthal & March, 1994). Due to the fundamental importance of basic science discovery, product innovation and application, what Brandenburger and Nalebuff (1996) called "cooperative competition" or "co-opetition" appears to prevail in biotechnology fields.

Doz and Baburoglu (2000) posit a process model of the emergence of collaborative activity in R&D cooperatives, or consortia. Although the model is based on the private sector, it can be used to examine collaborative activity in multi-sectorial contexts. Their starting assumption is that consortia must overcome specific barriers that can make the shift from a competitive to a collaborative ethos difficult. Doz and Baburoglu identify nine preconditions for successful collaborative process, paraphrased as follows:

(1) *Common ground*: Stakeholders and potential participants must identify sometimes subtle interdependencies that may exist in the shared field. This helps to build common ground. An external threat to the field can also serve the same function, triggering collaborative activity.

(2) *Norms*: Differences in behavioral norms can make communication difficult, and differences in values and ethical standards can make agreement difficult. Thus shared norms and the ability to identify and acknowledge differences must be fostered.

(3) *Initiators*. Even in conditions where is may be clearly beneficial, collaboration may not occur unless triggered by legitimate actors. The legitimacy and relevance of initiators in the eyes of potential participants may determine the trajectory and success of the cooperative effort.

(4) *Inclusiveness*: It is important to include primary contributors and stakeholders in the field without diluting the focus of the collaborative effort.

(5) *Future orientation*: Collaboration is bolstered when participants believe that mutually beneficial interaction will be sustained into the future. Trustworthiness, efficiency and effectiveness (Doz, 1996), and reputation in the existing network play a role (Gulati, 1995).

(6) *Contributions and payoffs*: Securing the participants' ability and willingness to contribute to the collaboration in the future is important. Equally important is that they recognize each other as effective contributors. This involves extensive negotiation around the balance of contributions and payoffs.

(7) *Governance*: The structure and process utilized to govern and implement the collaboration are essential.

(8) *Learning and adjustment*: Continual learning about expectations, processes, members, commitments, and governing rules and bodies – and making adjustments over time – is essential for long-term success of the collaboration (Doz, 1996).

(9) *Outcomes and evolution*: Successful outcomes consolidate the legitimacy and effectiveness of the collaborative venture. This provides opportunities to deepen commitments and expand the scope of collaborative activities.

Doz and Baburoglu note that these preconditions are most effective when formal structures of collaboration emerge from an already existing network of actors. Below we use their list as a basis for examining the relationships among research teams, organizations and their collaborations in the Australian biotechnology consortium.

Research Teams

The work of scientists has been likened to the work of sailors who "continually rebuild their ships amid the turbulence and resource scarcity of the high seas" (Otto Neurath quoted in Cartwright, Fleck, & Uebel, 1996). Numerous organizational forms and capabilities have emerged recently in attempts to manage scientists, teams and organizations working together in this turbulent sector. Such forms and capabilities are continuously rebuilt on the team and inter-organizational levels. Most research on biotechnology fields has found that collaborations are essential to the survival and development of these fields, and of the organizations, research groups and scientists within them (inter alia, Powell et al., 1996). As the President of the U.S. Biotechnology Industry Organization remarked, "strength...is reflected in the proliferation of collaboration and partnerships, which are the lifeblood of biotechnology..." (Feldbaum, 2001).

Research teams in the Australian biotechnology field increasingly span organizational boundaries. Project-based research teams simultaneously engage in extensive boundary spanning as well as multiple internal activities (Cohen & Bailey, 1997). Team boundary activity is a key construct in team research and is conceptualized as activities that involve interactions external to the team, as well as boundary management between the core aspects of the team and external to the team (Ancona & Caldwell, 1992, 2000). Boundary activity can include, but is not restricted to, collaborative activity. Boundary activity is a key indicator of the performance of R&D teams (Ancona & Caldwell, 1992, 2000). Beyerlein, Freedman, McGee, and Moran (2003) suggest that research teams contribute directly to the building of collaborative capital at the inter-organizational level through boundary activity, and the recognition and development of interdependencies with other groups.

Collaborative capital "includes both the process of collaboration and the relationships to make that collaboration work" (Beyerlein et al., 2003, p. 22). It is a "process and relationship system representing a key [organizational] asset" that "rests on a foundation of competencies, structures and culture that enables collaborative practices" (ibid., pp. 21–22). Collaborative capital develops over time as an organization participates in research, gains experience and develops a capability to orchestrate further collaborative endeavors. Building collaborative capital can be expected to enhance an organization's ability to navigate the turbulent "high seas" of its industry. The new concept of collaborative capital is situated between good team process (for example, effective intra-group communication and conflict management) and successful substantive and process outcomes, such as a new patentable molecule or a new innovation in team design.

The research team is the essential unit that carries out biotechnology research. There are multiple definitions of teams in organizational settings, we adopt a socio-technical systems definition: A team is a collection of individuals who are interdependent in their tasks, share responsibility for outcomes, see themselves and are seen by others as an intact social entity embedded in one or more larger social systems, and manage their relationships across organizational boundaries (see Beyerlein, 2000; Hackman, 2002; Sundstrom et al., 1990). The well-established principle in group dynamics that "[t]here are two basic types of needs and issues that arise in a team – task and [social] relationship" (Fisher, Rayner, & Belgard, 1995) is especially important in biotechnology collaborations because of IP issues, as discussed below.

Learning, Knowledge and Intellectual Property

Organizational learning "... is both a function of access to knowledge and the capabilities for utilizing and building such knowledge" (Powell et al., 1996; see also Kogut & Zander, 1992). As noted above, the knowledge base of the biotechnology sector has become increasingly complex, with widely dispersed sources of expertise. Learning in biotechnology occurs primarily through inter-organizational networks (Powell et al., 1996). The learning can be about process or content. An example of process learning is how to better organize a multi-disciplinary research team. An example of content learning is gaining understanding about a new molecule and procedures for producing it. As organizations become more experienced in collaborative relationships with a wide variety of partners and contexts, routines develop that increase its collaborative capabilities. The same applies at the level of the research team. Loveridge (2000, p. 135) calls this "appropriative learning" as it involves the "absorption, adaptation and application of information along socio-technical networks in a manner that expands the existing capabilities of the firm." We propose it also expands the capabilities of the *field* as cross-boundary learning systems take shape (Levin, 2004).

IP is about *content* learning. It consists of patents, trademarks, copyrights and trade secrets owned by a corporation or an individual; it is generally directed at perceived potential commercial use rather than actual use (Gans, Williams, & Briggs, 2002). IP is an asset that can be protected on an international basis; as an asset it has economic value similar to real and personal property. Consequently, IP can be sold, licensed, exchanged or gifted, and the owners hold rights to prevent its unauthorized use or sale. The fundamental value of IP in biotechnology is that it grants exclusive ownership over a technology or discovery, and its resulting products (Schneider, 2002).

IP rights are an increasingly important path to profits in innovation-driven industries, so firms in such industries compete intensely for exclusive rights to technologies, processes and resulting end products. Such exclusivity may generate monopoly returns and block further innovation and invention by others. From an economic point of view, IP rights are essential for the creation, production and distribution of innovations in markets (Gans & Stern, 2003); this is the value associated with the "capitalization of knowledge" (Etzkowitz, 1998). Traditional practices of science include contributing new discoveries to a body of knowledge. Scientists prefer to distribute their discoveries into the public domain relatively freely via peer-reviewed publications and conference presentations. From a scientific point of view, such avenues provide acknowledgement, prestige and a benchmark for productivity; this is the value associated with the "extension of knowledge" (*ibid.*). Insofar as IP grants exclusive rights to an individual or organization, it may restrict diffusion of discovery or innovation into society if monopolized. Conversely, if managed well, it can speed the diffusion of discovery and innovation for the public good. In general, tensions between these different ways of valuing IP create friction at the interfaces among actors in high-velocity innovation industries like biotechnology.

These frictions may affect the dynamics of collaboration in biotechnology fields. Collaborations between public institutions, such as universities and research centers, and pharmaceutical companies and public research groups in the biotechnology sector can stimulate complex IP issues. Scientific goals and values grounded in the "pursuit of truth" meet up against commercial goals of profit making. IP rights can be an important strategic asset contributing to profitability (Gans & Stern, 2003), but may cause tension with university-based academic goals of getting biomedical science into the public domain. For example, the exclusivity granted by IP to an owner group or individual may compel an industry player, such as a large pharmaceutical firm to partner with the biomedical research team, research institute or university, in order to gain legal access to a technology and its ensuing stream of products. This may produce divergent effects. On the one hand, the group that owns the IP can further advance a stream of research and develop the material without fear that a better resourced organization may expropriate the IP. On the other hand, IP rights can serve to monopolize ideas and block further innovation and invention by others. The public good may thus be trumped by private interests.

In summary, IP is a crucial, multi-faceted issue in biotechnology collaborations. It influences how knowledge and learning can be mobilized in biotechnology fields, given the institutional framework of practices and rules, how those practices and rules are transmitted across settings and how they change. How IP is negotiated also influences how collaborations – at the team, organizational and field levels – might evolve over time.

FIELD SETTING: AN AUSTRALIAN BIOTECHNOLOGY CONSORTIUM

Spurred by federal policy changes, opportunities presented by the growth of biotechnology in Australia, the sophistication required to meet these opportunities, global competitiveness and perceived fragmentation of the sector, several senior scientists, senior managers in research organizations and a public health expert began to work toward establishing a consortium in the late 1990s. After approximately 1 year of discussions the consortium was incorporated in 2000 as a not-for-profit company in one of the states of Australia. At its inception the consortium consisted of two major universities and two research institutes as founding members. The new company attracted more than 60 million Australian dollars of government- and commercial-funding commitments during its first 2 years. Membership currently (as at August 2004) stands at seven major universities and research institutes, and their numerous affiliates. The majority of affiliates are university departments of clinical research based in hospitals. The company has continued to attract government funding and industry partnerships.

The scope of the consortium involves the life sciences, or biosciences, sub-sector of the biotechnology sector and includes numerous facets of health and medical research. Membership is available to universities, research institutes, research groups or teams in the country; membership is not available to for-profit companies. The consortium's board consists of 12

members with a mix of scientific and commercial expertise. Board members
are either directors of academic institutions, or independents with company
director experience in commercial environments.

The consortium's purposes, extracted from its annual report and
interviews with its management and founding members, are best expressed
in terms of its commitments to:

(1) Innovation, infrastructure and invention leading to major scientific
    discoveries in its biotechnology field.
(2) Creation of investment and partnership opportunities in major
    collaborative research programs.
(3) Promotion and mediation of large-scale collaborative research pro-
    grams.
(4) Generation and commercialization of IP.
(5) Transfer of research findings into 'spin-off' companies.
(6) Support and employment for scientists.

The consortium is based on the recognition of a need to create a critical
mass of scientists working on complementary research programs, to develop
a distributed network of public research organizations, in addition to the
need for integrated access regimes to technologies and to move science
sufficiently from idea to market. For the near future, the consortium hopes
to maintain and improve the position of biotechnology research in Australia
in a competitive and volatile international industry by finding ways to
collaborate, develop expertise, innovate, identify discoveries with commercial potential, and effectively market products on a global scale.

FINDINGS

Interviewee Profile

All 18 interviewees were senior scientists, had extensive experience as leaders
of research groups in the life sciences and were currently in leadership roles.
Those roles were as project team leaders, program leaders or directors of
departments or institutes. (Programs consist of multiple project teams
with each team working on complementary aspects of a larger research
question.) All had extensive experience with research collaborations across
disciplines, teams and organizations. Seven individuals reported extensive
experience with industry; they had undertaken research partnerships with a
range of industry partners, either directly or through public research

institute–industry linkages. They also showed significant experience in publishing, patenting and licensing, both nationally and internationally. More than half of the interviewees had been involved with the creation of start-up companies either directly or through their research team. All had long histories of obtaining public-funding grants and depended greatly on these grants to finance their core research objectives. A small number remarked that their dependence on various types of philanthropic funding is sometimes more substantial than public or commercial funding.

A Fragmented and Uncoordinated Field

Interviewees commented that the life sciences sub-sector of the biotechnology sector in Australia was too fragmented and uncoordinated. Rather than relying on relatively loose networks and partnerships, they deemed it important to coordinate teams and organizations in a more structured and inclusive manner. Interviewees remarked that the idea and practice of collaboration has long been a part of the common beliefs about what makes for effective and creative science. However, collaboration has mostly occurred between isolated individuals and was somewhat haphazard. Interviewees said that public research in the past had been directed by sole researchers and appeared to be uncoordinated. However, medical and social problems required some "direction" to balance scientific output with the public good. Similarly, it became widely recognized in the past decade that a more directive approach was required to take advantage of the wide range of expertise in the biosciences in Australia. Interviewees' widely held belief was that Australia performs excellent research in the biotechnology sector. By coordinating the sector, resources might be better leveraged for competitive advantage both nationally and internationally.

Several ways of achieving some direction, not mutually exclusive, were mentioned. One way was coordinating basic research with applied research to "engender an iterative process between pure and applied research" as opposed to the "linear model of pure to applied research." This would "lift the profile of the sub-sector to government groups and funding sources, both public and private."

A second way involved program-based research. As mentioned above, increasingly complex research questions and broader requirements for expertise and resources have demanded multi-disciplinary approaches, and collaboration between teams and institutions has become necessary. One interviewee reported that this "evolved naturally but was still haphazard in approach." A more concerted approach would be to form large program-based research groups. Such groups involve a number of research teams working on specific aspects of a research question. The group is directed by an executive team of senior researchers, with each leading a sub-unit of three to twenty researchers. Federal-funding initiatives for program-based research have been implemented only recently, thus collaborative activity between research teams on this level was considered by some interviewees as "learning in progress." Program grants have not only provided a concrete and well-resourced opportunity for collaborative activity on the inter-organizational level, but also for a coordinated approach to attracting commercial interest and creating spin-off companies.

A third way of achieving coordination and direction was to create a consortium. We highlight this option below.

Collaboration to Enhance the Funding Base

Senior scientists and senior managers commented that they now attend to and engage in inter-organizational and inter-sectorial interactions to a much greater extent than before. Collaborations among teams, organizations and private sector research firms not only have improved the efficacy and inventiveness of the scientific process, but have attracted more funds from both public- and private-funding sources.

Interviewees reported that the nature and structure of public funding in Australia had changed considerably in the past decade. For example, public funds have become more competitive and grant funding has become more conservative. These trends have made it more difficult for young researchers and innovative projects to successfully obtain public funds. In addition, teams and individual scientists who are unsuccessful in renewal of their project funding have difficulty surviving professionally. Funding for personnel expenses was considered to be generous; however, costs toward infrastructure and equipment were minimal. Conversely, scientists noted that more flexibility and improved accountability have been brought into the public-funding system. Federal and State governments have encouraged collaborative research among disciplines, teams and institutions, and have directed funding toward such projects. Peer-reviewed competitive funding from public sources, especially from the National Health and Medical Research Council and the Australian Research Council, was still considered as the most prestigious form of funding. However, scientists have looked to other sources.

There is an emphasis by Federal and State governments to develop industry–research institute relationships. "Public institutions now have to show commercial outcomes as well as develop large-scale collaborative research." Some interviewees commented that there is pressure from their institutions for their research groups to show collaborations with industry. Conversely, industry has sought to gain access to science in universities and institutes to enhance their own base capabilities for new product development and other innovations. One senior scientist commented that industry is "increasingly aware of creative, inventive and quality research conducted in public research institutions." However, the biotechnology industry presence in Australia is small, so onshore commercialization opportunities were considered limited. A strong theme in the interviews was that researchers' thinking about industry partnerships has been changing. "Researchers appear to be more comfortable with the commercial dollar; however, it is not considered as prestigious as peer-reviewed competitive funding [from public sources]." Experience and sophistication in dealing with industry has improved dramatically over the years, for example, in contract negotiations and managing IP.

There was agreement among interviewees that industry–researcher interaction was in its infancy in Australia compared to the U.S.A. or Europe. They noted that the relationship between the public and private sectors in Australia had a different history from the U.S.A., and that Australia does not have the breadth of societal and industry resources to follow the same trajectory of industry–academic partnerships as in the U.S.A. Therefore, Australia had to "learn its own lessons." This "learning in progress" was regarded by all as a necessary and inevitable process. A notable difference from the American context was the "lack of flow [or] permeability" between the public and private sectors. This was described in two ways. First, it was difficult in Australia for scientists to move between the sectors and mechanisms were lacking to translate scientific productivity. Second, it was difficult in Australia to translate performance indicators such as patents and publications across the sectors; this indicated a difference in value systems. For example, peer-reviewed publications, conferences and public grant winning were thought of as important in academic research, whereas patents and value for dollar innovations with commercial potential were thought of as important in the industry sector. One scientist commented that "this lack of mechanism to translate scientific productivity between the academic and industry sectors seriously diminishes scope for job flexibility and career development. However, the landscape is changing."

One indicator of this changing landscape is that public research institutions have shifted from an emphasis on publishing scientific results to protecting IP. A majority of interviewees said that industry partnerships were necessary for the biosciences, but that the generation of IP of commercial value was only one aspect of science and should be balanced with public research. A number of senior scientists commented that Australia has started from a "low base of public–private sector interaction" which is only now being redressed.

Most interviewees saw positive outcomes to collaborating with industry. These were articulated as: "increased awareness by the government and the public of bioscience, and the intellectual resource it can contribute to the national economy," "stronger position to grow and survive in a commercial network" and "with better finance, the ability to attract newcomers to science." However, the interviewees, all of them academics or former academics, generally believed that bringing about commercialization and industry partnerships with the academic sector was difficult, and current infrastructure and procedures for doing so needed to be re-thought and reorganized. Some commented that the administration of collaboration with the private sector can take as much effort as managing the science itself. Legal supports, business professionals and adequate administration supports were argued as essential for successful technology transfer to the private sector.

The Consortium

Two of the founding members interviewed stated that the consortium was created to address the two main issues noted above, namely coordination of effort and enhancing the funding base. At its inception the consortium was to provide to its members an "administrative structure with the capacity to establish and manage large [multi-organizational research] programs," to "provide funding for key enabling technologies that are expensive" and to "provide seed funding for large programs that have a good chance of technology transfer." The consortium has taken strides to fulfill these purposes by implementing cross-institutional protocols for IP management, establishing platform technologies to support the scientific community and enabling industry access to these technologies. A number of collaborative projects have been established in numerous research areas, with combined public- and private-funding sources. One scientist commented that "by researchers coming together in a cohesive sense, it has proved to be attractive to international industry and local biotechnology companies."

As noted above, prior to the consortium some individual scientists and teams did forge partnerships directly with commercial entities. These scientists and teams researched specialist areas that were several steps away from a product, some of which had limited experience with commercial interactions. Founding members of the consortium recognized that there might be valuable discoveries hidden in some pockets of local biotechnology research that had IP of potential commercial value. Hence, one role that the consortium took on was to assist in the identification of that IP, and to assist in further development of promising projects. The consortium, for example, provided infrastructure and funding for proof-of-concept research. It also provided the necessary infrastructure to manage and negotiate industry partnerships and contracts, and provide legal administrative and administrative assistance. By providing such assistance, the consortium expected to enhance the efficiency of the research process from scientific discovery to market, using its intermediating capacity to mobilize new public and industry funding without risking existing public sources.

Interviewees commented that the consortium is still very young and is still learning. So far, it has acted as a focal point for building and encouraging collaborative activity. This has manifested in the creation of large-scale multi-institutional research programs, and the creation of a major research facility offering infrastructure and technology platforms. The consortium is co-located in this facility and provides management to the facility. Within this facility are co-located management representatives of a number of member research institutes and some research teams.

Some tensions were articulated around collaborative activity managed by the consortium. For instance, the existence of the consortium as an intermediate has added another layer of bureaucracy, which has eaten into the time available to the scientist for research. In addition, differences in operational processes between institutions were stated as hindrances to the collaborative process.

Intellectual Property

A number of scientists commented that IP was important for two distinct reasons. Two distinctive ways were articulated. IP served *commercial* interests by protecting discoveries for patenting, licensing options, etc.; IP served *scientific* interests by ensuring that discoveries were able to be publicly disseminated, resulting in prestige and better public grant-winning capacity.

One senior scientist with much industry experience commented that commercialization was all about the creation of IP, developing a portfolio and a channel to commercialize it. Difficulties arise once someone wants to transfer IP to other institutions. The technology transfer landscape has changed dramatically in the last decade with the advent of companies created specifically to assist in the strategic development of research (such as the Australian company Biocomm Ltd.). Such companies identify IP that might have commercial potential and attract or inject funds for high-risk research. All scientists commented that good regulation and administration of public–private sector interactions with IP implications was essential to them. Although the creation and development of IP was seen as a potential road to wealth by many scientists, they articulated the danger of over-committing to industry with its focus on commercialization of research. Tensions between academic and industry values were articulated a number of times by interviewees: the long-term perspective of science vs. the short-term perspective of industry, industry as a "black box of secrecy for competitive advantage" vs. scientists needing to publish to win promotions and grants, and "curiosity-driven vs. goal-directed research." One said, "some discoveries have been considered by the inventor as very important breakthroughs in the treatment of a rare disease, or a disease in the third world country. And the inventor was correct, it did provide a breakthrough in treatment. However, to the commercial world the IP had minimal market value for the treatment of a rare disease, as the customer base was low. Or in the case of the third world country, financial returns would be low. This is an example of differences in meaning." A number of senior scientists considered these tensions to be manageable and thought they actually created intellectually stimulating environments. They considered public and commercial funding as supporting each other, and "by leveraging IP, the value of moving a discovery to treatment is realized."

The social value and prestige of scientific findings may diverge from market value. It was strongly apparent in the interviews that clear decision points over whether to publish or patent were often contentious. Researchers and their host institution or agent (the consortium) needed to choose the appropriate time to begin cooperating with an industry partner, this was often a choice as to whether to patent. What influenced these decisions was the uncertain value of the technology vs. investment costs incurred as the invention/innovation moves down the value chain. In addition, the bureaucracy and costs of patenting was a consideration. For example, one scientist cited an instance in which his team had discovered a major breakthrough in his specialization with potential commercial value. They decided to go down the commercial route and patent the discovery. Just before the patent was defined and filed, another group announced they had made the same discovery and published their results. Thus the patent had no commercial value, and his team did not even get the acknowledgement and prestige for making the breakthrough in the first place.

DISCUSSION

In this section, we draw on the findings from the Australian consortium case to identify themes and to build new understandings of collaborative capital in inter-organizational fields of biotechnology research.

How Collaboration Emerged and Evolved

As noted above, the Australian biotechnology sector has been characterized by the turbulence also encountered by biotechnology fields in other countries. However, the Australian context presents additional problems, such as the "tyranny of distance," a more dispersed base of public institutions and limited industrial avenues to bring ideas to market (Wills, 1998). Scientists and administrators interviewed recognized that the Australian industry could only stay at the forefront if it positioned itself at the cutting edge of knowledge production and technology development. In fact, the country seems to be attempting such positioning. The Australian biotechnology sector has seen an unprecedented growth in inter-organizational partnering and external collaboration. Findings from the interviews and government documents confirm that network relations have been used extensively for competitive and strategic advantage to enhance legitimacy and prestige, and even survival prospects (see Powell et al., 1996).

Federal policy has clearly contributed to the recent growth of collaboration. The interviews identified changes in federal policy as drivers spurring the establishment of the consortium. In the past decade federal sources of funding were restructured and redirected toward large-scale collaborative research. A greater number of federal-funding opportunities became available, such as for collaborative research centers, academic–industry linkage grants, proof-of-concept studies and entrepreneurial scientific activities. Part of the rationale for such policy and funding changes was to improve national innovative capacity, and thus increase the global competitiveness of the Australian biotechnology industry. Over the past 25 years public policies and private sector initiatives have transformed Australia's innovative capacity from a classic imitator to an innovator economy (Gans & Porter, 2003).

In the remainder of this section, we describe the activities undertaken by the consortium and its member organizations in terms of Doz and Baburoglu's (2000) list of preconditions for collaborative activity in R&D consortia, described earlier in this chapter.

(1) *Common ground*: Collaboration in this field emerged and evolved in specific ways, structured and implemented in particular forms of formal and informal relationships. The consortium has been a key institution in this regard. The groundwork for the consortium was laid through the activity of leading scientists and directors of public research institutions that had a previous history of working together. Prior cooperation and ties resulted in common ground (Gulati, 1995) based on functional interdependencies and shared views on many issues. The founders of the consortium undertook a deliberate and concerted effort to initiate the entity and further develop common ground with potential members. From the outset, the founders identified certain interdependencies to justify the need for the consortium. As the consortium has evolved, the issues have been continually revisited, deliberated and classified. Moreover, contextual factors, such as federal policy and funding restructures, impelled them to pool and mobilize resources to take advantage of new and emerging research and funding opportunities.

(2) *Norms*: Three areas of difference were highlighted by the interviews. First, universities, research institutes and hospitals have different governance and organizational processes. Differences in processes have impacted on the management of science, technology transfer and teamwork. Second, perceptions within the scientific community of commercial funding are divergent. It was considered important to access commercial funding but not at the expense of driving science to commercial imperatives. The consortium's structure was considered an experiment in trying to meld traditional scientific values of "extension of knowledge" with newer commercial values of "capitalization of knowledge" (Etzkowitz, 1998). Third, the nexus between the public sector and the private sector showed even more divergent organizational processes, cultures and values. The interviewees

highlighted that understandings of efficiency, accountability and the profit motive were the most different between the sectors.

(3–4) *Initiators and inclusiveness*: The founding members created a boundary, direction and identity for the group, which then became a more permanent structure (Trist, 1983), and the consortium became a focal point for building and encouraging collaborative activity in the field. Importantly, with its infrastructure of technology platforms, hosting multi-disciplinary and multi-institutional research groups, and forming strategic partnerships with industry groups, it seeks to build a reputation of sustained mutually beneficial collaborative activity. The management of the consortium recognizes that the track record it builds for itself in these early years will help it attract new participants in the future (Doz & Baburoglu, 2000).

(5–6) *Future orientation, contributions and payoffs*: Some tensions have arisen between member organizations with regard to some aims and activities of the consortium, namely increasing levels of bureaucracy, differences in opinion about the role of public institutions vis-à-vis industry, and operational differences. Fluctuations in the balance of effort/contributions and payoffs to be created by collaboration were evident between members. These tensions were described as contributing to the growth and evolution of the field, and essential "learning experience." Those interviewed indicated a certain level of commitment and willingness to contribute. Moreover, the consortium was still considered as somewhat young and was yet to prove itself in the long term.

(7) *Governance*: Interviewees reported that the design of structures and processes to govern and implement collaborative activity were essential for effective collaborative endeavors. Examples included the management of IP, accountability and administrative issues associated with the science. A strong theme from the interviews was that the particular form of cooperation manifested by the consortium was new in the biotechnology sector in Australia.

(8) *Learning and adjustment*: The interviewees generally recognized that the concept and process of the consortium is experimental, and there is much room for learning and development. Adjustments over time in value expectations, processes and commitment were expected by most interviewed.

(9) *Outcomes and evolution*: Although the consortium is a relatively new entity, some broadening of commitments by collaborative partners are already evident. Over 4 years there has been movement from less

structured collaborative activities in the network to a legal entity with four founding member organizations to the current seven members and their numerous affiliates. Undoubtedly other factors have contributed to this movement, but we consider this consistent with Doz and Baburoglu's (2000, p. 180) assertion that "successful collaboration feeds on itself, on its effectiveness and legitimacy." The ability to form more common ground between old and new partners over time, and the fulfillment of commitments over time by both academic and industry partners, allows collaborative activity to develop in scope and duration (*ibid.*).

In sum, the consortium emerged from a pre-existing informal network and has yielded specific formalized collaborative agreements. The participants appear to have met all nine preconditions for collaboration to some degree. Obviously this aids successful initial collaborative activity, as claimed by Doz and Baburoglu (2000). It is important to note however, that based on evidence gathered through this study, these preconditions *continue to be relevant* as the field widens to include more diverse members. Further formalized agreements are implied by "visibly identified and publicly stated commitment to goods and allocation of resources" (Doz & Baburoglu, 2000, p. 184), such as technology platforms, shared facilities and infrastructure for collaborative research, infrastructure for the management of IP and the negotiation of industry partnerships. The cooperation between members has thus evolved through various phases, from common ground to contractual program research. Learning and adjustment cycles in specific projects have served to deepen common ground, redefine specific issues and inform future frameworks for collaborative agreements.

How Intellectual Property is Crucial

An overriding objective in establishing the consortium was to enhance the base of funding sources for scientists and institutions in the biotechnology sector, as described in the interviews. As noted above, new Australian federal policy and funding restructures have created incentives for academic–industry partnerships and the consortium is specifically geared to collaboration with the commercial sector. The findings suggest that IP acts as the *key-orienting agent* in this field. The prospect of future or potential IP helps to align the behavior of various stakeholders. Once attained, IP helps to shape subsequent behavior by legitimating a certain scientific path and a certain commercial path. In this iterative way, IP serves as the key resource for leveraging both collaborative and entrepreneurial activity. We justify this unobvious insight in the following paragraphs.

The creation, identification, development and marketing of IP are crucial issues to all the major players. The interfaces among the consortium, member organizations and research teams have been structured to address these issues. Interviewees experienced in dealing with commercial interests expressed two valuable outcomes from consortium-driven interactions: "the realization of discovery to treatment" and "wealth creation for their research." The creation of formal IP with its protections enables them to go to market with their discovery or product, and is thus highly valued as a key resource. Competitive advantage for most biotechnology firms and research organizations is fostered by knowledge-related competencies; that is, developing ideas that can attract IP protection along with strategic cooperation with partners who can commercialize the IP (Gans & Stern, 2003). Commercialization partners bring costly complementary assets to the partnership, such as distribution networks, manufacturing and technologic capabilities, to develop the discovery further.

The most salient difference in the value of IP between the academic and industry sectors is related to the "disclosure paradox" (Gans & Stern, 2003). Trading in ideas differs from trading in traditional economic goods. The negotiated price a buyer is willing to pay for an idea is dependent on the buyer having perfect information about the idea. But if the buyer knows the idea, she/he need not pay for it. Disclosure may increase the value the buyer puts on the idea but at the same time reduces the vendor's bargaining power. Three mechanisms can minimize the effect of the disclosure paradox: strong IP protection with non-disclosure agreements prevents expropriation, buyers can establish a reputation for fairness and avoid expropriation, and third-party brokers can intermediate the transaction, preserving the parties' bargaining power and managing the IP more efficiently (Hsu, 2000).

Academic culture encourages disclosure and dissemination of discoveries and ideas through publications and conference presentations. Indeed, academic performance indicators are often based on these media of disclosure. On the other hand, industry culture discourages disclosure and is increasingly wary of expropriation of the key assets of knowledge and information. Interviewees emphasized that researchers and research institutions require experience and sophistication in managing and negotiating the value of IP with the industry sector, in order to navigate the gap between such divergent views of disclosure and dissemination of ideas. The consortium has positioned itself as a broker of ideas between the academic and industrial sectors, and attempts to bridge that gap with protocols for IP management across institutions and across sectors.

That IP can leverage collaborative and entrepreneurial activity is an example of how collaboration and institutional fields co-evolve, as discussed early in this chapter (Phillips et al., 2000). The rules for IP are embedded in the institutional field, providing a context for collaborative actions to leverage it. This causal relationship between IP and field activity is less obvious than the converse, namely that collaboration and entrepreneurship stimulate new IP. Our insight derives from an institutional interpretation of this case and close attention to field-level processes.

How Collaboration Interacts among Three Levels

The research team is the essential unit that carries out biotechnology research, it was described by a leading scientist as the "key to the whole creative process and work of science, and key to sustaining collaborative work between disciplines, groups and institutions, both nationally and internationally." Collaborative activity, a specific form of team boundary activity, was considered by most interviewed as a key indicator of good science and high levels of team performance. This is consistent with recent research on team performance and effectiveness (Ancona & Caldwell, 1992, 2000).

As stated earlier, collaboration in a turbulent and competitive field may not arise spontaneously and often requires key individuals with specific capabilities to initiate collaborative processes. These proactive individuals locate and resonate with other individuals who are moving in the same direction. When they pool their energies they can become important forces for change in the field (Trist, 1983). Acting as "institutional entrepreneurs" (Rao, Morrill, & Zald, 2000) they diffuse new practices in a field through industry and other networks (see Holm, 1995; Greenwood, Suddaby, & Hinings, 2002). In this case, the founders of the consortium have operated around three change themes: coordinating research, mobilizing resources to access multiple-funding sources, and reconciling scientific and commercial values. These themes were evident at the initiation of the consortium, and driving these changes in the field continues as the consortium develops.

We found that in this biotechnology field, proactive individuals were mostly senior scientists who lead or are intimately involved with research teams and groups. Pre-existing network relations (going back many years in many instances) among these individuals and their teams had left trails of important connections and affordances. As the consortium emerged and developed to include new members, it appropriated those connections and developed them further in order to drive change in the field conducive to collaboration. That is, the consortium acted as a "proto-institution" in its field (Lawrence, Hardy, & Phillips, 2000). For example, previous informal relationships between research teams were formalized into large program research contracts with a specific research question designed to access public and/or industry funding. In several instances these contracts have evolved into formal inter-organizational collaborations. Interviewees reported that companies were often looking for collaborations involving senior scientists with a reputation, prestige and a track record of productivity. The scientists' prestige was a strong factor in winning public grants and commercial contracts. Contracts, IP issues and negotiations were often formalized and agreed directly with the researchers and their teams, and their employing institutions. As the senior scientist is the principal investigator on the contract or grant, she/he is directly responsible for the work carried out; however, the legal relationship for accountability is between the (public or private) funding body and the employing institution.

Research teams are sourced from host institutions, and research teams get assembled through the network of such institutions. Organizational norms, values, practices and resources provide a foundation for collaborative activity, which team members use as they interact (Phillips et al., 2000). Over time, these interactions between research teams and between organizations would drive the process of institutional definition and shape ongoing interactions. Collaborative outcomes at the field level involve the reproduction and innovation of practices, as well as the migration of practices and resources from one setting to another. For example, interviewees indicated that professional staff and scientists were now moving between research institutes and between industry and academia more frequently. The more permeable boundary between the two worlds has increased their exposure to industry values of performance, efficiency and accountability. They considered this good discipline for science.

How Collaborative Capital is Created at the Field Level

In an important expression of the resource-based view of the firm, knowledge is seen as a key resource and strategic asset of an organization (Grant, 1996). It is increasingly recognized that an organization's knowledge and its ability to appropriate it as a product of its relationships in learning networks or clusters (Baum, Calabrese, & Silverman, 2000; Levin, 2004; Powell et al., 1996; Zaheer & George, 2004). Knowledge and learning are social and embedded (Levin, 2004) distributed fields rather than tightly encapsulated in any organization. However, the free flow of knowledge in networks is constrained by formal IP, which is institutionally fixed at the level of the firm, or in some cases individual scientists. Commercial IP tries to control innovation, and the rents that flow from innovation, by attempting to control its distribution in and across inter-organizational fields.

We argue that if IP in a biotechnology field is solely driven by commercial imperatives and values, it would be unable to stimulate new field-level practices like collaboration and innovation. In the Australian biotechnology case, because IP helps to orient the behavior of *diverse* stakeholders with different values attached to IP, it can and does stimulate innovation and collaboration in the field beyond specific collaborations. We justify this assertion below.

Phillips, Lawrence, and Hardy (2000, p. 289) claim that inter-organizational collaboration "can have important 'second-order' effects that go beyond the innovations and direct connections established within the collaborative relationship... It can contribut[e] to the creation of new institutions and changes in inter-organizational networks." We argue that one of these second-order effects is collaborative capability. In this case, as organizations and teams interact, and become more experiences in collaborative relationships with a wide variety of partners and contexts, each organization and team builds its skills and capabilities in collaborating across boundaries. This is the first-order effect. In addition, the consortium is attempting to be the vehicle for diffusing new practices and a new ethos of collaborative practice in the field; that is, mobilizing a cross-boundary learning system (Levin, 2004). It acts as an enabling agent for science and commerce to talk to each other, and provides an operating framework for collaborative research. This field-level work of the consortium is the second-order effect.

Thus, we argue that in this field, the locus of innovation is found in networks of learning rather than in individual organizations. Collaboration in these networks – in the form of multi-organizational research teams – contributes to organizational learning (Dodgson, 1993), and that learning is a function of participation in relevant networks (Levinthal & March, 1994). Collaborative capability is not only a resource of a single organization in its competitive operations, but is also a *collective* resource of a field of organizations. Collective collaborative capacity is increased when information is absorbed, adapted and applied by means of appropriative learning by many members of a field (Loveridge, 2000). In that collaborative capabilities build collaborative capital, the consortium facilitates the building of collaborative capital not only within member organizations, but also across the biotechnology field (see Beyerlein et al., 2003).

In sum, based on the findings from this case, collaborative capital can be understood as a *field-level phenomenon*, in addition to the prior under-standings ascribed to it at the organizational level (*ibid.*). This insight helps us to see collaborative capital not as an entity or fixed asset, but as a field-level dynamic process. This process may be embodied in particular organizations through the work of research teams (facilitated by adminis-trators and other actors). That is, research teams are the essential units for scientific creativity, productivity and accountability; they also constitute nodes in networks of collaborative activity in the field. In this way, *research teams serve as building blocks for collaborative capital at the field level.* Further, *these building blocks are assembled in distinctive ways in each such field in a network of interacting organizations.* In this case, actors' behavior in the network was found to be oriented by IP but in general other factors, namely customer service, market share, social justice, etc., may also orient behavior, depending on the dynamics of the particular field.

CONCLUSION

This case study provides a fine-grained understanding of the processes involved in building collaborative capital that is often missing from studies of teams or institutional change. Issues of fragmentation, coordination of research and enhancement of the funding base were the main themes articulated in the interviews.

The key lessons from this study are:

(1) IP acts as the key-orienting agent in this field to align the behavior of various stakeholders. That is, IP serves as the key resource for leveraging both collaborative and entrepreneurial activity.

(2) IP has different meanings for the two main stakeholder groups; that is, *private sector actors* (such as pharmaceutical companies, biotechnology companies and venture capital firms) and *public research sector actors* (such as academic scientists and administrators in public research institutes and universities).

(3) The consortium serves as a key infrastructural element in the creation of collaborative capital in the biotechnology field. It enables science and commerce to talk to each other, provides an operating framework for

collaborative scientific research, and enables collective capability to be increased through "appropriative learning" (Loveridge, 2000).

It is through the "building block" process that inter-organizational collaboration has been able to begin restructuring the biotechnology field under study in Australia and contribute to the consortium's birth and development. Research teams were found to be assembled in distinctive ways in a rich and evolving network of interacting organizations. The consortium focused on the mobilization of resources for strategic advantage and global competitiveness, stimulated collaboration, and helped it evolve at three interacting levels: the research team, organization and field (the consortium).

The insight that collaborative capital needs to be explored as a field-level dynamic has important implications for managing innovation more holistically, both in local fields and at national levels. It suggests that there may be important implications for the design and management of research teams and consortium-like entities in complex inter-organizational fields. Further research may help to uncover these implications. In addition, further research on collaborative capital as a field-level concept would help to clarify the interactions among the three levels identified in this study. Such research would resonate with Davis and McAdam's (2000) notion that the locus of strategic advantage is not the individual autonomous organization but the field. Finally, a broader policy-relevant implication of this study that would reward future research is that a consortium approach to stimulating collaboration in complex innovation fields may enable the creation of new intellectual capital at the *national* level.

ACKNOWLEDGMENTS

This work is supported by an Australian Research Council Linkage grant. The industry partners in the grant are the Hay Group Ltd. and Neurosciences Victoria Ltd.

REFERENCES

Ancona, D. G., & Caldwell, D. F. (1992). Bridging the boundary: External activity and performance in organizational teams. *Administrative Science Quarterly, 37*, 634–665.
Ancona, D. G., & Caldwell, D. F. (2000). Compose teams to ensure successful boundary activity. In: E. Locke (Ed.), *The Blackwell handbook of principles of organizational behavior*. Oxford: Blackwell.

Baum, J., Calabrese, T., & Silverman, B. (2000). Don't go it alone: Alliance network composition and startups' performance in Canadian biotechnology. *Strategic Management Journal, 21,* 267–294.

Beyerlein, M. M. (Ed.) (2000). *Work teams: Past, present and future.* Amsterdam: Kluwer Academic Publishers.

Beyerlein, M. M., Freedman, S., McGee, C., & Moran, L. (2003). *Beyond teams: Building the collaborative organization.* San Francisco, CA: Jossey-Bass/Pfeiffer.

Brandenburger, A., & Nalebuff, B. (1996). *Co-opetition.* New York: Currency Doubleday.

Cartwright, N. J., Fleck, C. L., & Uebel, T. (1996). *Otto Neurath: Philosophy between science and politics.* Cambridge, UK: Cambridge University Press.

Cohen, S. G., & Bailey, D. E. (1997). What makes teams work: Group effectiveness research from the shop floor to the executive suite. *Journal of Management, 23*(3), 239–290.

Contractor, F., & Lorange, P. (1988). *Cooperative strategies in international business.* Lexington: Lexington Books.

Davis, G., & McAdam, D. (2000). Corporations, classes, and social movements after managerialism. *Research in Organizational Behavior, 22,* 193–236 Greenwich: JAI Press.

DiMaggio, P. J., & Powell, W. W. (1983). The iron cage revisited: Institutional isomorphism and collective rationality in organizational fields. *American Sociological Review, 48,* 147–160.

Dodgson, M. (1993). Learning, trust, and technological collaboration. *Human Relations, 46*(1), 77–95.

Doz, Y. (1996). The evolution of cooperation in strategic alliances: Initial conditions or learning processes? *Strategic Management Journal, 17,* 55–83.

Doz, Y., & Baburoglu, O. (2000). From competition to collaboration: The emergence and evolution of R&D cooperatives. In: D. O. Faulkner & M. De Rond (Eds), *Cooperative strategy,* (pp. 173–192). Oxford, UK: Oxford University Press.

Emery, F. E., & Trist, E. L. (1965). The causal texture of organizational environments. *Human Relations, 18,* 21–31.

Etzkowitz, H. (1998). The norms of entrepreneurial science: Cognitive effects of the new university–industry linkages. *Research Policy, 27,* 823–833.

Faulkner, D. O., & De Rond, M. (Eds) (2000). *Cooperative strategy: Economic, business and organizational issues.* Oxford, UK: Oxford University Press.

Feldbaum, C. (2001). *Deal-making with the biotechnology industry.* Speech before the Licensing Executives Society. Biotechnology Industry Organization. Retrieved January 10, 2004, from http://bio.org/speeches/speeches/20011029.asp?p = yes&

Fisher, K., Rayner, S., & Belgard, W. (1995). *Tips for teams.* New York: McGraw-Hill.

Freeman, C., Sharp, M., & Walker, W. (1991). *Technology and the future of Europe: Global competition and the environment in the 1990s.* London, New York: Pinter.

Gans, J., & Porter, M. (2003). *Assessing Australia's innovative capacity in the 21st century.* Intellectual Property Research Institute of Australia.

Gans, J. S., & Stern, S. (2003). *Managing ideas: Commercialization strategies for biotechnology.* Working Paper no. 01/03, Intellectual Property Research Institute of Australia.

Gans, J. S., Williams, P. L., & Briggs, D. (2002). *Intellectual property rights: A grant of monopoly or an aid to competition?* Working Paper no. 7/02, Intellectual Property Research Institute of Australia.

Grant, R. (1996). Toward a knowledge-based theory of the form. *Strategic Management Journal, 17,* 419–439.

Greenwood, R., Suddaby, R., & Hinings, C. R. (2002). Theorizing change: The role of professional associations in the transformation of institutional fields. *Academy of Management Journal, 45*(1), 58–80.

Gulati, R. (1995). Does familiarity breed trust? The implications of repeated ties for contractual choice in alliances. *Academy of Management Journal, 38*(1), 85–112.

Hackman, J. R. (2002). *Leading teams: Setting the stage for great performances.* Boston, MA: Harvard Business School Press.

Holm, P. (1995). The dynamics of institutionalization: Transformation processes in Norwegian fisheries. *Administrative Science Quarterly, 40*, 398–422.

Hsu, D. (2000). *Do venture capitalists affect commercialization strategies at startups?* Globalization Working Paper 00-006 MIT IPC.

Kogut, B., & Zander, U. (1992). Knowledge of the firm, combinative capabilities, and the replication of technology. *Organizational Science, 3*(3), 383–397.

Lawrence, T., Hardy, C., & Phillips, N. (2000). Institutional effects of inter-organizational collaboration: The emergence of proto-institutions. *Academy of Management Journal, 45*(1), 281–290.

Levin, M. (2004). Cross-boundary learning systems. *Systemic Practice and Action Research, 17*, 151–159.

Levinthal, D. A., & March, J. G. (1994). The myopia of learning. *Strategic Management Journal, 14*, 95–112.

Loveridge, R. (2000). The firm as differentiator and integrator of networks: Layered communities of practice and discourse. In: D. O. Faulkner & M. De Rond (Eds), *Cooperative strategy,* (pp. 135–169). Oxford, UK: Oxford University Press.

McCann, J., & Selsky, J. (1984). Hyperturbulence and the emergence of type 5 environments. *Academy of Management Review, 9*, 460–470.

Meyer, A., Goes, J., & Brooks, G. (1993). Organizations reacting to hyperturbulence. In: G. P. Huber & W. H. Glick (Eds), *Organizational change and redesign: Ideas and insights for improving performance* (pp. 66–111). New York: Oxford University Press.

Moore, J. (1996). *The death of competition: Leadership and strategy in the age of business ecosystems.* New York: Harper Business.

Nelson, R. (1994). The co-evolution of technology, industrial structure, and supporting institutions. *Industrial and Corporate Change, 3*, 47–63.

Phillips, N., Lawrence, T., & Hardy, C. (2000). Inter-organizational collaboration and the dynamics of institutional fields. *Journal of Management Sudies, 37*, 23–41.

Powell, W., Koput, K., & Smith-Doerr, L. (1996). Inter-organizational collaboration and the locus of innovation: Networks if learning in biotechnology. *Administrative Science Quarterly, 41*, 116–145.

Powell, W., Koput, K., Smith-Doerr, L., & Owen-Smith, J. (1999). Network position and firm performance: Organizational returns to collaboration in the biotechnology industry. *Research in the Sociology of Organizations, 16*, 129–159.

Rao, H., Morrill, C., & Zald, M. (2000). Power plays: How social movements and collective action create new organizational forms. *Research in Organizational Behavior, 22*, 237–281.

Schneider, J. (2002). Intellectual property: The driving force of growth and funding. *Journal of Commercial Biotechnology, 8*(4), 320–324.

Selsky, J. W., & Smith, A. E. (1994). Community entrepreneurship: A framework for social change leadership. *Leadership Quarterly, 5*(3/4), 277–296.

Smith-Doerr, L., Owen-Smith, J., Koput, K. W., & Powell, W. W. (1998). Networks and knowledge production: Collaboration and patenting in biotechnology. In: R. Leenders & S. Gabbay (Eds), *Corporate social capital.* Norwell, MA: Kluwer Academic Publishers.
Sundstrom, E., De Meuse, K. P., & Futrell, D. (1990). Work teams: Applications and effectiveness. *American Psychologist, 45,* 120–133.
Trist, E. (1983). Referent organizations and the development of inter-organizational domains. *Human Relations, 36,* 269–284.
Wills, P. J. (1998). The virtuous cycle: Working together for health and medical research. *Health and medical research strategic review.* Department of Health and Aged Care, Canberra.
Zaheer, A., & George, V. (2004). Reach out or reach within? Performance implications of alliances and location in biotechnology. *Managerial and Decision Economics, 25,* 437–452.

CREATING CULTURES OF COLLABORATION THAT THRIVE ON DIVERSITY: A TRANSFORMATIONAL PERSPECTIVE ON BUILDING COLLABORATIVE CAPITAL

Nancy L. Southern

ABSTRACT

This chapter discusses the personal and organizational risk factors of collaboration and shows the necessity of creating organizational cultures that support collaborative action. Building collaborative capital is presented as a transformative process requiring a shift in individual and collective beliefs and assumptions and new patterns of action and supporting structures that encourage communicative competence and risk taking. Collaboration is viewed through a relational lens, incorporating hermeneutic concepts. A process is offered that begins a cultural change by strengthening communicative relationships among senior leaders. A city government and public utility in a major city in the United States provide examples of actions taken by senior leaders committed to the endeavor of creating cultures of collaboration.

Collaborative Capital: Creating Intangible Value
Advances in Interdisciplinary Studies of Work Teams, Volume 11, 33–72
Copyright © 2005 by Elsevier Ltd.
All rights of reproduction in any form reserved
ISSN: 1572-0977/doi:10.1016/S1572-0977(05)11002-4

INTRODUCTION

I have had the good fortune to work with organizational leaders who want to create cultures in their organizations where collaboration among stakeholders is expected and practiced. These leaders envision people working together to accomplish organizational goals without needing direction from above. Conversations abound in the organization about the successful results of collaborative planning and action. People are excited about what they can create when there is an endless supply of diverse perspectives and ideas. Functional departments and organizational boundaries do not create limits for collaboration, but rather serve as containers for people with expertise in their fields. People work together for a common purpose, sharing resources, learning with and from one another, respecting and embracing difference, and engaging disagreement productively. Energy and enthusiasm are contagious as people recognize that any and all goals and challenges can be met by drawing from the knowledge, skills, and talents of a diverse group of people who have a shared vision and commitment to serving customers, community, and each other. These senior leaders recognize that achieving this vision creates collaborative capital that results in greater efficiency, more intangible resources, and the ability to not only reach their goals, but to exceed their expectations of what is possible. They also realize that the work of creating this culture begins with them.

Collaborate is defined by Webster's as "to work, one with another; to cooperate." Maybe the simple definition of this complex human relationship contributes to the minimal usage of this concept in organizations. Books and articles have focused more on collaboration across sectors, such as between business and education or for-profit and non-profit. Much of the focus of learning to collaborate is about how to build strategic partnerships through exchanging information. The term collaboration is also used commonly with network technology, focusing on the flow of information between people and organizations, enabling people to communicate and make collaborative decisions across distance. Not enough research and work has been done to understand the complexity of developing organizational cultures where collaboration is a pattern of action that is expected, facilitated by supporting structures and recognized as critical to organizational success and sustainability.

The focus of this volume is the development of collaborative capital. Since business continues to promote its primary purpose as the development of capital, those of us who work with developing people and organizations are often forced to present our work in the terms of economics. While I continue to hold the perspective that the value of human relationships should not be reduced to the purpose of making money, I do believe that increased profitability is an outcome of how effectively people work together in support of an organization's purpose and mission. In this regard, we are looking at the intangible capital that is derived from increased collaboration among stakeholders of any type of organization. The organizations I reference in this chapter are a large metropolitan city government and a water district that serves the county in which the city resides. I have worked with the senior leadership teams of both organizations as they strive to develop cultures of collaboration. These leaders understand the importance of collaboration among their staff, their partners, and the customers they serve. They recognize that collaboration is critical to working with the complexity that is inherent in the services they provide to a diverse population. Both organizations strive to be recognized as leaders in their field. They believe that only by creating cultures in which collaboration among diverse constituents is the norm, they will be able to achieve the level of stewardship expected of public servants.

Collaborative capital is not fully realized unless organizations can work together with stakeholders outside the organization. These may include board members, customers, students, suppliers, and the community. The public institutions that I profile in this chapter are learning just how important collaboration is with the residents they serve. The complexity of managing a city cannot be handled alone by the staff it employs or by the public officials elected. Water projects cannot be completed unless the residents support the project and understand the value that will result from the disruptions the project may cause. Oftentimes, these relationships that exist outside the visible or invisible walls of the organization are the most challenging. They require that each person hold a strong belief in the value of collaboration and have an orientation to collaborative action. Personal development and often transformational changes are needed. Interpersonal communication skills and ways of working with different perspectives and disagreement need to be developed. And the organizational culture needs to support collaborative action.

Rosabeth Moss Kanter (2004) posits that teams and organizations that overcome challenges and thrive on success rely on individual and organizational confidence. Her research of many successful organizations and individuals shows that three cornerstones are critical to developing and sustaining confidence: accountability, collaboration, and initiative. She has found that confidence exists on four levels: self-confidence, confidence in others, confidence in organizational systems, and external confidence in the network of relationships and resources. Understanding this interconnection between the individual, team, organization, and community helps senior leaders create the conditions that cultivate collaborative capital.

Kanter's research shows the importance of collaborative capital to organizational success. While collaboration may be a cornerstone of confidence, confidence is also a cornerstone of collaboration. Confidence spurs action and risk taking and supports collaboration. Collaboration builds and reinforces confidence. To extend our understanding of how to develop collaborative capital, this chapter shows the importance of understanding collaboration from a relational perspective where cultural consciousness and communicative competence result in the confidence that builds collaborative capital.

Creating collaborative capital is a complex cultural change process that is transformational by nature, as it requires change in fundamental beliefs and assumptions, patterns of action, and supporting structures. If we, as people striving to foster change in organizations and communities, take an integral approach to the changes needed for collaboration, then we create a greater possibility that people will change the way they participate in life both inside and outside the organization. Marvin Brown's book, *Corporate Integrity: Rethinking Business Ethics and Leadership* (2005) posits that the meaning of integrity must be integrative of five dimensions: the cultural, interpersonal, organizational, civic, and environmental. Rather than integrity being an individual concept, Brown places it within a civic context that draws upon shared values of meeting human needs and respecting human rights. "This allows an examination of how these values are realized not only in interpersonal relationships, but also in corporate relationships with other groups in civic society as they struggle to work together to design a sustainable world" (p. 25). Towards this purpose, I would like to extend the idea of collaborative capital outside the organizational context to providing greater possibilities for working together to create a sustainable global community. The two organizations I reference are doing just that. While they realize that collaboration begins with them, their purpose is much larger than creating a better organization. They want to contribute to creating a better community and be an example for other organizations.

My approach to building collaborative capital is built upon a set of beliefs and assumptions about the human experience that I have developed through my study of hermeneutic philosophy and Chinese culture. The following section provides a brief introduction to a few core concepts of hermeneutics which you will see reflected throughout this chapter.

A HERMENEUTIC PERSPECTIVE

While we can choose to think of collaboration for strategic economic purposes, I believe that the primary purpose is the desire to create meaningful life through relationships of care. As human beings, we come to know who we are and what is important through our relationships with others. These relationships create the possibility for making meaning as we expand our understanding through embracing that, which is different from us. When we live and work with care for those we serve and the work we do, we can build authentic relationships based on shared values, truthfulness, and trust and new worlds of understanding within which we can participate together. Our ability to encounter "the other," that which is truly different, is our gateway to transformation. Collaboration, from this perspective, is a transformational change process for persons and organizations.

Hermeneutics views one's life experience as interpretive and relational. As such, we come to know who we are within the context of our history, culture, and relationships. Martin Heidegger, a German philosopher who published his seminal work *Sein Und Zeit* (*Being and Time*) in 1927, described the nature of Being, which he called *Dasein*. Heidegger's understanding of the nature of Being was greatly influenced through his study and conversation with Asian teachers and philosophers. He was seeking to overcome the limitations of the mind–body dualistic thinking that had pervaded Western thought since the days of Descartes. The nature of Dasein is an integration of mind, body, and spirit. It represents a way of being in the world that is aware of self as connected to larger meaningful context. It is a way of being "in care" of self and the world. Paul Shih-yi Hsiao comments in his chapter in *Heidegger and Asian Thought*,

> In my attempts to understand Heidegger's ideas, I have first to learn why his thinking was so difficult for many of his Western contemporaries to understand, or appeared so sensational. What he "brought to language" has frequently been said similarly in the thinking of the Far East. For example, temporality has always been understood differently in China than in the West. For us the duck does not need any paranormal powers: everything is connected with everything else, and in each moment there is concealed the entire past and also the open future.
>
> (see Parkes, 1987, p. 94)

As in Chinese philosophy, in Heidegger's concept of being, thinking, speaking, and acting are inseparable. Care, expressed through concern, reflection, and action creates the possibility for meaningful existence and proactive change.

Heidegger's contributions along with his student, Hans Gadamer, and other philosophers that embraced the hermeneutic tradition offer a bridge between Eastern and Western thinking and ways of being. Hermeneutics offers a way out of the limitations of mind–body dualistic thinking and an opportunity to think and act from a place of being connected with others and the world as whole. Heidegger (1927/1962) posited that we are always already in relationship, meaning that we are born into a context of relationships that constitute our being in the world. Life begins with a union and we come to know who we are in relationship with others and with our world. Heidegger's perspective was influenced both by the many philosophers and students of life dating back to Plato and Aristotle and through his encounter with Eastern philosophy. Hermeneutics creates a bridge between Eastern and Western thinking and as such creates possibilities for understanding that which is foreign to us. As a philosophy of interpretation, hermeneutics was originally used to interpret the Bible and other texts. An understanding of hermeneutics helps one understand the nature of being from a human systems perspective, and take action in ways that are relational. Hermeneutics invites us into a meaningful inquiry into the context of our relationships with others, our work, our organizations, and the world.

Embedded in Heidegger's work is also the understanding that we live in language. As relational beings, we construct our world through language. Language is the fabric of cultures and we need to recognize its importance in human communication. Words are meaning-laden and shape how we think about concepts. For example, the common use of the word "tool" to describe language or skills related to communicating with others supports the assumption of separateness. The very idea of picking up and using a tool to accomplish a task is incongruent with the idea of two persons talking and working together. Establishing cultures of collaboration requires changing the way we understand ourselves in relationship with others and changing the language to be congruent with that understanding.

THE CHALLENGE OF COLLABORATION

Collaborative capital can only be fully realized within cultures that foster collaboration. Cultures define and reinforce how people act. The shared assumptions, group norms, unwritten rules, and climate communicate whether the culture is individually oriented or collaboratively oriented. While the espoused values may speak to the importance of collaboration, the stories of who gets recognized or punished and the metaphors used to describe how people interact communicate the actual values. People cannot and will not act collaboratively when the culture encourages competitive, individual behavior.

Cultural change is transformational change: a change in values, beliefs and assumptions, and patterns of action. Schein (1992) believes that "the ability to perceive the limitations of one's own culture and to develop the culture adaptively is the ultimate challenge of leadership" (p. 2). Developing cultures of collaboration requires leaders to understand organizations from a cultural perspective and develop cultural competence to work cross-culturally. As a leader, I need to recognize the gaps between the existing values, beliefs and assumptions, and patterns of action, and those that are needed to support collaboration. Then I need to employ transformational change efforts to close that gap.

Changing and developing supportive structures, such as technology, performance measures, and rewards is an important part of the process, but these alone will not sustain collaboration. People need to think differently about their relationships with others and value aspects of the relationship that are uncommon in our Western culture. We need to care about each other on both a personal and a professional level. We need to care about our customers. And we need to care about the work we do together in service of the organization's purpose. While the term love might be substituted for care in these statements, I find that care is a more appropriate term. I believe we can live our lives in care and do our work with care. That does not mean that we have to like everyone, love our work, or agree with all ideas and decisions, as care involves the willingness to speak out in disagreement. Rather, we see the importance of our relationships to support our common mission and to provide opportunities for continued learning. Without relationships of care, I doubt if true collaboration can be achieved.

Changing our own sense of self and our relationships with others and the organization involves personal risk. Collaboration involves risk. We need to acknowledge how difficult it is to collaborate with others. Even when we want to collaborate, we often find ourselves crossing boundaries we did not realize would create tensions, having our ego bruised when others offer a different perspective on our work, or having our intentions questioned based on erroneous assumptions. Collaboration requires that we prepare ourselves and our organizations to engage in ways that are unfamiliar and uncomfortable.

When we ask people to do this work, do we recognize that we are asking them to engage in transformational change? Are we, as change leaders, ready to support that transformational change? The field of transformative learning in adult education provides research and theory that informs our understanding of how to foster transformative learning and change at the personal level. Jack Mezirow, considered the *Father* of this field of inquiry, defined transformative learning as deep shifts in our frame of reference (Mezirow, 2000). Cranton (2000) describes frames of reference as "complex webs of assumptions, expectations, values, and beliefs that act as a filter or screen through which we view ourselves and the world" (p. 181). These frames of references are shaped by our experiences, cultural and religious beliefs, and provide a context for our sense of self and our interpretation of the world in which we live. When we understand that in asking people to collaborate, we are asking them to do so much more than behave differently; we can begin to see the level of personal risk associated with this change. We are asking them to reconsider and change some of the beliefs, values, and assumptions that have shaped their understanding of who they are in relationship with others and their world. Are they willing to take this risk, make this change? Are we willing to invest the resources in changing our organizations to support this risk taking?

LIMITS TO COLLABORATION

The term collaboration still has negative connotations for Europeans who endured the occupation of their countries during World War II and were old enough to understand the concept of aiding the enemy. To be considered a "collaborateur" by one's own people was to be branded a traitor in the worst sense. This points to the fact that although we generally assume that collaboration is a positive action, there are war-torn regions in today's world where collaboration with the enemy is taking place and the negative associations still exist. Many cultures, including organizational cultures have boundaries around collaboration. These boundaries often are not clearly stated. They may be part of what Schein (1992) refers to as unwritten rules. As a leader, employee, and organizational consultant, I have traversed unknowingly across these boundaries in more than one organization and have suffered the consequences. Most often these boundaries are related to power and authority issues and involve people in the hierarchy who are not comfortable sharing leadership. Once we have suffered punishment for traversing the boundaries of power and authority, most of us are more cautious about taking risks in the future.

How many people in organizations survive by keeping their heads down? As a consultant, I find that most people want to speak out and want to collaborate with each other. They realize the necessity of collaboration as they struggle to manage the complexity of their responsibilities without having the ability to create the changes needed to do their best work. Yet, they have learned to be cautious, to avoid disagreement and present little challenge to the current system.

John Locke (1998) argues that Americans continue to become de-voiced as our culture evolves toward more individualism. He points out that as we spend less time in conversation with others and more time at our computers, in our cars, and in front of the television, we become isolated and lose our ability to communicate. Locke makes an important connection between less socialization and a decline in trust. Fukuyama (1995) points out that when people distrust each other, they only co-operate under a system of formal rules and regulations agreed to and enforced, often by coercive means. The contractual relationship governed by policies is the basis of relationships in organizations. People do not often get to know each other well enough to develop trust. More people are working at home and communicating through e-mail. More teams are comprised of people who span great distances. While I do not believe that distance and technology have to foster a decline in relationships, I do think that more emphasis must be placed on fostering relationships in organizations, as collaboration requires trust and communicative competence.

I often tell my students of my experience working inside a large telecommunications company. The building is enormous, with four wings of three floors each spanning a quarter mile distance. Each of the three floors has a great deal of uniformity and it is easy for newcomers to lose sight of where they are in the building. A few offices surround the perimeter of each floor and most people sit in cubicles. Most communication, including meetings occurs on the phone or through e-mail and web technology. People sitting next to each other often do not work in the same group and often do not know each other. I have walked through the building many times during the middle of the day and it seemed as though no one was there. White noise is piped in to drown the sound and the cubicles are high enough so you cannot see people inside of them. If someone likes working anonymously, is easy to do there. Except around the cafeteria, I rarely saw people gathered and talking together. Often I saw managers walking the halls while participating in meetings on their cell phones. This is not the type of environment that fosters collaboration and I did not experience much of it while I was there. Rather, the separation and isolation created a level of distrust that not only inhibited open, honest communication, but created hostile competition and risk avoidance.

A pattern of behavior that reinforces risk avoidance and distrust exists within cultures where fear and powerlessness abound. As fear and power-lessness increase, distrust emerges between organizational members, and between members and the organization as a whole, eroding personal and professional relationships, and fostering risk avoidance and blame. A pattern or cycle of blame is one I have observed in many organizations and in our society. This pattern is often seen between competing groups, departments, and subcultures.

When we get stuck in this cycle of blame, we have a difficult time seeing our own responsibility for the problem. Fig. 1 shows how when people continuously avoid risk and collude to reinforce assumptions and beliefs, they feel powerless. Fear and powerlessness fuel blame and breakdown relationships. When this culture takes hold, open communication, truthful-ness, and trust cease to exist. A culture of blame results in a suspicion of intent. Even though other people may be doing their best and doing what they believe is right, their actions may cause others to believe that they do not have the best interests of the organization in mind. As distrust grows, people begin to take more independent and defensive action, thus

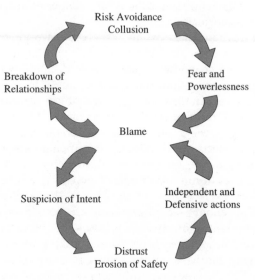

Fig. 1. Cycle of blame.

reinforcing the blame and continuing to damage relationships, inhibit collaboration, and erode organization potential.

This cycle of blame is one of many defensive routines that keep us from working collaboratively and living our lives in ways that support the greater good. Understanding what causes us to develop these patterns of actions is important to finding ways to change them. Chris Argyris' (1985, 1990, 1991, 1993) work in understanding defensive routines is helpful. Argyris defines a defensive routine as a habitual way of acting, individually and collectively, to prohibit embarrassment and threat. We can see how the cycle of blame fits into this definition, as it protects us from acknowledging, even believing, that we are wrong. Unfortunately, these defensive routines also inhibit learning as they continue to reinforce existing beliefs, assumptions, and patterns of action.

Argyris (1977) described a key to factor in supporting individual and organizational learning as the ability to move from the more common single-loop learning, correcting a problem and making appropriate changes to continue down the predetermined path, to double-loop learning, questioning the underlying assumptions of the path and the thinking that created the path. Argyris (1991) applied this concept to the challenge that professional people have engaging in double-loop learning as they tend to feel embarrassed and threatened by critically examining their own beliefs, assumptions, and role in organizations. Argyris posits that everyone develops a "theory of action – a set of rules that individuals use to design and implement their own behavior as to understand the behavior of others" (p. 103). The challenge he stated is that most people are not fully aware of the beliefs and assumptions behind their theories of action and thus unable to recognize the gap between their espoused theories and theories-in-action. So, while we may often accuse people of not "walking their talk," we may not understand that the challenge of doing so is much more complex than we realize.

Robert Kegan's work lends a perspective on this challenge. Kegan (1982) defined levels of consciousness in relation to a developmental self. While Kegan's work differs from the hermeneutic perspective in that it is grounded in subject–object relations, it offers important insight to the personal development process and our capacity for transformational learning. Kegan sees the development of persons as a process of differentiation, as we form a self, and integration, as we learn to relate to others. Hermeneutics, on the other hand, posits that we are always, already in relationship, questioning the very idea of a self-separate from others. While I prefer not to think of individuals as being stuck in certain stages of development, considering these stages can inform our understanding of the personal challenges of engaging the transformational change needed for collaboration, a new understanding of self in relation to others and to our world.

Kegan's work builds on the work of Piaget and others who have studied person development. His levels of consciousness actually begin with a Stage 0 which Kegan refers to as the incorporative stage, a reflexive stage occurring during infancy. Stage 1, or the first order of consciousness, is the impulsive stage, described as a time when the person, normally a 2-year old, "comes to have reflexes rather than to be them" (p. 85). This is when the subject–object relationship begins. The second order of consciousness constitutes a time when a person becomes aware of the needs and wants of others as different from those of oneself. This stage brings an understanding that we have some control over our reality and that our actions have consequences. What does not exist at this stage is the ability to create a shared reality. We understand that we need others to help us meet our own needs and our relationships are grounded in a need for control and a fear of losing control. Our interactions with others are focused on what response we might get to what we say and do. The third order of consciousness is the development of the interpersonal self and consciousness of a shared reality within a subject–object relationship. This shared reality, as Kegan describes, is not what I have described as creating a shared reality in the hermeneutic sense, where the relationship is between two subjects. Rather, Kegan's description of the interpersonal self embraces the other as a completion of the self from a deficit perspective. One's concern is about being accepted and appreciated and as a result may inhibit the full expression of emotions such as anger, even in situations where it is justified. Adults that live primarily within this stage of development are less likely to assert their influence. Kegan's fourth order of consciousness, the institutional self, broadens one's relationship with the other beyond just other people, to a relationship with institutions. As a self-authoring stage, we define who we are by the work we do and our meaning in life comes, not only through our relationships with family and friends, it also extends to our work and civic relationships. We care about the purpose and success of the organization and of our community or government and are willing to take risks in support of that larger purpose. A key limitation to this ego phase is that the individual is defined by the work or the institution and its belief system, thereby is not fully able to question those beliefs and redefine oneself.

The movement into the fifth order of consciousness, the interindividual stage, signals a new balance of self and other that enables what Kegan describes as the ability to "hear, and to seek out information which might cause the self to alter its behavior" (p. 105). He further describes it as developing the capability for intimacy while maintaining one's individual self, resulting in the capacity to "give oneself up" to another. I interpret this stage of development as gaining the self-confidence to question one's assumptions and those of others, including institutions, and to take action, interdependently with others to promote learning and change. In Kegan's view, this is the order the consciousness needed for persons to engage in relationships where dialog, granting authority, and sharing knowledge create an opportunity for our own transformation in thinking and being.

While we can consider how to work with individual development toward higher levels of consciousness, we can also think about this from a cultural context. A question I hold in considering these levels of consciousness in tension with a hermeneutic perspective is not so much whether there is a developmental aspect to the ability of persons to engage in true collaborative action, but rather, can the invitation to participate in cultures that promote and support knowledge sharing, dialog, continuous learning, and collaborative action, create the conditions that enable the development of one's personal capacity? In essence, can the right cultural context support one's ability to reach Kegan's fifth order of consciousness? I also wonder to what extent we are stuck in what Senge (1990) refers to as a "limits to growth" archetype. Our institutions are constructed to structure and control behavior, and people, beginning in childhood, adapt to the limits of that structure and thus limit our own ego development and ability to participate in ways that can change the institutions. It is a bit of the chicken and egg syndrome. How and where do we begin to develop the capacity to change individuals and cultures?

MEETING THE CHALLENGE OF COLLABORATION

Understanding the challenges we face to transform ourselves and our organizations for collaboration, provides us a better opportunity to construct change processes that support collaborative action. We must go far beyond the teambuilding activities, processes, and structural changes focused on creating behavioral change. We need to develop new ways to build and strengthen relationships, change the way we communicate with one another, and create new organizational cultures that support collaboration. We all need to develop a greater capacity for transformational learning.

The process of transformation begins with an invitation to participate in new ways, to change the nature of our relationships. With the intention of making meaning together, we can learn to talk together in new ways that encourage reflection on beliefs and assumptions, and invite multiple perspectives. Language is a powerful medium which shapes how we think and act, and how we engage with one another. We do not just use language, we participate in it. It shapes who we are and how we construct our world. Kegan and Lahey's book, *How the Way We Talk Can Change the Way We Work: Seven Languages for Transformation* (2001) offers a practical approach to working on this change through coaching, mentoring, and group activities. *The Fifth Discipline Fieldbook* (Senge et al., 1994) and the other companion books have provided me with approaches to working with transformational change. Whitney and Trosten-Blooms's book, *The Power of Appreciative Inquiry: A Practical Guide to Positive Change* (2003), provides a good road map to using appreciative inquiry (AI) as a way to transform the way people talk and work together.

As we work to change organizational culture, we need to remember that it is a creative process. Schein's book, *Organizational Culture and Leadership* (1992), is a great resource in understanding the aspects of organizational culture. We cannot succeed unless we develop an understanding of the current culture, the challenges facing the organization, and the hopes and dreams of the members. Then, as leaders, consultants, and educators, we can work together with members of the organization to construct a change process with the intention of building the organization's capacity to create the change themselves.

There is no toolbox for building collaborative capital. The remainder of this chapter offers what I have come to understand about collaboration and how I have used that understanding to construct a process that engages senior and mid-level managers in this transformational change.

NATURE OF THE COLLABORATIVE RELATIONSHIP: BALANCING RESPECT AND AUTHORITY

The Chinese art of *Guanxi*, which literally means "relationship," is closer to my idea of collaboration than how we generally think about collaboration in the United States. Guanxi is a mixture of strategic relationships and humanness, the simple honoring and respecting of others. It is a different way of being in relationship with others than that which is common in the

United States. Hofstede's (1997) research described a primary difference between the cultures of the United States and China as the orientation toward individualism and collectivism. Guanxi is based on the mental model of collectivism where the interest of the group prevails over the interest of the individual. I will share a story of my experience with Guanxi when I traveled to China for my dissertation research.

My doctoral study included three trips to Southeast Asia and China. During my first trip to China, I decided that I wanted to go back to adopt a daughter and to engage in conversations with business leaders and educators that would inform my dissertation. I wanted to know and understand what was different about being in relationship in the United States and China. I had experienced the difference through teaching students from China and Taiwan. I noticed that my relationships with Chinese students were often closer than with American students, contributing to a greater opportunity for mutual learning. Yet at the same time there was what Hofstede (1997) refers to as "power distance," and defines as "the extent to which the less powerful members of institutions and organizations within a country expect and accept that power is distributed unequally" (p. 28). My Chinese students accepted my authority as their teacher and were still comfortable establishing a close relationship with me that, at times, involved social activities outside of school. In the United States, we often view this type of relationship as strategic, hoping it will result in our benefit. I do not believe that was their primary motive. Their practice of Guanxi seemed to be primarily based on their honoring of me as a person of knowledge. They cared for me and expected some care in return. While that expectation can evolve into preferential treatment, that was a boundary I was responsible for maintaining.

This experience challenged a basic assumption I held that power distance weakens relationships and creates a barrier to communication and learning. These students were comfortable with the power distance between us and were willing to grant me authority as their teacher. In doing so, they situated themselves as learners and were also comfortable being my teachers of Chinese culture. Our relationship existed within a context of respect for what we could offer each other. As a result, they received more of my attention and understanding of the challenge of studying in another language and culture. My willingness and ability to engage in this relationship created mutual trust and acknowledgment.

When I met with business and political leaders and educators in China to discuss learning organizations, I experienced Guanxi again and understood the grace and the art of being in relationships where the individual is not the center of the universe. My experience was that the acceptance of power distance actually creates less power distance. This sounds like a paradox and challenges our either/or thinking. It also challenges a basic assumption about authority as something we must struggle against. I now believe that granting authority to others graces a relationship and gives us more collaborative and personal power. Holding on to authority creates alienation, distancing us from those with whom we work. Granting authority creates a space for belonging, as we welcome the knowledge and expertise that others bring to our work.

Gadamer (1960/1993) speaks of how unfortunate it is that the concept of authority is most often related to domination and blind obedience rather than to knowledge. He comments that authority rests on our acceptance and recognition that understanding and judgment of others can be superior to one's own in certain situations. Authority, he states, "cannot actually be bestowed, but is earned and must be earned, if someone is to lay claim to it" (p. 279). Holding this perspective of authority is critical to effective collaboration. For true collaboration means that we come into a relationship acknowledging our strengths and weaknesses, and those of others with the intention to create an outcome that is much greater than anyone can achieve independently.

The field of organizational development has fought hard to influence a change in the nature of authority relationships between managers and employees, and between peers. While this stance is important to support a shift in the nature of the relationships away from the traditional command and control, the idea of granting authority to others has been lost along the way. Striving for relationships of total equality, where no person has considerable influence over the other, can create a situation where people do not have the opportunity to excel in their areas of strength. Striving for equal voice and not allowing those with knowledge and experience to influence us can result in groupthink or poor decision-making. It is important to consider that all opinions are not always equal. Some opinions are solely based on values and beliefs and others based on knowledge and experience. While both are important to consider, if we recognize the importance of informed opinions, we might allow ourselves to be influenced by others regardless of the positional authority they or we may hold. An often-used example of groupthink is the challenger disaster. The engineers with the most technical knowledge about the O-rings warned the management team about the danger of launching when temperatures were below those that had been safely tested. Yet, these warnings were not heeded. Rather the decision was made from a management perspective, focused on the objective of launching the space shuttle on time over the objective of a safe launch and return. How many times have we seen decisions made in this way? Over time, those with knowledge come to accept that their informed opinions have little authority and they become less likely to share them in an influential way.

Granting authority requires self-confidence and awareness. To admit that others, whether they are in positions superior to ours or not, have authority based on their knowledge, requires that we feel secure in who we are and what we know. This security is fostered through cultures that appreciate and recognize the gifts and talents that each person brings. Max DePree, in his book, *Leadership is an Art* (1989), told a touching story of a millwright who had worked in his company for many years. Not until DePree attended the funeral of this millwright did he discover that the man was a talented poet. DePree writes that the learning from this story is that "it is fundamental that leaders endorse a concept of persons (that) begins with an understanding of the diversity of people's gifts and talents and skills" (p. 7). In speaking to the idea of granting authority, DePree powerfully connects this to the true value of diversity.

Understanding and accepting diversity enable us to see that each of us is needed. It also enables us to begin to think about being abandoned to the strengths of others, to admitting that we cannot *know* or *do* everything... Recognizing diversity helps us understand the need we have for opportunity, equity, and identity in the workplace (1989, p. 7).

This recognition of persons as unique and talented engenders the self-confidence needed to grant authority to others and to speak with authority when we are the ones who can best do so. Collaboration invites us into a democratic relationship, and as such, we are asked to listen to one another, consider each other's opinions, and grant authority when appropriate, regardless of the authority of the positions we hold. Organizational cultures that support collaboration respect the different and unique values, perspectives, and talents brought by people from diverse backgrounds and cultures.

CULTURAL CONSCIOUSNESS: ENCOUNTERING "THE OTHER"

Although some people in the United States think we have come a long way in our efforts to value diversity, this perspective seems to be held more by people of Caucasian heritage rather than by people of color. Although laws exist that prohibit racism in employment, housing, and public access, people of color continue to face racism and discrimination in many ways. Organizations often feel that have met their responsibility for diversity if they hire a certain percentage of people of color and espouse a value of respecting diversity. Yet, when I talk with people of color in organizations, they continue to feel pressure to conform to the normative beliefs and practices. Rarely do I meet people of color who feel free to express themselves in ways unique to their culture or feel their voice is equally heard.

Laws and policies promote compliance. And while there is the potential for compliance to grow into respect and recognition, that shift comes through relationships where a common purpose provides opportunities to develop knowledge and trust of one another. Diversity training programs may only scratch of the surface of understanding and valuing difference. For the most part, they too promote compliance. Edward E. Hubbard (2003) emphasizes the importance of measuring the effect of diversity efforts to their contribution to the bottom line. Similar to the concept of collaborative capital, diversity capital is important, yet we need to question if tying human relationships to economic advantage is serving the purpose of bringing us closer to valuing each other as persons with unique gifts, talents, and skills. Emphasizing the economic value of people and relationships reinforces how, in the Western tradition, we commonly hold others as objects rather than subjects. When people working in organizations are considered assets, it is easier to discard them when they become too heavy on the balance sheet. When an organization hires people of color for the purpose of economic advantage, the persons and what they bring tend to lose value. The challenge we face is that we have not yet reached the point where we do not need these justifications to drive decisions and actions because many people do not yet understand how critical diversity is to our continued learning and growth individually and organizationally. It is time to change the way we hold others in relationship, personally and within organizations.

While diversity begins with recognition and value of people from different walks of life, it is so much more. The core of diversity is our encounter with "the other," that which is different than us. Collaboration that values and thrives on diversity requires a curiosity about "the other" and a willingness to be vulnerable. This encounter with "the other" is a gateway to transformation if we are willing to question our own assumptions and those commonly held within the culture. Questioning these assumptions and exposing ourselves to very different realities can create disorienting dilemmas that shake the very fabric of our sense of self in the world as they call into question that which we thought we understood and from which we have based our relationships and actions. A disorienting dilemma can result in a major life transformation and leave one situated at the threshold of a new understanding, but not yet able to appropriate it. Being in this place of unknowingness and vulnerability can help us reach out to others in a way that creates openness and trust, and encourages new understanding.

All too often, diversity is discussed from a perspective that focuses on ethnic, gender, lifestyle, and physical ability differences. A broader perspective is important to consider as diversity involves working with any difference that is core to our beliefs, assumptions, and patterns of action. For instance, a public organization may have a diversity challenge of fully integrating people who have come from private industry. An organization which has a culture of people who are middle aged may have a challenge integrating young people. Schein (1996) discusses the challenge of working across the managerial cultures in organizations. He describes three cultures that are present in almost all organizations as executive, operations, and technical. The technical culture refers to people who have a specific expertise that clearly differentiates their work from others. Depending on the organization, this culture might include engineers, information technology people, scientists, doctors, or teachers. My observation has been that another subculture exists in many corporate organizations that is comprised of the sales and marketing people. Collaboration requires the ability to work effectively across these multiple cultures, to respect and value the different perspectives that each brings and to know when to grant authority based on knowledge and experience. The integration of these diverse perspectives creates an opportunity for knowledge sharing and creation.

A PLACE FOR KNOWLEDGE
SHARING AND CREATION

Krogh, Ichijo, and Nonaka (2000) speak to the importance of the cultural context for creating a space for knowledge creation. They state that "effective knowledge creating depends on an enabling context... a shared space that fosters emerging relationships" (p. 7). They refer to the Japanese idea of *ba*, which means place in the sense of context. So the space created refers to physical, virtual, and mental space. They discuss the difference between sharing information, which is what we see happening most often, and sharing knowledge. Sharing knowledge from a contextual perspective means that we think of knowledge, as these authors describe as "dynamic, relational, and based on human action" (p. 7). Sharing knowledge contextually requires us to consider communication from a contextual perspective. Brown (2005) describes the difference between an individualist perspective on communication, which he calls the post-office model, and a relational or contextual perspective.

> In the post-office model, one isolated individual has an idea in his head, puts it in some form, and then sends it to another. The other receives the "message," decodes it, and sends back a response. It is like sending and receiving mail. Communication is a process of "getting one's views across," or "exchanging ideas." In the contextual model of communication, on the other hand, individuals participate in communication, and the context is seen as an integral part of the communicative process. The space between persons, which seems like an empty space in the post-office model, becomes laden with meaning in the contextual model. Speakers and listeners are seen as continually relying on, as well as continually maintaining and changing, their context (p. 33).

We can see in Brown's description of these two different perspectives on communication how the individualist perspective supports communication based on information sharing and instrumental learning, rather than knowledge sharing and communicative learning. When we understand how someone came to their knowledge, we can see their opinion as an informed one and choose to grant them authority in that area. We can also question the assumptions upon which they base their knowledge. Knowledge creation requires interpersonal relationships that support the granting of authority and the ability to engage in dynamic dialog. Working in this collaborative space requires confidence on all four levels described by Kanter (2004). It also requires new ways of communicating that support collective learning and collaborative action.

Brown's work on disagreement as a resource for decision-making is important to reference here, as we consider the space we need to create for building collaborative capital. Traditionally, teamwork has focused more reaching agreement than engaging disagreement. Yet, disagreement is a critical resource for collaborative action. Brown uses W. Barnett Pearce's (1989) cultural communication model to show how different cultural perspectives and practices of communication ignore or engage disagreement as a resource for learning and change. Pearce's model includes four different cultural types: monocultural, ethnocentric, modernistic, and cosmopolitan. Brown (2005) states that while the modernistic communicator may engage disagreement, it is generally in the form of "us and them." The cosmopolitan communicator sees disagreement as an opportunity for learning different ways of constructing reality, and interprets disagreement as a resource as long as it does not completely block coordination. Disagreements about what should be done are seen as conflicts between different views of what is right. In such cases, they explore the background of the different views and try to increase their knowledge to see which "right" might be more appropriate, or if there might be a third way of resolving the conflict (p. 53).

Collaboration requires that we be cosmopolitan communicators, people who can consider different points of view and bridge those differences to create new perspectives.

We cannot speak of collaborative capital without acknowledging the importance of how we communicate and take action. Once we recognize the importance of diverse perspectives, disagreement, and a cultural environment that supports learning and knowledge sharing, we need to develop processes for engagement. Dialog, as a way to engage in conversations that are contextual and meaningful, is an important strategic resource.

THE ROLE OF DIALOG AND CONVERSATION

The ability to explore alternative perspectives and challenge assumptions comes through the engagement in dialog. While the term dialog is loosely used, I like to reserve it for a conversational process which engages a deep level of inquiry to explore new thinking and make new meaning. Dialog assumes a respect for diverse perspectives which is demonstrated through listening with care and curiosity. Buber (1947/1955) describes "the basic movement of the life of dialog is the turning toward the other" (p. 22). He sees the necessary relationship as one of "I-thou," showing respect and honoring of the other. Dialog is much more than an exchange of words. It is exchange of meaning from which new meaning is made collectively. There is presence required where all participants focus their awareness to the conversation and the context that surrounds it. Friere (1992/1994) describes dialog as a democratic relationship, an "opportunity available to me to open up to the thinking of others, and thereby not wither away in isolation" (p. 119). Dialog engages us in a communicative relationship that has the power to transform how we live and work together.

While the act of dialog has the power to transform, the nature of the dialog process is counter-cultural to the way we have learned to communicate in the United States. Issacs (1999) describes dialog as "a conversation in which people think together in relationship" (p. 19). Dialog creates an open space where we can share and explore our ideas and come to new understanding. It allows for questions to be asked that have not been asked before. It provides an opportunity to say what we have never before said. The process invites people into a shared inquiry, a learning conversation that is dynamic and creative. Dialog by nature is collaborative process. As people think together, take risks by raising questions and challenging assumptions, they develop closer relationships that appreciate diverse perspectives.

Dialog involves personal risk as it creates an expectation that assumptions and beliefs will be challenged. It provides a forum for engaging disagreement and finding common ground. Through working with dialog, I have discovered how difficult it can be to bring people into a space where they can learn and practice dialog. One of the key challenges is time; another is the lack of orientation toward reflective conversation, especially within organizations. As a result of the post-office perspective, many people see communication as a means to an end. They only want to hear what they believe is relevant and say what they think is important, based on what they already know. Most people spend more time-sharing their opinion than asking questions.

Since the intent of dialog is inquiry and learning, it does not always have a clear intended result. And while it is generally not considered an efficient process, in reality it saves time and results in better decision-making. Dialog provides the context that enables us to understand not only what others think, but also why they think what they do and how they came to think that way. As such, we begin to be able to think and act together. I will give an example. I have worked with one senior management team on strategic planning for 4 years. My approach is more on strategic conversation than planning per se. Yet, I hold the intention that the team will create plans for change. This particular senior management team did not want to walk away from the planning retreat with a long list of to-do items and so were hesitant to create an action plan. The retreats created a space when the team could engage in a strategic conversation in ways that did not occur during their regular meetings. They shared their different perspectives and challenged some of the prevailing assumptions. Yet, they continued to be resistant to creating an action plan. I discovered at our third planning retreat that they really did not seem to need a formal plan. The conversation and dialog at the retreat provided them with enough common ground, an understanding of how they wanted to take action so that they were able to take appropriate action in the course of their regular work. They had developed a greater capacity to act collaboratively through the quality of their conversations and relationships. My realization of this phenomenon gave me more confidence in the power of dialog to prepare people to take collaborative action.

Understanding that dialog can be a transformative process, I have sought to understand what makes it so and how to bring people into relationships that support dialog. How can we develop enough confidence in ourselves and enough trust in our relationships to challenge and shift individual and collective assumptions? Habermas' (1981/1985, 1981/1987) theory of communicative competence has helped me understand how the communicative act of dialog is transformative on an individual level and how it creates an opportunity for shared meaning and action.

COMMUNICATIVE COMPETENCE

Communicative competence takes place when the principles of *comprehensibility*, *shared values*, *truth*, and *trust* are met in conversation. These principles of communication are based on the work of Jurgan Habermas (1981/1985), a critical theorist whose work has informed transformative learning in adult education. This work creates a foundation for communication that is meaning centered, and creates an opportunity for reflection and critique that leads to communicative learning. Mezirow (2000), drawing from the work of Habermas, differentiates instrumental learning from communicative learning. Mezirow sees instrumental learning as "learning to control and manipulate the environment or other people, as in task-oriented problem solving to improve performance" (p. 8). While this may sound a bit negative, if one reflects upon the types of learning that take place in schools and organizations, much of it is about understanding facts and processes to gain more control. Communicative learning, on the other hand, is about understanding meaning. While instrumental learning is more focused on explanation, communicative learning, as Mezirow describes, is focused on understanding context.

Understanding in communicative learning requires that we assess the meanings behind the words; the coherence, truth, and appropriateness of what is being communicated; the truthfulness and qualification of the speaker; and the authenticity of expressions of feeling. That is, we must become critically reflective of the assumptions of the person communicating (2000, p. 9).

And, I would add, at the same time, we need to be critically aware of our own assumptions as we are interpreting what is communicated through the filters of our own beliefs and assumptions. Mezirow's description is focused on the individual aspect of communicative learning, whereas, dialog is focused on the collective aspect. To participate in a collective communicative process such as dialog, we must develop our individual capacity for communicative learning.

I believe communicative competence begins with an orientation of being situated within a cultural context, *the world* of diverse perspectives, patterns of action, and belief systems. We see ourselves as part of something much larger than that which is familiar to us. We have a curiosity to explore that which is unknown (Fig. 2).

When people with different perspectives and experiences come together with an orientation to learn and reach new understanding through conversation, sharing their thoughts, experiences, questions, and learnings, they create the possibility for authentic relationships and collaborative action. Gadamer (1975/1994) refers to this as a *fusion of horizons*, an enlargement of our own horizon (*my world*) through understanding that which is different, giving us the ability to co-create *our world*.

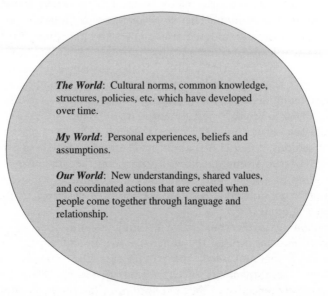

The World: Cultural norms, common knowledge, structures, policies, etc. which have developed over time.

My World: Personal experiences, beliefs and assumptions.

Our World: New understandings, shared values, and coordinated actions that are created when people come together through language and relationship.

Fig. 2.   Cultural context. Adapted from the work of Habermas (1985, 1987).

Habermas' (1981/1985, 1981/1987) proposed the four principles of mutual comprehension, shared values, truthfulness, and trust to overcome the problem of distorted communication. I have interpreted Habermas' proposal in a way that has enabled me to share it with others to influence improvement in the quality of conversation and communication. The following model can be understood by placing communication within the world of language and action (Fig. 3).

The core of communicative competence is the intention of communication to reach new understanding for the purpose of informing individual and collective action. It assumes that all people are communicative by nature and, as such, at the core of our being is our desire to make meaning and engage in relationships that support mutual learning. Communication is considered an art, something we practice and perfect over time. The four principles support communicative learning in the following way. *Mutual comprehension* requires us to bridge the differences in language, the cultural beliefs, and assumptions that influence how we think and what we say. It requires the ability to listen and hear one another's intention as well as interpret the words and body language. Mutual comprehension requires the ability to speak openly and be understood. It requires us to listen to other perspectives, consider them, ask questions that aid in understanding, and respond respectfully. We need to use language that can be understood by others and have the ability to speak and write clearly. Much of the

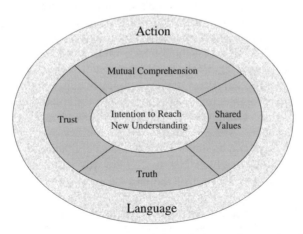

Fig. 3. Communicative competence. Adapted from the work of Habermas (1985, 1987).

communication today is done in writing through e-mail messages. The importance of one's ability to communicate in a way that aids mutual comprehension through this medium cannot be underestimated, as it has become an important way to build and support collaborative relationships.

Shared values are the common threads that bring us together toward a shared purpose. They help in bridging cultural gaps as they give us a reason to listen and try to understand. No matter how different our life experience may be, I have always been able to find shared values with others when we engage in meaningful conversation. The element of *truth* in communicative competence acknowledges that we discover truth in the communicative relationship. If we understand that we are all participants in the world with our own experiences and interpretations of those experiences, the possibility of discovering truth comes through engaging in conversation and dialog with others who hold different perspectives. Discovering truth through communicative relationships requires individuals to feel free to speak truthfully. Speaking truthfully puts us in a place of vulnerability, creating an opening that invites others into an authentic relationship. Speaking truthfully enables us to discover a collective truth. *Trust* requires each of us to be open to learning from the other, trusting that we have something to offer and something to accept.

While each of these principles needs to be present for communicative competence, each communicative event has differing qualities of principle. We may enter a relationship from a place of trust, yet experience a breakdown in mutual understanding as a result of different interpretations of an event. The existence of trust enables a higher degree of truthfulness to support the exploration of the misunderstanding. Recently I was doing some collaborative work with a colleague where we experienced a breakdown in our communicative relationship. We have been friends and colleagues for many years and share values on the importance of collaboration and dialog. Most of our work together met our expectations for collaboration. Then we ran into a problem. During my colleague's vacation, I was acting alone in supporting our client. Some of the action I took was not the same as my colleague would have taken in the same situation and he believed it created a problem that could have been avoided. There was a breakdown in mutual comprehension and as a result of the lack of understanding, an erosion of trust, causing him to question my intentions.

Had our relationship not been grounded in communicative competence, this event could have destroyed it. We see this happen often in organizations with disastrous results. Fortunately, we had a strong desire to continue as friends and colleagues and knew we needed to strive for mutual understanding and regaining trust. The conversation that followed drew heavily upon our willingness to learn from the event and our openness to learn more about ourselves in relationship with the other. We both needed to consider the assumptions behind our actions and question the validity of them. We needed to speak truthfully about our intentions, what we did and why, to help bring understanding to our actions. We needed to seek to understand each other's point of view and allow that to inform our understanding of the actions we both took in this event. All of this helped us regain trust and confidence in our ability to continue to collaborate.

This personal example shows the interconnection of the personal capacity, the interpersonal communication ability, and the desire to act on our shared value of collaboration. The complexity involved in this concept of collaboration cannot be underestimated. I stated earlier that even if people want to collaborate, they do not necessarily have the capacity to do so. My colleague and I have a strong desire to collaborate, we have a strong personal and professional relationship that supports collaboration, and we have communicative skills to help us along the way. Yet, as the above example shows, collaboration tests us all. Creating the capacity to collaborate calls all of us into a place of continued learning and development, a place where we are vulnerable and where we must be willing to take risks. How we engage with others in this work is important to its success. As learners, collaborators, and mentors, we take this journey together, learning and changing along the way.

The following process shows how I have used these ideas to construct a way of working with senior leaders to develop their capacity for collaboration among themselves and to take action that supports creating cultures of collaboration in their organizations. The process incorporates a way of working with organizational transformation that supports the development of communicative learning and collaborative capital.

DEVELOPING ORGANIZATIONAL CAPACITY FOR COLLABORATION

Building collaborative capital is both complex and challenging. The question organizations often ask is "How do we start?" My experience has been that a process for sustainable cultural change needs to start with senior leaders developing their own capacity to collaborate. While pockets of collaboration can exist within units or departments, if collaboration is not supported throughout the organization, those people dedicated to working collaboratively eventually become frustrated and leave. Cultural change involves change in collective and individual beliefs and assumptions, organizational patterns of action, supporting structures, and events. Drawing from work of Senge et al. (2000) and Schein (1992), I use a pyramid model to show how these four elements are addressed concurrently. I find this model easy to understand and work with in communicating my approach and in engaging the organization in defining the desired change (Fig. 4).

The pyramid shape shows how beliefs and assumptions create the foundation of a culture. Schein (1992) discusses how basic assumptions are so embedded within a culture that they are rarely recognized or discussed. Behavior based on basic assumptions is often taken for granted, as over time we become unaware of how our thinking has shaped our actions. Individual behavior based on collective assumptions, over time forms patterns of interaction, communication, and decision-making. When new people enter the culture with a different set of assumptions and act differently, they are often distrusted, ignored, and even punished for their differences. Supporting structures are constructed on the basic assumptions to support the existing patterns of actions. Events, planned or unplanned, publicly communicate what the organization believes and how it carries out its work. Cultural change involves consciously changing each of the four elements in an interconnected way.

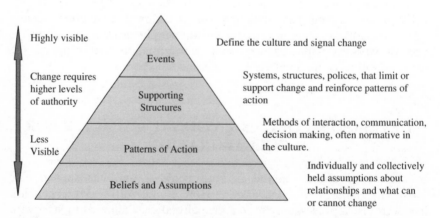

Fig. 4. Transformational change pyramid. Adapted from the work of Senge et al. (2000) and Schein (1992).

To illustrate this approach to building collaborative capital, I use examples from two of my public sector clients, one a city government serving a diverse, rapidly growing population of over 925,000, and the other a water district that provides drinking water resources and coordinates flood protection for its 1.7 million residents. Both of these organizations are making great strides in their efforts to build collaborative cultures. By presenting some of the ways I have worked with them and some of the actions they have taken on their own, I hope to demonstrate how this approach builds collaborative capital. Both of these organizations invited me to work with their senior management teams recognizing that they were the stewards of cultural change. They understood that without developing their own ability to collaborative, they could never institute a culture of collaboration throughout the organization. Additionally, these two organizations exist within the same county and are extending their collaborative efforts in working together as well as to working with the communities they serve and with other stakeholders.

Both of these organizations are led by men committed to collaboration. They are leaders willing to take risks and to support risk taking in their organizations. They invited me to help them engage their senior management teams, both of which are approximately 30 people, in a process where they could build a shared vision and work collaboratively to change the organizational culture. In their invitation to me to help them carry out their objectives, they had already determined that an event was an important part of the initial effort. I was able to offer them a way to leverage an event into an ongoing transformational change process using the transformational change pyramid model. The following description of process and events is a compilation of activities that have taken place over time, not necessarily within one event. I have grouped them together to show how the process leads to collaborative action and organizational change. Important to this work is that it is creatively co-constructed working with the client's needs and current situation.

In planning the initial event, a senior management retreat, I spoke to the importance of giving each participant a voice in shaping it. This effort of co-construction ensures that the organization's objectives are met and that all participants see their perspectives and objectives reflected in the design. The process began with a series of interviews that served as an invitation to participate in an important effort to create a new culture. During the interviews I was able to uncover limiting beliefs and assumptions held by the participants and invite them to challenge those. For instance, a participant told me that he had never fully participated in previous retreats. He described his pattern of showing up at some point during the first day, observing the process, confirming his belief that it would not create change, and returning to his more important work back at the office. If he had extra time, he might show up for a short time toward the end of the retreat. He described how he felt his work did not require the same type of collaboration as did others who performed more central tasks. His previous experience led him to believe that this retreat would be the same as all the others and he was pretty certain he would not have time to attend the entire session. I asked him to challenge his assumptions and consider participating fully, stressing the importance of his contribution. Although he made no commitment to do so, he showed up at the beginning of the retreat and stayed until the end, fully participating throughout.

The invitation to participate in co-creating a new reality is the beginning of the journey to build collaborative capital. The helix in Fig. 5 displays the increasing arenas of participation from invitation to collaboration and ultimately engagement within a learning community.

Once people accept an invitation to hold their beliefs and assumptions in question and participate in a new way, they create the possibility to change both their minds and their actions. As their beliefs and assumptions change, their patterns of action change. The man I described and a number of other managers, in accepting the invitation to participate in new ways, shifted their sense of self in relation to their colleagues and their organization. They engaged with each other in new ways and their commitment grew to

Fig. 5. The collaborative journey.

co-creating a collaborative culture, one where they are learning and changing together.

Shifting mental models, the deeply held beliefs and assumptions that filter what we see and determine how we act, is often the first step in moving people into a collaborative space. The following are assumptions I hold about collaboration which shape how I engage others in this work:

- I can be more successful with the help of others.
- Diversity makes us more creative and capable.
- Disagreement adds value to a conversation.
- Talking about what we have learned is more valuable than talking about what we have done.
- I can speak freely and truthfully to anyone in the organization.

Exploring these beliefs and assumptions in dialog, discussing the personal and organizational experiences that support and inhibit each, helps people reflect on their own beliefs and assumptions and creates tension between the current reality and desired future. Just talking about the assumptions will not create a change of mind. People need to have experiences that confirm the possibility for change. These experiences take place when people begin to form relationships where mutual comprehension, shared values, truthfulness, and trust support new understanding.

The first part of working with my client organizations engages them in meaningful conversation with the intent of sharing aspects of themselves and their lives that are not normally shared. The questions that shape the conversation are the type of questions that might spur a meaningful conversation with someone you recently met and want to get to know better. Questions such as "What influences (people, culture, events) have shaped you?", "What do you value most about yourself, your personal life, your work life?", "What are your passions, talents, hobbies?", and "What are your aspirations?" lead people to reveal aspects of themselves that are unknown even by those they have worked with for years. These conversations enable people to see each other differently, as real people, rather than as the roles they fill in the organization. As small groups share their stories, then share what they have learned about each other with the larger group, a sense of closeness and connection emerges. The values and commitment they share form bonds that extend beyond their contractual relationships. This experience begins to create new beliefs about how they can work together in new ways and forms a basis for communicating using the principles of communicative competence. Their engagement in this meaning-laden process and their surprise and elation at the personal connections made, moves the group solidly into the engagement arena. They are then ready to continue to explore the possibilities of working together in a more challenging and authentic way.

This initial process of relationship building highlights the diversity within the group in a way that can be appreciated. It shows that within that diversity are shared values that have brought this group together and that support them in achieving their common goals. Unfortunately, many people believe that diversity presents an obstacle to collaboration. Diversity, rather than an obstacle to overcome, brings strength to collaboration. Without different perspectives and disagreement, we tend to follow a path which leads to little exploration and learning. And no matter how similar we are, we will always encounter obstacles to collaboration.

After creating an atmosphere of connection and shared values, the group moves into a process that defines the current culture and creates a shared vision of their desired culture of collaboration. I work with Senge's (1990) idea of creative tension, as I believe that change is often created when we can work within the gap between the current reality and the vision of a desired future. I find that there is power in naming the aspects of the current reality that are not serving the organization. Recognizing them and coming to understand why they exist is the first step in taking action to change them. Talking about the current reality can also be threatening and draws upon the trust and shared values that were established in the previous process. Speaking openly about what is not working continues to build recognition that the people are able to speak truthfully and that their experience and observations are valued. This in turn builds trust supporting a higher degree of communicative competence.

I would like to add a comment about how this process both incorporates and differs from AI, as many people are drawn to AI as an alternative approach to problem-solving. The work of Cooperrider and Srivastva (1987), Whitney and Trosten-Bloom (2003), and others, who have developed and advanced the appreciative approach, has influenced my approach as it draws upon the appreciation of human relationships and possibilities of what we can construct through those relationships. Gergen's (1994) work in the theory of social construction draws upon hermeneutics and the interpretative nature of being. Yet, I find that in many situations, a pure appreciative approach does not support a full understanding of the nature of the systems we live and work in and as such does not always fully prepare the ground for change. In my opinion, AI does not require the same level of openness, truthfulness, and trust as when a group seeks to understand the nature of their current situation and how each person contributes to either reinforcing the current reality or taking action to create the desired change. The risk taking and tension created by holding what is and seeking what is desired willingly places people in a vulnerable space where they are often inspired by the great challenge before them. Facing challenges together, taking risks together, and being vulnerable together, takes people beyond the shared values and vision to a place where truthfulness and trust foster closer relationships and strengthen communicative competence.

The next step in my process of working with these groups brings them face-to-face with some of the tensions they are experiencing which surface during the interviews. I call this process "courageous conversations" because the engagement is high risk and requires the courage to speak truthfully. This process places people in groups where they most often associate and where natural tensions exist. Often these groups are comprised of individuals from operations and administration, or manufacturing and sales and marketing. Each group is asked to discuss questions, such as "How do we add value?", "How can we better collaborate?", "How can we better serve our colleagues?", and "What do we need from others to enhance our effectiveness?" These questions bridge a problem-solving and appreciative approach. They call people to develop new patterns of action, while recognizing that current practice is not fully supportive of the new vision. Once the group discussions are complete, each group is asked to speak to the other groups, responding to each of the questions. The insights gained from these conversations are critical to developing a collaborative mental model. People recognize how they often blame the other groups for problems that they contribute to creating and maintaining, and they realize that by changing their own patterns of action, they can change the nature of the relationship. They come away from the process feeling that they have faced a mirror, have seen their reflection, and have spoken the truth. They often comment that they never thought they could say out loud what was said.

The final key step in this initial work of senior management teams is to talk together about the changes they need to make within the organization to move toward their vision of a collaborative culture. Working with the transformational change pyramid (Fig. 4), the group defines new beliefs and assumptions, patterns of action, supporting structures, and events that will foster collaboration among themselves and their relationships with staff and other stakeholders, and that will enhance the organization's capacity to collaborate. When working with the city's senior staff, they determined that a key action was to have their direct reports go through a similar process and then talk together about their shared vision and ways to implement it. They also committed to working more closely together on their initiatives to engage the city's citizens in the Strong Neighborhoods Initiative and redevelopment efforts.

The water district senior managers committed to using the Baldrige criteria as a supporting structure to further their vision. Other important actions included strengthening relationships with their board, community, staff, and partners. With all employees, except senior managers represented by bargaining units, the CEO recognizes that an important aspect of realizing their vision is to develop strong relationships with the bargaining units. Although he has encountered a perspective from both union and management employees that collaboration is a sign of weakness, continuing collaborative efforts are beginning to shift that belief into one that values the partnership. A yearlong collaborative process resulted in a redesign of the Classified Employee Performance Program that is cited by both union and management as one of the organization's key accomplishments. The collaborative process strengthened the relationships between the three bargaining units and with the senior management team. The district is also involved in the Water Resources Protection Collaborative that brings together representatives from 15 municipalities, the county, and private and public interest groups to jointly develop and implement guidelines, standards, and measures to protect the water resources.

These senior management teams discussed other key supporting structures that would help reinforce collaborative patterns of actions. Meetings are generally a place where change is needed. They are a leverage activity that can propel the group toward their collaborative vision, or if left unchanged, can cause the group to shift back to their old assumptions and fall back into old patterns that limit collaboration. Meetings need to be dynamic and provide a space for talking openly and truthfully about the continued tension between the current reality and desired future. People need to develop skills to challenge assumptions and to use disagreement effectively and the climate needs to support different perspectives and disagreement. There needs to be a willingness to discuss behaviors that do not support collaboration and to listen to constructive criticism, regardless of the power structure. Carefully considering who needs to be involved in conversations, meetings, decisions, and projects, is critical in a collaborative effort. Exclusion of key members tends to kill collaboration. Yet, we all know that having too many people involved can make collaborative action difficult. Carefully deciding who participates, clearly communicating how those decisions are made, and extending an invitation that clarifies expectations are all-important patterns of action.

Other important supporting structures for collaboration include hiring practices, training and development, recognition, technology improvements, procedures, and policies. An additional supporting structure is an effective mentoring process. Mentoring most often takes place between individuals, yet it can better support collaboration when done within mentoring communities. Mentoring calls us into relationships of care, where we provide support and guidance, challenge, and opportunity to others who want to learn. When done well, mentoring provides a supporting fabric for the transformative changes that we are asking people to make as they move into collaborative relationships. Daloz (1999) offers an in-depth look at the mentoring relationship as one that fosters transformation through encounters with "otherness." In his work with adult students, he proposes guiding principles of mentoring including engendering trust, recognizing movement, giving voice, introducing conflict, and taking care of the relationship. As a teacher and mentor of adult students, I have been fortunate to have relationships where my support and guidance have helped others transform their lives. In return, my life has also been transformed. Mentoring is an intimate relationship that builds communicative competence, supports risks, and results in mutual learning. Placing the mentoring relationship within a community, a group of people committed to learning and teaching together, creates an important supporting structure for building collaborative capital.

Important to any culture change are events that signal the beginning of something new and different. The senior leadership retreats I described have provided an opportunity for the senior managers to work together in new ways. They have been events that signaled a change in the nature of their relationship. The city has held two economic summits that bring together scholars, technology leaders, real estate brokers, merchants, and representatives from arts and non-profit groups. The city manager considers the summit a significant catalytic event as it brought stakeholders into a dialog that could support collaborative action in improving the economic future of a city hard hit by the technology downturn. While many leaders might shy away from taking a risk to hear criticisms voiced by constituents, the mayor, city manager, city council members, and city staff not only listened, they also made commitments to act on recommendations.

These senior leadership teams have made great progress in their efforts to create the culture and conditions in their organizations that support collaboration. They are committed to the collaborative journey. The retreats have provided a time when they can strengthen their relationships, reflect on their progress and the challenges they overcame together. They engage with each other as equals, even though their positions place them in varying levels of authority. Their participation demonstrates a willingness to be vulnerable as they acknowledge privately and publicly where they need to improve and what they have learned. They engage in dialog, questioning assumptions, and using inquiry to explore new territory. They raise critical questions that challenge existing beliefs and assumptions, and thus create the possibility for new thoughts and actions. They see themselves as one, a group of senior leaders, committed to the common good of the organization and the people and communities they serve.

LEARNING FROM THE COLLABORATIVE JOURNEY

Ultimately, the result of creating cultures of collaboration is the development of learning communities. The ability to work together, take risks, disagree, make mistakes, learn from those mistakes, and continue the collaborative efforts results in collaborative capital. If collaboration does not extend into a learning community, then chances are that when difficulties arise, people will revert to independent action. What does it take to keep these efforts going? When I asked the city manager to reflect on what he had learned from his efforts, he offered the following insights:

- *Collaboration is built upon the professionalism of department heads and staff.* The right people with the desire to work together and the knowledge that they are all serving the same constituency can accomplish great things. He gives these senior managers total accountability and expects them to work together to meet the needs of the constituents. Recently he put his job on the line in his commitment to hire a fire chief that he believed would work well within the culture. The person he wanted was not the popular choice and the city council split their votes in confirming the appointment. His belief in this person and willingness to take a personal risk resulted in creating a strong collaboration between police and fire to better serve the city.
- *When people embrace collaboration they are willing to make personal sacrifices for the good of the whole.* He spoke about his recent budget process, where the city faced a $70 million shortfall. He described the organization as "breezing through it" as the managers worked together to make the cuts that were best for the city. Rather than taking the common

position of protecting one's turf, he stated that the managers offered to make the necessary cuts, negotiated with one another, and committed to support each other. The collaborative spirit of this difficult task extended to the elected officials, and they too worked collaboratively to best meet the needs of their constituents.

- *Bring your enemies close.* Ideally in a collaborative culture we would like to envision everyone working together, yet there may be groups that chose not to participate. He found himself in the middle of a difficult situation when a contract with a local technology company to provide technology for the new city hall was called into question by the city council. The council appointed an independent investigator to determine if inappropriate actions were taken. In reflecting on what happened, he believes at the core of the problem was the lack of collaborative relationship with their city attorney's office. The attorney's office had issued concerns about the bidding and contracting process, but the department heads did not heed them. Since a strained relationship had existed for a long time, the city attorney's office was considered the enemy, placing the relationship outside the sphere of communicative competence. And since the culture does not promote an escalation of issues to the top, the concerns were not raised with the city manager. The department heads worked collaboratively with each other and with their preferred vendor. Unfortunately, the way the collaboration was engaged fell outside the acceptable guidelines of the city contracting process. He believes the investigation will show that the city obtained the best technology for a good price, yet he also recognizes that he and others may lose their jobs as a result of the error. However, he realizes that there needs to be improvement in the relationship between the city attorney's office and the city staff and a way to make sure that issues and concerns are raised for discussion within the senior management team. The situation was a challenging one and was used as an opportunity to learn how to best serve the organization while fostering collaboration within the city offices and with supporting organizations.
- *Trust the people and the process even when mistakes are made.* Even when faced with the difficult situation described above, he expressed no hesitation in continuing to pursue his vision of a collaborative culture and to trust the people whom are close to the work. He is committed to making sure the group learns from the mistake, reviews the patterns of action that created the problems, and establishes supporting structures to avoid similar situations in the future. Although some people are calling his culture into question and would like to see him revert to a command and

control style of leadership, I do not think this leader will yield to that pressure.

SUMMARY

Collaboration is a way of working together for the purpose of contributing to the common good. The quality of the relationships and what is created through them defines successful collaboration. Relationships are both strategic in the need to achieve a common purpose and authentic in the desire to learn from others. Relationships exist within the sphere of communicative competence, a way to be in conversation with the intention of expanding horizons through mutual comprehension, shared values, truthfulness, and trust. These four principles promote understanding through language and action that supports collaboration. At the core of this way of being in conversation with others is the intention to reach new understanding. Understanding a different perspective creates an opportunity to explore our assumptions and expand or change our perspective. Gadamer (1975/1994) refers to this as a *fusion of horizons*, the enlargement of my own horizon by understanding another. As our personal and collective horizons expand, so too does our ability to create transformational change.

Collaborative capital is built over time as organizational cultures are created that thrive on diversity and continuous learning. As people challenge existing assumptions and limiting beliefs, take personal and collective risks, disagree, and learn from both success and mistakes, trust and confidence is strengthened and the organizational builds the capacity to meet challenges and serve the greater good. Senior leaders serve an important role in creating cultures of collaboration as they model the way and create the conditions for collaboration within the organization and with external stakeholders. When people can speak truthfully and act together toward a shared purpose, their inspiration is contagious.

Much more research and work needs to be done to understand the transformative challenges of collaboration. How do we best work in organizations to build and sustain a collaborative culture? How can we prepare ourselves, leaders, managers, and employees for this work? How can we change the way we communicate to increase our ability to consider different perspectives and shift our thinking, creating greater possibilities for collaborative action? There are no tools to make this process easy. Rather, as people committed to this work, we can only embark on the collaborative journey and learn from each other along the way.

REFERENCES

Argyris, C. (1977, September–October). Double loop learning in organizations. *Harvard Business Review, 55*(5), 115–125.

Argyris, C. (1985). *Strategy, change and defensive routines*. Boston: Pitman.

Argyris, C. (1990). *Overcoming organizational defenses. Facilitating organizational learning.* Boston: Allyn and Bacon.

Argyris, C. (1991, May–June). Teaching smart people how to learn. *Harvard Business Review, 69*(3), 99–109.

Argyris, C. (1993). *Knowledge for action. A guide to overcoming barriers to organizational change.* San Francisco: Jossey Bass.

Brown, M. (2005). *Corporate integrity. Rethinking organizational ethics and leadership.* London: Cambridge University Press.

Buber, M. (1955). *Between man and man.* Boston: Beacon Press (original work published 1947).

Cooperrider, D., & Srivastva, S. (1987). Appreciative inquiry in organizational life. *Research in Organizational Change and Development, 1,* 129–169.

Cranton, P. (2000). Individual difference and transformative learning. In: J. Mezirow & Associates (Eds.), *Learning as transformation: Critical perspectives on a theory in progress.* San Francisco: Jossey-Bass.

Daloz, L. (1999). *Mentor: Guiding the journey of the adult learner.* San Francisco: Jossey-Bass.

DePree, M. (1989). *Leadership is an art.* Melbourne, Australia: BRW Business Library.

Friere, P. (1994). In: R. Barr (Trans.), *Pedagogy of hope: Reliving pedagogy of the oppressed.* New York: Continuum (original work published 1992).

Fukuyama, F. (1995). *Trust: The social virtues and the creation of prosperity.* New York: The Free Press.

Gadamer, H. (1993). In: J. Weinsheimer, D. Marshall (Trans.), *Truth and method,* 2nd revised ed. New York: Continuum (original work published 1975).

Gergen, K. (1994). *Realities and relationships: Sounding in social construction.* Cambridge: Harvard University Press.

Habermas, J. (1985). In: T. McCarthy (Trans.), *The theory of communicative action, vol. 1: Reason and the rationalization of society.* Boston: Beacon Press (original work published 1981).

Habermas, J. (1987). In: T. McCarthy (Trans.), *The theory of communicative action, vol. 2: Lifeworld and system: Functionalist reason.* Boston: Beacon Press (original work published 1981).

Heidegger, M. (1962). In: J. Macquarrie, & E. Robinson (Trans.), *Being in time.* [Translation of 7th edition of *Sein und zeit.*] San Francisco: Harper Collins (original work published 1927).

Hofstede, G. (1997). *Cultures and organizations: Software of the mind.* New York: McGraw-Hill.

Hubbard, E. (2003). *Diversity scorecard: Improving human performance.* Boston: Butterworth-Heinemann.

Issacs, W. (1999). *Dialogue and the art of thinking together.* New York: Doubleday.

Kanter, R. M. (2004). *Confidence: How winning streaks and losing streaks begin and end.* New York: Crown Publishing.

Kegan, R. (1982). *The evolving self: Problem and process in human development.* Cambridge: Harvard University Press.

72   NANCY L. SOUTHERN

Kegan, R., & Lahey, L. (2001). *How the way we talk can change the way we work: Seven languages for transformation.* San Francisco: Jossey-Bass.

Krogh, G., Ichijo, K., & Nonaka, I. (2000). *Enabling knowledge creation.* New York: Oxford University Press.

Locke, J. (1998). *The devoicing of society: Why we don't talk to each other.* New York: Simon & Schuster.

Mezirow, J., Associates (2000). *Learning as transformation: Critical perspectives on a theory in progress.* San Francisco: Jossey-Bass.

Parkes, G. (Ed.) (1987). *Heidegger and Asian thought.* Honolulu: University of Hawaii Press.

Pearce, W. B. (1989). *Communication and the human condition.* Carbondale and Edwardville: Southern Illinois University Press.

Schein, E. (1992). *Organizational culture and leadership* (2nd ed.). San Francisco: Jossey-Bass.

Schein, E. (1996). Three cultures of management: The key to organizational learning. *MIT Sloan Management Review, 38*(1), 9–20.

Senge, P. (1990). *The fifth discipline: Art and practice of the learning organization.* New York: Doubleday.

Senge, P., et al. (1994). *The fifth discipline fieldbook: Strategies and tools for building a learning organization.* New York: Doubleday.

Senge, P., et al. (2000). *Schools that learn. A fifth discipline fieldbook for educators, parents and everyone who cares about education.* New York: Doubleday.

Whitney, D., & Trosten-Bloom, A. (2003). *The power of appreciative inquiry: A practical guide to positive change.* San Francisco: Berrett-Koehler.

EXPLOITING INTELLECTUAL AND COLLABORATIVE CAPITAL FOR INNOVATION IN KNOWLEDGE-INTENSIVE INDUSTRIES

Anne H. Koch

ABSTRACT

Development of intellectual capital, in conjunction with collaborative capabilities, is particularly important to continuously generating innovation. In the literature to date, the link between collaborative and intellectual capital, although key assets in knowledge-intensive industries, has rarely been investigated. This chapter introduces a model illustrating the interaction between human, intellectual, and structural capital, and their interplay. Several propositions are also derived in view of the need for companies to harness these three types of capital which are integral to implicit knowledge generation and leveraging the dynamic capabilities of the organization. As a consequence, team-based organizational forms are considered to be the most appropriate collaborative pattern for knowledge-intensive industries. This suggests that companies must increasingly focus on building valuable collaborative capital using flexible forms of organization in order to perpetuate successful product innovations.

Collaborative Capital: Creating Intangible Value
Advances in Interdisciplinary Studies of Work Teams, Volume 11, 73–90
Copyright © 2005 by Elsevier Ltd.
All rights of reproduction in any form reserved
ISSN: 1572-0977/doi:10.1016/S1572-0977(05)11003-6

INTRODUCTION

Collaborative capital is one of the essential drivers for success in knowledge-intensive industries. Knowledge-intensive industries are now at the core of industry growth. It is widely held that we have entered into a new type of knowledge-driven economy or even a completely new form of "knowledge society" (Smith, 2000). Open innovation is suggested as a new paradigm for organizing and managing research and development. The way businesses develop new ideas and bring them to market is shifting from a closed approach, in which a company develops innovation internally and maintains control of it, to an open approach in which companies draw ideas from outside sources (Chesbrough, 2003; Narula, 2004). The capability to collaborate efficiently and effectively becomes even more important in an increasingly interconnected world, with certain industries spanning their innovation activities across branches and firm boundaries to alliances and cooperative arrangements with business partners. The body of knowledge regarding collaboration, innovation, and new product development is only currently beginning to expand (cf. Bougrain & Haudeville, 2002; Chiesa & Toletti, 2004; Love & Roper, 2004; Parker, 2000).

The quality of a firm's collaborative capital is evident in its role in the firm's ability to bring about radical innovations in the form of technologic breakthroughs. A number of questions around this phenomenon are becoming increasingly obvious. For example, how can collaborative capital and the firm's resulting innovative capabilities be described? What forms of capital interact to make a firm really competitive and innovative? Which collaboration patterns are most appropriate for knowledge-intensive industries? The interplay of different capital forms has already been described by Bounfour (2003) and Amidon (2003) as coexistent, but has not been further linked to collaboration. Additionally, the interplay has not been connected to firms seizing opportunities in knowledge-intensive industries. Thus, collaboration as a capital asset has been neglected in the literature, especially with regard to organization of the workflow of innovation processes.

This chapter explores how collaborative capital in knowledge-intensive companies can be defined, especially, what it consists of and under which conditions it is valuable. Rather than reducing the concepts of human, intellectual, and structural capital to mere assets, they are placed in their dynamic entrepreneurial context and elucidated by a discussion of the efforts undertaken to generate product innovations. Thus, in this chapter, a model introducing the interplay of different capital forms is developed. Next, propositions on the design of flexible collaborative forms are derived.

The arguments on this topic are linked to the resource-based view of the firm's perspective on the exploitation of a firm's innovative and dynamic capabilities (cf. Hamel & Prahalad, 1994; Teece, 2000). Finally, highlights of the implications for future research and practice are offered, and final conclusions drawn.

Definition and Reflections on Collaborative Capital

Beyerlein, Freedman, McGee, and Moran (2003) have introduced the term collaborative capital as a process and relationship system representing a key asset of the organization. Effective collaboration means working together efficiently and effectively. This is not a new requirement for business success, but it has become a critical success factor that applies to all the relationships that create a business, including those with customers, business allies, suppliers, divisions, departments, functions, projects, specialties, vertical levels, and employees (Beyerlein et al., 2003). Collaboration in terms of open innovation might also imply that stakeholders are taken into consideration more than in traditional business models. The broad definition of collaborative capital can be applied to many different contexts and all imaginable work surroundings. These include:

(1) Abstract categories for the purposes of discussion such as networks and teams.
(2) Standard cooperative forms such as joint ventures or franchises which embody different legal forms.
(3) Internal and external organizational collaborative forms such as cross-functional teams and inter-company partnerships or alliances.
(4) Collaborative forms linked electronically across dispersed geographic locations, thus illustrating the distinction between local and international collaboration (Oliver, 2004).

In this chapter, all of the above-mentioned collaborative forms are addressed.

When linked with the term capital as prefix, the terms intellectual, knowledge, and human are sometimes hard to decipher. The resulting terms intellectual capital, knowledge capital, and human capital describe intangibles, not assets on the standard balance sheet. Contrary to the concepts of social and human capital, financial capital is indeed tangible (Bollingtoft, Ulhoi, Madsen, & Neergaard, 2003). Thus, the frequent use of the word capital for less easily defined factors reflects the shift from the traditional basic production factors of land, labor, material, and financial capital to more intangible assets in knowledge-based economies. In addition to the traditional variables of cost and time (Amidon, 2003), new indicators of progress can be found in the intangible values of the firm.

In knowledge-intensive industries, knowledge has tremendous significance as a competitive strategy. Lev and Zambon (2003) state that companies are increasing their investments in intangible assets because "products have to be differentiated and innovated and then embody increasing amounts of knowledge, so that the phases of the production process where intangible assets are particularly present (research, organization, and marketing) become essential to managers and investors" (p. 598). For some types of fairly routine services, idea generation, and utilization may not be costly relative to other production factors.

However, in knowledge-intensive industries, what is considered capital-intensive is not the raw or fabricating materials of the products, but the knowledge-producing labor force which increasingly infuses service firms of all types as well as the shop floor. The term capital as used in collaborative capital no longer connotes capital in the traditional sense of financial, easily measurable assets, although it is surely harnessed for profit gains. Rather, collaborative capital as we use the term today resides ultimately in the heads of the employees and consists of their knowledge, skills, and competencies.

Collaboration is easily linked with the terms assets and capital, when addressing the notion of the exploitation of intellectual capital. Knowledge-intensive industries are rapidly increasing their operations resulting in new forms of value-added organization exploding daily on the global business scene. On the other hand, certain industries still require large infusions of venture capital (tangible financial capital). Intellectual and human capital as knowledge sources are the major future resource of knowledge-based industries. Furthermore, knowledge-based industries are increasingly designed around new collaborative forms (e.g. biotechnology clusters involving universities, government agencies, and biotechnology firms) due to increasing vertical disintegration (Langlois, 2003), and the tendency to partner across the new product development supply chain. It is evident that in modern industry, there are many possibilities and opportunities for developing new structural capital and organizational configurations.

In general, increased knowledge content is evident among employees because more knowledge is embedded in products (Narula, 2004). Narula suggests that it is necessary to recognize that products have an intellectual component as well as a physical component. The relative balance between tangible and intangible (intellectual) value added is shifting inexorably toward the intellectual. Many of the fastest growing companies in the past 20 years (e.g. Microsoft, Intel, and Oracle) are successful in part due to the fact that their businesses are based much more on knowledge intensity rather than on the physical content of their products (Nonaka & Nishiguchi, 2001). It is becoming clear that the more knowledge is integrated into a product, the more difficult it is to capture and quantify the value of a product, thus pointing to an increasing awareness of the integrative value of human, intellectual, and structural capital in new product offerings.

CHARACTERISTICS OF DIFFERENT CAPITAL FORMS

Human Capital

Human capital is a general concept that is considered to be the foundation of intellectual capital. Sanchez, Chaminade, and Olea (2000) define human capital as "the knowledge that employees take with them when they leave the firm at the end of the day ... for example, their expertise, educational level, etc." (p. 320). The knowledge, skills, and competencies of outstanding personnel are vital to developing successful products and improving total production efficiency (Chen, Zhu, & Xie, 2004). Human capital is also the point of departure for developing the organizational structures and collaborative processes for promoting creativity leading to exploiting intellectual capital for organizational success. This applies to permanent employees as well as additional hires with complementary skill sets employed on a short-term basis to work on ideas and develop new products. Furthermore, the dynamics of collaboration among employees is extremely critical in the initial phase of innovation. In the start-up phase, creativity is paramount, and collaborative work processes begin to emerge as to how to best explore and harness team capabilities around new product ideas and concepts.

According to Sanchez et al. (2000), relational capital is firm specific and is defined as "all the intellectual capital linked with the external relationships of the firm, as, for example, the relation with customers" (p. 320). In this context, relationship capital, with the implied component of trust and understanding between and among company employees and customers, is extremely important. According to Dawson (2000), relationship capital is mutually created and shared, especially by individuals who work in collaborative ways. Human capital overlaps with intellectual capital in the sense that ideas and experiences are not simply confined to archived written material but are dynamic and alive, as tacit knowledge and expertise held in the minds and accrued experience of employees. Thus, human capital, while contributing to the value of the organization, remains in the possession of the individual, and can be schematically associated with the tacit knowledge of individuals (Bounfour, 2003). Individuals can and do learn, develop, and acquire knowledge both independently and within the organization. In other words, they are not necessarily dependent on organizational assets in order to learn, whereas it is a fact of organizational life that the organization cannot develop, learn, or flourish independent of its human capital (Bogdanowicz & Bailey, 2002). Furthermore, the organization cannot grow by depending solely on the intellectual capital embodied in legal forms such as its copyrighted and patented ideas.

Intellectual Capital

A concise definition of intellectual capital is knowledge that can be converted into value (Shaikh, 2004). Beyerlein et al. (2003) offer a more detailed definition along the same lines: "intellectual capital represents one key capability of the organization – the ability to produce, capture and synthesize information into knowledge that *can be used* to produce some product or service" (p. 22). Clearly, the knowledge, experience, and ideas of people at every level of a firm impact its products, services, processes, and customers. Combining intangible resources can facilitate the development of intellectual capital and the realization of specific desirable outcomes such as collective knowledge, patents, and trademarks (Bounfour, 2003). And according to Bakhru (2004) and Stewart (1997), the knowledge and skills embedded in individuals are integral components of an organization's human capital as well as its intellectual capital.

As an organization builds and expands its knowledge base, both tacitly and explicitly, it builds its intellectual capital, and consequently, enhances its competitive advantage (Bogdanowicz & Bailey, 2002). According to Bounfour (2003), human and structural capital can be seen as components of intellectual capital involved in an ongoing dynamic dialogue. Similarly, Roos, Roos, Dragonetti, and Edvinsson (1997), and Lövingsson, Dell'Orto, and Baladi (2000) subordinate human and structural capital to intellectual capital. A parallel model of the integrative nature of the three types of capital, namely human, intellectual, and structural, underscores this chapter, although the discussion goes somewhat further with the notion of the interface of all three, termed collaborative capital. And for purposes of discussion, intellectual capital is distinguished from human capital with the former referred to as the knowledge assets already embodied in legal forms (e.g. trademarks, licenses, patents, and copyrights).

Current new product development lore suggests that in order to continually update the intellectual property of a firm, as well as develop new ideas which may have potential as future new product offerings, an effective idea generation process is critical. It is common knowledge that only a small percentage of the many ideas unearthed in individual or team-based efforts make it beyond the initial product conceptualization and design stage to prototyping and testing. Technologic research aids in moving the new product idea through the steps of product innovation into eventual marketable products and services. While it varies by industry, in general only a very small percentage of initial ideas generated are realized. However, the ongoing interplay of new ideas and existing intellectual capital within the organization keeps employees up-to-date in their areas of expertise. In addition, with knowledge becoming more complex and necessary for the design of products and services, it is essential to be aware that intellectual capital only becomes accessible through human capital (i.e. knowledge, skills, and competencies) for exploitation into innovative product solutions.

Structural Capital

Unlike the terms intellectual and human capital, the term structural capital is used less often. Sanchez et al. (2000) suggest that structural capital is industry specific, defining it as "the pool of knowledge that stays at the firm at the end of the working day, as for example, the firm's routines, culture, databases, etc." (p. 320). Structural capital resides in the knowledge processes and systems of a company (Dawson, 2000). According to Bounfour (2003), structural capital corresponds to all intangible items that are separable from people's tacit knowledge, for example, trademarks, patents and licenses, databases other than those related to customers, procedures, and software – more or less formalized methodologies. The overlap of intellectual and structural capital becomes readily apparent.

Systematic management of intellectual capital is accomplished, among other things, through the continuous recycling and creative utilization of shared knowledge and experience. This, in return, requires the structuring and packaging of competencies with the help of technology, process descriptions, manuals, networks, and so on, to ensure that this competence remains with the company after the employees leave. Once packaged, these become a part of a company's structural capital, or more precisely, its organizational capital (Stewart, 1999). The term capital in this context expresses the value of a structural design with regard to the firm's performance.

The term structural capital is conveyed in a relatively passive way in all the aforementioned descriptions which deal with restoring existing structural components (e.g. databases), whereas the phases of the innovation cycle demand a more active conceptualization. Especially at the beginning of the innovation cycle, it is important to invent structures since this phase of the innovation process is often informal and not very structured. Human capital can only effectively exploit archived intellectual capital when the structural capital provides the possibility to seize opportunities. The interlinking of the different capital forms is illustrated in the visual model which follows. Further implications of the arguments are derived in the form of propositions.

Interlinking Different Capital Forms

In all three capital forms, that is human, intellectual, and structural, knowledge is integrated to a great extent. Implicit and explicit knowledge are important components of the intersection of the three capital forms. In this chapter, collaborative capital is introduced as a form of synergy which binds the structural, intellectual, and human assets of an enterprise (Fig. 1). The capital assets of each of these capital forms have to be taken up and transferred into a fluid workflow. It is especially valuable for an organization if the different capital forms can enhance their value around the actions of individuals in cross-functional teams during the early phases of emergent innovation. The formation of the interrelations between intellectual, human, and structural capital can be seen as a continuing dynamic process where different actors develop ideas independent of the organization's knowledge base, or build on ideas residing in organization's existing storehouse of knowledge. Along this continuous innovation pipeline, employees shape, form, and design collaborative forms through self-direction. The cultural space affording such development of collaborative work processes is key if organizations are to compete and survive in knowledge-intensive industries.

Each of the forms of capital provides stability for the model (represented by propeller blades). If companies possessing valuable human, intellectual, and structural capital focus on developing innovative products and services, and bringing them to market, the investment will produce substantial profit returns. The dynamic nature of the innovation cycle from inception to product offerings in the marketplace is captured in the propeller blades that rotate and are constantly in movement. This is analogous to the fact that

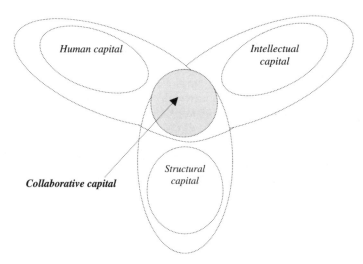

Fig. 1. Propeller model: the interlinking of different capital forms.

human, intellectual, and structural capital of a company that continuously innovates has of necessity to be in flux. A company's success is reflected through its dynamic capability in using its collaborative capital which the model suggests is the interrelations of all three types.

The underlying driving force for innovation success is lodged in the intersection of all three capital forms; that is, collaborative capital, as distinct from tangible forms such as fixed financial capital. That the assets are not fixed becomes apparent, for example, since employees are selected for an innovation project according to their skill sets. In the model, a propeller's rotation velocity is related to the velocity of its movement. This velocity of change capability mirrors conditions in rapidly changing, knowledge-intensive industries such as consumer electronics where the ability to retool rapidly based on developments in the various asset types illustrated in the model is increasingly necessary.

Companies combining the three capital forms in a way which stabilizes each of them may have a better chance of experiencing positive market performance. A company should strive to keep a balance between the three capital forms and thereby avoid instability in the whole system. Underdeveloped human, intellectual or structural capital can result in unexploited opportunities and unsatisfactory market performance.

Without appropriate structures designed to enhance natural forms of capital embedded in the organization, work efforts will not be sufficiently exploited in terms of generating intellectual capital. In order to achieve effective collaboration, the structures need to be appropriately matched to the type of firm as well as industry. In the future, the power of organizations will derive from their ability to combine their human capital and intellectual assets, enabling employees to work in flexible structures such as cross-functional teams which can enhance their innovation efforts. Also, inter-organizational arrangements of organizations can be established for each project in order to "bring in new blood", thereby opening up the introduction of new ideas and possibly the development of new products. Organizational design flexibility for the purpose of exploiting innovation opportunities is based on various factors outlined below.

Design of Flexible Collaborative Forms for Exploiting Opportunities

Explicit and tacit knowledge lodged in different work areas (as in a cross-functional arrangement) needs to be brought into the work setting and more importantly into the creative process. Technologic knowledge is often tacit; that is, hard to document in writing, and instead resides within individuals, systems, and processes of the firm (Tyler & Steensma, 1995). In order to also incorporate and process employees' tacit knowledge, the special team form of multifunctional teams is a very appropriate way of integrating knowledge from distant sites within the organization. Sometimes the fruitful exploitation of knowledge can even demand that a collaboration form be adapted to a specific situation. For example, often consultants are drawn into a project session, making their implicit knowledge as external experts explicit in the context of the visited team for a special task or as an additional information source. Knowledge is created by means of a dynamic that involves the interplay between the explicit and the tacit, that is, the knowledge-conversion process (Nonaka & Teece, 2001). Managers need to champion the development of internal structures such as work teams to enable employees to easily make their tacit knowledge public, thereby increasing its reach and potential in innovation activities. As sharing implicit knowledge helps to make it explicit and therefore a useful factor in the production process, it is proposed that:

Proposition 1. The value of structural capital to the organization is enhanced when it allows the use of the implicit knowledge embedded in human capital for leveraging the intellectual capital of the organization.

Two conditions useful in exploiting the knowledge assets of the company which form the foundation for a strong collaborative organization are the following: First, the truly collaborative organization tends to create flatter, more flexible organizations (Beyerlein et al., 2003). Second, collaboration and/or networking can be principally seen as a means of speeding up the process of bringing new products to market (Love, 2001; Roper, 1997). Individuals do not work in isolation to produce and exploit ideas, intellectual capital and property, but are embedded in a net of opportunities which can be exploited to a greater or lesser extent, depending on suitable collaboration forms.

New and progressive organizational forms in knowledge-based industries are burgeoning for a couple of reasons. First, due to an increase in corporate restructuring, competition, and globalization, virtual teams have become an integral part of the organization. This is due in large part to declining costs of computing and communication technologies (e.g. groupware) and ease of access (Baker, 2002). The biotechnology industry is a good example of external collaborative alliances between government agencies and private sector laboratories (Rothaermel & Deeds, 2004). Second, collaboration between industry organizations, universities (Nursall, 2003; Siegel, Waldman, Atwater, & Link, 2003), and other research contractors is becoming widespread due to the general movement away from competition to collaboration, related changing attitudes around partnerships as "win–win" propositions, and the obvious ease and accessibility of electronic communication.

All three forms of capital aim at mobilizing the combination of intellectual and human assets in the most effective way for conducting research and doing business. All collaboration patterns mentioned are based on teamwork or at minimum on networking which tends to be coupled somewhat more loosely. These collaboration forms all point to the work setting and operation of an "open" innovation mode where companies no longer innovate simply as closed systems but share their knowledge resources across internal and external boundaries through various collaborative arrangements. Therefore, it is proposed that:

Proposition 2. Creation of valuable structural capital in knowledge-intensive industries demands the flexibility to innovate in an open mode across internal and external organizational boundaries.

Dynamic capabilities have been described by Teece (1987) as the interplay of human, intellectual, and relational capabilities. He states, "the foundation of a firm's competitive position is the set of capabilities (material resources, human skills and relationships, and relevant knowledge) the firm uses to build the product features that appeal to the marketplace" (p. 61). In most sectors of today's global marketplace, sustaining competitive advantage requires dynamic capabilities as well as knowledge assets. He suggests that development of dynamic capabilities enable organizations to identify and capitalize on new opportunities and update intellectual assets, with the objective of achieving competitive dominance in the marketplace. According to Teece, the ability to sense and seize opportunities is intimately tied to creating appropriate collaborative forms along the value chain. And part of the logic of capitalizing on opportunities in the marketplace is of course timing. Opportunities in the marketplace tied to the inception of innovative activity may result in the development of very successful new venture and innovation projects.

To facilitate the creation of effective, flexible organizational forms, an organization needs to create both structured and unstructured avenues for individuals to come together in the collaborative process. As mentioned previously, the organizational form which seems best suited to knowledge-intensive industries in terms of idea generation, knowledge creation, and exploitation is the team-based organization consisting of multiple teams. As Beyerlein et al. (2003, p. 14) state: "within a team-based organization, many forms of teams are utilized, both temporary and permanent, functional and cross-functional, local and distributed. This wide array of team forms shows that collaborative work is being organized in creative ways to fit the situation". Nonaka and Takeuchi (1995) further suggest that organizational knowledge creation operates in a spiral fashion and is thus dependent on mechanisms in place for sharing tacit knowledge among organizational members. Thus, it is proposed that:

Proposition 3. The value of collaborative capital to the organization is enhanced, and knowledge creation and leveraging more effective, when organizations are designed around team-based structures.

Effective collaboration also concerns how companies attract, train, and retain skilled people. Highly skilled personnel are an essential precondition for valuable collaborative capital. The role of human capital in an organization with regard to collaborative capital is attuned to combining forces with skilled people quickly when a window of opportunity opens. Another perspective related to the team-based approach suggests that knowledge-intensive industries are most effective when organized using the standard communication design of distributed networks with multiple, dynamic nodes of interaction. With this type of arrangement, the workers are empowered and called to innovative action (Amidon, 2003). It may be that collaborative work structures can best capitalize on opportunities in the marketplace in flexible ways through reliance on teams *and* network organizational designs.

An important leadership task for the future calls for a promotion of the interplay between the human, intellectual, and structural types of capital so that individual innovation actors feel the urgency to constantly improve their work processes. If we can take a cue from the history of empowerment initiatives in industry over the last several decades, the collaborative capital within teams and in cooperation with other teams will probably evolve naturally with a little organizational design push in the form of team building as a precondition for effective innovation (Skopec & Smith, 1997). This can take the form of a social process where employees create their own innovation teams, or are assigned to innovation or project teams where they have the latitude to use their potential and possibilities for self-organization in an independent fashion. On the other hand, there may be situations where collaboration is less a self-organizing process and more a centralized process, mandated from the top of the organization. The former scenario applies, especially in knowledge-intensive industries, since specialized experts come together where it can be assumed that a large part of knowledge-intensive tasks unfold in self-organizing ways.

One reason for this state of affairs in knowledge-intensive industries is that innovation processes are based to a large extent on implicit knowledge, increasingly possessed at all levels of the organization. In other words, the term expert is becoming commonplace throughout the organization. Thus, the traditional planning, organizing, leading, and controlling tasks of administration as well as work process decisions need to be relocated within the work units where the work is performed and the expertise resides. This entails empowerment and self-organization processes. Employees cannot be forced to work well together, they can only do so voluntarily, and this is more likely when individuals have a say in how best to design the work processes for results. Thus, based on the assumption that collaborative capital is a resource which cannot be effectively mandated by top or middle management, it is proposed that:

Proposition 4. The value of collaborative capital to organizations is enhanced when organizations provide their employees with the opportunity for self-organization and self-management.

Implications for Future Research and Practice

The intent of this chapter has been to examine the interplay of different capital forms resulting in collaborative capital in the knowledge-intensive industries. The work was undertaken partially in response to the Ittner and Larckners' (2003) claim that a better understanding of value creation can be used as the basis for validation as well as decision-making in organizations. In this vein, the chapter highlighted the potential to improve collaborative capital by using structural capital to combine human and intellectual capital in such a way that they optimally complement each other in terms of knowledge creation and exploitation. The lesson for knowledge-intensive companies is, of course, that it is smart to begin building up their collaborative capital in order to leverage their human and intellectual assets.

In addition, one current perspective on entrepreneurial success is that it lodged solidly in collaborative capital consisting of a combination of human and intellectual capabilities, as well as structural capital. Intention is to able to explore new terrain, seize opportunities, and exploit new knowledge. This combination of capital forms can unleash a major driving force as we have seen among many successful young entrepreneurs in the last decade. Team-based organizational forms also can play a central role in facilitating successful new product innovations in the entrepreneurial arena.

Underlying these examples of collaboration are industry- and firm-specific structures which need to be investigated in future research. More research is needed particularly on structural capital in the early-stage innovation phase. Intellectual and human capital is essential, especially in knowledge-intensive industries which depend very much on radical innovations. Without these assets, a firm would be unlikely to put anything of value into motion. To obtain and leverage the best of these assets, intelligent unit, organizational, and inter-organizational designs are necessary for specific industries and firms.

Another implication of the arguments offered in this chapter is that future organizational design forms will need to continue to empower employees to be intimately involved in work process design and strategic thinking around opportunities. Being able to flexibly capitalize on opportunities is becoming one of the most important drivers for the knowledge-based industries of the future. The structural design of organizations will be based on collaborative forms which rely on experts in certain stages of a project, and then shift appropriately to those with the expertise for the next stage. That we are all becoming experts in a knowledge work sense, in this high-velocity age of communication and computing, suggests that each employee will have the opportunity to contribute to the collaborative capital of the organization. This opportunity to organize and design informal and dynamic work structures that capitalize on all the knowledge in the organization is especially needed in times of increased specialization. Despite the fact that the work in some knowledge-intensive industries like biotechnology is largely based on very long product life cycles and research phases, the old collaboration patterns will of necessity increasingly break down as new ones emerge tailored to the specific knowledge and innovation needs of the particular project stage.

Examining these issues raises the question as to whether emerging organizational collaborative forms have enough stability to allow an innovation to succeed. In other words, is sufficient structure available to contain the circuitous design process? The answer might be just that collaborative capital multiplies when the underlying collaborative structure is stable. The degree of stability needed might be another issue (posited against the dynamics of the creative process and the inherent tensions, e.g. creative destruction). These ideas could be investigated in further research. Finally, another line of future inquiry might be to investigate if changing collaborative structures are time saving or merely time consuming (and therefore costly to the organization), considering the time required for new partners at any level to become socialized to the requirements of the innovation project.

SUMMARY AND CONCLUSIONS

This chapter has conceptually examined the interdependencies of different capital forms. The conclusion has been drawn that team-based organizations operating with shifting team structures for specific innovation phases and projects is the way to success for dynamic firms of the future. The possibility to shift teams and their constellations according to situation-specific tasks exploits intellectual capital thoroughly and determines the value of collaborative capital. Through changing team and collaborative structures, firms will constantly learn to adapt their collaborative capabilities and to design work settings in the best ways to facilitate steps in the innovation process.

The asset base of companies competing for growth in the knowledge-based economy will continue to shift away from equipment, buildings, and other fixed assets to corporate knowledge assets (Beck, 1998). Since knowledge in the knowledge-intensive industries is constantly growing and changing, the major driving force is collaborative capital consisting of human, intellectual and structural capital suitable to a particular innovation project phase. Team-based organizational designs incorporating empowerment as an organizing principle will help to unfold the benefits of collaborative capital, and are the keys to exploiting future opportunities in knowledge-intensive industries.

In conclusion, it is desirable to build a stronger theoretical framework for the integration of collaborative capital and its dynamics in the initial stages of product innovation. Using existing theory and practice, the integrative framework illustrated in Fig. 1 provides a possible foundation for empirical research aimed at uncovering the importance and interrelations of collaborative capital in research and development organizations. The model illustrating the major components of collaborative capital may serve as an initial conceptual basis for exploring its characteristics. It may also serve as a starting point to further identify how organizational structures in a team-based organization continually evolve, while at the same time leveraging the human and intellectual capital of the organization. Future findings may ultimately converge with collaboration patterns which support different innovation processes.

REFERENCES

Amidon, D. M. (2003). *The innovation superhighway: Harnessing intellectual capital for sustainable collaborative advantage*. Amsterdam, Boston: Butterworth-Heinemann.
Baker, G. (2002). The effects of synchronous collaborative technologies on decision making: A study of a virtual team. *Information Resources Management Journal, 15*(4), 79–93.
Bakhru, A. (2004). Managerial knowledge to organizational capability: New e-commerce businesses. *Journal of Intellectual Capital, 5*(2), 326–337.
Beck, N. (1998). *The next century: Why Canada wins*. Toronto: Harper Collins Publishers Ltd.
Beyerlein, M., Freedman, S., McGee, C., & Moran, L. (2003). *Beyond teams: Building the collaborative organization*. San Francisco: Jossey-Bass.
Bogdanowicz, M. S., & Bailey, E. K. (2002). The value of knowledge and the values of the new knowledge worker: Generation X in the new economy. *Journal of European Industrial Training, 26*(2–4), 125–128.
Bollingtoft, A., Ulhoi, J. P., Madsen, H., & Neergaard, H. (2003). The effect of financial factors on the performance of new venture companies in high tech and knowledge-intensive industries: An empirical study in Denmark. *International Journal of Management, 20*(4), 535–547.
Bougrain, F., & Haudeville, B. (2002). Innovation, collaboration and SMEs internal research capacities. *Research Policy, 31*(5), 735–748.
Bounfour, A. (2003). *The management of intangibles: The organisation's most valuable assets*. London, New York: Routledge.
Chesbrough, H. W. (2003). *Open innovation: The new imperative for creating and profiting from technology*. Boston: Harvard Business School Press.

Chiesa, V., & Toletti, G. (2004). Network of collaborations for innovation: The case of biotechnology. *Technology Analysis and Strategic Management, 16*(1), 73–96.

Chen, J., Zhu, Z., & Xie, H. Y. (2004). Measuring intellectual capital: A new model and empirical study. *Journal of Intellectual Capital, 5*(1), 195–213.

Dawson, R. (2000). *Developing knowledge-based client relationships: The future of professional services.* Woburn, MA: Butterworth-Heinemann.

Hamel, G., & Prahalad, C. K. (1994). *Competing for the future.* Boston: Harvard Business School Press.

Ittner, C. D., & Larckner, D. F. (2003). Are non-financial measures leading indicators of financial performance? An analysis of customer satisfaction. *Journal of Accounting Research, 36*, 1–35.

Langlois, R. N. (2003). The vanishing hand: The changing dynamics of industrial capitalism. *Industrial and Corporate Change, 12*(2), 351–385.

Lev, B., & Zambon, S. (2003). Intangibles and intellectual capital: An introduction to a special issue. *European Accounting Review, 12*(4), 597–603.

Love, J. H. (2001). Patterns of networking in the innovation process: A comparative study of the UK, Germany and Ireland. In: O. Jones, S. Conway & F. Steward (Eds), *Social interaction and organisational change: Aston perspectives on Innovation networks.* London: Imperial College Press.

Love, J. H., & Roper, S. (2004). The organisation of innovation: Collaboration, cooperation and multifunctional groups in UK and German manufacturing. *Cambridge Journal of Economics, 28*(3), 379–395.

Lövingsson, F., Dell'Orto, S., & Baladi, P. (2000). Navigating with new managerial tools. *Journal of Intellectual Capital, 1*(2), 147–154.

Narula, R. (2004). R&D collaboration by SMEs: New opportunities and limitations in the face of globalisation. *Technovation, 24*(2), 153–161.

Nonaka, I., & Nishiguchi, T. (2001). *Knowledge emergence: Social, technical, and evolutionary dimensions of knowledge creation.* New York: Oxford University Press.

Nonaka, I., & Takeuchi, H. (1995). *The knowledge-creating company: How Japanese companies create the dynamics of innovation.* New York: Oxford University Press.

Nonaka, I., & Teece, D. (2001). *Managing industrial knowledge: Creation, transfer and utilization.* London, Thousand Oaks: Sage.

Nursall, A. (2003). Building public knowledge: Collaborations between science centres, universities and industry. *International Journal of Technology Management, 25*(5), 381–389.

Oliver, A. L. (2004). Biotechnology entrepreneurial scientists and their collaborations. *Research Policy, 33*, 583–597.

Parker, H. (2000). Interfirm collaboration and the new product development process. *Industrial Management and Data Systems, 100*(6), 25–31.

Roos, J., Roos, G., Dragonetti, N., & Edvinsson, L. (1997). *Intellectual capital.* New York: Macmillan Business.

Roper, S. (1997). Product innovation and small business growth: A comparison of the strategies of German, UK and Irish companies. *Small Business Economics, 9*, 523–537.

Rothaermel, F. T., & Deeds, D. L. (2004). Exploration and exploitation alliances in biotechnology: A system of new product development. *Strategic Management Journal, 25*(3), 201–221.

Sanchez, R., Chaminade, C., & Olea, M. (2000). Management of intangibles: An attempt to build a theory. *Journal of Intellectual Capital, 1*(4), 312–327.

Siegel, D. S., Waldman, D. A., Atwater, L. E., & Link, A. N. (2003). Commercial knowledge transfers from universities to firms: Improving the effectiveness of university–industry collaboration. *Journal of High Technology Management Research, 14*(1), 111–133.

Shaikh, J. M. (2004). Measuring and reporting of intellectual capital performance analysis. *Journal of American Academy of Business, 4*(1–2), 439–448.

Skopec, E., & Smith, D. M. (1997). *How to use team building to foster innovation throughout your organization.* Lincolnwood: Contemporary Books.

Smith, K. (2000). What is the "knowledge economy"? Knowledge-intensive industries and distributed knowledge bases. Paper presented to *DRUID summer conference on the learning economy – Firms, regions and nation specific institutions,* June 15–17.

Stewart, T. A. (1997). *Intellectual capital: The new wealth of organizations.* New York: Doubleday.

Stewart, T. A. (1999). The case for managing structural capital. *Health Forum Journal, 42*(3), 30–33.

Teece, D. (1987). *The competitive challenge: Strategies for industrial innovation and renewal.* Cambridge, MA: Ballinger.

Teece, D. (2000) Managing intellectual capital. *Organizational, strategic, and policy dimensions.* Oxford, New York: University Press Oxford.

Tyler, B. B., & Steensma, K. H. (1995). Evaluating technological collaborative opportunities: A cognitive modeling. *Strategic Management Journal, 16*(Special Issue), 43–70.

CONNECTING ACROSS MILES AND WIRES: EXAMINING COLLABORATIVE CAPITAL DEVELOPMENT IN VIRTUAL SPACES

Lindsey Godwin and Julie Rennecker

ABSTRACT

Collaborative capital, or the capacity to work effectively with others toward shared goals and outcomes, reflects an accumulation of both skills and resources by individuals or groups. Traditionally, these skills and resources represented products of experiences in face-to-face task or interest groups. More recently, reflective of organizational trends to collaborate more often across both geographical and organizational boundaries, these experiences have been mediated by technologies designed to facilitate collaborative work. Often, however, the people using the technologies already know one another and interact face-to-face periodically. In contrast, in this chapter, we focus on a new technology-enabled social form, the multi-day online conference enabled by iCohere, an emerging groupware technology supporting the conference, to examine how collaborative capital might be built in and among previously unacquainted, globally distributed individuals. Using Erickson and Kellogg's

Collaborative Capital: Creating Intangible Value
Advances in Interdisciplinary Studies of Work Teams, Volume 11, 91–113
ISSN: 1572-0977/doi:10.1016/S1572-0977(05)11004-8

notion of "social translucence" we explore the case of one online conference attended by over 600 participants in 50 countries to identify technologic and social infrastructures conducive to the generation of new collaborative capital through participation in virtual spaces. By design, the technology and conference plan replicated common conference experiences conducive to collaborative capital development, but conference attendees also interacted and participated in ways that transcended the possibilities of a face-to-face conference. We anticipate these findings to be interesting for both managers and project team leaders seeking to foster collaborative capital development with the aid of modern communication and collaboration technologies.

Technology makes the world a new place.   –Shoshana Zuboff

INTRODUCTION

While organizations often measure their success in terms of physical, human, or market capital, it is the collaborative capital of an organization's members that enables the organization's achievements. Collaborative capital, or the capacity to work effectively with others to achieve shared goals and outcomes, is a cornerstone for effective organizations. However, facilitating collaborative capital development can be a daunting challenge in today's globally distributed organizations. Many contemporary organizations consist of networks of people distributed around the world who connect, often temporarily, to achieve a shared goal, posing significant obstacles to both collaboration and collaborative capital development. To manage this challenge, organizations have employed a variety of communicative technologies, such as e-mail, pagers, cellular telephones, and instant messaging, to facilitate interaction and information sharing across space and time. Yet, collaborative capital development requires more than information exchange.

Collaboration, the objective of collaborative capital building, has been a fertile research topic for several decades. Authors in different fields have created a variety of definitions, including, public management administration which has suggested that collaboration entails "multi-organizational arrangements to solve problems that cannot be solved by single organizations" (Agranoff & McGuire, 2003, p. 4); conflict resolution which has defined collaboration as "a process of joint decision-making among key stakeholders of a problem domain about the future of that domain" (Grey, 1989, p. 11); and community development which suggests that collaboration is a complex form of interaction which includes a commitment to mutual relationships and goals, shared responsibility and mutual authority, and accountability for success (Mattessich, Murray-Close, & Monsey, 2001, p. 59). While each of these various definitions adds insight to the growing conversation on collaboration, for this chapter, we draw upon the work of Himmelman, a scholar-practitioner whose work has explored transformational collaboration in social systems and various organizational contexts. Himmelman offers a schema for beneficial relationships, suggesting an interaction continuum with collaboration at one end. He defines collaboration as the "exchanging of information, altering activities, sharing resources, and enhancing the capacity of another for mutual benefit and to achieve a common purpose" (Himmelman, 1996, 1997). However, each of these definitions, including Himmelman's, implies a context of proximal social relationships among people who are already in relationship with one another.

Using Himmelman's definition as our foundation, we build upon and extend the existing work on collaboration to consider how technology can be used to facilitate the activities necessary for collaborative capital development in virtual spaces between individuals who have not previously met. As mentioned above, technologies are opening the possibility for networks of people distributed around the world to connect and collaborate even if they have never met before. However, research has shown that the technical capabilities of a tool do not in themselves ensure its adoption (Grudin, 1988; Markus & Connolly, 1990) but rather that the effective use of a technology also depends on social structuring actions by the users. Therefore, we will focus on the interplay between the technologic and social infrastructures involved in the use of a technology to create a viable virtual space to support collaboration on a global scale.

We begin our discussion by differentiating collaboration from other forms of reciprocal social activity and considering the mechanisms by which collaborative capital develops. Then we introduce the Erickson and Kellogg (2000) social translucence theory to discuss technology affordances that facilitate collaboration by mirroring natural social processes. Using this framework to analyze the use of iCohere, a relatively new groupware technology, to support a multi-day online conference attended by over 600 participants in 50 countries, we show how the framework can also be used to analyze and identify social interventions that enhance the use and collaborative outcomes of the technology. Based on this case study, we identify technologic and social infrastructures conducive to the generation of new collaborative capital in virtual spaces. Our analysis is aimed at informing managers and team leaders who seek to foster collaborative capital development via technology-mediated forums, as well as technology designers seeking to better understand the collaborative process.

COLLABORATION AND COLLABORATIVE CAPITAL

Collaboration has been defined differently by a number of researchers (Grey, 1989; Mattessich et al., 2001; Agranoff & McGuire, 2003), and the term "collaboration" has often been used synonymously with other reciprocal interpersonal activities, such as cooperation. However, Himmelman (1996) suggests, that these various other terms actually refer to different levels of reciprocity, with collaboration entailing the greatest personal investment, potential benefit, and potential risk. As shown in Table 1, Himmelman's hierarchy of "mutually beneficial" relationships is useful for differentiating collaboration from other exchange relationships. For our discussions, we will assume this integrated definition of collaboration, which captures the dynamic exchange of a collaborative relationship.

Collaboration is not synonymous with collaborative capital, however. Collaborative capital refers to the *capacity* to work effectively with others to achieve mutually beneficial goals. Thinking about collaboration in terms of "capital" suggests a figure-ground shift with respect to the phenomena of interest. Whereas collaboration focuses on the dynamics and current actions among collaborators, the notion of collaborative capital foregrounds an

Table 1. Typology of Mutually Beneficial Relationships.

	Definition
Networking	Exchanging information for mutual benefit
Coordinating	Exchanging information and altering activities for mutual benefit and to achieve a common purpose
Cooperating	Exchanging information, altering activities, and sharing resources for mutual benefit and to achieve a common purpose
Collaborating	Exchanging information, altering activities, sharing resources, and enhancing the capacity of another for mutual benefit and to achieve a common purpose

individual's, group's, or organization's *potential* to collaborate in the future based on past collaborative relationships. This "potential" consists of both skills and resources that can be used or "accrued" to facilitate future collaboration. These skills and resources are a result of the exchanges (both relational and informational) that occur during networking, coordinating, and cooperating, which in turn foster both the likelihood of collaboration among the interacting parties and the development of collaborative capital. While their work focuses on the development of metropolitan regions, a recent report from the MetroBusinessNet, a national learning network composed of regional business-civic organizations, supports the assertion that increased reciprocal interactions lead to an increased likelihood of collaboration. They state that "trust is built through proximity and repeated interaction, which in turn stimulates collaboration. The growth of the computer and software industry in Northern California's Silicon Valley is an example of this cooperative model" (MetroBusinessNet, 2003, p. 3). In this example, collaboration between companies A and B helps to not only foster future collaboration between those companies, but also helps company A acquire knowledge, skills, and networks which become their collaborative capital, aiding them in and making them more attractive partners for future collaborations with company C.

Collaboration is unique among the reciprocal relationships in that it involves an investment in the capacity of another (Himmelman, 1996). So while networking, coordinating, and cooperating each contribute to the accrual of one's own skills and resources, collaborating contributes to both one's own collaborative capital and to that of the participating others, enhancing all parties' potential for effective collaboration in the future both with each other and with unspecified others. This dynamic process and its potential serial effects are illustrated in Fig. 1.

COLLABORATIVE CAPITAL BUILDING IN CYBERSPACE

As discussed above, technologies are helping collaborators transcend geographic boundaries. Despite this emerging reality, most of the research on collaboration to date, is founded on an assumption of co-location or at least periodic face-to-face contact. For instance, several studies have investigated the roles of physical proximity and the arrangement of physical space in determining who collaborated with whom. In a seminal study of an

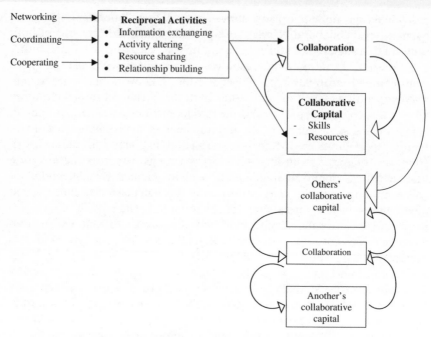

Fig. 1. The collaborative capital development process.

engineering research and development organization, Allen (1977) found that the researchers collaborated almost exclusively with others whose desks were located within 30 meters of their own, a finding that was later replicated by Kraut, Fish, Root, and Chalfonte (1990), and Kraut, Fussel, Brennan, and Siegel (2002). Building upon this finding, others such as Hillier and Penn (1991, p. 26) have suggested that the physical organization of space can either facilitate or hinder the generation of new knowledge by using spatial organization to create or deter "new relational patterns by maximizing (or minimizing) the randomness of encounters through spatial proximity and movement."

However, the modern organizational landscape is no longer confined by space and time. The globalization of work means that individuals often find themselves needing to work with a person across the globe as frequently as the one in the next cubicle (Hayes, 2004). In addition, many organizations are discovering that collaboration with other organizations is a necessary component of contemporary business (Stiles, 1995). One recent survey indicated that 75% of executives consider collaboration with other organizations to be a top priority (Kontzer, 2002).

The combined increases in both geographic distribution and multi-organizational partnerships have placed new and growing demands on the collaborative capacity of both individuals and organizations. To cope with these escalating demands, organizations are employing various combinations of communication and information technologies to aid collaboration, both within and between organizations (Hinds & Kiesler, 2002). Forrester (2003) predicts that American and European firms will spend 28% of their information technology budgets on geographically distributed work in the next 2 years. At least some portion of that will go toward the purchase of groupware technologies that market themselves specifically as support tools for distributed collaborative work. For example, in an Internet advertisement, CoCreate says their collaboration software helps companies "unite the 'too many' into one place on the web ... Project members anywhere can access the right version of the data, view it in a meaningful way and engage with team members to coordinate ideas and changes" (CoCreate, 2004).

The capabilities of technologies designed to support collaborative processes, however, have often fallen short. One possible explanation is that many technologies employed as collaboration solutions support only single social processes, such as networking, coordinating, *or* information exchange rather than a combination of all these activities. Bernstein (2000) noted that "most collaboration support systems have focused on either automating fixed work processes or simply supporting communication in ad hoc processes," resulting in either inflexibly structured systems incompatible with the variability of collaborative work or in systems providing no facilitative structure at all. Again, drawing on Himmelman's definition, collaboration requires mechanisms to both support communication and to augment communicative processes with mechanisms for networking, coordinating, and resource sharing.

Erickson and Kellogg (2000) proposed the social translucence of technology (STT) framework as a guide for the design of effective collaborative technology systems. They argue that computer-mediated communication (CMC) is most effective when it mimics natural communication processes and use the term social translucence to indicate the degree to which a technology does so. They proposed three characteristics that differentiate socially translucent collaborative technologies, namely visibility, awareness, and accountability. Quan-Haase, Cothrel, and Wellman (2004, p. 2) further developed Erickson and Kellogg's work by refining the definitions of each characteristic:

1. *Visibility*: movements and changes are used to guide interactions and exchanges.
2. *Awareness*: knowing that others are present or available for communication. This knowledge can be used for starting communication and changing communicative behaviors.
3. *Accountability*: knowing that others know that they are there, making participants accountable for their behavior.

Erickson and Kellogg (2000) assert that in addition to these three characteristics, a technology, which is going to effectively foster collaboration must also support the *persistence* of the conversation occurring in cyberspace. They state, "persistence expands conversation beyond those within earshot, rendering it accessible to those in other places and at later times" (p. 8). Thus, technology creates the possibility of creating lasting conversations which "opens the door to a variety of new uses" for the conversation beyond the original exchange, thus making collaboration in the future possible. To support the persistence of conversations, socially translucent technologies also need to provide activity support, conversation visualization and restructuring, and organizational knowledge spaces.

Activity support, Erickson and Kellogg contend, is necessary to support the initiation of social activity and it includes the support of long-running, reflective, and coherent conversations which are participant directed. *Conversation visualization and restructuring* characteristics are those which allow knowledge within a conversation to be reusable, with members able to search, navigate, and visualize their conversations by having the freedom and tools available to summarize, highlight, and link ideas within a given discussion. Finally, the system must allow for the *creation of organizational knowledge spaces*, or semi-private areas that allow smaller, sub-communities to exercise control over the ways they share their knowledge with the larger organization.

These six principles comprise the STT framework for collaborative technology design. Though initially intended to guide the design process, the framework can also be used as an analytic lens for understanding the capabilities and limitations of a technology in use, which is where we turn next.

A CASE OF VIRTUAL COLLABORATIVE CAPITAL BUILDING: THE FIRST INTERNATIONAL CONFERENCE FOR BUSINESS AS AN AGENT OF WORLD BENEFIT

On January 24, 2004, over 600 people in 50 countries logged onto their computers to listen to the welcome address for the First International Online Conference on Business as an Agent of World Benefit (BAWB). The conference, convened by an academic center by the same name, was held as a free public gathering. For 3 days, academics, business leaders, independent consultants, and activists came together to explore the role of business in society and to begin collaborating around ways to advance corporate citizenship.

The conference was enabled by iCohere, a technology designed to replicate and support natural conversation processes to facilitate collaboration. Fig. 2 shows a screen shot of the conference site. Similar to a location-based conference, the virtual space included scheduled presentations, a "café" for

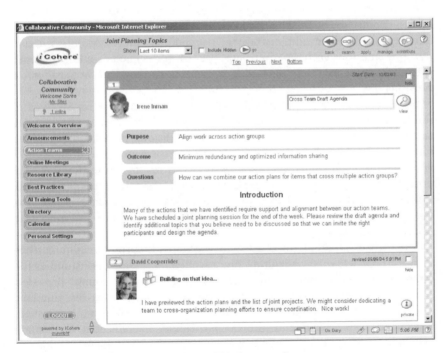

Fig. 2. Screen shot of iCohere conference space.

unscheduled informal conversation, an "exhibition hall" where sponsors displayed information about their organizations, and a live chat area for both scheduled and unscheduled conversations that could be joined by anyone who logged onto the conference. A set of menu buttons accessible from any of these activity spaces allowed participants to navigate among the spaces, following their own interests at their own pace, just as someone might move among presentations, in and out of the vendors' exhibitions, or among conversations during a reception at a traditional conference.

Participants registered online prior to the conference and received an e-mail with a login ID and password to access the conference space. When logging on for the first time, the application prompted the participant to configure the space to reflect his or her own time zone and to fill out a personal profile, including a photo. A "participant directory" provided hyperlink access to these profiles, including photos, for anyone participating in the conference.

A daily agenda posted on the conference welcome page detailed the day's planned events, including the scheduled live chats and the "opening" of new presentations or workshops for viewing. The presentations consisted of Power Point slides with pre-recorded voiceover and automatic slide advance. Conference administrators "opened," or made available, a few new presentations each day, but once opened, participants could access the presentations at any time, including presentations they had "missed" on a previous day.

In contrast to the ephemerality of conversations in a physical café, the threaded discussions in the "Collaboration Café" were archived and accessible to participants at any time. In addition, contributors' names, photos, and a hyperlink to their respective personal profiles automatically accompanied each contribution. So participants reading or responding to a posted comment could also peruse the profiles of the contributors as context for the posted remarks. From the profile view, a participant could also initiate a private or public "chat" with or send an e-mail to anyone who sounded interesting.

A real-time, hyperlink directory of all participants currently online further increased participants' visibility to one another, increasing opportunities for impromptu synchronous conversations. Again, each name provided a hyperlink connection to the participant's personal profile, but this link also offered the possibility of sending the person an instant message. The instant messaging feature allowed participants to connect in "real-time" via spontaneous live chat sessions with one or many participants. Similar to other instant messaging or chat technologies, iCohere allowed participants to participate polychronically, engaging simultaneously in as many asynchronous and synchronous conversations as they wanted. Thus, someone could be engaged in a live chat with three separate people while contributing to a discussion thread.

Other conference features designed specifically to facilitate networking and collaboration made each participant's interests and contribution to the conference visible. In addition to the author-identifier and personal profile hyperlink associated with each posting, clicking on a person's name in one area, such as the discussion forum, produced a listing of the contributor's postings in other conference areas, including other discussion threads. If a participant were so inclined, he or she could read all contributions made by a particular person.

A "resource" area provided a space for spontaneous sharing of participant-developed materials, links to relevant web sites, announcements of upcoming events and commentary on available publications. The contributor's photo and a hyperlink to his or her profile accompanied these postings as well. Finally, any participant could spontaneously poll the other participants on a particular question of interest. Unlike live conferences, the electronic medium made this task easy. The question (which could be open ended or forced choice) was posted in the announcement area of the conference so that everyone could easily access it, and as participants responded, the question originators could track the results in real time. Participants commonly used this function to test for consensus around a particular topic or to gather demographic or opinion data from participants.

The conference facilitators also played an active role in keeping participants engaged. Each evening of the conference, the BAWB conference team e-mailed a summary of the day's activities and discussions, and an overview of the following day's events to all registered participants, whether they had been logged on that day or not. During live chats, one of the team members served as a discussion facilitator helping to keep the conversation flowing by summarizing, inviting questions, and welcoming new participants as they joined the chat. Team members also "floated" around the conference, visiting the various discussion threads, adding comments, making links, or posting announcements as appropriate to help disseminate ideas that were emerging throughout the conference. The BAWB conference team worked in conjunction with the iCohere staff to answer technical questions that arose, from login difficulties to confusion about how to contribute. In a few cases, a conference team member or one of the iCohere help desk staff, also made him- or herself available via telephone to resolve participants' questions.

Each day of the conference, new people contacted the BAWB team to register for the event indicating that they had been encouraged to attend by a friend or colleague who was already participating. By the last day, more than 600 individuals had visited the space. The conference closed with an invitation for participants to continue visiting and using the site, which remained open to them for an additional 60 days. Anecdotal reports by conference participants and queries sent to the BAWB team after the conference described the array of new relationships that were formed at the conference.

In addition to the anecdotal feedback, at the conclusion of the conference, participants were asked to complete a survey to share their impressions of the conference and to make suggestions for improving future conferences. While only 55 participants completed the survey, the results suggest that participants were pleased with their experience. When asked if they would participate in another online conference, 38 (69%) indicated "absolutely," 16 (29.1%) indicated they were "likely," 1 (1.8%) indicated "unsure," and no one responded "unlikely" or "definitely not." When asked to rate their over all conference experience, 15 (27%) rated it as "excellent," 27 (49%) rated it as "very good," 10 (18.2%) indicated it was "good," 1 (1.8%) indicated it was "fair," and only 2 (3%) rated it as "poor." When asked about the online conference environment provided by iCohere, 23 (44.2%) indicated it was "excellent," 18 (34.6%) indicated it was "very good," 8 (15.4%) indicated it was "good," 2 (3.8%) indicated it was "fair" and only 1 (1.8%) indicated it was "poor." In addition to various satisfaction scales, the survey also asked participants for qualitative feedback. These remarks were overwhelmingly positive, indicating excitement about the conference environment, as shown by the sampling of comments provided in Table 2.

Table 2.   Illustrative Comments from Participants.

Question: What additional feedback do you have about the conference?

I loved the possibility of being together in a virtual space but with very real people.

Would not have believed an online conference could simulate the real thing so well.

This is the best set of online discussions I have seen.

I like that the presentations and information was/is available 24 h per day so that I could work around my schedule.

I loved the live chats, very energizing, and the information was generously shared.

More video and audio links ... voice connections ... typing is not the easiest.

I would like there to be a distinction when invited to chat between a personal invitation and one that goes to everyone.

The synergy of the live chats has great potential. Better facilitation is needed, maybe by offering a more targeted focus for discussion.

I liked the pictures. It added a human touch to a high-tech environment.

The design of the technology and the actions of the facilitators combined to create a "socio-technical infrastructure" that enabled the conference to transcend an online information exchange to further enhance the collaborative capacity of geographically distributed people by fostering exchanges between and developing relationships among people who would likely not have otherwise "met." As one participant wrote "(I enjoyed) the communication capabilities that allowed me to meet new people and engage in meaningful dialog which will continue beyond the conference."

BUILDING A VIRTUAL FORUM FOR COLLABORATIVE CAPITAL

As overviewed above, the iCohere space had many features that aided in the creation of a vibrant collaborative space. In addition to the structure of the technology itself, the facilitative actions of the BAWB team and iCohere staff, as well as user initiatives, contributed to the success of the conference. This case illustrates the importance of both technologic and social infrastructure that need to be present in order to enable activity conducive to collaborative capital development. We now turn our attention to each of the six elements suggested by the STT framework to further analyze the case.

Visibility

Many features of iCohere alerted participants to changes in their virtual space to help them navigate events and interactions more effectively. New postings not yet read by a participant were marked with a blue star on the posting itself and a number on the navigation menu indicating the number of unread postings in each conference area. So a participant signing on after several hours away from the conference could see at a glance on the Welcome page that he or she had four unread e-mails, two unread announcements, and perhaps as many as 30 new posts in various discussion threads. This information allowed the participants to navigate to the new information quickly and in the order of their choosing.

A dynamic directory of currently online participants (discussed in more detail in the next section) reflected the comings and goings of individuals, similar to the way a person might monitor others attending a reception or paper session at an academic conference when trying to connect with a particular person. Finally, pop-up messages notified participants when each new "chat" conversation began. These indicators of changes in the content, participation, and activities in the conference space served as cues, interpreted idiosyncratically by each participant to support self-directed movement within the conference space.

The facilitators also helped foster a sense of visibility throughout the conference. At the end of each day, they created a summary of the day's events as well as an updated agenda for the following day. This information was then e-mailed to every participant so that they had the current schedule for when activities were happening each day of the conference. As needed, they would also post announcements within the conference space, updating the agenda or calling attention to upcoming activities, such as live chats.

Awareness

Several features of iCohere facilitated presence' awareness among conference participants. The dynamic directory of currently online participants accessible via the navigation menu made it possible to determine at a glance who and how many participants were available for synchronous interaction. The tool also allowed participants to indicate when they were online but unavailable for chatting. Finally, within the chat area, iCohere automatically generated announcements signaling each participant's arrival or departure. It was not possible however, when browsing the asynchronous areas to identify whom else was browsing the same spaces at the same time or who had read the same postings as one's self without querying each participant individually. Facilitators also helped promote awareness throughout the conference by acting as a hosts, "introducing" individuals to one another through live chats or postings in discussion threads.

Accountability

The iCohere environment has a built in accountability structure. Each person is assigned a unique login ID and password and must use these identifiers to enter the virtual space. Upon logging in, the technology recognizes a person as present, announces his or her presence to the world, and tracks each person's behavior within the space. As mentioned in the description of the conference experience, this tracking function of the technology makes it possible to view a summary of each participant's asynchronous contributions, i.e. discussion board postings, resource suggestions, etc. and to view the personal profile associated with any posting. While these features do not rule out the possibility of participants supplying fraudulent profile information, the use of names, pictures, and other identifying information increases the possibility that participants may recognize one another from offline contact, identify mutual acquaintances, or recognize one another in a future encounter, intimating an environment of accountability.

Activity Support

From a technologic perspective, the iCohere space allows for a wide array of activity configurations. For each area of the conference (i.e. each discussion area, live chat, announcement board, calendar, etc.) administrative rights could be given to conference facilitators only, facilitators and identified group leaders only, or to all participants. While the technology was infinitely flexible regarding how it was set up to support both self-initiated and facilitated activity, the conference facilitators played an integral role in the activity support. They determined how many synchronous chat and asynchronous discussion "rooms" to initially open and whom to grant administrative rights to. For example, during the conference, only facilitators were allowed to post on the announcement board because the facilitators wanted to retain control over that space, using it to garner attention to the items they moderated. However, the main discussion hall, called the "Collaboration Café," was configured to allow any participant to initiate their own threaded discussion topic, as well as contributing to existing threads. As a result, participants created 20 distinct discussion forums in this area without ever needing a facilitator's help.

Conference facilitators also worked prior to the conference to "seed" each area with materials and discussion starters, so that participants would enter an area that "felt" like there was activity going on. For example, prior to the conference, they created a "Welcome and introduction" area, which not only invited participants to introduce themselves but already contained the facilitators' greetings, personal information, and picture.

Conversation Visualization and Restructuring

In accord with Erickson and Kellogg's notion of creating persistent conversations, one of the benefits of technology-mediated collaboration, in contrast to face-to-face interaction, is the ability to visualize, structure, and restructure interactions, both as they are occurring and retrospectively. Several iCohere features combined to allow participants to structure, visualize, search, and navigate their conversations. The first was a tool to help structure conversations. A conversation template included fields for a title of the discussion area, a purpose statement for the discussion, desired outcomes (if any) for the discussion, guiding questions, and a conversation introduction or overview to help the initiator frame the discussion. When posted, the template contents made it possible for participants to quickly visualize the range of conversations taking place and to navigate through multiple conversations on similar or related topics.

The technology also included a template for framing each contribution to the conversation. When creating a new posting a participant could choose to create a title or to begin with one of several suggested openings, such as "Yes, I agree," "I have a different perspective", or "Let me summarize". In addition to having all the asynchronous threaded discussions available to all conference participants, iCohere automatically archived all transcripts from the live chat sessions, allowing them to "persist" beyond the synchronous discussion to be available asynchronously to any participant as well. A final technology feature that enabled conversation navigation was a "search" option, which allows participants to do a text search throughout the conference if desired.

Conference facilitators also helped "connect the dots" between related conversations by monitoring discussions throughout the conference and posting summaries and/or making links across the conference space to other conversations when appropriate. Once the conference was over, they also created a conference proceedings document which included both a text-based summary of the conversations at the conference as well as graphic illustrations to provide additional context cues about the experience of the conference for both participants and non-participants alike.

Organizational Knowledge Spaces

The final STT element suggests that allowing semi-autonomous knowledge communities to exist within the larger community helps promote conversation and collaborative sharing within a safe space, a process that the iCohere technology was able to facilitate. The technology allowed for private conversations to occur within the public conference space, including private responses to individuals during public live chats, as well as creating private live chats, which outsiders could not enter unless invited. Also, the technology allowed for the creation of private sub-groups within the conference, which would be able to create threaded discussion areas that could only be seen by other members of the sub-group. Conference facilitators worked to not only make participants aware of these features, but they also used them themselves during the conference. For example, the facilitators created a sub-group for all conference facilitators and technical support staff, so that they could have a threaded discussion about the technical issues, which were emerging, as well as to track feedback from participants. The rest of the conference was unaware that these posts were even created, since they did not have access to see them.

Table 3 summarizes the key STT characteristics of the technology and social infrastructures enabling the online conference and facilitating the development of collaborative capital at the individual, group, and (in this case) conference level.

One characteristic that the STT framework does not explicitly capture, but that proved to be an important feature of the BAWB conference was the multi-media components of the technology space. The iCohere technology was designed to go beyond just text-based exchanges, with the ability to support the sharing and accessing of audio files, multi-media clips, pictures, and other graphics. For example, every keynote and workshop presentation not only had a visual slide show, but also a voiceover component that participants could audio stream onto their computers as if they were watching the presentation live. As the conference feedback indicated, these features made the conference space "come alive" and feel more "human" than simply sitting in front of a computer. Therefore, based on our data, we propose a seventh STT element necessary for successful collaborative capital development, *sensory flexibility*. Sensory flexibility is presentation of information and communication via multiple sensory modes (i.e. text, graphics, audio). Since individuals process information differently through their senses, we argue that sensory flexibility as a technical feature enables individuals to better visualize and restructure their conversations, and thus better exchange information, which is one key foundation for collaboration.

However, as the table illustrates, the iCohere collaboration technology, in concert with the social facilitation of the conference, largely embodied the six qualities of social translucence. From the feedback comments and survey results discussed earlier, there is support that various features were not only made available to, but were effectively used by participants and found to be useful. This is not a minor point, since a technology's features are not really "features" unless the users find them usable and useful (Grudin, 1988). In addition to the feedback, the rich threaded discussion halls and resource

Table 3. Summary of STT Features within the iCohere Conference.

Social Translucence Principle	Purpose Networking	iCohere Technology Features	Facilitative Activities by Conference Staff	Participant Reactions
Visibility	Using movements and changes in the space as a guide for interactions and exchanges	Indicator displayed for new information posted "pop-up" invitations to join live chats Current # online displayed	Sent e-mail summary of daily activity Posted announcements with updates to agenda and to call attention to certain activities	I appreciate the daily e-mails and I also appreciated being invited to join the discussions
Awareness	Knowing that others are present or available for communication encourages exchange	Announcement of person entering/leaving live chat Directory of online participants available for live chat and networking	Acting as a host, introducing individuals to each other throughout the conference	(I enjoyed) the opportunity to review the profiles of the participants so I could select people with similar interests for follow-up
Accountability	Knowing that others know that they are there encourages participation	Shared profiles so that everyone had access to everyone Attached author name to each contribution		(I enjoyed) the communication capabilities that allowed me to meet new people and engaged in meaningful dialogue which will continue beyond the conference
Activity support	Supporting the initiation and conduct of social activity within the space	Granting administrative rights in areas to participants to begin their own discussion	Seeded the site with materials and initial discussions Facilitated live chats Available at help desk to answer technical questions	(One of the conference facilitators) was wonderful ... very helpful getting me involved, set up online, and tuned into the ways and means of this online conferencing....

Conversational visualization and restructuring	Making conversations reusable; allowing participants to add structures to conversations: summarizing, highlighting, linking, etc.	Transcripts available from all live chats Availability of all threaded discussions to be seen 60 days after the conference Templates for posts with headings for contributions such as: "building upon that idea"; "let me summarize"; "I have a different perspective" Text-search capability	Monitored discussions, posting summaries and making links across the conference space Created conference proceedings document and circulated it to participants	(I appreciated the conference's) structure and organization. (I) would not have believed an online conference could simulate the real thing so well
Organizational knowledge spaces	Allowing semi-autonomous knowledge communities to exist within the community, with each exercising control over the ways and means they share their knowledge with the larger group	Allows for private sub-groups with private discussion areas Allows private live chats Allows private responses within open live chat Allows anonymous contributions	Informing participants about the features that allow private conversations	(During a live chat) I just realized that I can send private messages within this conversation, that is very helpful, so you and I can talk "offline" if needed

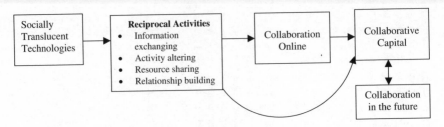

Fig. 3. STT impact on collaboration and collaborative capital.

area which participants populated serve as indicators for collaboration that occurred online during the conference. While we do not have systematic data on the collaborative exchanges that occurred after the conference, we received many anecdotal stores describing offline collaborative exchanges triggered by the conference. One author of this chapter has even personally enjoyed several collaborative relationships with individuals met during the conference.

As illustrated in Fig. 3, socially translucent technologies create an environment within which the reciprocal activities necessary for collaboration can occur. However, the online conference demonstrates that even if immediate collaboration does not occur within the confines of the online space, collaborative capital can be accumulated. The exchange of information, resource sharing, and relationship building that does occur online, can greatly increase an individual's *potential* to collaborate in the future, thus increasing their collaborative capital.

CONCLUSION: GOING BEYOND THE CASE

It is important to recognize that the technology structure provides space for, enables, and supports particular types of interactions, but whether or not these interactions occur depends primarily on human choice and the intentional actions of both the conference hosts and the participants. In the case of the event studied here, participants were motivated by a shared interest in exploring business and society issues, and participation was completely voluntary. The BAWB case illustrates how new collaborative technologies are opening the door for the development of virtual communities comprised of previously unacquainted and unassociated others, who share no immediate task, but rather come together on the grounds of common beliefs and shared mission. As online communities have emerged over the past decade, people are no longer limited to collaborating with others whom they have previously met, but instead they can connect with others whom they have met only in cyberspace (Smith & Kollock, 1999; Rheingold, 2000). However, as online communities and virtual conferences illustrate, even in the absence of an assigned task, such virtual connections set the stage for collaboration between individuals with a multitude of organizational affiliations and interests. Individuals are now coming together with others to exchange information and create networks that extend around the globe. The wake of these virtual exchanges has implications for an individual's collaborative capital even beyond the immediate online interaction. The virtual connections may spark collaboration between strangers, or an individual may simply become better prepared (with increased information or social skills) to collaborate with someone sitting beside them.

On the other hand, using this same technology to support collaboration in an organizational context, where participation would reflect one's role responsibilities as much or more than one's personal affinities, one can imagine that the nature of the collaborative space may differ from the case described here. The same technologic features would be beneficial, but one might expect to see, more focused conversations as deadlines and productivity factor into the collaborative equation.

Whether for inter-organizational collaboration or for online conferencing, the iCohere technology is one example of an emerging generation of collaborative groupware that supports virtual interactions to enable new ways of collaborating across time and space. As the BAWB online conference illustrates, creating a successful interactive, online collaborative experience requires both a human presence of facilitation, and an effective virtual environmental design. Together, these two components set the stage for collaborative capital building within a virtual environment.

As globalization increases, collaborative technologies are poised to play an increasingly important role in organizational processes. In order to best support effective collaborative capital development, both the design of the technology and the actions of facilitators need to be considered. Together, these elements create a "socio-technical infrastructure" that enables natural interactions to occur in a virtual environment. Social translucence theory offers a framework for structuring technology to mirror natural interaction processes, creating better collaborative forums. Building upon STT, the case study presented here illustrates how the ideas of visibility, awareness, accountability, activity support, conversation visualization and restructuring, and organizational knowledge spaces can be applied to the phenomenon of online conferencing. The insights derived from this case are applicable for practitioners and technology designers alike, who look into tomorrow and see the endless possibilities virtual spaces hold for collaborative capital building.

REFERENCES

Agranoff, R., & McGuire, M. (2003). *Colborative public management: New strategies for local governments (219pp)*. Washington, DC: Georgetown University Press.

Allen, T. J. (1977). *Managing the flow of technology: Technology transfer and the dissemination of technological information within the R&D organization*. Cambridge, MA: MIT Press.

Bernstein, A. (2000). How can cooperative work tools support dynamic group process? *Proceedings of the 2000 ACM conference on computer supported cooperative work*.

CoCreate (2004). Web site: http://www.cocreate.com/

Erickson, T., & Kellogg, W. A. (2000). Social translucence: An approach to designing systems that mesh with social processes. *ACM Transactions on Computer–Human Interaction*, 7(1), 59–83.

Forrester Research cited by the *Associated Press* (2003) Tech jobs leave U.S. for India, Russia, reported on 14 July 2003.

Grey, B. (1989). *Collaborating: Finding common ground for multiparty problems*. San Francisco, CA: Jossey-Bass.

Grudin, J. (1988). Why CSCW applications fail: Problems in the design and evaluation of organizational interfaces. Paper presented at the *Conference on computer-supported cooperative work*.

Hayes, B. (2004). Project management marries collaboration: A new technology for distributed project teams. *Proceedings of the PMI global congress*.

Hillier, B., & Penn, A. (1991). Visible colleges: Structure and randomness in the place of discovery. *Science in Context*, 4(1), 23–49.

Himmelman, A. T. (1996). On the theory and practice of transformational collaboration: From social service to social justice. In: C. Huxham (Ed.), *Creating collaborative advantage* (pp. 19–43). London: Sage Publishers.

Himmelman, A. T. (1997). Devolution as an experiment in citizen governance: Multi-Organizational partnerships and democratic revolutions. A working paper for the *Fourth international conference on multi-organizational partnerships and cooperative strategy*. Oxford University, 8–10 July.

Hinds, P., & Kiesler, S. (Eds) (2002). *Distributed work*. MIT Press.

Kontzer, T. (2002). Benefits of colboration: A new survey indicates companies that are linking their processes with third-party partners and suppliers are enjoying a variety of benefits. *Information week*. Online source. Retrieved October 1, 2004 from http://www.informationweek.com/story/IWK20021125S0012

Kraut, R. E., Fish, R. S., Root, R. W., & Chalfonte, B. L. (1990). Informal communication in organizations: Form, function, and technology. In: S. Oskamp & S. Spaccapan (Eds), *Human reactions to technology: The claremont symposium on applied social psychology* (pp. 145–199). Beverly Hills, CA: Sage Publications.

Kraut, R. E., Fussel, S. R., Brennan, S. E., & Siegel, J. (2002). Understanding effects of proximity on implications for technologies to support remote collaborative work. In: P. Hinds & S. Kiesler (Eds), *Distributed work* (pp. 137–164). Cambridge, MA: MIT Press.

Markus, M. L., & Connolly, T. (1990). Why CSCW applications fail: Problems in the adoption of interdependent work tools. Paper presented at *The conference on computer-supported cooperative work*, Los Angeles, CA, U.S.A

Mattessich, P. W., Murray-Close, M., & Monsey, B. R. (2001). *Collaboration: What makes it work* (2nd ed). St. Paul, MN: Amherst H. Wilder Foundation.

MetroBusinessNet. (2003). *It takes a region to raise a new economy*. Online source. Retrieved November 1, 2004 from http://www.regionalstewardship.org/ARS_enews/November2003.php

Quan-Haase, A., Cothrel, J., & Wellman, B. (2004). Instant messaging as social mediation: Case study of a high-tech firm (forthcoming).

Rheingold, H. (2000). *The virtual community*. Cambridge, MA: MIT Press.

Smith, M., & Kollock, P. (Eds) (1999). *Communities in cyberspace*. New York, NY: Routledge.

Stiles, J. (1995). Collaboration for competitive advantage: The changing world of alliances and partnerships. *Long Range Planning, 28*(5), 8–9 109–112.

STRIVING FOR A NEW IDEAL: A WORK ENVIRONMENT TO ENERGIZE COLLABORATIVE CAPACITY ACROSS EAST AND WEST BOUNDARIES

Jill Nemiro, Stefanus Hanifah and Jing Wang

This chapter is dedicated to Shu Wang, whose life embodied the very core values of collaboration and love in raising three inspirational daughters. May her collaborative soul and loving spirit be an inspiration to us all.

ABSTRACT

Contemporary organizations have realized the importance of creating work environments that energize and sustain collaborative capacity. Nowhere is the need for collaborative capacity more apparent than when business interactions and collaborative work efforts cross country boundaries. Collaborative capacity is the foundation to an organization's key resource, the collaborative capital. Creating a work environment or climate that supports, enhances, and maintains collaborative capacity is essential for achieving high levels of collaborative capital. In this chapter, we review an exploratory, cross-cultural investigation of the work environments that guide organizations (public and private universities)

Collaborative Capital: Creating Intangible Value
Advances in Interdisciplinary Studies of Work Teams, Volume 11, 115–159
Copyright © 2005 by Elsevier Ltd.
ISSN: 1572-0977/doi:10.1016/S1572-0977(05)11005-X

in the United States and in several Asian countries. One hundred and ninety-four staff from a university in the United States and a combined total of 976 individuals from eight universities throughout Asia (Malaysia, Singapore, South Korea, and Taiwan) were asked to assess their organizations' work environments using the Performance Environmental Perception Scale (PEPS; David Ripley (1998) The development of the performance environment perception scale and its underlying theoretical model. Unpublished Doctoral Dissertation, University of Tennessee, Knoxville). We describe what work environment factors were viewed the same across Eastern and Western cultures, and what factors were viewed differently. Additionally, we present a model of work environment factors that can be used to enhance and sustain collaborative capacity across Eastern and Western cultures.

As Director, Far East for MCI International from 1988 to 1999, I had the responsibility of negotiating operating agreements with a number of Asian countries to provide international telephone service between those countries and the United States. My most important mission was to obtain the agreement from the governmental authority of China to jointly provide service with MCI. Starting in the late 1980s, MCI sent a series of proposals to the Chinese telephone authority. At that time, AT&T was the only USA carrier offering direct telephone service with China. MCI's initial written proposals to China and numerous follow-ups over time went unanswered. It appeared to us that China had no interest in dealing with a 2nd USA telephone company. From their point of view, they were quite satisfied to operate only with largest USA telephone company. Our arguments of economic benefits to China that would result from an expanded MCI customer base in the USA went unheeded for several years. We could not even get a face-to-face meeting to present our proposal in China or the USA.

Subsequently, we devised a different strategy. MCI would offer China, without charge, microwave telephone equipment they could use in their domestic network. The equipment was valued at nearly $1 million. We requested a meeting to discuss the equipment as well as our earlier proposals for direct service. Eventually, the Chinese agreed to meet with us in Beijing. We presented our case for direct operations and our offer of free equipment. China finally agreed to start operating with MCI. But strangely, to us, they insisted on paying MCI for the equipment. From their point of view, giving them the equipment outright was not a viable means of negotiation. They insisted on keeping the equipment and operations as separate matters. MCI eventually started operating telephone service with China in 1991. Afterwards, China purchased over $1M worth of equipment from MCI. What did we learn from our years of negotiating with China? In one word - PATIENCE.

Sy Scharff, Retired Director, Far East, MCI

In American corporations, workers are expected to be interactive, creative, and participatory if they want to move up the corporate ladder. Many Asian American workers have a different view on the road to success in corporate America. We believe if we are quiet and obedient, and do not question our supervisors, these are the factors for career advancement. For instance, Asian American workers may avoid eye contact with supervisors as a sign of respect. However, it represents inappropriate nonverbal expression in the United States. In some Asian cultures, people are taught to use a soft-spoken voice because a loud voice sends a signal of disrespect. Humility and self-criticism are also considered virtues by many Asian cultures. In American corporations, a worker with these personal characteristics is seen as weak and low in confidence and not fit to take on leadership roles. In the last twenty years, the Asian American population has grown faster than any other minority group in America. In my personal view, American corporations can take full advantage of talented Asian Americans by learning more about their cultures and providing a working environment where they feel less marginalized and can view themselves as constructive members of the corporations.

Hai Dang, GIS Technician, Gulf Coast Electric Cooperative

INTRODUCTION

The quotes above illustrate a major challenge facing contemporary organizations, that of how to effectively collaborate across boundaries. Such forms of collaboration, referred to as complex collaboration (Beyerlein, Beyerlein, & Johnson, 2004; Mankin & Cohen, 2003), have become a critical topic for organizations as demonstrated by the increase in research, popular books, and consulting groups dealing with the subject. In 1994, O'Hara-Devereaux and Johansen wrote *Global Work*. The focus of this book was to outline the problems facing organizations that need to bridge distance, culture, and time to accomplish their work, and to lay out a set of "third-way strategies" to assist with these new challenges. Ten years later, answers are still being offered for how to effectively collaborate across boundaries. For example, in Mankin and Cohen's (2003) *Business without Boundaries*, the authors describe an action framework for collaborating across time, distance, organization, and culture. Why has complex collaboration sustained as an important area in organizational research over the last decade? Because organizations need to be able to engage in complex forms of collaboration to survive. To meet the needs of a global economy, competitive market pressures, new technology, government regulation, demographics and consumer preferences, and labor force trends companies have realized the importance of complex collaboration and of tapping into knowledge and information from wherever they exist across the globe.

Globalization of our economy and of the organizations that make up that economy challenges virtually all leaders, managers, and employees to become more internationally aware. Nowhere is this need for internationally aware workers more apparent than in the business interactions between those who live and work in the West and the East. The United States has for some time held a strong role in the world of business. But at the same time, there has also been a steady economic and cultural bloom in Asia. Asia is a dynamic force to be appreciated, embraced, and partnered with. Workers in the United States have been, are, and will continue to be thrust into international relations by working for foreign-owned companies, or by dealing with foreign suppliers, customers, and co-workers and vice versa. Thus, the decade-long search for answers on how to effectively achieve complex collaboration will most likely continue into the next decade as well.

The organizational designs that structure contemporary organizations are changing into forms that support and foster teaming and collaboration. These new collaborative organizations and work systems are the structures from which collaborative capital – the topic of this volume – may emerge. Collaborative capital is a valuable resource that organizations can use to create strengths and opportunities with the greatest potential for timely impact and financial payoff. One way to bolster an organization's collaborative capital is to build up the very foundation of this essential resource. We, and others (Beyerlein, Freedman, McGee, & Moran, 2003; Fitzgerald, 2003), call that foundation, the collaborative capacity. Collaborative capacity refers to the practices, values, and processes that foster working with others at all levels within an organization and beyond. Thus, collaborative capital can be increased by assessing and changing an organization's work environment to more fully energize and strengthen that same organization's collaborative capacity. (The emerging trend of collaborative organizational forms, collaborative capacity, and collaborative work environments will be discussed in more detail later.)

The work environments that guide these new collaborative organizations are becoming more complex and sophisticated. Typically, we enter a work environment as a young adult with most of our values solidly ingrained. We become oriented and subsequently socialized to the practices of our new work environment, but only in the context of the national culture in which we have grown up and lived. National cultures differ in basic values and assumptions held, and these differences impact the ways in which the management in those countries guide their organizations. Westerners hold deep-rooted values of individualism, which influence employee attitudes and perceptions. Asian companies tend to have a more communal corporate culture. The more leaders, managers, and workers from these cultures understand the basic differences and similarities in the factors that guide their work environments, the more successfully these leaders, managers, and workers will be able to communicate with, learn from, and be able to collaborate with one another.

In this chapter, we describe an exploratory, cross-cultural investigation of the work environments that guide organizations in the United States and several Asian countries: Malaysia, Singapore, South Korea, and Taiwan. Using survey methodology, workers in each country assessed their organization's work environment. We describe what work environment factors were viewed the same across Eastern and Western cultures, and what factors were viewed differently. Additionally, we present a model of work environment factors that we propose will lead to high levels of collaborative capacity, and as a result, collaborative capital, across organizations and the employees within them, in Eastern and Western cultures.

Confucianism

"The superior man wishes to be slow in his speech and earnest in his conduct. He is modest in his speech, but exceeds in his actions. In every action he considers righteousness to be essential. He performs it according to the rules of propriety. He executes it with humility. He completes it with sincerity. This is indeed the way of a superior man."

Confucius

To better understand what work environment factors are important to employees in Asia and to evaluate the processes that manage Asian organizations, we first need to understand and appreciate the cultural beliefs that guide behavior in these countries. Confucianism is a key belief system in Asian culture, and Confucian ideas are incorporated into the fabric of life in many areas of Asia.

Classical Confucianism was derived from Confucius's teachings around 500 B.C. After taking hold in Imperial China, Confucianism underwent various modifications, and later came to have some influence in Korea and Japan. Confucian beliefs were also carried by Chinese migrants to Singapore and the Malacca Straits (and elsewhere in Southeast Asia) in the nineteenth and twentieth centuries. The Confucianist was "bound in the first place to maintaining the harmony of the divine and to an ideal of self-perfection which precluded the mere means-end calculation of utilitarian advantage" (Schroeder, 1992, p. 48). The classic texts of Confucianism have been less widely read among Asians than the Bible among Europeans and Americans, or the Koran among Islamic communities, and during the periods in history when the texts were studied, this was usually only among the literate elites.

Nevertheless, it is claimed that Confucian ethical codes of conduct within relationships are rigidly adhered to in day-to-day behavior among Japanese, Koreans, and Chinese. In essence, there has been a "collective programming of the mind" (Wilkinson, 1996).

Confucianism holds that the family unit is the root of social stability and political order, and that an individual's identity is in terms of the family or group. It teaches that the human condition can be improved, that hard work and self-cultivation in the context of group achievement is one's objective and that education is the key to human development. The Confucius ideology is based on values such as the respect for authority, family/group orientation, and preference for social relations (Redding, 1980, 1987; Redding and Ng, 1982). Hofstede and Bond (1988) referred to a Confucian work ethic. They identify a "cluster of values" which they refer to collectively as "Confucian dynamism": these are perseverance, thrift, a sense of shame, and the hierarchical ordering of relationships by status.

Cultural Dimensions

An important initial step in developing an appreciation of the different work environment factors valued by those in the East and the West is to examine what contemporary research has already offered in terms of how these populations score along a variety of cultural dimensions. Hofstede (1980; 1983a, b, c, d) developed a model of cultural dimensions to help us understand how and why people from various cultures behave as they do. Hofstede used an existing data bank covering matched populations of employees in national subsidiaries of IBM in 53 countries, and his findings indicated that national culture consisted of four key dimensions: power distance, individualism, masculinity, and uncertainly avoidance. All are briefly described below:

- *Power distance* deals with the acceptance of unequal power in organizations; the degree of inequality among people which the population of a country considers normal. It ranges from extremely unequal to relatively equal.
- *Individualism* refers to the tendency of people to look out only for themselves and their immediate families; the degree to which people in a country have learned to act as individuals rather than as members of cohesive groups. It ranges from individualist to collectivistic.
- *Masculinity* deals with the degree to which "masculine" values such as

aggressiveness, assertiveness, success and competition, and materialism exist in a culture versus such "feminine" values like concern for relationships, quality of life, service, and caring. It ranges from predominantly masculine to predominantly feminine.

- *Uncertainty avoidance* has to do with the extent to which people feel threatened by ambiguous or uncertain situations; the degree to which people in a country prefer structured over unstructured situations. It ranges from extremely rigid to relatively flexible.

More recently, Hofstede (2001) added a fifth cultural dimension:

- *Long-term/short-term orientation*: Long-term orientation contains values such as persistence, ordering relationships by status, thrift, and having a sense of shame. Short-term orientation includes values such as personal steadiness and stability, protecting your "face," respect for tradition, and reciprocation of greetings, favors, and gifts.

The difference between the East and the West is marked for all five of Hofstede's dimensions. In our study, Malaysia, Singapore, South Korea, and Taiwan fall into one group with regards to Hofstede's dimensions, while the United States' sample falls into another group. The two groups, according to Hofstede's (2001) data, practically cement themselves on opposite ends of the scale for at least three of his cultural dimensions: namely power distance, individualism, and masculinity. For the dimension of uncertainty avoidance, however, South Korea and Taiwan rank above the United States, while Malaysia and Singapore rank below. With respect to the more recent long-term orientation dimension, Singapore, South Korea, and Taiwan group together, and distinctly differ from the United States (Hofstede, 1997). In fact, the highest scores on the dimension of long-term versus short-term orientation are all found in Asian countries such as Hong Kong, Taiwan, and Japan. Data is not yet available for Malaysia.

The cultural dimension most widely noted is that of *individualism versus collectivism*, perhaps because it impacts both business and social interactions between Americans and Asians. Individualism is extreme in the West. Emphasis is placed upon individual achievement. Westerners are expected to achieve success through their own hard work and individual efforts, and to overcome obstacles by themselves. People in Western cultures, such as the United States, value and in fact cherish their freedoms (i.e. the right to free speech, the right to protest). Westerners value candor and directness in business, and are used to making independent decisions and taking independent action. They strive to stand out from the crowd. In sharp contrast, in Asia collectivist values predominate. Personal goals are subordinate to group goals. Individuals must not stand out from the crowd. Rather, one's duty and obligation is to the group. Harmony among organizational members is important. Instead of striving for personal achievement, modesty and humility are emphasized (Maccoby, 1994).

Another cultural dimension in which Eastern and Western cultures can be distinguished is that of **high context and low context**. Context has to do with how much one has to know before effective communication can occur, how much shared knowledge is taken for granted. Hall (1976, 1989) suggests that in a high-context culture, much of the important information is not found in the actual words transmitted in a communication, but rather in the context in which those words are used. People in high-context cultures rely heavily on situational cues for meaning when communicating with another person. Nonverbal cues, such as position or status, convey messages more powerfully than do spoken or written words. Typically, Asian cultures (i.e. Japan and China) tend to be high context. Nearly all communication takes place within an intricate, vertically organized structure in which people know who is above and below them. These distinctions carry implications for the form of address, choice of words, physical distance, and demeanor. On the other hand, in low-context cultures, such as the United States, the important information in a communication is transmitted through the words themselves, whether written or spoken. Perceptions and assumptions from nonverbal cues are in fact double-checked verbally. When viewed from this dimension, the countries in our study can be classified into two groups: Malaysia, Singapore, South Korea, and Taiwan as countries with high-context cultures; and the United States as a country with a low-context culture.

Another dimension that differs between Eastern and Western cultures is **locus of control**, which refers to a belief about where individuals view control over life events. The belief that an individual is basically in control of one's life events and can influence what happens is *internal* locus of control. The belief that life events are the result of chance, luck, or fate and one does not have much influence over what happens refers to *external* locus of control (Rotter, 1966). Asians tend to accept fate and believe they have less control over their environment (external locus of control). In contrast, Westerners tend to have a more internal locus of control, viewing themselves as the masters of their fate (Asian Studies Development Program, 1995).

Eastern and Western cultures can also be distinguished by their differing emphasis on rituals, suggesting another cultural dimension of **high ritual/low ritual**. Asian cultures tend to be highly ritual, where human interactions

Table 1. Cultural Dimensions.

Dimension	East	West
Power distance	Unequal	Equal
Individualism	Collectivist	Individualist
Masculinity	Feminine	Masculine
Uncertainty avoidance	Rigid	Flexible
High/low context	High	Low
Locus of control	External	Internal
High/low ritual	High	Low

follow a pattern with rigid rules of behavior. Western cultures, on the other hand, tend to be low ritual. It is often unclear and ambiguous as to what is the correct social behavior. Each new human interaction entails a degree of new ritual or pattern of behavior (Asian Studies Development Program, 1995).

In sum, the collection of cultural dimensions reviewed can be used to distinguish, characterize, and better understand organizational members from the East and West. Table 1 reviews the cultural dimension distinctions for East and West cultures.

As our study samples from both the East and West, two cultures markedly different on a variety of cultural dimensions, we expected that these differences would be reflected in the employees' perceptions about their work environment as well. *Specifically, we expected that work environment ratings would be more similar among those Eastern countries that tended to group naturally in the above cultural dimensions: Malaysia, Singapore, Taiwan, and Korea. We also expected that the Eastern work environment ratings would tend to differ from those of the United States, a country that did not group naturally in the above dimensions with the Eastern countries.*

Business Practices of the East and West

Eastern and Western cultures differ not only with respect to specific cultural dimensions (as previously discussed) but also on the business practices that guide their organizations. The ideal Western organization stems from the historical struggle for individual rights and freedom from authoritarian domination. Employees and managers are not "compliant organization men (or women)." Rather, they attempt to maximize autonomy and control of turf. The ideal Asian organization is based on good interpersonal relationships rather than individual rights. Similar to a caring family, a leader is like a good father who accepts responsibility for the development and well-being of employees. In return, leaders expect obedience and personal loyalty (Maccoby, 1994). What follows is a review of some prevalent differences in business practices in the East and West in terms of leadership style, interpersonal relations, autonomy versus belongingness, recognition, trust, and motivation and compensation systems.

Leadership Style

Organizational norms, specifically in China, prefer a centralized structure in which decisions are made at the top. Under such norms, the organization is perceived as a family unit and individuals in managerial positions are supposed to play a father-like role and preserve the "face" of subordinates (Redding & Ng, 1982). Like the head of a family, a direct and authoritarian leadership style is expected and preferred, and participate management is not valued. Leaders are highly valued and the status of management is respected. Management often oversees tasks and employees tend to rely on group interaction and shared assignments. Due to the importance on status, the leadership systems tend to be more authoritarian, even in the face of consultative decision-making. The higher the manager, the more status and respect he or she commands, and to disagree would be disloyal. Leaders are expected to lead, and employees are uncomfortable with being delegated even discretionary decision-making. Triandis and Gelfand (1998) have found that vertical collectivism emphasizes the headman style of leadership, both for organizational and political leaders. While the headman, or national political leader, has much greater authority, power, and prestige than others, he or she is also responsible for ensuring that cultural values are upheld and that members of the group are provided for. The leaders of Asian organizations more closely resemble leaders in organizations with vertical collectivism. In many organizations in Asia, decisions are still centralized at headquarters. Chinese management systems in particular tend to maintain the authoritative position, and keep tight control of information. Subordinates are dependent on owners for information, and there is a large power distance maintained between the managers and the subordinates. Major decisions are made by owners and upper management, and there is limited delegation of power.

Traditionally, organizations in the United States took on mechanistic and bureaucratic structures. Leaders were authoritarian figures who issued commands and controlled from the top. However, organizational designs have become flatter, meaning less corporate hierarchy (Dutton, 1998).

Leadership styles have also changed from the more traditional top-down, command-and-control style, to a more collaborative leadership style, with team leaders and members working "side by side" (Romig, 2003). The emphasis in Western culture on autonomy and individualism has allowed these flatter organizational designs to emerge, and these designs have lead to more efficient and less costly management systems. Westerners want to minimize authoritarian control and maximize individual autonomy and initiative. The best leader is the "one-minute manager" who communicates clear goals and delegates' decisions about how to implement them.

Emphasis on Relationships
Another essential difference between business practices in Asia and the United States is the emphasis placed on establishing relationships. Interaction between individuals in an Asian organization is built on trustworthy relationships that tend to be highly personalized (Peng, Lu, Shenkar, & Wang, 2001). The need to build highly personalized relationships in an organization is one of the characteristics of Confucian values striving for *guanxi* (personal relationships). As a result, economic exchanges are more likely to be reinforced though social exchanges that stress reciprocity rather than rational transactions typically found in the West (Yeung & Tung, 1996). The quality of such relationship is expected and valued. This need to create good *guanxi* is the foundation of the saying – "it's not what you know but whom you know that matters."

In business dealings, Asians tend to pay more attention to relationships than contracts. Westerners, by contrast, pay more attention to deadlines and schedules than social protocol. In the Asian culture, it is important to establish relationships first, before focusing on the specifics of a business deal. Specifics come only after relationships have been established. However, in Western cultures, and the United States in particular, business dealings are more direct. Only if time permits will someone seek to establish a relationship with those one is doing business with.

Belongingness Versus Autonomy
Being a part of an organization unique with Confucian values means valuing one's place and role in the organization. When a firm is perceived as an extended family, employees are encouraged to develop a strong sense of belonging, which may boost productivity. On the contrary, individualistic cultures place value more on autonomy, the sense of individual freedom, and power. Autonomy has also been shown to be essential for Western worker job satisfaction (Hackman & Oldham, 1980).

A high level of autonomy leads to intrinsic motivation that enhances the importance of one's job. More autonomy means more freedom and as a result, leads to higher levels of work performance and job satisfaction, and less turnover.

Recognition

As Asian philosophy stresses that the individual is only important as part of the group, Asians are more willing to accept their fate and their status in society. They are less inclined to seek personal recognition or strive for high status. In addition, the emphasis is on recognition of elders as authority figures in a family or group. On the other hand, in the competitive, individualist culture of the United States, recognition becomes very important because it is a reflection of one's social status within an organization. Recognition also is important because it makes one feel a part of an organization, rather than a tool for organizational success. Recognition helps people to have dedication, and to have a positive attitude about their job (Pollock, 2002).

Trust

In the West as in the East, collaboration requires developing trust. In the East, trust has been created by strong protective father figures (leaders) and a communal organization. It has been supported by shared ownership of networks of companies (i.e. the Japanese *keiretsu*) which value product quality and employment security, open and honest sharing of information, and acceptance of one's ideas. In the West, trust has resulted from a combination of enforceable contracts and mutual understanding. Trust is maintained by open dialog about expectations in an ever-changing environment. Trust has also been increased by involving employees in the strategic planning process, so that they can influence change to take account of their interests. Rather than create a caring family (as in the East), systems are in place in the West to create a winning team assessed by achieved financial outcomes.

Reward and Compensation

According to Atchison (2003), people are motivated by money. This is particularly true for Western cultures (i.e. the United States). Unlike workers in the 1970s and 1980s who valued interesting work above everything else, the results of a 1998 study suggest that contemporary workers place the highest value on good wages and job security (Karl & Sutton, 1998). Rewards and compensation are typically viewed as the key driver for work motivation. However, compensation becomes less of an issue for employees when the work is challenging (Herzberg, 1966; Atchison, 2003).

In corporate America, the concept of merit pay or pay for performance (reward based on performance) has taken hold, shifting from the traditional direct reward only (Amsler, Beadles II, Lowery, Petty, & Thompson, 2002). This type of compensation elicits higher levels of performance because the rewards individuals receive increase as their work performance goes up. Even though merit-pay systems tend to be a stable fixture in American business, they are not without controversy (Amsler et al., 2002). However, in general rewards play an important part in the corporate culture of Western organizations, in relation to job satisfaction and work performance.

For Asian workers, compensation (rewards and benefits) is also important to ensure employee job satisfaction and high work performance, particularly in Hong Kong (Yam & Yam, 1993). However, promotions for recognized achievements and pay-for-performance programs are viewed as less effective with Asian workers, because these programs assume the individual seeks to be set apart from the group, and that their colleagues approve of this. It also assumes that the contribution of any one individual is easily distinguishable, and that no problems arise from singling out an individual for praise. However, as previously stated, one overriding aspect of the Asian culture is the importance of belonging to the group, thus any system that rewards an individual for standing out from the group may be ineffective. Employees may not readily accept that individual members of groups should excel, thus revealing the shortcomings of the other members. Rather, the Asian definition of an outstanding individual is one who benefits those closest to him or her. A promotion as a reward for hard work may be detrimental to an employee's performance, as harmony, a highly cherished value, may be disrupted between the promoted person and his or her colleagues. Pay-for-performance systems also imply that individuals are solely responsible for what they have accomplished, even though they may have had help from co-workers or supervisors. To an Asian employee, to claim most or all of a reward for oneself denies the importance of the relationships with superiors and peers with whom one has worked, been instructed by, or inspired by.

In sum, the collection of business practices reviewed can be used to distinguish, characterize, and better understand organizational members in the East and West. Table 2 reviews the business practice distinctions for Eastern and Western cultures.

Table 2.   Business Practices in the East and West.

Business Practice	East	West
Organizational design	Centralized hierarchy	Flatter, decentralized design
Leadership style	Father-like leader who takes care of subordinates and in return expects obedience and compliance, has direct and authoritarian leadership style	One-minute leader who works side by side with members, communicating clear goals and delegating how to accomplish them
Relationships	Strong emphasis on developing highly personalized relationships in an organization, based on one of the characteristics of Confucian values striving for *guanxi* (personal relationships)	Attention to direct business dealings, contracts, schedules, and deadlines over personal relationships
Belongingness/autonomy	Value is placed on developing in employees a strong sense of belonging	Value is placed on autonomy, the sense of individual freedom, and power
Recognition	Employees are less inclined to seek personal recognition or reach for high status; desire not to stand out from group	Recognition is important because it reflects one's social status within an organization, makes one feel a part of an organization, and helps to create dedication and a positive attitude on one's job
Trust	Trust is built around personal relations and networks	Trust is built based on accountability, and involving employees in decision-making
Reward and compensation	Sole and individually based rewards are not well accepted. Claiming most or all of a reward for oneself denies the importance of relationships with superiors and peers with whom one has worked, and who may have inspired or instructed the individual	Although team-compensation programs are on the rise, typically, pay for performance or merit pay systems are based on an individual's successful efforts

As such, we predicted that those work environment factors that tap into autonomy, power, and recognition and reward would be rated higher in agreement in the United States than in the Asian countries. We also predicted that those work environment factors dealing with personal bond, relationships, group process, and leadership would be rated higher in agreement in the Asian countries.

The Emergence of Collaboration and Collaborative Work Environments

After examining the cultural belief systems and business practices that distinguish those who live in the East and West, one may anticipate potential difficulties in creating a work environment in which these two cultures can effectively work together and collaborate. Yet, collaboration, defined as "the collective work of two or more individuals where the work is undertaken with a sense of shared purpose and direction that is attentive, responsive, and adaptive to the environment" (Beyerlein & Harris, 2004, p. 18) has become important because it helps organizations to effectively integrate and align their human resources, to better tap into the external environment, to adapt a flexible stance, and ultimately to achieve a competitive advantage in the fast-paced, global marketplace (Beyerlein & Harris, 2004). More and more, organizations are transforming into what are termed *collaborative organizations*. These new organizational forms support both informal and formal forms of collaboration, use teams to accomplish work when needed, and are designed to support collaboration (Beyerlein & Harris, 2004). Broader still is what has been referred to as a *collaborative work system* (CWS). These types of systems are defined as systems "in which a conscious effort has been made to create structures and institutionalize values and practices that enable individuals and groups to effectively work together to achieve strategic goals and business results" (Beyerlein, McGee, Klein, Nemiro, & Broedling, 2003, p. 1). A CWS may range from a co-located team to a global, multi-organizational strategic alliance.

Collaborative organizations and work systems serve as catalysts to build *collaborative capacity*, the extent to which collaboration is fostered both internally with human resources and externally with customers, suppliers, and other stakeholders (Fitzgerald, Nemiro, Fry, & Murrell, 2003). The emerging literature on collaborative capacity suggests a variety of levels and dimensions that lead to its existence. For example, Foster–Fishman, Berkowitz, Lounsbury, Jacobson, and Allen (2001) indicated that colla- borative capacity includes four critical levels: member capacity, relational capacity, organizational capacity, and programmatic capacity. Gardner

(1998) outlined another set of four levels as ingredients for collaborative capacity: information exchange, joint projects, changing rules, and changing systems. Fitzgerald (2003) developed a comprehensive framework for collaborative capacity, which included 10 relational constructs reflecting fundamental structural dimensions of collaborative entities: context, composition, core, scope, complementarity, competence, character, consequences, catalyst, and course. In Fitzgerald's framework, each of the 10 dimensions may affect or be affected by the others, either positively or negatively.

Collaborative capacity is the foundation to an organization's key resource – *collaborative capital*, broadly defined as "who we know and how well we work together" (Beyerlein et al., 2003, p. 22). Creating a work environment or climate that supports, enhances, and maintains collaborative capacity is essential for achieving high levels of collaborative capital. Collaborative capital can lead organizations to such valued outcomes as increased innovation and creativity, commitment and involvement, flexibility and adaptability, better use of knowledge, and enhanced learning.

Collaborative Work Environment
Limited empirical research has been done on exactly what factors are needed to create the appropriate work environment or climate for complex collaboration.

Organizational climate as an area of study has generally been defined as the nature of the work environment itself. It is considered to be a more limited concept than organizational culture. Organizational climate typically explains "what we do" and organizational culture explains "why we do what we do" (Burnside, 1990, p. 271). Culture refers to the deeper values, norms, beliefs, and assumptions which enable shared meaning and understanding to occur and be maintained (Morgan, 1986). Organizational climate is comprised of the attitudes, feelings, and behaviors that comprise the life within a particular organization. Each organizational member perceives the climate and can describe it based on his or her own perception. Thus, climate can be determined by assessing employees' perception of their work environment (Ekvall, Arvonen, & Waldenstrom-Lindblad, 1983). Having the ability to assess and evaluate the work environment assists employees and their organizations in better understanding one another and in creating an overall organizational work environment that leads to optimal worker performance.

Researchers have found that climates or work environments may exist at the group level as well as the organizational level (Powell & Butterfield,

1978). Sackmann (1992) found that while some aspects of an organization's environment were homogeneous throughout the organization, other aspects differed considerably across subgroups within the organization. Gersick (1988) found that the success or failure of a work team depended heavily on the environment of the group. Amabile, Conti, Coon, Lazenby, and Herron (1996) suggested that different teams within an organization may experience different work environments. Researchers of organizational climate distinguish between more holistic, omnibus measures of organizational climate, and those which attempt to study specific climates of interest. Schneider (1975) stated that organizations actually have many climates, and that it is important when discussing or studying organizational climate to identify the particular climate of interest. Similarly, Schneider and Reichers (1983) suggested that "to speak of organizational climate, per se, without attaching a referent is meaningless ... climate is not an 'it', but a set of 'its,' each with a particular referent" (pp. 21–22). Thus, organizations may have numerous referent climates. Some examples from the organizational climate literature include a climate for service (Schneider, Parkington, & Buxton, 1980), for safety (Zohar, 1980), or for creativity (Nemiro, 2003; Taylor, 1972; Witt & Beorkrem 1989). Of particular relevance to our discussion is a referent climate or work environment for collaboration. Beyerlein and Harris (2004, p. 230) offer a list of characteristics for such a climate or work environment:

- Time and energy spent looking for partners
- Spontaneous problem solving
- Cooperation mindset where collaboration is efficient and habitual
- When a problem arises, impulse is to solve it in a group of appropriate individuals
- Committed to cooperation and collaboration
- Understand how to pull a group together to work on something
- Respect for expertise over position
- Continuous improvement
- Shared responsibility
- Decision-making, responsibility, and authority placed where work is actually done
- Employees fully engaged mentally (challenged), physically, and emotionally in work
- Commitment of all employees to success of company
- Not "me" but "we" mindset
- Open atmosphere of trust and respect

- Partnership instead of dictatorship
- Decisions made collaboratively
- Employees are involved in decision-making
- A natural tendency to select collaborative methods for reaching solutions
- A focus on relationship building
- Formal and informal collaboration promoted
- Support for natural, informal processes of learning, and communication
- Different functions and departments work together without disruptive conflict
- People of different races, gender, and religions work together in harmony.

Collaboration in the East
Collaboration and working in teams has taken hold across the globe, both in the West and the East. Initially it was felt that CWS and team-based organizations would never work in Asia, that the cultures that guided these countries were more suited for authoritarian and rigid organizational structures, rather than more participative methods. However, the past decade has seen many changes in Asian and American business due to the growth of a global economy, a more complex business environment, increased labor turnover and labor market shortages, a need to develop local staff rather than relying on short-term expatriate staff, a trend toward specialization, and mobility of the workforce. A number of Asian corporations, laden with debt, nearly collapsed during the financial crisis in the late 1990s. Companies that once survived based on personal ties and location in a developing region had to make fast changes to survive. As a result, some of the most respected companies in Asia are now talking more about empowering employees, more flexible organizational structures, team management, and the values of collaboration (i.e. Singapore Airlines, Bangkok Bank, Malaysia Airlines, and in Korea – Daewoo and Samsung) (Davies & Mead, 1996).

Organizations across the globe and the leaders that guide them now recognize that in the next century they will not have a monopoly on all knowledge and wisdom. These same leaders also realize that business innovation, which is increasingly becoming more complex, is and will continue to be critical for company survival. In September 2001, *People's Daily* reported that business innovation was critical for Asian companies to survive and stay abreast of their competition in order to build world-renowned brands. Experts and entrepreneurs attending *The Asia's Future Summit* (an economic conference organized by the Asian *Wall Street Journal* to celebrate its 25th anniversary) agreed that in the global marketplace, appropriate strategy and organizational design are key. Mark Daniell, Managing Director of Bain & Company in Southeast Asia, said Asian companies are increasingly testing different management models and beginning to embrace such ideas as maintaining flexibility, listening to and respecting workers, and creating collaborative work environments. Calling managers by their names instead of titles and using offices without walls are just symbolic of the types of innovative ideas and values that are occurring in these progressive Asian companies. In fact, the major concerns facing Chief Executive Officers (CEOs) of Asian companies today are issues such as stimulating innovation and acquiring top talent (according to a global survey of chief executives released by the Conference Board, CEO Challenge, 2004).

Summary of Expectations

In the preceding sections, we highlighted and described the key cultural belief systems and dimensions, and business practices that differentiate Eastern and Western cultures, and the organizations that reside within them. We also emphasized the importance of collaboration, and discussed the emergence of new collaborative organizational forms and work environments. We now restate our expectations that guided our examination and analysis of the study's data:

- *Expectation 1*: We expect that work environment agreement ratings will tend to be similar among the Asian countries (those countries that grouped naturally according to Hofstede's cultural dimensions): Malaysia, Singapore, Taiwan, and South Korea. Work environment agreement ratings within the United States will tend to differ from those ratings of the Asian countries, as the United States did not group naturally with Asian countries when scored on traditional cultural dimensions.
- *Expectation 2*: We expect that work environment factors that tap into autonomy, power, and recognition and reward will be rated higher in the United States than in the Asian countries. Work environment factors dealing with personal bond, relationships, group process, and leadership will be rated higher in the Asian countries.

We are particularly interested in seeing if our expectations hold true in light of the emerging need for all companies across the globe – whether from the East or West – to pursue business innovation in order to survive in the fast-paced economy. To the extent that our findings are not in keeping with our above expectations, important questions will be raised concerning the extent

to which the determination of an appropriate collaborative work environment should be based on cultural considerations without due regard for
other organizational contextual aspects.

METHODOLOGY

Design
A cross-sectional survey research design was used. As this was an
exploratory study, we wanted to generate questions and hypotheses for
future research, rather than seek and draw firm conclusions.

Participants
The study's participants included staff members from a Southern California
University in the United States and eight universities located throughout
Asia. Two of the eight universities were located in South Korea; one
university was in Malaysia (but data was collected from two different sites);
two universities were located in Singapore, and three universities from
Taiwan were sampled.

We chose to sample only university staff members, rather than academic
personnel (faculty) mainly because we felt staff members would better
represent a true "working employee" in a generalized work setting. In
addition, by limiting the participants to staff employees, we attempted to
avoid limitations that may have arisen from differences in academic
departments.

There were 194 staff members from the United States site and a combined
total of 976 individuals from the eight universities in Asia that participated in the study. Table 3 lists the number of participants by university site
and country. (Please note codes listed in Table 3 next to each university
site name. For ease, these codes may be used, rather than the full university cite name, at times throughout the chapter to indicate a specified
university site.)

Overall, the total sample (of those participants who provided this
information) had slightly more females (56%). Within the Asian universities,
South Korea's participants were 60% male and 36% female. In Malaysia,
males and females were evenly divided with each gender comprising 37% of
the sample. For the two university sites in Singapore, 41% of participants
were male and 57% were female. Within the three Taiwan academic settings,
30% of the participants were males and 70% females. In the United States

Table 3.   Number of Participants by Site and Country.

Country	University Site (Code)	No. of Participants
South Korea	Korea University (K1)	66
	Pusan National University (K2)	80
		Total: 146
Malaysia	Multimedia University, Site 1 (M1)	144
	Multimedia University, Site 2 (M2)	155
		Total: 299
Singapore	Nanyang Technological University (S1)	214
	Singapore Management University (S2)	44
		Total: 258
Taiwan	National Chung Cheng University (T1)	139
	National Dong Hwa University (T2)	52
	Shu-Te University (T3)	82
		Total: 273
United States	California State Polytechnic University, Pomona (Cal Poly Pomona)	194

site, the sample was made up of 15% males and 80% females. (Percentages for each country may not add up to 100% because gender data was collected on a voluntary and anonymous basis. We could not determine the gender of those who chose not to provide that data.)

The sample population of the East group was generally younger than that of the West. Table 4 shows the number of participants in each age range category by country. However, it must be noted that data on participants' age was not collected from two of the three sites in Taiwan (National Chung Cheng University [T1] and Shu-Te University [T3]).

University sites were also classified by size (number of full-time enrolled students), age (years since university was founded), and whether the site was private or public owned. Five of the nine East universities indicated private ownership. However, participating scholars shared that governments may be significantly involved in the funding of private institutions and exert major influence on their operations. The university in the United States is a public university and is older than all but one of the East sites (Korea University, founded in 1905). See Table 5 for a list of the participating universities' names, and the ownership (public or private), size, and age of each university site.

Table 4. Number of Participants in Each Age Range Category by Country.

Country	<20	20–29	30–39	40–49	50–59	60+	Unknown
South Korea	0	16	49	57	21	1	2
Malaysia	2	160	64	11	1	0	64
Singapore	6	68	101	74	6	0	3
Taiwan	0	24	18	10	0	0	216[a]
United States	1	16	28	67	69	8	6

[a]Age data was not available for T1 and T3 sites. For T1 and T3, refer to Table 3.

Table 5. Ownership, Size, and Age of Each University Site.

Site	Year Founded	Ownership	Size (FTEs[a])
Korea University	1905	Private	>20,000
Pusan National University	1946	Public	>20,000
Multimedia University, Site 1	1993	Private	5–10,000
Multimedia University, Site 2	1993	Private	5–10,000
Nanyang Technological University	1991	Public	>20,000
Singapore Management University	2000	Private	<5000
National Chung Cheng University	1986	Public	5–10,000
National Dong Hwa University	1994	Public	<5000
Shu-Te University	1997	Private	<5000
Cal Poly Pomona	1938	Public	10–20,000

[a]FTEs means full-time enrolled students.

Research Instrument

Participating employees completed the Performance Environmental Perception Scale (PEPS), developed by Ripley (1998). The PEPS instrument asks employees to assess their work environment by indicating their degree of agreement with 60 elements in the work environment that have previously been shown to impact employee performance (Ripley, 2003). Each of the 60 elements is reflected in a situational statement that characterizes that particular work environmental element present in an organization. These statements are either positively phrased (i.e. "Employees here want to get ahead") or negatively phrased (i.e. "A lot of people often don't turn up for work around here"). A 1 to 7 response scale is used, with "7" indicating total agreement with the statement and "1" indicating total disagreement with the statement.

For three of the Asian countries (South Korea, Malaysia, and Taiwan), the PEPS instrument was translated under the direction of the participating scholars, using appropriate procedures to ensure that original meaning of the statements were retained. The participating scholars in Singapore chose to use the U.S. English version with minor changes to reflect word usage more common to Singapore. Employees in both the East and West groups all responded to the same instrument (with the exception of minor wording changes previously mentioned). To avoid any misinterpretation across cultures, for our study, we chose to analyze only those statements that were positively stated (50 out of the 60 items on the original PEPS instrument). This allowed for comparison of results and was considered appropriate for exploratory research.

Data Collection
Our data collection process was part of a larger effort by David Ripley and his colleagues (Ripley, Hudson, Turner, & Osman-Gani, 2004) to investigate the importance of context beyond culture in human resource development. Ripley and 13 participating scholars collected PEPS survey data from a total of 17 sites in New Zealand, Australia, Asia, and the United States. The first and third authors of this chapter collected data from California State Polytechnic University, Pomona (Cal Poly Pomona). We distributed 1000 PEPS surveys to all Cal Poly Pomona staff members (not faculty). One hundred and ninety-four completed surveys were returned. Each staff member received a packet through campus mail, including a cover letter, instructions sheet, the PEPS survey, and a return envelope. Staff members who participated returned their surveys via campus mail. All returned surveys were anonymous. No names or department listings were asked for or indicated on the returned envelopes or surveys. Individual data from the PEPS instrument was strictly used for the purpose of this research and was not seen or used by university administration.

We then solicited and received permission from Ripley (the Principal Investigator of the larger effort) and each of the Asian participating scholars to use the data collected from the Asian university locations for cross-cultural comparison with our U.S. Cal Poly Pomona data.

RESULTS

Initially, descriptive statistics (mean and standard deviations) were generated for all PEPS items for each university site within each country, for all individual country sites combined (all Korea, all Singapore, U.S. data came from only one site, and Malaysia data from two divisions of the same university), and for all Asian countries combined. See the appendix for a listing of the mean ratings of PEPS items by site, country, and East and West groups.

Comparison Across Universities Within a Specific Country
We first examined any notable differences in the way different sites within the same country viewed the work environments of their organizations. Reviewing the mean ratings for each PEPS item for the two universities within Korea, there were no distinctive differences between how employees from these two organizations rated their work environments. The same holds true for the three universities within Taiwan. Across the three universities in Taiwan, there were no marked differences in the mean ratings of each individual PEPS item.

On the other hand, the work environments of the two universities in Singapore were rated somewhat differently. Overall, employees of Singapore Management University (S2) rated their work environment more positively than those employed at Nanyang Technological University (S1). Out of 50 PEPS items, the S2 site had higher mean ratings of agreement than the S1 site on 44 items. The only items that S2 employees rated lower in agreement (however, only minimally lower) than the S1 site were (S2 scores listed first, followed by S1 scores) career planning (3.59; 3.84), job design (3.70; 4.30), empowerment (4.07; 4.32), feedback (3.75; 4.14) goals (3.95; 4.02), and role clarity (3.52; 3.63). On the other hand, there were several PEPS items that were rated markedly higher in agreement by S2 employees, than S1 workers, including accommodation (5.09; 3.50), attitude (5.02; 2.73), commitment (5.16; 3.50), task/job importance (5.19; 3.14), responsibility (5.14; 3.02), job security (4.68; 2.90), technology/structure fit (5.20; 2.83), and working conditions (5.11; 3.07). The work environment ratings for Singapore Management University indicated that employees were more committed, were engaged in tasks that they felt were more important, and had higher levels of responsibility. Those in the S2 site also felt they had better working conditions, a better fit between technology and organizational structure, and more reasonable job security as well. A plausible explanation for these differential ratings may be due to the fact that the S1 site was publicly owned and rather large in size (>20,000), while the S2 site was privately owned and somewhat smaller in size (<5000). Whatever the reason for these differences, they are important because they suggest that organizational culture may supercede national culture as a determinant of an organization's work environment. Comparisons could not be made for Malaysia and the United States, as data in each of these countries was only collected from one university.

Comparison Across Countries
Some intriguing themes emerged from the work environment ratings across countries. Probably due to the lower work environment ratings for the S1 site, Singapore generally had lower scores in agreement with the PEPS items than any of the other countries, with attitude (3.12), job security (3.20), technology/structure fit (3.24), satisfaction (3.35), and responsibility (3.39) rated the lowest in agreement.

Employees within Korea agreed that their work environments had employees with ambition (5.58), a positive attitude (5.31), and commitment (5.08). Employees saw their jobs as important, were involved, responsible, were high performers, and clear about the roles they played (task/job importance, 5.21; job involvement, 5.44; responsibility, 5.01; peer group characteristics, 5.20; and role clarity, 5.11). On the other hand, those in Korea did not view the organization as assisting them with career development, and did not see themselves as particularly being able to be involved in setting job-related goals (career planning, 2.54; goals/goal setting, 3.44). In addition, employees did not strongly identify with the organization (organizational identification, 3.45). All other PEPS items were rated somewhat neutrally by Korean workers.

Malaysian employees perceived their work environment for the most part positively, with only one mean rating (out of 50) below 4–3.91, accommodation (the willingness of the organization to accommodate reasonable special needs on the job). The most positively rated items (highest in agreement with) were ambition (5.12), attitude (5.29), autonomy (5.24), job characteristics (5.16), task/job importance (5.64), participative problem solving (5.15), responsibility (5.77), satisfaction (5.22), performance standards (5.04), structure (5.28), support (5.12), and technology/structure fit (5.46).

In Taiwan, those work environment items that received relatively high-mean ratings in agreement were ambition (5.06), attitude (5.69), job characteristics (5.13), commitment (5.11), familiarity (5.24), peer group characteristics (5.22), reliance on co-workers (5.16), resources (5.04), responsibility (5.60), technology/structure fit (5.08), and working conditions (5.03). Taiwanese staff only minimally disagreed with the following items: career planning (3.87), job enrichment (3.88), structure (3.95), and autonomy (3.98). All other PEPS items had mean ratings above 4.00, indicating either neutral or agreeable ratings.

The work environment that characterized the United States site was, for the most part, rated positively. Only two of the 50 PEPS items had mean ratings indicating slight disagreement: career planning (3.56) and job enrichment (3.78). All other PEPS items received either a neutral or agreeable mean rating. Those PEPS items receiving the highest ratings of agreement were acculturation (5.25), attitude (5.31), job characteristics (5.34), commitment (5.27), expectations (5.07), familiarity (5.44), task/job importance (5.57), peer group characteristics (5.02), quality of work life (5.04), responsibility (5.69), satisfaction (5.17), scheduling (5.02), job security (5.51), performance standards (5.24), support (5.09), technology/ structure fit (5.09), values fit (5.25), variety (5.11), and working conditions (5.27).

Overall, the U.S. work environment was rated most positively, and the Singaporean work environment was rated the least positively, as determined by the number of PEPS items that received a 5.00 or above score (indicating agreement): South Korea (8); Malaysia (13), Singapore (0), Taiwan (11), and the United States (20).

Comparison Between East and West Groups
To compare the work environments between East and West, we generated a list of PEPS item mean ratings in descending order (see Table 6) for the East group (all Asian sites) and the West group (U.S. site). It is interesting to note again that overall the U.S. work environment was rated more positively than the Asian work environment, as 20 out of 50 were rated 5.00 or above (indicating agreement) and none were rated below 3.56. The highest level of agreement with a PEPS item in the East group was with peer group characteristics (4.69), indicating modest agreement with the notion that most employees in the organization are good performers. The lowest mean rating for the East group was for career planning (3.55), indicating that employees did not feel their organization helped them plan how to move ahead (get promoted). However, recall that promotions may be viewed in Asia as standing out from the crowd. Interestingly, the PEPS items that received the lowest mean ratings in each group were the same for East and West groups: job enrichment (which received the same mean for both groups, 3.78), and career planning (with a mean of 3.55 and 3.56 for the East and West groups, respectively).

Table 6. Means of PEPS Items Listed in Descending Order for East and West.

East (All Asian Sites)		West (U.S. Site)	
PEPS Item Code	Mean	PEPS Item Code	Mean
Peer group characteristics	4.69	Responsibility	5.69
Ambition	4.64	Task/job importance	5.57
Responsibility	4.63	Job security	5.51
Attitude	4.62	Familiarity	5.44
Commitment	4.59	Job characteristics	5.34
Familiarity	4.57	Attitude	5.31
Job involvement	4.51	Commitment	5.27
Reliance on co-workers	4.45	Working conditions	5.27
Computer systems use	4.40	Values	5.25
Acculturation	4.40	Acculturation	5.25
Information	4.38	Performance standards	5.24
Leadership	4.37	Satisfaction	5.17
Job characteristics	4.35	Variety	5.11
Role clarity	4.35	Support	5.09
Resources	4.34	Technology/structure fit	5.09
Freedom	4.33	Expectations	5.07
Culture	4.30	Quality of work life	5.04
Quality of work life	4.29	Scheduling	5.02
Integration (of employees)	4.23	Peer group characteristics	5.02
Technology/structure fit	4.22	Freedom	5.00
Accommodation	4.22	Accommodation	4.99
Support	4.22	Participative problem solving	4.98
Task/job importance	4.22	Organizational climate	4.90
Empowerment	4.20	Autonomy	4.84
Clarity	4.19	Computer system use	4.82
Participative problem solving	4.19	Reinforcement	4.82
Expectations	4.18	Leadership	4.76
Working conditions	4.17	Structure	4.73
Satisfaction	4.16	Resources	4.65
Processes	4.14	Integration (of employees)	4.65
Task settings (complexity)	4.12	Processes	4.62
Organizational climate	4.11	Job involvement	4.59
Job design	4.11	Environment	4.57
Performance standards	4.11	Information	4.40
Feedback	4.10	Training	4.40
Job security	4.10	Clarity	4.39
Reinforcement	4.07	Culture	4.39
Organizational identification	4.06	Task settings (complexity)	4.38
Goals/goal setting	4.06	Innovation	4.38
Participation	4.03	Ambition	4.36

Table 6. (*Continued*)

East (All Asian Sites)		West (U.S. Site)	
PEPS Item Code	Mean	PEPS Item Code	Mean
Innovation	3.99	Feedback	4.31
Environment	3.95	Role clarity	4.27
Values	3.95	Participation	4.22
Scheduling	3.93	Organizational identification	4.22
Structure	3.89	Goals/goal setting	4.20
Variety	3.85	Reliance on co-workers	4.18
Autonomy	3.83	Job design	4.14
Training	3.78	Empowerment	4.09
Job enrichment	3.78	Job enrichment	3.78
Career planning	3.55	Career planning	3.56

Analysis of Expectations

- *Expectation 1*: With regard to our first expectation – that work environments would tend to be more similar among Eastern countries, and would tend to differ from those of the United States – the evidence is only somewhat supportive. From the comparisons discussed previously, it can be deduced that there is an overall difference between the Eastern and Western work environments. As previously stated, the PEPS items were rated higher in agreement by U.S. staff, than by Eastern personnel.

On the other hand, when we examine the PEPS mean ratings within the different countries in the East group, there are more divergent ratings than we expected. Most notably, the work environment in Singapore received overall relatively lower ratings in agreement than those of Korea, Malaysia, and Taiwan. In addition, even a cursory glance at the appendix reveals some noted differences among the different Asian countries on the mean ratings of individual PEPS items. A few of the more noted differences are listed below:

- Malaysians indicated higher agreement with autonomy (5.24), satisfaction (5.22), performance standards (5.04), structure (5.28), support (5.12), technology/structure fit (5.46), and task/job importance (5.64, although Koreans were close with a mean score of 5.21), and participative problem-solving (5.15) than other Asian countries.
- Koreans indicated higher agreement on role clarity (5.11) and job involvement (5.44), and lower agreement on career planning (2.54) than other Asian countries.

- Taiwanese rated higher agreement with reliance on co-workers (5.16), available resources (5.04), and good working conditions (5.03) than respondents from the other Asian countries.

In sum, while the work environments of the East and West may differ, there may also be influential differences between individual Asian countries as well. The organizational culture (and other related variables) may impact the work environment of a company within a particular country (i.e. the different ratings received from the two sites within Singapore).

- *Expectation 2*: In our second expectation, we predicted that those work environment factors that tap into autonomy, power, and recognition and reward would be rated higher in agreement in the United States than in the Asian countries. We also predicted that those work environment factors dealing with personal bond, relationships, group process, and leadership would be rated higher in the Asian countries. Table 7 lists the PEPS items that assessed the above-mentioned work environment factors and the mean ratings from the East and West groups.

Table 7. Mean Ratings of Selected PEPS items by East and West Groups.

Items[b] Expected Would Be Higher in West				Items Expected Would Be Higher in East			
Item Code	West	East	Difference[a]	Item Code	West	East	Difference
Scheduling	5.02	3.93	1.09	Familiarity	5.44	4.57	0.87
Autonomy	4.84	3.83	1.01	Support	5.09	4.22	0.87
Freedom	5.00	4.33	0.67	Acculturation	5.25	4.40	0.85
Ambition	4.36	4.64	0.28	Integration of employees	4.65	4.23	0.42
Participation	4.22	4.03	0.19	Leadership	4.76	4.37	0.39
Goals	4.20	4.06	0.14	Reliance on co-workers	4.18	4.45	0.27
Empowerment	4.09	4.20	0.11	Organizational Identification	4.22	4.06	0.16
				Culture	4.39	4.30	0.09

[a]Difference between highest and lowest mean rating for an item.
[b]Items were selected based on our expectations that items assessing autonomy, power, and recognition and reward would be rated higher in agreement in the United States than in the Asian countries; and those items dealing with personal bond, relationships, group process, and leadership would be rated higher in the East than in the West.

Our second expectation was only partially confirmed; 5 (out of the 7) items that we thought would be rated higher in agreement by the West group actually did yield higher scores, although not notably higher. Flexibility of schedule and freedom in one's job elicited the most difference. Interestingly, ambition was rated slightly higher in the East than in the West. Only one of the items we thought would be rated higher in agreement by the East group (reliance on co-workers) was, but the difference was minimal.

Potential Limitation
The findings between East and West group ratings should be viewed with care. The ratings on any given PEPS element do not differ substantially in any direction (higher or lower) between East and West groups. The fact that many of the elements were scored slightly lower by the East group as compared to the West group may be due to cultural differences in assessment. In other words, Asians may be more prone to not overrate or underrate. There may be a tendency to assess near the middle or neutral rating. As previously discussed, in a collectivistic culture, it is rare to be out of the ordinary, and in fact, is frowned upon and avoided so as to save "face." With this in mind, we urge caution in interpreting differences in ratings between the East and West groups on the PEPS elements.

Examining Collapsed Factors
In order to move toward a model for a work environment for cross-cultural collaborative capacity, we collapsed most of PEPS items into broader factors that have been found by previous research to encourage collaboration and creativity (Amabile, 1983, 1989, 1995; Nemiro, 2004). We then took the summated mean rating of all the items we collapsed within these factors. Results are shown in Table 8.

What Table 8 reveals is that although ratings on these work environments factors vary between the East and the West, they certainly *do not vary greatly or in any significant way*. Both the West and the East rated their environments relatively similar (about neutral in agreement) with respect to empowerment, trust, information sharing, goal/role clarity, and career advancement. Also, the lowest-rated factor was the same for both the East and the West (career advancement) indicating that staff from both the East and the West viewed their organizations as not doing enough to advance their careers or provide appropriate training. Resources, personal bond/ connection, and innovation/creativity were also rated relatively similar

Table 8. Mean Ratings of Collapsed Work Environment Factors for East and West Groups.

Work Environment Factor	PEPS Item Code (*Statement*)	East (All Asia)	West (United States)
Job/task importance	Task/job importance (*The work I do is important to the organization*) Responsibility (*My job is an important responsibility*)	4.42	5.63
Freedom	Freedom (*We have the freedom we need to do our jobs*). Scheduling (*Our work schedule give me the flexibility when I need it*)	4.13	5.01
Empowerment	Empowerment (*We are able to have a say about decisions that affect us*) Goals/goal setting (*We are involved in setting goals for our jobs here*) Participation (*We routinely participate in decisions about our jobs*) Autonomy (*We are able to make the decisions when we need to in getting our jobs done*)	4.03	4.36
Resources	Computer systems use (*We have the tools and equipment we need to get the job done*) Resources (*Resources to do the job are available when needed*) Technology/structure fit (*We are able to take advantage of the technology available to us*)	4.32	4.85
Trust	Reliance on co-workers (*I can count on my co-workers in getting my work done*)	4.45	4.18
Information sharing	Feedback (*We often receive feedback about our work*) Information (timely, relevant) (*We get information when we need it*)	4.24	4.36
Personal bond/ connection	Acculturation (*As a new employee, I was welcomed into the work group and made to feel at home*) Culture (*There is a family feeling to the work group*) Familiarity (*We all know each other and know our way around the place*) Integration of employees (*People get integrated into the organization in a short time*)	4.37	4.93

Table 8. *(Continued)*

Work Environment Factor	PEPS Item Code (*Statement*)	East (All Asia)	West (United States)
Goal/role clarity	Clarity (*We normally get clear instructions about what is expected of us*) Role clarity (*Everyone's role is clear in the organization*)	4.27	4.33
Employee satisfaction/ organizational commitment	Attitude (*I have a positive attitude about working here*) Job characteristics (*I like most things about my job*) Commitment (*The people I work with are committed to doing a good job*) Organizational identification (*We all identify strongly with the organization*) Job involvement (*Employees here tend to get deeply involved in their jobs*) Satisfaction (*I find my job satisfying*) Variety (*There is enough variety in my job to satisfy me*)	4.31	5.01
Career advancement (planning/ training)	Career planning (*The organization works with us to help us plan how to get ahead in the organization*) Training (*Training is provided when conditions on the job change*)	3.67	3.98
Job security	Job security (*We have a reasonable degree of job security*)	4.10	5.51
Work processes	Environment (*Our work and tasks are organized so things run pretty smoothly around here*) Processes (*Our processes are effective*) Structure (*We are well organized for the work we have to get done*)	3.99	4.64
Innovation/ creativity	Innovation (*Most jobs require innovation*) Participative problem solving (*Part of our job is to get involved in solving problems*)	4.09	4.68
High performance expectations/ standards	Expectations (*Expectations are generally pretty high here*) Peer group characteristics (*Most people here are good performers*)	4.27	5.04

Table 8. (*Continued*)

Work Environment Factor	PEPS Item Code (*Statement*)	East (All Asia)	West (United States)
	Quality of work life (*This is a high-quality work environment*)		
	Reinforcement (*When we do good work, we are encouraged to keep it up*)		
	Performance standards (*We have high performance standards*)		
Management/ leadership support	Leadership (*Our supervisors take the time to work with us when we need help*)	4.29	4.92
	Support (*I receive the support I need from my supervisor*)		
Overall work environment	Working conditions (*Working conditions are good here*)	4.14	5.09
	Organizational climate (*We have an atmosphere that most people feel comfortable working in*)		

between the East and the West, although West ratings tended to be slightly higher. Western employees tended to rate freedom, employee satisfaction and organizational commitment, effective work processes, high-performance expectations and standards, and management and leadership support a bit higher in agreement than the East group. The widest difference in assessment of work environment factors in the East and West was with respect to job/task importance, with employees in the West viewing their jobs as having more important responsibility, and more job security. (*Note*: This rating of job security seems particularly odd, as the East is a collectivistic culture. However, this result should be treated with caution, as it may have to do with the fact that the U.S. sample included only a public organization, while the East sample included both private and public organizations.) The overall work environment factor (good working conditions and comfortable working climate) was rated somewhat higher for the West than the East. In the next section, we integrate our results and present our working model for the factors that we propose need to be in place for collaborative capacity between those in Eastern and Western cultures.

A MODEL FOR A WORK ENVIRONMENT FOR
CROSS-CULTURAL COLLABORATIVE CAPACITY

Traditionally, Asian organizations have taken a structured and pragmatic approach to business. The concept of team-based organizations, collaboration, and team management may have seemed foreign to this culture. However, Asian businesses, like all other cultures in the world, are changing in the way their organizations are structured and the processes through which work gets accomplished to allow for more flexibility so as to cope with the international competitiveness that is central to contemporary business (Davies & Mead, 1996). In this section, we offer a model for a work environment for energizing cross-cultural collaboration capacity, based on our findings. Collaborative capacity will emerge when an organization has the right blend of work environment factors to enhance collaboration, along with the right individuals selected to work collaboratively as well. We suggest that this model may function as a palette from which an organization can select, develop, and maintain the needed blend of structural and interpersonal work environment factors. The model is graphically represented in Fig. 1.

Our model contains two major types of work environment factors: *structural factors*, which deal with job design and work processes; and *interpersonal factors*, which deal with elements involved in organizational member exchanges. Within each of these types of factors (structural and interpersonal) are a set of what we refer to as core and variable elements. High levels of core elements are needed for any successful collaborative effort, no matter what country boundaries the collaboration crosses into. On the other hand, variable elements are those which may need to be adjusted depending on the special needs of a particular national culture. For example, personal connection may need to be higher when collaborating in the East versus the West. When the proper blend of work environment factors is in place, members tend to be satisfied and committed to the collaborative effort and to the organization. As a result, a synergistic collaborative capacity emerges.

Certainly, there has been a myriad of empirical studies investigating some of the links we propose between our structural and interpersonal variables and employee satisfaction and organizational commitment. In fact, employee satisfaction and its determinants and outcomes has been one of the most intensely studied topics by organizational researchers (Gruneberg, 1979). An in-depth review of this literature is beyond the scope of this chapter. [We do, however, refer the reader to Ripley (2003) for a thorough

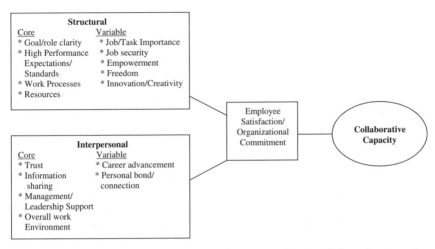

Fig. 1. A model for a work environment for cross-cultural collaborative capacity.

discussion of each of the 60 items on the PEPS instrument and its link to employee performance. We also offer a list of selected classic readings that deal with the relationship between some of the structural variables and employee satisfaction and organizational commitment: Becker, Billings, Eveleth, and Gilbert (1996), Hackman (1990), Hackman and Oldham (1980), Herzberg (1968), Randall (1987), and Staw (1986). Additionally, some readings of interest in examining the relationship between some of the interpersonal variables (i.e. leadership and empowerment) and employee satisfaction and organizational commitment include Conger and Kanungo (1987), Cotton, Vollrath, Froggatt, Lengnick-Hall, and Jennings (1988), Manz and Sims (1989), and McGregor (1957).]

In today's turbulent and complex business climate, the importance of employee satisfaction and organizational commitment needs to be seen from a new perspective. Employees no longer remain in one organization for the majority of their working lives. Not only that but employees may be members of or interact with more than one organization in pursuing their day-to-day working responsibilities. Contemporary employees are required to interact more intensely with employees from other organizations, customers, suppliers, and stakeholders than ever before. Future researchers will want to have on their agenda the examination of our proposed link between employee satisfaction and organizational commitment and collaborative capacity. A preliminary scan for relevant literature revealed no specific investigations of the direct link between employee satisfaction and organizational commitment and collaborative capacity. However, some exploratory research (Ali, Pascoe, & Warne, 2002; Pascoe, Ali, Warne, 2002) has begun to demonstrate the role of employee satisfaction as an enabler of collaborative (or social) learning, knowledge creation, and knowledge sharing. In essence, these preliminary studies suggest that employees, who are more satisfied and have higher levels of morale, will be more willing to collaborate with others by sharing knowledge and voicing their ideas with others as well. In addition, Pascoe et al. (2002) indicated that the following overarching values facilitate collaborative learning: empowerment, trust, forgiveness, cultural cohesiveness, organizational commitment, openness of the decision-making process, and a culture of information sharing. The authors further identified five basic constructs that enable collaborative learning: organizational culture, employee satisfaction and morale, knowledge management, team building, and professional career development of individuals. Many of these values and constructs overlap with some of the factors offered in our own proposed model of structural and interpersonal variables (i.e. empowerment, trust, information sharing, and career advancement). These initial studies, along with our own findings, provide some, even if scant, evidence for the potential link between employee satisfaction and organizational commitment and collaborative capacity. (We note that collaborative learning and collaborative capacity are not the same construct, but suggest that they both go hand in hand.) Thus, we reiterate that employee satisfaction and organizational commitment are important in today's business climate not merely because of the established links with high levels of work performance, but also because they may lead to the willingness to engage in collaborative relationships with other employees, customers, suppliers, and stakeholders.

Our study has lead to a theoretical basis for understanding what factors need to be in place to create high levels of employee satisfaction and organizational commitment, and as a result, collaborative capacity, in the East and West. Future empirical research is needed to test each of our proposed links (between each structural and interpersonal variable and employee satisfaction and organizational commitment, and between employee satisfaction and organizational commitment and collaborative capacity). In addition, investigation of the required levels of what we propose as variable elements in specific cultures will assist in discerning to what degree we can vary these elements and still achieve highly collaborative conditions in a cross-cultural context.

Can One Model Fit All?

In proposing any model for cross-cultural use, one must question its applicability across the globe. We have designed our model to include work environment elements that can be adjusted depending on a particular organization's needs (which may vary depending on organizational and/or national culture). However, some researchers are now questioning the very idea that national culture has an impact on a company's performance. Harvard Business School Professor Rohit Deshpandé and John Farley of Dartmouth's Amos Tuck School have examined organizational culture factors in companies across several Asian countries (China, Hong Kong, India, Japan, Thailand, and Vietnam), and in Great Britain, France, Germany, and the United States. Deshpandé and Farley (2001) found that the most successful firms in these diverse countries had remarkably similar corporate cultures. They suggested that organizational culture may in fact "trump" national culture in determining performance. Successful firms exhibit greater innovativeness and market orientation, more entrepreneurial organizational cultures and participative climates. Future researchers should continue to modify and add to our proposed model, as it will be important to search for the factors *beyond* national culture, particularly at the specific organizational level, that are of a significant concern for creating a work environment for collaboration across cultures.

DEVELOPING THE HUMAN ELEMENT

Managers and leaders that guide collaborative work are like architects. They possess the ability to transform and shape the work environment into one that supports collaboration. They must also recognize the importance of developing the human element – those individuals who are involved in the collaborative effort. Many organizational members are technically well trained but lack appropriate lateral skills (Mankin & Cohen, 2003) to function effectively in complex collaborative work. Lateral skills include such things as – a high level of emotional intelligence, good communication skills, sensitivity to others and other cultures, a desire to help others, maturity, and patience under pressure. Pat Feely, CEO and President of Radica Games Limited, a producer of electronic games and toys with operations in China, the United States, and in the UK, suggests that "experience and talent are almost meaningless without strong lateral skills" (Feely, 2004). In truly collaborative spaces, risk taking, experimentation, careful listening, intuition, building on others ideas and exploration are also critical skills to develop in the human element (O'Hara-Devereaux & Johansen, 1994). Selecting the right individuals and further developing these critical lateral skills in those individuals are just as important to collaborative capacity, as appropriate work environments and organizational designs. No amount of organizational redesign can result in organizational learning unless supported by solid personal relationships, built through lateral skills.

ACKNOWLEDGMENT

We extend grateful thanks to the efforts of the other participating scholars who made this study possible: David E. Ripley, Irene Hudson, and Robin Turner, *The University of Canterbury, New Zealand*; Dae-Bong Kwon, *Korea University, Korea*; Yet Mee Lim, *Multimedia University, Malaysia*; Hsin-yi Chen, *National Dong Hwa University, Taiwan*; Hui-chin Chu, *Shu-Te University, Taiwan*; Lien Ya-hui, *National Chung Chen University, Taiwan*; Tan Wee Liang, *Singapore Management University, Singapore*; and Aahad Osman-Gani, *Nanyang Technological University, Singapore*.

REFERENCES

Ali, I. M., Pascoe, C., & Warne, L. (2002). Interactions of organizational culture and collaboration in working and learning. *Educational Technology and Society*, 5(2).

Amabile, T. M. (1983). *The social psychology of creativity*. New York, NY: Springer-Verlag.

Amabile, T. M. (1989). *How work environments affect creativity*. Paper presented at the IEEE International Conference on Systems, Man, and Cybernetics, November. Cambridge, MA.

Amabile, T. M. (1995). *KEYS: Assessing the climate for creativity*. Greensboro, NC: Instrument published by the Center for Creative Leadership.

Amabile, T. M., Conti, R., Coon, H., Lazenby, J., & Herron, M. (1996). Assessing the work environment for creativity. *Academy of Management Journal*, 39(5), 1154–1184.

Amsler, M. G., Beadles II, N. A., Lowery, M. C., Petty, M. M., & Thompson, W. J. (2002). An empirical examination of a merit bonus plan. *Journal of Managerial Issue*, 14, 100–117.

Asian Studies Development Program (1995). *Impact of culture on business behavior: Module for Asian studies*. Curriculum Online Project, University of Hawaii, East–West Center and Kapiolani Community College. ASDP@lama.kcc.hawaii.edu

Atchison, A. T. (2003). Exposing the myths of employee satisfaction. *Healthcare Executive*, 18, 20–24.

Becker, T. E., Billings, R. S., Eveleth, D. M., & Gilbert, N. I. (1996). Foci and bases of employee commitment: Implications for job performance. *Academy of Management Journal*, 39, 464–482.

Beyerlein, M. M., Beyerlein, S. T., & Johnson, D. (Eds) (2004). *Complex collaboration: Building the capabilities for working across boundaries.* Oxford, UK: Elsevier.

Beyerlein, M. M., Freedman, S., McGee, C., & Moran, L. (2003a). *Beyond teams: Building the collaborative organization.* San Francisco, CA: Jossey-Bass/Pfeiffer.

Beyerlein, M. M., & Harris, C. L. (2004). *Guilding the journey to collaborative work systems: A strategic design workbook.* San Francisco, CA: Pfeiffer.

Beyerlein, M. M., McGee, C., Klein, G., Nemiro, J. E., & Broedling, L. (2003b). *The collaborative work systems fieldbook: Strategies, tools, and techniques.* San Francisco, CA: Jossey-Bass/Pfeiffer.

Burnside, R. M. (1990). Improving corporate climates for creativity. In: M. A. West & J. L. Farr (Eds), *Innovation and creativity at work* (pp. 265–284). New York, NY: John Wiley & Sons.

CEO Challenge (2004). *Top 10 challenges.* The Conference Board. www.conference-board.org.

Conger, J. A., & Kanungo, R. (1987). Toward a behavioral theory of charismatic leadership in organizational settings. *Academy of Management Review, 12,* 637–647.

Cotton, J. L., Vollrath, D. A., Froggatt, K. L., Lengnick-Hall, M. L., & Jennings, K. R. (1988). Employee participation: Diverse forms and different outcomes. *Academy of Management Review, 13,* 8–22.

Davies, R., & Mead, N. (1996). *Team management systems in the Asian banking system.* Institute of Team Management Studies. http://www.orientpacific.com/bnk-itms.htm.

Deshpandé, R., & Farley, J. (2001). *The country effect: Does location matter?* HBS Working Knowledge, President and Fellows of Harvard College. http://hbswk.hbs.edu.

Dutton, G. (1998). The re-enchantment of work. *Management Review, 87,* 51–54.

Ekvall, G., Arvonen, J., & Waldenstrom-Lindblad, I. (1983). *Creative organizational climate: Construction and validation of a measuring instrument* (Report 2). Stockholm: Swedish Council for Management and Organizational Behavior.

Feely, P. (2004). Collaboration in a fast changing, multicultural environment. Keynote speaker presentation. The 15th annual international conference in organizational effectiveness through collaborative excellence, sponsored by the University of North Texas' Center for Collaborative Organizations, Fort Worth, Texas.

Fitzgerald, S. (2003). *Exploring collaborative capacity in a global chaordic alliance – The united religions initiative.* Unpublished Doctoral Dissertation. Alliant International University.

Fitzgerald, S., Nemiro, J., Fry, R., & Murrell, K. (2003). Using an appreciative design compass to uplift collaborative capacity. *AI Practitioner, May,* 22–26.

Foster-Fishman, P., Berkowitz, S., Lounsbury, D., Jacobson, S., & Allen, N. (2001). Building collaborative capacity in community coalitions: A review and integrative framework. *American Journal of Community Psychology, 29*(2), 241–261.

Gardner, S. (1998). *Beyond collaboration to results.* Phoenix, AZ: Arizona Prevention Resource Center.

Gersick, C. (1988). Time and transition in work teams: Toward a new model of group development. *Academy of Management Journal, 41,* 9–41.

Gruneberg, M. M. (1979). *Understanding job satisfaction.* New York: John Wiley.

Hackman, J. R. (1990). *Groups that work and those that don't.* San Francisco, CA: Jossey-Bass.

Hackman, J. R., & Oldham, G. R. (1980). *Work redesign.* Reading, MA: Addison-Wesley.

Hall, E. T. (1976). *Beyond culture.* Garden City, NY: Doubleday.

Hall, E. T. (1989). *Beyond culture.* New York: Anchor Books.

Herzberg, F. (1966). *Work and the nature of man.* Cleveland, OH: World.

Herzberg, F. (1968). One more time: How do you motivate employees? *Harvard Business Review*, 46, January–February, 53–62.

Hofstede, G. (1980). *Culture's consequences*. Beverley Hills, CA: Sage.

Hofstede, G. (1983a). Dimensions of national cultures in fifty countries and three regions. In: J. B. Deregowski, S. Dziurawiec & R. C. Annis (Eds), *Explications in cross-cultural psychology* (pp. 335–355). Lisse, Netherlands: Swets and Zeitlinger.

Hofstede, G. (1983b). National cultures in four dimensions. *International Studies of Management and Organization*, *13*, 46–74.

Hofstede, G. (1983c). The cultural relativity of organizational practices and theories. *Journal of International Business Studies*, *14*, 75–89.

Hofstede, G. (1983d). National cultures revisited. *Behavior Science Research*, *18*, 285–305.

Hofstede, G. (1997). *Cultures and organizations: Software of the mind.* New York: McGraw-Hill.

Hofstede, G. (2001). *Culture's consequences* (2nd ed.). Beverly Hills, CA: Sage.

Hofstede, G., & Bond, M. (1988). The Confucius connection: From cultural roots to economic growth. *Organizational Dynamics*, *16*(4), 4–21.

Karl, K., & Sutton, C. (1998). Job values in today's workforce: A comparison of public and private sector employees. *Public Personnel Management*, *27*(4), 515–528.

Maccoby, M. (1994). Creating quality cultures in the East and West. *Research Technology Management*, *37*(1), 57–59.

Mankin, D., & Cohen, S. (2003). *Business without boundaries: An action framework for collaborating across time, distance, organization, and culture.* San Francisco, CA: Jossey-Bass.

Manz, C. C., & Sims, H. P. (1989). *Superleadership: Leading others to lead themselves.* Upper Saddle River, NJ: Prentice Hall.

McGregor, D. M. (1957). The human side of enterprise. *Management Review*, *46*(11), 22–28.

Morgan, G. (1986). *Images of organization.* Beverly Hills, CA: Sage Publications.

Nemiro, J. (2003). Developing and assessing a climate for creativity in virtual teams. In: M. Beyerlein, C. McGee, G. Klein, J. Nemiro & L. Broedling (Eds), *The collaborative work systems fieldbook: Strategies, tools, and techniques.* San Francisco, CA: Jossey-Bass/Pfeiffer.

Nemiro, J. (2004). *Creativity in virtual teams: Key components for success.* San Francisco, CA: Pfeiffer.

O'Hara-Devereaux, M., & Johansen, R. (1994). *Global work: Bridging distance, culture, and time.* San Francisco, CA: Jossey-Bass.

Pascoe, C., Ali, I. M., & Warne, L. (2002). Yet another role for job satisfaction and work motivation – Enabler of knowledge creation and knowledge sharing. *Proceedings of the Informing Science+IT Education Conference*, June 19–21, Cork, Ireland, pp. 1239–1248.

Peng, M. W., Lu, Y., Shenkar, O., & Wang, D. (2001). Treasures in the china house: A review of management and organizational research on Greater China. *Journal of Business Research*, *52*(2), 95–110.

People's Daily (2001). Roundup: Business innovation key for Asian companies to stay ahead, September 12. http://english.peopledaily.com.cn

Pollock, T. (2002). Three ways to motivate people. *Automotive Design and Production*, *114*, 10–11.

Powell, G., & Butterfield, D. (1978). The case for subsystem climates in organizations. *Academy of Management Review*, *3*, 151–157.

Randall, D. M. (1987). Commitment and the organization: The organization man revisited. *Academy of Management Review*, *12*(3), 460–471.

Redding, S. G. (1980). Cognition as an aspect of culture and its relation to management processes: An exploratory review of the Chinese case. *Journal of Management Studies*, *17*(2), 127–148.

Redding, S. G. (1987). The study of managerial ideology amongst overseas Chinese owner/ managers. *Asia-Pacific Journal of Management*, May, 167–177.

Redding, S. G., & Ng, M. (1982). The role of 'face' in the organizational perceptions of Chinese managers. *Organization Studies*, *3*(3), 201–219.

Ripley, D. (1998). *The development of the performance environment perception scale and its underlying theoretical model.* Unpublished Doctoral Dissertation, University of Tennessee, Knoxville.

Ripley, D. (2003). A methodology for determining employee perceptions of factors in the work environment that impact employee development and performance. *Human Resource Development International*, *VI*(1), 85–100.

Ripley, D., Hudson, I., Turner, R., & Osman-Gani, A. (2004). *The importance of context beyond culture in human resource development: An exploratory study in 17 work settings across seven countries.* Manuscript under review. The University of Canterbury, New Zealand.

Romig, D. (2003). Side-by-side leaders promote breakthrough results. In: M. Beyerlein, C. McGee, G. Klein, J. Nemiro & L. Broedling (Eds), *The collaborative work systems fieldbook: Strategies, tools, and techniques* (pp. 121–133). San Francisco, CA: Jossey-Bass/Pfeiffer.

Rotter, J. B. (1966). Generalized expectancies for internal versus external reinforcement. *Psychological Monographs*, *80*(Whole No. 609).

Sackmann, S. (1992). Culture and subcultures: An analysis of organizational knowledge. *Administrative Science Quarterly*, *37*, 140–161.

Schneider, B. (1975). Organizational climates: An essay. *Personal Psychology*, *36*, 19–39.

Schneider, B., & Reichers, A. (1983). On the etiology of climates. *Personnel Psychology*, *36*, 19–39.

Schneider, B., Parkington, J., & Buxton, V. (1980). Employee and customer perception of service in banks. *Administrative Science Quarterly*, *25*, 252–267.

Schroeder, R. (1992). *Max Weber and the sociology of culture.* London: Sage.

Staw, B. M. (1986). Organizational psychology and the pursuit of the happy/productive worker. *California Management Review*, *28*(4), 40–53.

Taylor, C. W. (1972). *Climate for creativity.* New York, NY: Pergamon Press.

Triandis, H. C., & Gelfand, M. J. (1998). Converging measurement of horizontal and vertical individualism and collectivism. *Journal of Personality and Social Psychology*, *74*, 118–128.

Wilkinson, B. (1996). Culture, institutions and business in East Asia. *Organizational Studies*, *17*(3), 421–447.

Witt, L. A., & Beorkrem, M. N. (1989). Climate for creativity productivity as a predictor of research usefulness and organizational effectiveness in an R&D organization. *Creativity Research Journal*, *2*, 30–40.

Yam, S., & Yam, P. (1993). Coping with labor discontent: Strategies of Hong Kong companies. *International Journal of Manpower*, *14*(5), 87–97.

Yeung, M., & Tung, L. (1996). Achieving business success in Confucianism societies: The importance of Guanxi (connections). *Organizational Dynamics*, *25*(2), 54–66.

Zohar, D. (1980). Safety climate in industrial organizations: Theoretical and applied implications. *Journal of Applied Psychology*, *65*, 96–102.

APPENDIX. MEAN RATINGS (AND STANDARD DEVIATIONS) OF PEPS ITEMS BY SITE, COUNTRY AND EAST/WEST GROUPS

PEPS Item Descriptor	Korea			Malaysia	Singapore			Taiwan				East	West
	K1	K2	All	M1M2	S1	S2	All	T1	T2	T3	All	All Asia	United States
Accommodation	4.12	4.12	4.12	3.91	3.50	5.09	3.77	4.84	4.67	4.55	4.72	4.22	4.99
	(1.83)	(1.78)	(1.80)	(1.58)	(1.49)	(1.31)	(1.58)	(1.60)	(1.58)	(1.75)	(1.64)	(1.71)	(1.68)
Acculturation	5.29	4.54	4.88	4.94	3.44	4.98	3.70	4.87	5.17	4.49	4.81	4.40	5.25
	(1.54)	(1.80)	(1.72)	(1.57)	(1.62)	(1.11)	(1.65)	(1.69)	(1.40)	(1.68)	(1.65)	(1.75)	(1.91)
Ambition	5.26	5.85	5.58	5.12	3.49	4.64	3.68	4.76	4.92	5.63	5.06	4.64	4.36
	(1.61)	(1.91)	(1.80)	(1.57)	(1.42)	(1.62)	(1.52)	(1.63)	(1.59)	(1.27)	(1.57)	(1.78)	(1.48)
Attitude	5.53	5.13	5.31	5.29	2.73	5.02	3.12	5.74	5.62	5.67	5.69	4.62	5.31
	(1.36)	(1.63)	(1.52)	(1.58)	(1.26)	(1.36)	(1.54)	(1.28)	(1.24)	(1.14)	(1.23)	(1.85)	(1.64)
Autonomy	3.92	3.92	3.92	5.24	3.46	4.59	3.65	3.92	3.80	4.12	3.98	3.83	4.84
	(1.81)	(1.86)	(1.83)	(1.65)	(1.59)	(1.37)	(1.61)	(1.72)	(1.66)	(1.62)	(1.68)	(1.69)	(1.78)
Career planning	2.21	2.81	2.54	4.18	3.84	3.59	3.80	3.81	4.00	3.87	3.87	3.55	3.56
	(1.39)	(1.65)	(1.56)	(1.68)	(1.55)	(1.70)	(1.57)	(1.73)	(1.77)	(1.66)	(1.71)	(1.71)	(1.82)
Job characteristics	4.71	4.22	4.45	5.16	3.20	4.91	3.49	5.21	4.85	5.20	5.13	4.35	5.34
	(1.45)	(1.65)	(1.58)	(1.51)	(1.32)	(1.44)	(1.48)	(1.33)	(1.41)	(1.29)	(1.34)	(1.62)	(1.54)
Clarity	4.21	4.15	4.18	4.58	3.84	4.09	3.88	4.47	4.79	4.35	4.50	4.19	4.39
	(1.36)	(1.36)	(1.36)	(1.59)	(1.57)	(1.70)	(1.59)	(1.50)	(1.64)	(1.31)	(1.48)	(1.52)	(1.67)
Organizational climate	3.32	3.81	3.59	4.33	3.58	4.77	3.78	4.57	5.08	4.73	4.72	4.11	4.90
	(1.53)	(1.52)	(1.54)	(1.70)	(1.61)	(1.38)	(1.63)	(1.62)	(1.52)	(1.37)	(1.53)	(1.65)	(1.71)
Commitment	5.29	4.91	5.08	4.84	3.50	5.16	3.78	5.00	5.58	5.00	5.11	4.59	5.27
	(1.24)	(1.62)	(1.46)	(1.63)	(1.61)	(1.27)	(1.67)	(1.41)	(1.16)	(1.31)	(1.35)	(1.64)	(1.63)
	4.95	4.96	4.96	4.71	3.32	4.75	3.57	4.96	4.98	4.73	4.90	4.40	4.82

Computer system use	(1.82)	(1.67)	(1.48)	(1.50)	(.151)	(1.46)	(1.81)	(1.20)	(1.58)	(1.72)	(1.48)	(1.58)	(1.37)
Freedom	5.00 (1.66)	4.33 (1.61)	4.97 (1.44)	4.90 (1.45)	5.12 (1.46)	4.96 (1.44)	3.75 (1.54)	4.66 (1.40)	3.56 (1.50)	4.73 (1.66)	4.17 (1.59)	4.29 (1.70)	4.02 (1.44)
Culture	4.39 (1.87)	4.30 (1.99)	4.60 (2.40)	4.18 (1.58)	4.90 (1.57)	4.73 (2.99)	4.00 (1.62)	4.32 (1.43)	3.93 (1.65)	4.83 (1.73)	4.29 (1.65)	4.00 (1.65)	4.65 (1.58)
Job design	4.14 (1.58)	4.11 (1.47)	4.19 (1.38)	3.93 (1.27)	4.56 (1.42)	4.22 (1.39)	4.20 (1.54)	3.70 (1.53)	4.30 (1.52)	4.43 (1.61)	3.80 (1.47)	3.81 (1.46)	3.79 (1.49)
Empowerment	4.09 (1.66)	4.20 (1.65)	4.24 (1.66)	4.51 (1.54)	4.42 (1.66)	4.01 (1.71)	4.27 (1.64)	4.07 (1.35)	4.32 (1.69)	4.56 (1.70)	3.98 (1.66)	4.13 (1.66)	3.80 (1.65)
Job enrichment	3.78 (1.72)	3.78 (1.60)	3.88 (1.70)	3.99 (1.55)	4.21 (1.87)	3.69 (1.70)	3.74 (1.56)	4.16 (1.64)	3.66 (1.53)	4.47 (1.63)	3.65 (1.46)	3.63 (1.40)	3.68 (1.53)
Environment	4.57 (1.64)	3.95 (1.48)	4.25 (1.52)	3.89 (1.49)	4.52 (1.35)	4.36 (1.57)	3.64 (1.37)	3.84 (1.48)	3.60 (1.35)	4.49 (1.60)	3.93 (1.48)	3.73 (1.50)	4.18 (1.42)
Expectations	5.07 (1.54)	4.18 (1.59)	4.66 (1.49)	4.52 (1.46)	4.90 (1.35)	4.66 (1.55)	3.62 (1.54)	4.77 (1.41)	3.39 (1.45)	5.00 (1.68)	4.28 (1.55)	4.20 (1.51)	4.36 (1.61)
Familiarity	5.44 (1.45)	4.57 (1.62)	5.24 (1.33)	5.20 (1.22)	5.19 (1.41)	5.28 (1.37)	3.66 (1.64)	4.98 (1.47)	3.39 (1.54)	4.97 (1.60)	4.93 (1.32)	4.63 (1.46)	5.30 (1.02)
Feedback	4.31 (1.66)	4.10 (1.49)	4.14 (1.56)	4.38 (1.37)	4.29 (1.51)	3.93 (1.67)	4.07 (1.63)	3.75 (1.51)	4.14 (1.53)	4.60 (1.49)	4.09 (1.28)	3.99 (1.27)	4.21 (1.28)
Goals/goal setting	4.20 (1.83)	4.06 (1.59)	4.44 (1.52)	4.76 (1.22)	4.60 (1.72)	4.18 (1.56)	4.01 (1.62)	3.95 (1.66)	4.02 (1.61)	4.79 (1.48)	3.44 (1.45)	3.27 (1.39)	3.64 (1.51)
Organizational identification	4.22 (1.59)	4.06 (1.54)	4.55 (1.40)	4.67 (1.25)	4.87 (1.40)	4.36 (1.46)	3.90 (1.49)	4.18 (1.63)	3.85 (1.45)	4.48 (1.59)	3.45 (1.60)	3.62 (1.52)	3.23 (1.67)
Task/job importance	5.57 (1.49)	4.22 (1.70)	4.39 (1.55)	4.50 (1.40)	4.59 (1.58)	4.25 (1.61)	3.48 (1.72)	5.19 (1.42)	3.14 (1.56)	5.64 (1.49)	5.21 (1.31)	4.87 (1.38)	5.63 (1.08)
Information (timely, relevant)	4.40 (1.70)	4.38 (1.59)	4.85 (1.39)	4.67 (1.36)	5.02 (1.51)	4.89 (1.36)	3.73 (1.63)	4.09 (1.61)	3.66 (1.62)	4.52 (1.66)	4.66 (1.47)	4.49 (1.63)	4.86 (1.24)
Innovation	4.38 (1.57)	3.99 (1.52)	4.11 (1.55)	4.28 (1.62)	3.81 (1.51)	4.12 (1.52)	3.81 (1.46)	4.36 (1.30)	3.70 (1.47)	4.95 (1.43)	4.08 (1.56)	3.92 (1.72)	4.27 (1.33)

APPENDIX. (Continued.)

PEPS Item Descriptor	Korea			Malaysia	Singapore			Taiwan				East	West
	K1	K2	All	M1M2	S1	S2	All	T1	T2	T3	All	All Asia	United States
Integration (of employees)	4.23 (1.50)	4.10 (1.35)	4.16 (1.41)	4.51 (1.48)	3.90 (1.41)	4.50 (1.17)	4.00 (1.39)	4.47 (1.51)	4.44 (1.56)	4.62 (1.24)	4.48 (1.44)	4.23 (1.43)	4.65 (1.37)
Job involvement	5.74 (1.14)	5.19 (1.36)	5.44 (1.29)	4.42 (1.52)	3.84 (1.45)	4.48 (1.36)	3.95 (1.45)	4.41 (1.44)	4.65 (1.58)	4.67 (1.20)	4.54 (1.40)	4.51 (1.50)	4.59 (1.55)
Leadership	5.03 (1.49)	4.17 (1.75)	4.58 (1.69)	4.83 (1.64)	3.54 (1.53)	4.66 (1.71)	3.73 (1.62)	4.76 (1.65)	5.25 (1.56)	4.84 (1.54)	4.88 (1.60)	4.37 (1.70)	4.76 (1.75)
Participation	4.11 (1.64)	3.65 (1.55)	3.85 (1.61)	4.71 (1.57)	3.66 (1.55)	4.02 (1.55)	3.72 (1.55)	4.28 (1.45)	4.46 (1.71)	4.61 (1.45)	4.42 (1.51)	4.03 (1.58)	4.22 (1.73)
Participative problem solving	4.66 (1.36)	4.30 (1.34)	4.47 (1.36)	5.15 (1.57)	3.36 (1.53)	4.50 (1.52)	3.55 (1.59)	4.50 (1.64)	4.75 (1.69)	4.80 (1.44)	4.64 (1.59)	4.19 (1.62)	4.98 (1.69)
Peer group characteristics	5.48 (1.13)	4.96 (1.34)	5.20 (1.27)	4.92 (1.55)	3.71 (1.50)	4.61 (1.60)	3.86 (1.55)	5.13 (1.50)	5.35 (1.15)	5.28 (1.37)	5.22 (1.40)	4.69 (1.58)	5.02 (1.50)
Processes	4.56 (1.15)	4.14 (1.43)	4.33 (1.32)	4.46 (1.54)	3.53 (1.36)	4.27 (1.32)	3.66 (1.38)	4.50 (1.66)	4.46 (1.49)	4.48 (1.28)	4.49 (1.51)	4.14 (1.47)	4.62 (1.57)
Quality of work life	4.00 (1.35)	4.01 (1.47)	4.01 (1.41)	4.28 (1.63)	3.68 (1.45)	4.49 (1.37)	3.81 (1.47)	4.75 (1.57)	5.08 (1.29)	4.96 (1.18)	4.88 (1.41)	4.29 (1.52)	5.04 (1.67)
Reinforcement	3.98 (1.42)	4.16 (1.41)	4.08 (1.41)	4.82 (1.62)	3.59 (1.60)	4.84 (1.52)	3.81 (1.65)	4.19 (1.62)	4.62 (1.73)	4.29 (1.44)	4.31 (1.59)	4.07 (1.59)	4.82 (1.65)
Reliance on co-workers	4.69 (1.14)	3.81 (1.45)	4.21 (1.39)	4.79 (1.70)	3.64 (1.52)	4.84 (1.46)	3.85 (1.58)	4.96 (1.33)	5.60 (1.09)	5.21 (1.41)	5.16 (1.33)	4.45 (1.56)	4.18 (1.83)
Resources	4.38 (1.28)	4.25 (1.19)	4.31 (1.23)	4.54 (1.45)	3.42 (1.47)	4.50 (1.25)	3.81 (1.49)	5.00 (1.35)	5.29 (.96)	4.94 (1.06)	5.04 (1.20)	4.34 (1.46)	4.65 (1.60)

Responsibility	5.45 (1.29)	4.65 (1.56)	5.01 (1.49)	5.77 (1.36)	3.02 (1.44)	5.14 (.152)	3.39 (1.66)	5.25 (1.50)	5.65 (1.19)	6.16 (1.81)	5.60 (1.95)	4.63 (1.97)	5.69 (1.38)
Role clarity	5.20 (1.49)	5.04 (1.68)	5.11 (1.60)	4.55 (1.61)	3.63 (1.55)	3.52 (1.81)	3.61 (1.60)	4.78 (1.54)	4.78 (1.65)	4.32 (1.60)	4.64 (1.59)	4.35 (1.70)	4.27 (1.76)
Satisfaction	4.70 (1.61)	4.14 (1.85)	4.39 (1.76)	5.22 (1.45)	3.11 (1.35)	4.48 (1.58)	3.35 (1.48)	4.72 (1.45)	5.06 (1.56)	4.78 (1.47)	4.81 (1.48)	4.16 (1.68)	5.17 (1.59)
Scheduling	4.09 (1.85)	4.15 (1.75)	4.12 (1.79)	4.72 (1.60)	3.27 (1.57)	4.52 (1.50)	3.40 (1.62)	4.67 (1.64)	3.87 (1.80)	3.82 (1.81)	4.25 (1.77)	3.93 (1.75)	5.02 (1.88)
Job security	4.22 (1.40)	4.56 (1.60)	4.41 (1.52)	4.52 (1.57)	2.90 (1.32)	4.68 (1.41)	3.20 (1.50)	4.72 (1.80)	4.63 (1.66)	4.96 (1.38)	4.78 (1.65)	4.10 (1.72)	5.51 (1.65)
Performance standards	4.41 (1.29)	4.35 (1.30)	4.38 (1.29)	5.04 (1.41)	3.43 (1.34)	4.61 (1.35)	3.63 (1.41)	4.46 (1.45)	4.40 (1.51)	4.35 (1.35)	4.42 (1.43)	4.11 (1.44)	5.24 (1.56)
Structure	4.36 (1.39)	4.16 (1.49)	4.25 (1.44)	5.28 (1.42)	3.54 (1.44)	4.05 (1.45)	3.63 (1.45)	3.97 (1.61)	3.96 (1.51)	3.90 (1.70)	3.95 (1.61)	3.89 (1.53)	4.73 (1.65)
Support	4.94 (1.30)	3.87 (1.51)	4.36 (1.51)	5.12 (1.51)	3.23 (1.50)	4.93 (1.47)	3.53 (1.62)	4.74 (1.58)	4.96 (1.58)	4.83 (1.71)	4.81 (1.62)	4.22 (1.70)	5.09 (1.77)
Task settings (complexity)	4.09 (1.52)	4.26 (1.44)	4.19 (1.47)	4.85 (1.53)	3.55 (1.48)	4.34 (1.46)	3.69 (1.51)	4.58 (1.55)	4.69 (1.49)	4.28 (1.52)	4.51 (1.53)	4.12 (1.55)	4.38 (1.73)
Technology/ structure fit	4.42 (1.21)	4.34 (1.32)	4.38 (1.27)	5.46 (1.41)	2.83 (1.20)	5.20 (1.23)	3.24 (1.50)	4.87 (1.44)	5.19 (1.47)	5.35 (1.24)	5.08 (1.40)	4.22 (1.63)	5.09 (1.70)
Training	3.12 (1.55)	3.89 (1.58)	3.54 (1.61)	4.00 (1.78)	3.32 (1.55)	4.64 (1.60)	3.55 (1.63)	3.98 (1.63)	4.21 (1.73)	4.33 (1.47)	4.13 (1.61)	3.78 (1.64)	4.40 (1.79)
Values (individual/ organization fit)	3.61 (1.42)	3.58 (1.39)	3.59 (1.40)	4.68 (1.48)	3.52 (1.37)	4.34 (1.46)	3.66 (1.42)	4.35 (1.40)	4.56 (1.56)	4.41 (1.26)	4.41 (1.39)	3.95 (1.45)	5.25 (1.53)
Variety	4.00 (1.53)	3.50 (1.40)	3.72 (1.47)	4.53 (1.47)	3.33 (1.37)	4.66 (1.51)	3.56 (1.48)	4.02 (1.49)	4.31 (1.45)	4.44 (1.42)	4.21 (1.47)	3.85 (1.50)	5.11 (1.71)
Working conditions	3.85 (1.41)	3.96 (1.44)	3.91 (1.42)	4.54 (1.74)	3.07 (1.36)	5.11 (1.33)	3.42 (1.56)	4.89 (1.40)	5.31 (1.32)	5.09 (1.15)	5.03 (1.32)	4.17 (1.61)	5.27 (1.64)

TEAM-MEMBER EXCHANGE AND INDIVIDUAL CONTRIBUTIONS TO COLLABORATIVE CAPITAL IN ORGANIZATIONS

Melvin L. Smith

ABSTRACT

Given the suggested importance of collaborative capital to team and organizational performance, it is important that we develop a better understanding of potential processes by which it is developed in organizations. This chapter represents an attempt to explore one such process by examining why and how individuals contribute to the creation and maintenance of collaborative capital in the organizations for which they work. Drawing on social exchange theory and the norm of reciprocity, it is argued that individuals' perceived social exchange relationship quality with their coworkers will predict their contributions to collaborative capital. Results of a preliminary empirical examination supporting this prediction are shared and suggestions for future research are offered.

Collaborative Capital: Creating Intangible Value
Advances in Interdisciplinary Studies of Work Teams, Volume 11, 161–181
Copyright © 2005 by Elsevier Ltd.
All rights of reproduction in any form reserved
ISSN: 1572-0977/doi:10.1016/S1572-0977(05)11006-1

Much of the activity that occurs in organizations is centered on relationships of one form or another (Leana & Rousseau, 2000). Moreover, these relationships can represent significant value to an organization. This chapter is concerned with why and how individuals contribute to the creation and maintenance of the internal bonds among organizational members that facilitate collective action. These internal bonds have been described in the organizational literature as organizational social capital (Leana & Van Buren, 1999), communal social capital (Oh, Kilduff, & Brass, 1999; Pearce & Randel, 2000; Pil, Smith, & Leana, 2000), and more recently collaborative capital (see chapters in this volume).

Collaborative capital has been broadly defined in this volume as how well people work together. This form of capital represents a potentially valuable resource to organizations in that similar to organizational social capital, which can be argued that it fosters the development of intellectual capital (Nahapiet & Ghoshal, 1998) and facilitates successful collective action (Leana & Van Buren, 1999). Thus, there is inherent value in better understanding the factors that lead to its creation and maintenance.

In this chapter, I discuss how collaborative capital is related to the concept of social capital in organizations. I then draw on theoretical and empirical work across a variety of disciplines including psychology, sociology, social psychology, economics, and sociobiology, to provide insight into why individuals might contribute to collaborative capital in organizations. Ultimately, I draw on social exchange theory (Blau, 1964) and the norm of reciprocity (Gouldner, 1960) to suggest that individuals' perceived social exchange relationship quality with their coworkers will predict contributions to collaborative capital above and beyond any dispositional or instrumental reasons for making such contributions. Finally, I share the results of a preliminary empirical examination of this issue and discuss potential implications and future research suggestions.

COLLABORATIVE CAPITAL AS A FORM OF SOCIAL CAPITAL IN ORGANIZATIONS

The term "social capital" was first used by Hanifan (1920), who presented it as a property of communities based on goodwill, fellowship, sympathy, and social intercourse. Hanifan described social capital as a resource that could be utilized to improve community well-being. Social capital theory was further developed and popularized by Bourdieu (1985) and later Coleman

(1988).[1] Focusing on both the structure of network ties and the quality of those ties, Bourdieu (1985, p. 248) defined social capital as "the aggregate of the actual and potential resources which are linked to possession of a durable network of more or less institutionalized relationships of mutual acquaintance and recognition" (see Portes, 1998; Paxton, 1999 for additional discussion). In his initial introduction of the social capital construct to the sociology literature in America, Coleman (1988) suggested that social capital could be defined by its function. He asserted that it consists of social structures, facilitates actions of actors within the structure and, unlike other forms of capital, resides in the relations among actors and not in the actors themselves.

While Coleman's initial work generated considerable interest in the concept, his actual definition of social capital has been criticized due to its vagueness, which has resulted in differing and in some ways contradictory conceptualizations of the construct (Portes, 1998; Portes & Sensenbrenner, 1993). One such conceptualization, which is most commonly associated with the work of Burt (1992; 1997) focuses on the "private goods" aspect of social capital (see Leana & Van Buren, 1999). Burt (1992) offers that social capital is a property of individuals as he defines it in terms of the information and control benefits that accrue to individuals that are able to fill what he calls *structural holes* or gaps between non-redundant contacts in a network. Researchers who have adopted this structural view of social capital based on network position have found that social capital is significantly associated with a variety of individual outcomes such as promotions and bonuses (Burt, 1992, 1997), CEO compensation (Belliveau, O'Reilly, & Wade, 1996), and managers' assessment of career potential (Friedman & Krackhardt, 1997). This form of social capital is quite different from, and in fact nearly diametrically opposed to, collaborative capital as defined in this and other chapters in this volume.

A form of social capital more consistent with the concept of collaborative capital is that described by Putnam (1995, p. 67), who referred to social capital as "features of social organization such as networks, norms, and social trust that facilitate coordination and cooperation for mutual benefit." While this definition is still consistent with Coleman's (1988) presentation of the concept, it differs from Burt's (1992) definition in that it singularly focuses on what has been referred to as the "public goods" aspect of social capital (Coleman, 1990; Leana & Van Buren, 1999). Social capital as described by Putnam is based on dense networks of social interaction that reduce incentives for opportunism and broaden the individual participants' sense of self from "I" to "we," thus enhancing the appeal of collective benefits (Johnson, Smith, & Gambill, 2000). Whereas Burt's (1992) analysis and discussion are motivated by the individual benefits of social capital, Putnam's work is centered on the benefits to a collective. Researchers who have adopted this public goods view have found that social capital at the collective level favorably impacts a variety of collective outcomes (Fukuyama, 1995; Putnam, 1993).

Adler and Kwon (2002) note that most research on social capital has tended to adopt one of these perspectives or the other. Researchers who have adopted an external (private goods) perspective have typically focused on the structure of relations an individual maintains with others (e.g. Burt, 1992, 1997; Friedman & Krackhardt, 1997). Researchers who have adopted an internal view of social capital (public good perspective) have generally been more concerned with the nature and quality of relations that exist between members of a collective (e.g. Fukuyama, 1995; Leana & Van Buren, 1999; Portes & Sensenbrenner, 1993). Adler and Kwon (2002) describe the distinction between the external and internal perspectives as "bridging" and "bonding" forms of social capital, respectively. I offer that this bonding form of social capital represents the essence of collaborative capital.

In their theoretical development of the relationship between social capital and organizational competitive advantage, Nahapiet and Ghoshal (1998) draw on Granovetter's (1992) discussion of both structural and relational embeddedness. *Structural embeddedness* refers to the impersonal linkages between individuals within a social system (see also Burt, 1992). On the other hand, *relational embeddedness* considers the nature of personal relationships that individuals have developed with one another through a history of interactions. Both of these forms of embeddedness are concerned with network ties. However, while structural embeddedness considers the overall configuration of one's network ties, relational embeddedness is more concerned with the quality of those ties.

Nahapiet and Ghoshal (1998) further contend that social capital also has a cognitive component, representing systems of shared interpretations and meaning between individuals. They, therefore, describe social capital as a three-dimensional construct consisting of a cognitive, structural, and relational dimension. Drawing on this framework as well as the work of Jassawalla and Sashittal (1998, p. 239) who define collaboration as, "the coming together of diverse interests and people to achieve a common purpose via interactions, information sharing, and coordination of activities." I offer that collaborative capital comprises dense networks of information sharing, trust, and reciprocation norms that facilitate collective action within an organization.

UNDERSTANDING INDIVIDUAL CONTRIBUTIONS TO COLLABORATIVE CAPITAL

Biological View

In his introduction of the discipline of sociobiology, Wilson (1975, p. 343) offered that sociobiology is the "… systematic study of the biological basis of all behavior." Wilson (1978, p. 43) added that, "evidence is strong that a substantial fraction of human behavior is based on genetic differences among individuals." Accordingly, sociobiologists and evolutionary psychologists contend that many patterns of human behavior have a basis in evolution (Konner, 1999). More specifically, it has been suggested that there is a biological basis of the cooperative behavior that occurs among individuals in the absence of immediate incentives to cooperate. Cosmides and Tooby (1992) offer that humans may be evolutionarily predisposed to engage in social exchange using mental algorithms developed from millions of years of engaging in social interaction as a species. According to Cosmides and Tooby, although we are not born with the actual behavioral responses that promote cooperative outcomes, we are born with the capacity to learn such responses from social exposure. Along similar lines, Baumeister and Leary (1995) discuss the *need to belong* as a fundamental human motivation with an evolutionary basis, suggesting that the desire to form and maintain social bonds has implications for both individual and group survival. They contend that, over a period of time, groups select individual characteristics (e.g. social identity and group loyalty) that facilitate social group survival. Caporael (1997, p. 277) adds that, "in this view, individualistic self-interest is tempered by the requirements of group living."

In sum, the sociobiological and evolutionary psychological approaches suggest that there is a potential genetic explanation for contributions to collaborative capital on the part of individuals. However, while contemporary sociobiology has experienced growing visibility in a variety of fields, including psychology, anthropology, and economics, many sociologists are still skeptical of the discipline and as a result, few have attempted to incorporate its propositions into their work (Freese & Powell, 1999). Pierce and White (1999) further suggest that management researchers have not considered evolution as anything more than a metaphor with little theoretical work and even less empirical investigation appearing in the organizational literature. In addition, although evolution and the resulting genetic makeup of individuals may represent a plausible explanation for why humans as a species might engage in cooperative behavior in the absence of immediate individual reward, there remain other likely explanations for individual differences in such behavior. Thus, the further consideration of additional approaches seems warranted.

Dispositional View

Another potential explanation for why an individual might be motivated to contribute to an organization's collaborative capital is based on an individual differences or dispositional approach, based on the belief that personal characteristics can aid in explaining individual attitudes and behavior (Staw & Ross, 1985). In studying social dilemma situations where individuals are faced with a decision to act upon self-interest or in the interest of a collective, social psychologists have identified one such individual difference variable that has been referred to as social motives or social values (Messick & McClintock, 1968). Social values have been defined and measured in terms of the weights that individuals assign to their own and others' outcomes (McClintock & Allison, 1989). Messick and McClintock (1968) note that three particularly common social value orientations are *cooperative* (concerned with maximizing joint gain), *individualistic* (concerned with maximizing one's own welfare), and *competitive* (concerned with maximizing the difference between one's own outcomes and the outcomes of others in the same social environment). Previous research has confirmed that, as predicted, cooperative behavior is significantly more likely to be displayed by cooperators than by competitors or individualists (see Messick & Brewer, 1983 for a review). Thus, social value orientation is one individual difference variable that may potentially influence individual contributions to communal social capital.

Proponents of the dispositional or individual differences approach to understanding individual behavior also include personality theorists whose research is typically concerned with how individuals think, feel, and act (Ehrenreich, 1997; Funder, 1994), as well as cultural value theorists who contend that interpersonal behavior is influenced by values that are presumed to be formed in early childhood and are relatively stable over time (cf. Adler, 1997; Hofstede, 1980; Kluckhohn & Strodtbeck, 1961). One such individual difference variable likely to influence investments in communal social capital is collectivism, or a general orientation toward group goals and a proclivity to cooperate in group endeavors (Hofstede, 1984; Wagner, 1995). Eby and Dobbins (1997) suggest that collectivism differs from traditional group attraction constructs such as cohesiveness in that the former is context free. This supports the present conceptualization of collectivism as an individual difference variable rather than as a variable based on situational influence.

Nested within the collectivism construct is a specific value referred to as dispositional group loyalty, which is focused on predispositions related to motivation to achieve group goals and to defend group prestige (James & Cropanzano, 1994). James and Cropanzano (1994, p. 179) more specifically define group loyalty as, "... adherence to a social unit to which one belongs, as well as its goals, symbols, and beliefs." They argue that to the extent that groups tend to be important to an individual's self-perception, dispositional group loyalty will exist. Further, their research showed that dispositional group loyalty significantly predicted individual involvement in group-based organizational activities, favorable attitudes toward the organization, and the inclination to engage in behaviors for the benefit of the organization. These findings are consistent with the work of Triandis (1995) who suggested that individuals with a collectivistic orientation are more likely to define themselves in terms of group memberships and are also more likely to subordinate personal goals to the goals of the collective than are those with an individualistic orientation. In sum, it can be inferred that the greater an individual's collectivistic orientation, the more likely that individual would be to (1) engage in behavior that is directed toward benefiting the collective as a whole and (2) subordinate self-interests, if necessary, to the interests of the collective, both of which are behaviors in line with individual contributions to the collaborative capital of an organization.

While these individual difference arguments may be compelling in explaining collective-oriented behavior, many researchers also look beyond the various individual difference variables and consider as well the basic process of adaptation through which people interact with their social environment (Ehrenreich, 1997). Coleman (1987) suggested the need to move beyond an individual difference explanation for why some individuals might engage in behavior such as contributing to a collective good (e.g. collaborative capital) while others might not. He suggested that it is necessary to consider an explanation that accounts for the rational actions of individuals. Neoclassical economists, as well as expectancy theorists, have successfully utilized such an approach based on rational choice to explain a variety of work-related attitudes and behaviors. Thus, consideration of an instrumental explanation for individual contributions to the collaborative capital of an organization also seems warranted.

Instrumental View

A fundamental assumption of human rationality in neoclassical economics is that individuals behave in a self-interested manner and seek to maximize their expected individual returns (Becker, 1962; Gupta, Hofstetter, & Buss, 1997). Thus, the theory of rational choice might suggest that individuals would contribute to the collaborative capital of an organization when such an investment would result in greater personal outcomes. However, there are certain situations where the actual behavior of decision-makers appears to violate the basic assumptions of "rational choice" (cf. Becker, 1962; McCormick, 1997; Tversky & Kahneman, 1986). A specific example of this is when individuals make contributions to a public good from which they could conceivably benefit without making a contribution (Coleman, 1987). Collaborative capital is potentially one such public good.

Considerable research in the area of social dilemmas has been conducted in an attempt to better understand why individuals might contribute to a public good when it appears that doing so goes against self-interests (see for instance, Axelrod, 1984; Axelrod & Hamilton, 1981; Brewer & Schneider, 1990; Kramer & Brewer, 1984). The fundamental problem in a social dilemma situation is that while an individual can benefit from mutual cooperation (in this case collaborative capital contributions), each individual can conceivably do even better by "free-riding," thereby exploiting the cooperative efforts of others (Axelrod & Hamilton, 1981). Research in the area of social dilemmas has successfully drawn on relational arguments based on reciprocity (Axelrod, 1984; Axelrod & Hamilton, 1981), as well as collective identity (Brewer & Schneider, 1990; Kramer & Brewer, 1984) to explain individual behavior that appears to favor collective interests over individual rationality. The consideration of social context thus appears to be useful in explaining what, on the surface, appears to be irrational behavior. It follows that developing an understanding of why individuals might contribute to the collaborative capital of an organization is likely to benefit from the consideration of additional explanations that go beyond those provided by the purely instrumental approach.

Considering the social aspects of exchange in addition to the purely economic aspects may therefore enhance our understanding of why individuals might contribute to collaborative capital. Emerson (1987) draws a useful distinction between social and economic exchange that supports this view that social exchange theory may usefully inform the issue of collaborative capital contributions. Emerson states that,

"... social exchange theory is developing in a way that is radically different from the traditional study of economics. The major difference is this: At its core, neoclassical economic theory views the actor (a person or a firm) as dealing not with other actors but with a *market*. ... Thus, "rationality" in economic theory might be understood as a property of action taken in markets, rather than a characteristic of actors. ... By contrast, in various forms of social exchange theory, the *longitudinal exchange relation* between two specific actors is the central concept around which theory is organized" (pp. 11–12; italics added).

Based on this distinction, and given the degree to which collaborative capital is based on relationships between and among individuals, it seems vital to also consider a relational explanation for collaborative capital contributions on the part of individuals.

Relational View

As previously suggested, dispositional and/or instrumental explanations, while potentially informative, may be insufficient to adequately predict individual contributions to collaborative capital. Given that collaborative capital (like other forms of social capital) resides in the relationships between individuals rather than with individuals themselves (Coleman, 1988), it is essential to also consider a relational explanation for why individuals might be motivated to make such contributions.

Social exchange refers to the voluntary actions of individuals that are motivated by the returns they are expected to bring from others (Blau, 1964). According to Blau, the basic principle underlying social exchange is that by supplying rewarding services to another, one obligates that individual to furnish benefits in turn, thus discharging the obligation. However, since there is no way to assure what one considers to be an appropriate return for these rewarding services (favors), social exchange requires trusting others to reciprocate accordingly. By the same token, the act of discharging their obligations allows others to demonstrate their trustworthiness. Over time, the gradual expansion of mutual service is accompanied by the parallel growth of mutual trust (Blau, 1964). This process is largely fueled by a generalized *norm of reciprocity*, which suggests that we owe others certain things because of what they have done for us in our previous interactions with them (Gouldner, 1960). Many scholars over the years have noted the importance of reciprocity in exchange relationships. Reciprocity has been referred to as *the vital principle of society* (Hobhouse, 1906), *almost a primordial imperative which pervades every relation of primitive life* (Thurnwald, 1932), and *the schema upon which all contacts among men rest* (Simmel, 1950).[2]

Social exchange is distinguishable from purely economic exchange in that the former is characterized by unspecified obligations and requires (as well as promotes) trust, while the latter rests on formal contracts stipulating specific quantities to be exchanged (Blau, 1964). A further distinction between these two forms of exchange can be made in considering the manner in which obligations are discharged. With economic exchange, agreements are enforced and guaranteed. Whereas with social exchange, gratitude establishes a "bond of interaction" between exchange partners, leading to the reciprocity of service (Simmel, 1950).

Organizational researchers have frequently drawn upon social exchange theory (Blau, 1964) and the norm of reciprocity (Gouldner, 1960) in their examinations of the employment relationship and other relationships between individuals in the workplace. One line of research (leader-member exchange, LMX; Graen & Scandura, 1987) focuses on the quality of the relationship between a superior (leader) and a subordinate (member). A similar area of research (team-member exchange, TMX; Seers, 1989) considers the effects of an individual's perceptions of the quality of the exchange relationships with the members of his or her work group. It is TMX that is of particular interest in the present chapter as we consider potential influences on individual contributions to collaborative capital.

THEORETICAL MODEL AND HYPOTHESES

While prior research has not specifically examined the antecedents of collaborative capital contributions as defined here, considerable research has been conducted on the influence of various social exchange relationships on the individual components I have suggested comprise the collaborative capital contribution construct (i.e. information sharing, trust/trustworthiness, and helping behavior). Drawing on this research, I develop a model of collaborative capital creation offering specific propositions as shown in Fig. 1. Although dispositional and instrumental motivations are expected to influence collaborative capital contributions as previously suggested, the focus of this chapter is on the relational view described above. Thus, no hypotheses are offered on the relationship between the dispositional or instrumental factors and individual contributions to collaborative capital. Instead, I argue for the strength of TMX as a relational predictor of such contributions. It is not my intent to either challenge or confirm the

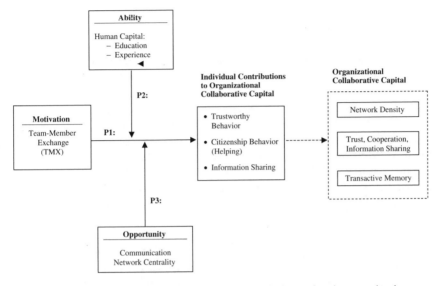

Fig. 1. Theoretical model of collaborative capital creation in organizations.

individual differences or the rational choice approaches to explaining collaborative behavior. I acknowledge that there is evidence that supports both views. However, I do contend that even after considering the effects of both of these approaches, individual perceptions of the quality of their social exchange relationship with their coworkers will explain additional variance in their contributions to collaborative capital.

Team-Member Exchange and Collaborative Capital

An important social exchange relationship in organizations is that between an individual and the other members of his or her work group. Recognizing that this exchange relationship had not been specifically addressed in the literature on social exchange in organizations, Seers (1989) introduced a measure of TMX, which he proposed as a way to assess the reciprocity between an employee and his or her peer group. Seers suggested that TMX measures an individual's perception of his or her willingness to assist other work group members, and to share ideas and provide feedback, as well as measuring perceptions regarding how readily information, help, and recognition are received from other members. In his development of the construct, Seers demonstrated that TMX is distinct from, although related to LMX. TMX is similar to LMX in that both constructs focus on the reciprocity between parties to an exchange relationship, and in both cases reciprocity is analyzed in terms of the resources each party brings to bear on the exchange process (Seers, Petty, & Cashman, 1995). However, whereas the LMX construct is designed to jointly assess employee role-making and supervisory leadership, the TMX construct is designed to jointly assess employee role-making and work group dynamics (Seers, 1989; Seers et al., 1995). In addition, while both TMX and LMX are based on role theory and social exchange theory, TMX differs from LMX in that it is not dyadic. Instead, it involves an individual's perceived relationship with a *group* of peers with whom he or she identifies as a member, rather than with each member individually.

Since TMX serves as an indicator of the perceived reciprocity between an individual and his or her peer group, it is likely to have implications regarding trust within the group. Trust and trustworthiness are highly intertwined and reciprocally related constructs. Therefore, perceptions of an exchange partner's trustworthiness are likely to influence one's willingness to trust that individual, as well as one's own trustworthy behavior in the relationship. In his review of the trust literature, Kramer (1999) suggests that these perceptions of exchange partner trustworthiness are, among other things, based on the history of prior interactions with that particular individual. Kramer (1999, p. 575) also states that, "a number of studies have demonstrated that reciprocity in exchange relationships enhances trust." Therefore, high-quality TMX relationships, which are characterized by a mutual willingness to share information and provide assistance when needed, should also be positively associated with trustworthy behavior on the part of individuals. Further, prior research suggests that high-quality TMX relationships are positively associated with greater cooperation, collaboration, and teamwork within a group of peers (Seers, 1989; Seers et al., 1995), all of which are consistent with the behaviors that I have suggested represent contributions to an organization's collaborative capital. I, therefore, propose the following:

Proposition 1. Individuals' perceptions regarding the quality of their social exchange relationship with their work group will be positively related to their contributions to collaborative capital as defined by (a) information sharing, (b) helping, and (c) trustworthy behaviors.

Ability and Opportunity as Potential Moderating Factors

According to Angle and Lawson (1994), any complex behavior is governed by a variety of factors, including one's knowledge, skills, and abilities; the resources to which one has access; and one's motivation to engage in the particular behavior. Similarly, previous theoretical work concerning the creation of intellectual capital (Moran & Ghoshal, 1996; Nahapiet & Ghoshal, 1998) and social capital (Adler & Kwon, 2002), suggests that contributions to the social capital of a collective are likely to depend not only on individual motivation, but also on individual ability and opportunity to make such an investment.

Drawing on the work of Cohen and Levinthal (1990), Nahapiet and Ghoshal (1998) suggest that organizational learning requires the ability to recognize new knowledge, as well as the ability to assimilate and use it. Along similar lines, Leana and Van Buren (1999) argue that a key component of organizational social capital is "associability" or "the *willingness* and *ability* of individuals to define collective goals that are then enacted collectively" (p. 542). They further suggest that, while the propensity to socialize may be largely universal, the ability to do so in order to achieve a collective purpose is not. Other authors have also discussed the role of ability in the creation of social capital. Lin (1999), for instance, offers that education and experience (indicators of ability) are sources of social capital in that they impact the resources to which one has access. Additionally, Adler and Kwon (2002), discuss the importance of ability as they suggest that individual motivation to contribute to social capital is of little use without the requisite ability or expertise to do so. Based on these prior theoretical arguments, I propose that individual knowledge, skills, and abilities will positively moderate the relationship between perceived social exchange relationship quality with one's coworkers (which I have argued represents individual motivation to contribute to collaborative capital), and one's actual contributions.

Proposition 2. An individual's knowledge, skills, and ability will have a positive moderating effect on the relationship between their perceived social exchange relationship quality with their coworkers and their contributions to collaborative capital.

Research on the social networks of individuals has stressed the importance of access to information. Coleman (1988) for instance, discusses a dimension of social capital that functions as an information channel used for acquiring valuable information. Similarly, Burt (1992) stresses the information benefits of social capital that result from (1) being made aware of opportunities, (2) before others, and (3) often through an indirect contact. Burt refers to these as access, timing, and referral benefits, respectively. In essence, these information channels, which may be utilized to give as well as receive information, are based on an individual's network position and arguably determine to an extent the individual's *opportunity* to contribute to the collaborative capital of an organization.

While Coleman (1988) and Burt (1992) both discuss the role of information access or opportunity in the creation of social capital, they approach the issue from different viewpoints. As discussed earlier, Coleman (1988) argues the benefits of network closure and dense networks of redundant contacts. According to Coleman, networks of this type facilitate the emergence and enforcement of norms, and promote trustworthiness, thereby strengthening social capital (Adler & Kwon, 2002). On the other hand, Burt (1992) argues the benefits of sparse networks of non-redundant contacts. According to Burt, individuals create social capital by spanning what he calls structural holes, or gaps between otherwise non-connected individuals in a network. Although the dense network arguments of Coleman (1988) and the sparse network arguments of Burt (1992) relative to the creation of social capital appear to be diametrically opposed, recent work has argued that both approaches can yield significant, albeit different, benefits (see Adler & Kwon, 2002; Oh, Kilduff, & Brass, 1999; Pil et al., 2000). However, I argue here that it is the approach based on network centrality that most accurately represents an individual's opportunity to contribute to the collaborative capital of an organization. By being centrally located in the communication network of the organization and having direct ties to a number of others, an individual is likely to have greater access to information, as well as greater potential outlets for sharing information. I thus propose the following:

Proposition 3. An individual's centrality in the organization's communication network will have a positive moderating effect on the relationship between their perceived social exchange relationship quality with their coworkers and their contributions to collaborative capital.

PRELIMINARY EXAMINATION OF PROPOSED RELATIONSHIPS

I have proposed in this chapter that the contributions of individuals to the collaborative capital of their organizations can be explained in part by the perceived quality of their social exchange relationship with their coworkers. I have suggested that this relationship will significantly predict collaborative capital contributions even after considering dispositional and instrumental explanations for such behavior. I have also proposed that this relationship would be moderated by the individual's ability and opportunity to contribute to collaborative capital. In a preliminary investigation of these proposed relationships, I examined data collected from 150 teachers at three schools in an urban public school district in the Midwestern United States.

As school administrators attempt to improve instructional quality within their school systems, a key factor that has been identified as instrumental to the achievement of that objective is the development of a professional learning community within schools, which includes the creation of an environment characterized by a clear, shared purpose for student learning, as well as collaboration among staff to achieve that purpose (King & Newmann, 2001). This has led in many cases to the creation of team-based organizational structures to facilitate the sharing of ideas and information among teachers with diverse backgrounds, perspectives, disciplines, and expertise. Senge, Cambron-McCabe, Lucas, Smith, Dutton, and Kleiner (2000) state that, "[s]chools are rife with team activity." They note that there are nested teams throughout a school system including curriculum teams, site teams, staff-development teams, and at the core, the teams of teachers who return to the classrooms and interact with students day after day.

The use of these team-based organizational structures in schools is largely predicated on the belief that teamwork offers the potential to achieve outcomes that could not be achieved with teachers working in isolation (Drach-Zahavy & Somech, 2002). In that regard, teams of teachers within schools are not unlike teams within any other organization in that they are often designed to increase members' responsibility for group performance and outcomes (Pounder, 1999). Pounder also suggests that teams within schools are designed to create work interdependence. At first blush, this may seem to be at odds with the organizational literature which suggests that teams are created to more effectively deal with the interdependencies that inherently exist in the work to be performed. However, in the case of schools where the work of teachers has often been viewed as solitary, it may that forming teams can actually enhance teachers' awareness of the interdependencies of the work involved in educating students. Nonetheless, a key issue facing administrators as they attempt to foster the development of collaborative, professional learning communities within their schools is encouraging individual teacher efforts aimed at creating and maintaining such a community, given that these efforts extend beyond their traditional classroom accountabilities. Thus, developing a better understanding of the factors that influence teacher contributions to the collaborative capital of the school should be of significant interest to school administrators, as well as researchers.

Findings from the data collected suggest that, as predicted, the more favorable their perceived social exchange relationship with their peers as a whole, the more likely a teacher was to contribute to the collaborative capital of the school as reported by other teachers. This was the case even when controlling for dispositional and instrumental factors (collectivistic orientation and expected returns from engaging in collaborative behavior, respectively). It was also predicted that even if teachers are motivated to engage in behaviors that contribute to the collaborative capital of their school, as gauged by the perceived quality of their social exchange relationships with their peers, the likelihood that they will actually engage in such behaviors will be positively influenced by their ability and opportunity to do so. Tests of the predicted moderating effects of ability (measured as highest level of education attained) and opportunity (measured as communication network centrality) failed to support the predictions. Instead, the data suggest that the effects of both ability and opportunity on contributions to collaborative capital are direct rather than moderating. Thus, regardless of perceived social exchange relationship quality with their peers, teachers with higher levels of education and those who are more centrally located in their school's network of communication appear to be more likely to contribute to the collaborative capital of their school.

Recent work by Settoon and Mossholder (2002) may offer potential explanations for the direct effect of network centrality, as well as education, on collaborative capital contributions. Although they did not specifically examine the collaborative capital construct as described in the present study, Settoon and Mossholder studied a similar construct (interpersonal citizenship behavior, ICB), that represents behaviors such as listening and being accessible, providing work-related advice, and supplying factual information and direct assistance to others. In discussing the results of their study in which they found a direct link between network centrality and ICB, Settoon and Mossholder (2002, p. 255) suggest that "... some individuals help more often because they are integral to the workflow, possess necessary expertise, or are simply more available in a temporal or physical sense." Contributing to the collaborative capital of an organization may thus be partially explained by being more available (network centrality) and/or possessing what is perceived to be more relevant expertise (education), both providing an individual with a greater opportunity to engage in such behaviors and a greater likelihood of being asked to do so.

CONCLUSIONS AND FUTURE RESEARCH DIRECTION

Given the suggested importance of collaborative capital to team and organizational performance, it is important that we develop a better understanding of potential processes by which it is developed in organizations. This chapter represents an attempt to explore one such process by examining why and how individuals contribute to the creation and maintenance of collaborative capital in the organizations for which they work.

By exploring the effects of perceived social exchange relationship quality with one's coworkers on one's contributions to the collaborative capital of an organization, this chapter has potential implications for both research and practice. Initially, it sheds additional light on the issue of why individuals might contribute to the creation and maintenance of collaborative capital (a public good) in an organization when the benefits received are likely to be indirect and non-specific. It appears that while dispositional or instrumental motivations may explain in part the individual behaviors that contribute to the organization's collaborative capital, a relational factor (i.e. TMX), significantly adds to the explanation of such behavior. Additionally, while ability and opportunity did not serve as moderating factors as predicted, they both did have a direct influence on individual contributions to collaborative capital. Achieving a better understanding of the relative strength of the various factors suggested to influence individual contributions to collaborative capital would be a potentially fruitful endeavor.

Another potential avenue for future research would be to explore the implications of social exchange relationship development (or deterioration) over time. Conducting longitudinal studies would allow the examination of how changing perceptions of TMX influence an individual's willingness to contribute to collaborative capital. It could be the case that changes in perceived relationship quality are as strong a predictor of collaborative capital contributions as the perceived quality of the relationship itself. Further extensions of this line of research might then also explore potential causes of favorable and/or unfavorable changes in perceived social exchange relationship quality.

Finally, while the focus of this chapter is on individual perceptions and related individual behaviors, the value of its contribution to the literature is partially predicated on the belief that individual contributions to collaborative capital as defined here actually lead to greater collaborative capital in the organization. Future cross-level research examining this relationship would be useful. Further, studies examining the relationship of collaborative capital to specific organizational outcomes are also needed. In essence, micro-, macro-, and meso-level studies are needed to truly enhance our understanding of the processes that facilitate the creation and maintenance of collaborative capital, as well as to further our understanding of the potential impact of collaborative capital on team and organizational performance.

NOTES

1. Coleman's work was largely influenced by the work of Bourdieu as well as that of economist Glen Loury (1977). See Portes (1998) for a detailed discussion.
2. See Gouldner (1960) for additional discussion on historical views of reciprocity.

REFERENCES

Adler, N. J. (1997). *International dimensions of organizational behavior* (3rd ed.). Cincinnati, OH: South/Western.

Adler, P. S., & Kwon, S. (2002). Social capital: Prospects for a new concept. *Academy of Management Review, 27*, 17–40.

Angle, H. L., & Lawson, M. B. (1994). Organizational commitment and employees' performance ratings: Both type of commitment and type of performance count. *Psychological Reports, 75*, 1539–1551.

Axelrod, R. M. (1984). *The evolution of cooperation.* New York: Basic Books.

Axelrod, R. M., & Hamilton, W. D. (1981). The evolution of cooperation. *Science, 211*, 1390–1396.

Baumeister, R. F., & Leary, M. R. (1995). The need to belong: Desire for interpersonal attachments as a fundamental human motivation. *Psychological Bulletin, 117*, 497–529.

Becker, G. S. (1962). *Human capital.* New York: Columbia University Press.

Belliveau, M., O'Reilly, C., & Wade, J. (1996). Social capital at the top: Effects of social similarity and status on CEO compensation. *Academy of Management Journal, 39*, 1568–1593.

Blau, P. (1964). *Exchange and power in social life.* New York: Wiley.

Bourdieu, P. (1985). The forms of capital. In: J. G. Richardson (Ed.), *Handbook of theory and research for the sociology of education.* New York: Greenwood Press.

Brewer, M. B., & Schneider, S. K. (1990). Social identity and social dilemmas: A double-edged sword. In: D. Abrams & M. A. Hogg (Eds), *Social identity theory: Constructive and critical advances* (pp. 169–184).

Burt, R. S. (1992). *Structural holes.* Cambridge, MA: Harvard University Press.

Burt, R. S. (1997). The contingent value of social capital. *Administrative Science Quarterly, 42,* 339–365.

Caporael, L. R. (1997). The evolution of truly social cognition: The core configurations model. *Personality and Social Psychology Review, 1,* 276–298.

Cohen, W. M., & Levinthal, D. A. (1990). Absorptive capacity: A new perspective on learning and innovation. *Administrative Science Quarterly, 35,* 128–152.

Coleman, J. S. (1987). Free riders and zealots. In: K. S. Cook (Ed.), *Social exchange theory.* Newbury Park, CA: Sage.

Coleman, J. S. (1988). Social capital in the creation of human capital. *American Journal of Sociology, 94,* S95–S120.

Coleman, J. S. (1990). *Foundations of social theory.* Cambridge, MA: Harvard University Press.

Cosmides, L., & Tooby, J. (1992). Cognitive adaptations for social exchange. In: J. H. Barkow, L. Cosmides & J. Tooby (Eds), *The adapted mind: Evolutionary psychology and the generation of culture* (pp. 163–227). New York: Oxford University Press.

Drach-Zahavy, A., & Somech, A. (2002). Team heterogeneity and its relationship with team support and team effectiveness. *Journal of Educational Administration, 40,* 44–66.

Eby, L. T., & Dobbins, G. H. (1997). Collectivistic orientation in teams: An individual and group-level analysis. *Journal of Organizational Behavior, 18,* 275–295.

Ehrenreich, J. H. (1997). Personality theory: A case of intellectual and social isolation? *The Journal of Psychology, 13,* 33–44.

Emerson, R. M. (1987). Toward a theory of value in social exchange. In: K. S. Cook (Ed.), *Social exchange theory.* Newbury Park, CA: Sage.

Freese, J., & Powell, B. (1999). Sociobiology, status, and parental investment in sons and daughters: Testing the Trivers–Willard hypothesis. *American Journal of Sociology, 106,* 1704–1743.

Friedman, R. A., & Krackhardt, D. (1997). Social capital and career mobility: A structural theory of lower returns to education for Asian employees. *Journal of Applied Behavioral Science, 33,* 316–334.

Fukuyama, F. (1995). *Trust: The social virtues and the creation of prosperity.* New York: Free Press.

Funder, D. C. (1994). Editorial. *Journal of Research and Personality, 28,* 1–3.

Gouldner, A. W. (1960). The norm of reciprocity. *American Sociological Review, 25,* 165–167.

Graen, G. B., & Scandura, T. A. (1987). Toward a psychology of dyadic organizing. *Research in Organizational Behavior, 9,* 175–208.

Granovetter, M. (1992). Problems of explanation in economic sociology. In: N. Nohria & R. Eccles (Eds), *Networks and organizations: Structure form and action* (pp. 25–56). Boston: Harvard Business School Press.

Gupta, D. K., Hofstetter, R. C., & Buss, T. F. (1997). Group utility in the micro motivation of collective action: The case of membership in the AARP. *Journal of Economic Behavior & Organization, 32,* 301–320.

Hanifan, L. J. (1920). *The community center.* Boston: Silver, Burdette & Co.

Hobhouse, L. T. (1906). *Morals in evolution: A study in comparative ethics.* London: Chapman & Hall.

Hofstede, G. (1980). *Culture's consequences: International differences in work related values.* Beverly Hills, CA: Sage.

Hofstede, G. (1984). The cultural relativity of the quality of life concept. *Academy of Management Review, 9,* 389–398.

James, K., & Cropanzano, R. (1994). Dispositional group loyalty and individual action for the benefit of an ingroup: Experimental and correlational evidence. *Organizational Behavior and Human Decision Processes, 60,* 179–205.

Jassawalla, A. R., & Sashittal, H. C. (1998). An examination of collaboration in high-technology new product development processes. *Journal of Product Innovation Management, 15,* 237–254.

Johnson, O. E., Smith, M. L., & Gambill, D. (2000). Reconstructing "We": Organizational identification in a dynamic environment. In: C. Leana & D. Rousseau (Eds), *Relational wealth: The advantages of stability in a changing economy* (pp. 153–168). New York: Oxford Press.

King, M. B., & Newmann, F. M. (2001). Building school capacity through professional development: Conceptual and empirical considerations. *The International Journal of Educational Management, 15,* 86.

Kluckhohn, F., & Strodtbeck, F. L. (1961). *Variations in value orientations.* Evanston, IL: Row, Peterson.

Konner, M. (1999). Darwin's truth, Jefferson's vision: Sociobiology and the politics of human nature. *The American Prospect, 45,* 30–38.

Kramer, R. M. (1999). Trust and distrust in organizations: Emerging perspectives, enduring questions. *Annual Review of Psychology, 50,* 569–598.

Kramer, R. M., & Brewer, M. B. (1984). Effects of group identity on resource use in a simulated commons dilemma. *Journal of Personality and Social Psychology, 46,* 1044–1057.

Leana, C. R., & Rousseau, D. M. (2000). *Relational wealth: The advantages of stability in a changing economy.* New York: Oxford University Press.

Leana, C. R., & Van Buren III, H. J. (1999). Organizational social capital and employment practices. *Academy of Management Review, 24,* 538–555.

Lin, N. (1999). Social networks and status attainment. *Annual Review of Sociology, 25,* 467–487.

Loury, G. (1977). A dynamic theory of racial income differences. In: P. A. Wallace & A. M. LaMonde (Eds), *Women, minorities, and employment discrimination* (pp. 153–186). Lexington, MA: Lexington Books.

McClintock, C. G., & Allison, S. T. (1989). Social value orientation and helping behavior. *Journal of Applied Social Psychology, 19,* 353–362.

McCormick, K. (1997). An essay on the origin of the rational utility maximization hypothesis and a suggested modification. *Eastern Economic Journal, 23,* 17–30.

Messick, D. M., & Brewer, M. B. (1983). Solving social dilemmas: A review. In: L. Wheeler & P. Shaver (Eds), *Review of Personality and Social Psychology* (pp. 11–44). Beverly Hills: Sage.

Messick, D. M., & McClintock, C. G. (1968). Motivational bases of choice in experimental games. *Journal of Experimental Social Psychology, 4,* 1–25.

Moran, P., & Ghoshal, S. (1996). Value creation by firms. *Academy of Management Best Paper Proceedings,* 41–45.

Nahapiet, J., & Ghoshal, S. (1998). Social capital, intellectual capital, and the organizational advantage. *Academy of Management Review, 23,* 242–266.

Oh, H., Kilduff, M., & Brass, D. J. (1999). Communal social capital, linking social capital, and economic outcomes. Paper presented at the *annual meeting of the Academy of Management*, Chicago, IL.

Paxton, P. (1999). Is social capital declining in the United States? A multiple indicator assessment. *American Journal of Sociology, 105*, 88–127.

Pearce, J., & Randel, A. (2000). Social capital: Mediating the negative relationship between an employability approach to human resource management and job performance. Paper presented at the *annual meeting of the Academy of Management*, Toronto Canada.

Pierce, B. D., & White, R. (1999). The evolution of social structure: Why biology matters. *Academy of Management Review, 24*, 843–853.

Pil, F. K., Smith, M. L., & Leana, C. R. (2000). Individual and organizational social capital: Implications for private good outcomes. Paper presented at the *annual meeting of the Academy of Management*, Toronto, Canada.

Portes, A. (1998). Social capital: Its origins and applications in modern sociology. *Annual Review of Sociology, 24*, 1–24.

Portes, A., & Sensenbrenner, J. (1993). Embeddedness and immigration: Notes on the social determinants of economic action. *American Journal of Sociology, 98*, 1320–1350.

Pounder, D. G. (1999). Teacher teams: Exploring job characteristics and work-related outcomes of work group enhancement. *Educational Administration Quarterly, 35*, 317–348.

Putnam, R. (1993). *Making democracy work: Civic traditions in modern Italy*. Princeton, NJ: Princeton University Press.

Putnam, R. (1995). Bowling alone: America's declining social capital. *Journal of Democracy, 6*, 65–78.

Seers, A. (1989). Team-member exchange quality: A new concept for role-making research. *Organizational Behavior and Human Decision Processes, 43*, 118–135.

Seers, A., Petty, M. M., & Cashman, J. F. (1995). Team-member exchange under team and traditional management. *Group & Organization Management, 20*, 18–38.

Senge, P. M., Cambron-McCabe, N., Lucas, T., Smith, B., Dutton, J., & Kleiner, A. (2000). *Schools that learn: A fifth discipline fieldbook for educators, parents, and everyone who cares about education*. New York: Doubleday.

Settoon, R. P., & Mossholder, K. W. (2002). Relationship quality and relationship context as antecedents of person- and task-focused interpersonal citizenship behavior. *Journal of Applied Psychology, 87*, 255–267.

Simmel, G. (1950). *The sociology of George Simmel*, translated and edited by Kurt H. Wolff. Glencoe, IL: Free Press.

Staw, B., & Ross, J. (1985). Stability in the midst of change: A dispositional approach to job attitudes. *Journal of Applied Psychology, 70*, 469–480.

Thurnwald, R. (1932). *Economics in primitive communities*. London: Oxford University Press.

Triandis, H. C. (1995). *Individualism and collectivism*. Boulder, CO: Westview Press.

Tversky, A., & Kahneman, D. (1986). Rational choice and the framing of decisions. *Journal of Business, 59*, S251–S278.

Wagner, J. A. (1995). Studies of individualism–collectivism: Effects on cooperation in groups. *Academy of Management Journal, 38*, 152–172.

Wilson, E. O. (1975). *Sociobiology: The new synthesis*. Cambridge, MA: Harvard University Press.

Wilson, E. O. (1978). *On human nature*. Cambridge, MA: Harvard University Press.

LEADING TOGETHER, WORKING TOGETHER: THE ROLE OF TEAM SHARED LEADERSHIP IN BUILDING COLLABORATIVE CAPITAL IN VIRTUAL TEAMS

N. Sharon Hill

ABSTRACT

Due to geographic dispersion and reliance on technology-mediated communication, developing collaborative capital can be a challenge in a virtual team. Knowledge sharing is one form of collaborative capital that has been identified as critical to virtual team success. This chapter develops a theoretical model that proposes that shared leadership in virtual teams is positively related to knowledge sharing between team members, and that this relationship will be partially mediated by trust. The model also shows that a team's degree of reliance on technology-mediated communication will moderate the relationships in the model.

Collaborative Capital: Creating Intangible Value
Advances in Interdisciplinary Studies of Work Teams, Volume 11, 183–209
Copyright © 2005 by Elsevier Ltd.
ISSN: 1572-0977/doi:10.1016/S1572-0977(05)11007-3

INTRODUCTION

An important trend in organizations is the increased use of virtual teams (Biggs, 2000; Gibson & Cohen, 2003). Virtual teams vary widely in their configuration. However, in this chapter the term virtual team refers to teams that have two primary characteristics: team members are (1) geographically dispersed, and (2) rely on technology (e.g. e-mail, instant messaging) to communicate much more than they use face-to-face meetings (Gibson & Cohen, 2003). Due to the geographic dispersion of team members and the reliance on technology-mediated communication, virtual teams face some unique challenges that can be potentially detrimental to the process of building collaborative capital within the team.

Collaborative capital has been broadly defined as how well people work together, and building collaborative capital requires intentional effort on the part of team members. Knowledge sharing is one important manifestation of collaborative capital in a team. Since the knowledge required to complete important organizational tasks is distributed across many individuals (Argote, Ingram, Levine, & Moreland, 2000), organizations are making increased use of teams to pool organizational knowledge. The assumption is that each group member brings different perspectives and information, which if shared and used within the group will improve group outcomes. The focus of this chapter is to examine the link between leadership processes within a virtual team and collaborative capital that is manifested as knowledge sharing within the team.

Paradoxically, the key benefit associated with the implementation of virtual teams, can also impact negatively on knowledge sharing behaviors between team members. As with conventional teams, virtual teams are seen as an opportunity to bring together different experts, often with specific knowledge and skills. Since team members do not have to be co-located, an important advantage of virtual teams is the opportunity to pool the best expertise without regard to location. On the other hand, geographic dispersion of team members and reliance on technology (e.g. phone, computer) for team communications can have a negative influence on knowledge sharing (Cramton, 2001; Cramton & Orvis, 2003; Gibson & Cohen, 2003; Griffith, Sawyer, & Neale, 2003). This dual-edged sword makes it imperative to better understand the factors that contribute to increased knowledge sharing in teams that operate in a virtual environment. Researchers, as well as practitioners, need to understand how virtual teams can be implemented without inhibiting knowledge sharing, and hence the development of virtual team collaborative capital.

This chapter argues that the way in which leadership develops within a virtual team, that is shared leadership, influences knowledge sharing in the team. Shared leadership refers to a phenomenon where responsibility for leadership activities is distributed between group members (Pearce & Conger, 2003; Pearce & Sims, 2000). For example, research has provided some evidence that rotating the leadership role between team members in a virtual team improves team process and outcomes (Jarvenpaa, Knoll, & Leidner, 1998). However, apparently, there is no research that relates the shared leadership construct from the leadership domain to knowledge sharing in a virtual team. The purpose of this chapter is to fill this gap and advance theoretical understanding of knowledge sharing dynamics in virtual teams.

The model shown in Fig. 1 describes the hypothesized relationship between shared leadership and knowledge sharing in a virtual team. The key premise of the model is that shared leadership has a direct influence on knowledge sharing; as well as an indirect influence, mediated by trust. The model also shows that reliance on technology-mediated communication

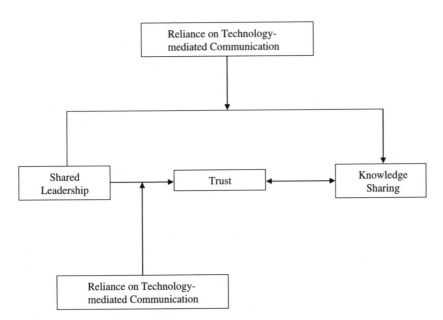

Fig. 1. The relationship between shared leadership and knowledge sharing in virtual teams.

moderates the relationship between shared leadership and trust, and the relationship between shared leadership and knowledge sharing, such that the greater the reliance on technology-mediated communication, the stronger the relationships.

The organization of this chapter is as follows. It first reviews the literature related to knowledge sharing in groups, and, more specifically, knowledge sharing in a virtual team context. Then findings from knowledge sharing and leadership research are integrated to develop the propositions in the model. Finally, implications for collaborative capital research and for practice are discussed.

KNOWLEDGE AND KNOWLEDGE SHARING

Knowledge Sharing Definitions

The knowledge possessed by individuals can be classified in several different ways. The first classification is according to task-related knowledge (i.e. knowledge about carrying out the task at hand), social knowledge (i.e. knowledge about individuals and their relationships that helps people interpret the behavior of others), and contextual knowledge (i.e. knowledge about the environment in which tasks, individuals and groups are embedded) (Cramton & Orvis, 2003). This chapter focuses on task-related knowledge, and follows Bartol and Srivastava's (2002) definition of knowledge as "information, ideas, and expertise relevant for tasks performed by individuals, teams, work units, and the organization as a whole" (p. 65).

Individual knowledge can also be conceptualized on a continuum from explicit to tacit (Leonard & Sensiper, 1998; Polanyi, 1966). Explicit knowledge can be articulated and thus is more easily shared with others. Tacit knowledge cannot be as easily shared through verbal communication, and is therefore considered to be more "sticky" and more difficult to transfer (Von Hippel, 1994). For example, to illustrate the difference between explicit and tacit knowledge, Griffith et al. (2003) provide the example of writing a research report. At the explicit end of the spectrum are the procedures that a researcher has for writing such a report. At the tacit end of the spectrum is the researcher's ability to "hook" the reader and argue a point persuasively. They describe the latter as a skill that is learned with experience and that is very difficult to fully articulate. Nonaka (1994) proposed several mechanisms through which tacit knowledge is shared, including an individual observing or working alongside another over a period of time, and a process of externalization, where more elaborate forms of communication (e.g. metaphors, stories, etc.) are used to communicate tacit knowledge. The propositions in this chapter are formulated to include knowledge in general, and do not make any distinction between explicit and tacit knowledge.

One final classification of knowledge, which is of relevance here, is the distinction between common vs. uniquely held knowledge. Many knowledge sharing research tasks involve a "hidden profile" (Stasser & Titus, 1985) in which group members differentially possess task relevant knowledge. In these experiments, researchers measure how much common vs. uniquely held pieces of information are shared. As was noted earlier, the benefits from knowledge sharing are a result of group members pooling their respective unique information.

Researchers have defined knowledge sharing in a variety of different ways. Some definitions appear more focused on explicit knowledge, for example, "oral and written discussion of information among group members" (Miranda & Saunders, 2003, p. 90), and others on tacit knowledge, for example, "the process by which one individual is affected by the experience of another" (Argote, McEvily, & Reagans, 2003, p. 3). This chapter uses Bartol and Srivastava's (2002) more general view of knowledge sharing as individuals sharing ideas, suggestions, and expertise with one another that are relevant to the organizational task. To understand how virtualness can impact knowledge sharing between team members, it is helpful to identify the mechanisms through which knowledge sharing occurs in a team context.

Mechanisms for Knowledge Sharing in Teams

Research has shown that despite the benefits of knowledge sharing, successful sharing can be difficult to achieve (Argote et al., 2000). For example, in their seminal study, Stasser and Titus (1985) used a hidden profile task to show that group members tend to exchange common or redundant information at the expense of information that is uniquely held by group members. Knowledge researchers (Argote et al., 2003; Nahapiet & Ghoshal, 1998) have identified several mechanisms that promote knowledge sharing. Based on a review of the knowledge sharing literature, Argote et al. (2003) suggested that these findings could be summarized as three primary mechanisms: ability, motivation, and opportunity. These mechanisms are briefly described below.

Ability refers to the capacity of team members to share know-ledge (Argote et al., 2003), and refers in part to the effectiveness of the communication process that occurs between knowledge sharing partners. Communication is the process of transferring information, meaning, and understanding from sender to receiver (Gibson, 1997). Fisher and Fisher (1998) describe an effective knowledge transfer process as one in which knowledge is (1) sent properly, (2) received properly, with (3) minimum noise (factors that distort the transfer process). Factors that interfere with effective communication process, will limit ability to share knowledge. For example, language differences between sender and receiver (Weber & Camerer, 2003), lack of experience with the task that prohibits the receiver from absorbing the knowledge that is shared (Cohen & Levinthal, 1990), differences in values and assumptions between sender and receiver that influence their perceptions and understanding of information (Fisher & Fisher, 1998), and use of technology that slows down the communication process or limits the ability to share information non-verbally (Straus, 1997; Straus & McGrath, 1994; Walther & Burgoon, 1992).

In addition to the ability to share knowledge, individuals must also be motivated to share (Argote et al., 2003). Factors that impact motivation to share knowledge include rewards and incentives (Bartol & Srivastava, 2002) and the interpersonal relationships between team members, such as social cohesion (Reagans & McEvily, 2003) and trust (Levin & Cross, 2004; Mayer, Davis, & Schoorman, 1995; McEvily, Perrone, & Zaheer, 2003; Scott, 2000; Szulanski, 2000).

Finally, apart from being able to communicate effectively, and being motivated to share knowledge, knowledge exchange requires that team members have the opportunity to interact and learn from each other (Argote et al., 2003). This is particularly important for tacit knowledge exchange where knowledge is difficult to articulate and is often transferred through non-verbal means, such as working alongside the individual who is the source of the knowledge. For example, physical proximity provides indi-viduals with greater opportunity to observe each other and share tacit knowledge (Nadler, Thompson, & Van Boven, 2003). Opportunities for informal as well as formal interaction can also increase the amount of knowledge that is shared (McEvily & Zaheer, 1999; Reagans & Zuckerman, 2001).

In summary, knowledge sharing in teams can be influenced by team members' ability to communicate effectively, motivation to share knowl-edge, and opportunity for interaction that leads to knowledge sharing. Vir-tual team researchers have suggested that knowledge sharing may be particularly difficult in a virtual team environment (Cramton, 2001; Cramton & Orvis, 2003; Hinds & Bailey, 2003; Hinds & Weisband, 2003).

> Effective teamwork depends on appropriate information sharing; identifying important pieces of unshared information and converting them into shared information when decisions have to be made, inferences drawn, or work is being coordinated. This is not an easy task in any team, and it seems to be more difficult in virtual than face-to-face environments.
>
> (Cramton & Orvis, 2003, p. 217)

The next section discusses how virtualness can impact knowledge sharing in virtual teams through the mechanisms described above.

KNOWLEDGE SHARING IN VIRTUAL TEAMS

As mentioned previously, two primary characteristics of virtual teams are their geographic distribution and reliance on technology-mediated communication (Gibson & Cohen, 2003). These characteristics impact knowledge sharing through each of the mechanisms discussed in the previous section. Table 1

Table 1. Impact of Virtualness on Knowledge Sharing Mechanisms.

Knowledge Sharing Mechanism	Impact of Virtualness on Knowledge Sharing Mechanism
Ability	Less effective communication process which reduces the ability to share knowledge: • Less able to use non-verbal cues and voice intonation to ensure effective communication of information • Communication occurs at a slower rate and is more cumbersome • Less able to share tacit knowledge through direct observation of actions
Motivation	• More difficult to develop strong interpersonal relationships (e.g. trust, social cohesion, shared identity) which provide motivation to share knowledge • Decreased social awareness of communication partner negatively impacts motivation for socially desirable behaviors, such as cooperation and rapport building
Opportunity	• Fewer day-to-day interactions (including impromptu meetings and discussions) that provide opportunities to share knowledge

summarizes the impact of virtualness on team members' ability to communicate effectively, motivation to share knowledge, and opportunity to share knowledge.

Impact of Virtualness on Ability to Share Knowledge

Virtual team researchers have proposed that virtual teams will have less effective communication processes as a result of reliance on technology-mediated communication (Cramton & Orvis, 2003; Fisher & Fisher, 1998; Hinds & Weisband, 2003). During face-to-face interaction, people rely heavily on non-verbal cues and voice intonation to grasp the full meaning of information. These cues play an important role in the communication process. They help the receiver to interpret the meaning of knowledge, and also help the sender to confirm that the communication partner has understood the knowledge received. These cues are largely absent in technology-mediated communication and as a result the ability to share more complex knowledge is likely to be negatively impacted.

In addition, technology-mediated communication is more cumbersome, and knowledge sharing that involves typing out complex ideas is likely to proceed at a slower rate (Straus, 1997; Straus & McGrath, 1994; Walther & Burgoon, 1992). If less information is exchanged, then there is less opportunity for unique information to become salient in the group, leading to an increased tendency to dwell on knowledge that is commonly shared rather than uniquely held by different team members (Cramton, 2001). Finally, virtualness limits the ability to share tacit knowledge, since tacit knowledge is frequently transferred through working alongside and observing others, team members who are not collocated will find it more difficult to share tacit knowledge (Griffith et al., 2003).

Impact of Virtualness on Motivation to Share Knowledge

Virtualness is also likely to impact motivation to share knowledge through its influence on the interpersonal relationships between team members. An established body of research has demonstrated that there is a positive relationship between proximity to others and interpersonal liking (Athanasiou & Yoshioka, 1973; Kahn & McGaughey, 1977). Research has also shown that communication via technology-mediated communication impedes the development of interpersonal liking (Siegel, Dubrovsky, Kiesler, & McGuire, 1986). McGinn and Croson (2004) defined the construct of social awareness as "the degree of consciousness of and attention to the other in the interaction" (p. 339). Research has shown that the greater social awareness that occurs in face-to-face communication compared to technology-mediated communication is more likely to lead to socially desirable behaviors such as cooperation (Dawes, Van de Kragt, & Orbell, 1988) and rapport building (Drolet & Morris, 2000). Virtual team researchers have also demonstrated that virtual teams are less likely to develop a shared identity, and be more likely to experience higher levels of conflict than face-to-face teams (Mortensen & Hinds, 2001). Finally, virtual teams also find it more difficult to develop trust (Gibson & Manuel, 2003). Alge, Wiethoff, and Klein (2003) found that teams communicating face-to-face who did not have a history together developed higher levels of trust and shared more unique information than groups interacting via technology-mediated communication.

Impact of Virtualness on Opportunity to Share Knowledge

Geographic dispersion impacts the opportunity that team members have to share knowledge. Proximity results in more frequent interaction and increased likelihood of collaboration (Keller & Holland, 1983; Kraut, Fussell, Brennan, & Siegel, 2002; Monge & Kirste, 1980; Olson & Olson, 2000). "It is much easier to coordinate activities with other team members when you see them frequently...some of the most important coordination and information sharing occurs informally in the halls, break rooms, and parking lots" (Fisher & Fisher, 1998). Research has shown that people who are physically distant communicate with each other less than people who are proximate and do not have opportunities for face-to-face interaction (Conrath, 1973; Monge & Kirste, 1980). As a result, they share less task-related information (Keller & Holland, 1983).

Taken together, the impact of geographic dispersion and technology-mediated communication is likely to be detrimental to knowledge sharing in a virtual team (Cramton & Orvis, 2003; Hinds & Weisband, 2003). How then might the leadership process within the team mitigate some of the negative effects of virtualness on knowledge sharing? This is the focus of the next section.

SHARED LEADERSHIP AND KNOWLEDGE SHARING
IN VIRTUAL TEAMS

There is some evidence from the research on face-to-face decision-making groups that leadership can influence how knowledge is shared in groups both negatively and positively (Cruz, Henningsen, & Smith, 1999; Henningsen, Henningsen, Jakobsen, & Borton, 2004; Larson, Christensen, Franz, & Abbott, 1998; Wofford, Calabro, & Sims, 1975). Leaders can improve knowledge sharing by asking questions and repeating unique information so that it gets the attention of the group (Larson et al., 1998; Henningsen et al., 2004). Leaders tend to have more influence than the average group member and appear to take a more active role than others in managing the information that is raised during discussion. Due to their influence in the group, the information possessed by leaders also receives more attention within the group; hence a leader with information supporting the best decision alternative can help the group share more unique information and come to a better decision outcome (Cruz et al., 1999; Henningsen et al., 2004).

On the negative side, a leader can also stifle information flow within the group (Cruz et al., 1999; Wofford et al., 1975). Groups with directive leaders advance fewer opinions and share less information than groups with no leaders or participative leaders. If leaders possess information supporting a less than optimal alternative, they can cause the group to share less unique information and make a poor decision (Cruz et al., 1999; Henningsen et al., 2004). Despite the evidence that leadership can play a role in influencing knowledge sharing in face-to-face groups, there has apparently been no research that examines the relationship between leadership and knowledge sharing in virtual teams.

The Influence of Leadership on Knowledge Sharing in Virtual Teams

Bell and Kozlowski (2002) stated in a recent discussion of the implications of virtual teaming for effective leadership, "There is little current theory to guide researchers on the leadership and management of virtual teams" (p. 15). However, virtual team researchers have proposed that leadership can play a critical role in overcoming knowledge sharing problems caused by technology-mediated communication and geographic dispersion in virtual teams (Cramton & Orvis, 2003; Hinds & Weisband, 2003). For example, leaders can increase information exchange between team members, by establishing norms for communication, monitoring and facilitating the communication process in the team, and by encouraging questioning of assumptions and reframing of thinking (Avolio, Kahai, Dumdum, & Sivasubramaniam, 2001; Cramton & Orvis, 2003; Hinds & Weisband, 2003).

Researchers have further suggested that because virtual teams operate in an environment in which team members are geographically distributed and have different work contexts, they require *more* leadership than conventional co-located teams (Lipnack & Stamps, 1997). One solution is for each team member to assume part of the leadership role. According to Lipnack and Stamps (1997), "a virtual team that attempts to operate with one formal leader is not going to make it" (p. 33). They further state that "virtual teams that deal with complex issues and problems invariably have shared leadership, regardless of the titles they use for convenience" (p. 176). Following a similar rational, Fisher and Fisher (1998) also recommend distributed leadership for effective virtual team functioning. They state that "managing these teams from a central hierarchy…is neither practical nor desirable." Based on this, it is worthwhile to consider the role that shared leadership can play in promoting knowledge sharing in a virtual team.

The Influence of Shared Leadership on Knowledge Sharing in Virtual Teams

Leadership researchers have conceptualized and defined leadership in several different ways (for a review, see Bass, 1990). This chapter uses Yukl's definition of leadership as "influence exerted… over other people to guide, structure, and facilitate relationships in a group…" (Yukl, 2002, p. 3). In more traditional conceptualizations of leadership, one individual projects influence downward on members of the team (Pearce & Conger, 2003; Pearce & Sims, 2000). This type of leadership is known as vertical or top-down. In contrast to vertical leadership, shared leadership is a leadership phenomenon within a group where responsibility for leadership activities is shared between group members, and involves a horizontal or lateral influence process between group members (Pearce & Conger, 2003; Pearce & Sims, 2000; Yukl, 2002). Shared leadership may be characterized by team members sharing some leadership functions or different people performing a particular leadership function at different times (Yukl, 2002).

The key distinction between shared leadership and traditional models of leadership is that the influence process involves more than just downward influence on subordinates by an appointed or elected leader. Rather, leadership is broadly distributed among a set of individuals instead of centralized in the hands of a single individual who acts in the role of superior.

(Pearce & Conger, 2003, p. 1)

This key difference between vertical leadership and shared leadership is depicted in Fig. 2(a) and Fig. 2(b). The presence of shared leadership within a team does not preclude vertical leadership. Locke (2003) described an integrated model, shown in Fig. 2(c), which includes both vertical, top-down leadership and horizontal, shared leadership among team members. He suggested that there are certain leadership tasks, for example, setting a single vision for the team, which should be done by the vertical leader. The vertical leader can also play a role in facilitating the development of shared leadership within the team.

The focus in this chapter is to examine the effects of the shared leadership component that exists within a team. Yukl (2002) has called for more research on distributed leadership in teams. In his view, "the leadership actions of any individual leader are much less important than the collective leadership provided by the members of the organization" (p. 432). Preliminary research in both face-to-face and virtual teams provides evidence that shared leadership can be a better predictor of team effectiveness than vertical leadership (Avolio, Jung, Murry, & Sivasubramaniam, 1996; Pearce & Sims, 2002; Pearce, Yoo, & Alavi, 2004; Taggar & Hackett, 1999). Studies that examine the influence of shared leadership in teams

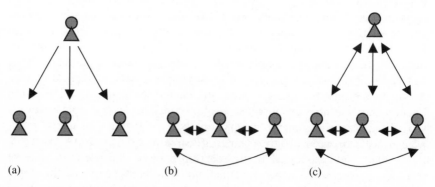

Fig. 2. Directions of influence in vertical, shared, and integrated leadership models. (a) vertical (top-down) leadership, (b) horizontal (shared) leadership, and (c) integrated model.

(e.g. Pearce & Sims, 2002; Pearce et al., 2004) have focused on teams that have a vertical leader. These studies have measured shared leadership by assessing to what extent the vertical leader and team members exhibited different types of leadership behaviors, for example, directive, transactional, transformational, and empowering leadership behaviors. They then compare the relative impact of leadership from the vertical leader with shared leadership from team members on team outcomes. Shared leadership has generally been found to be more influential than vertical leadership for team effectiveness.

In a face-to-face environment, for example, Pearce and Sims (2002) found that performance in change management teams with a formal, assigned leader was more strongly related to shared leadership within the team than to assigned vertical leadership. Taggar and Hackett (1999) investigated the relationship between leader emergence and team performance in face-to-face, self-managed teams, and found that leader emergence only increased team performance if "staff members" (which they defined as team members other than the emergent leader) also exhibited leadership behaviors. An important finding was that although one individual may clearly exhibit leadership, that individual cannot compensate for lack of leadership behavior in other team members. In discussing their findings, Taggar and Hackett (1999) did not refer to the shared leadership construct, but their description of leadership within the team fit the definition of shared leadership used in this chapter.

Shared leadership may be even more important than vertical leadership in the virtual team environment. Pearce and Sims (2000) developed a conceptual framework to guide research in the area of shared leadership, and suggested that shared leadership may be particularly important in virtual work groups as a day-to-day mechanism for group interaction that may not be possible for the vertical leader to provide. Bell and Kozlowski (2002) supported Pearce and Sims' (2000) view that shared leadership is important in virtual teams. They argue that "because leaders of virtual teams cannot monitor or interact with their team members, they need to create a self-managing team by distributing leadership functions to the team" (p. 28). Yoo and Alavi (2004) studied how leadership emerged in self-managed virtual teams and also concluded that the role of leadership was distributed among several team members, suggesting that the role of leadership be conceptualized as a "distributed leadership system" (p. 50).

In further support of the proposition that shared leadership influences virtual team process and outcomes, Pearce et al. (2004) found support for the positive influence of shared leadership on virtual team effectiveness.

They found shared leadership to be a significant predictor of team potency, social integration, problem-solving quality, and perceived effectiveness; whereas vertical leadership did not predict these outcomes. Moreover, shared leadership resulted in higher levels of initiative and proactivity among team members, behaviors that have been linked to team performance in the virtual team literature (Furst, Blackburn, & Rosen, 1999; Lipnack & Stamps, 1997; Townsend & DeMarie, 1998).

Although there is some evidence that shared leadership influences virtual team performance, the relationship between shared leadership and knowledge sharing has apparently not been specifically examined. However, there is reason to think that shared leadership will be an important determinant of knowledge sharing behaviors within a virtual team. Pearce and Conger (2003) suggested that shared leadership will increase communication and integration of knowledge between team members, because it leads to greater coordination of team member tasks. In other words, in a team where members are sharing the leadership role, there is more of an opportunity for team members to exchange knowledge. Team members that share the leadership role are likely to have a higher level of communication within the team and to share more information in the process of coordinating their various leadership activities. Research in face-to-face teams has shown that a leader with expertise in a certain task area can help the group share more unique information related to the task (Cruz et al., 1999; Henningsen et al., 2004). This suggests that when virtual team members with different areas of expertise, share the leadership role, higher levels of knowledge sharing will occur within the team.

From a motivational perspective, knowledge sharing can be either extrinsically motivated (Bartol & Srivastava, 2002), or intrinsically motivated (Osterloh & Frey, 2000). Extrinsic motivation comes from factors outside the team, for example, rewards, recognition, peer pressure (Deci, 1975; Hackman, 1987). Individuals are intrinsically motivated when they experience enjoyment, satisfaction, self-expression, or a sense of personal challenge as a result of performing the task itself (Deci, 1975; Deci & Flaste, 1995). There is evidence that shared leadership is positively related to levels of intrinsic motivation within the team. For example, Avolio et al. (1996) found shared leadership to be significantly related to the amount of extra effort team members exerted on their projects. Similarly, Pearce (1997) found a significant relationship between shared leadership and citizenship behaviors within the team. When members of a team take on the shared leadership role they are sharing responsibility for the effectiveness of the team. Fisher & Fisher (1998) argue that this will create a higher sense of allegiance and commitment to the team which in turn will have a positive impact on knowledge sharing.

In summary, shared leadership is predicted to positively influence the amount of interaction that occurs between team members, and therefore opportunity for knowledge sharing. It will also increase intrinsic motivation of team members leading to greater willingness to share knowledge.

Proposition 1. Shared leadership in virtual teams will be positively related to knowledge sharing between team members.

TRUST AS A MEDIATOR OF THE SHARED LEADERSHIP-KNOWLEDGE SHARING RELATIONSHIP

The model in Fig. 1 shows that the relationship between shared leadership and knowledge sharing will also be partially mediated by the trust that develops between team members, that is collective trust that exists within the team. Collective trust within a team can be defined as a shared psychological state in which team members accept vulnerability based on the expectations and intentions or behaviors of others within the team (Cummings & Bromiley, 1996; Rousseau, Sitkin, Burt, & Camerer, 1998). In short, trust is a form of willingness to take risk, based on the expectation that others will behave as expected (Jarvenpaa et al., 1998). As discussed below, shared leadership is likely to lead to higher levels of trust within the team, and this increased trust will provide team members with greater motivation to share knowledge.

Relationship Between Shared Leadership and Trust

Researchers have suggested that shared leadership will influence attitudes within a team, such as trust (Pearce & Conger, 2003). Also, Pearce and Sims (2002) showed that shared leadership was a better predictor of social integration within the team than vertical leadership. In virtual teams, trust develops differently than in face-to-face teams. Whereas trust is typically conceptualized as either an affective or a cognitive construct with emphasis on feeling, commitment and exchange (Mayer et al., 1995; McAllister, 1995), Jarvenpaa et al. (1998) showed that for virtual teams who are forming for the first time, trust is based less on these factors, and more on actions that the team members take. Jarvenpaa et al. (1998) studied the antecedents of trust in 75 global virtual teams in order to better understand the specific behaviors that lead to the development of trust. By studying the communication transcripts for the three teams with the highest final trust score, and the three teams with the lowest final trust score, they found that teams with high levels of trust were those with an action orientation in which team members were focused on the task. Action was an important antecedent to trust, and action that went beyond the call of duty strengthened trust.

Shared leadership relies on team members being proactive in assuming leadership responsibilities. In particular, when team members share task leadership responsibilities, they signal to other team members that they are proactive and task focused, resulting in higher levels of the task-based trust that has been found to be so important in virtual teams. Jarvenpaa et al. (1998) did indeed find that rotating leadership was an important characteristic of the high trust teams. The behaviors exhibited by team members were consistent with those associated with shared leadership, that is the "serial emergence" of multiple leaders over the life of the group (Pearce & Conger, 2003; Pearce & Sims, 2000). In these teams, all team members exhibited leadership behaviors throughout the course of the project, as they perceived a need arose. In contrast, teams that were low in trust had no shared leadership, that is, in these teams either one leader emerged with no sharing of leadership among the remaining team members, or no leader emerged.

Relationship Between Trust and Knowledge Sharing

As noted earlier, several knowledge management and organizational learning researchers have argued that higher trust leads to increased knowledge sharing (McEvily, Perrone, & Zaheer, 2003; Scott, 2000), and empirical research has supported this proposition (Levin & Cross, 2004; Mayer et al., 1995; McEvily et al., 2003; Scott, 2000; Szulanski, 2000). Team members are more willing to share information if they believe that other team members will reciprocate. (Argote et al., 2003). Also, trust creates a greater willingness to share knowledge, and to listen to and use the knowledge provided (Levin & Cross, 2004; Mayer et al., 1995; Tsai & Ghoshal, 1998).

Virtual team researchers have also suggested that trust is a critical element for effective virtual team functioning (Jarvenpaa et al., 1998). Building trust in a virtual team is more challenging than in a face-to-face team, but may be even more important for team functioning because in the virtual team environment, other forms of social control and psychological safety are less effective or feasible (Gibson & Manuel, 2003). Jarvenpaa et al. noted that "although trust is important in any type of team, trust is pivotal in preventing geographical distance from leading to psychological distance in a global team" (p. 30). In Jarvenpaa et al.'s study, the low trust teams were characterized by a low-level of communication and knowledge sharing among team members.

Hart and McLeod (2003) conducted a field study of seven virtual work teams in which they examined the relationships between team members and their communication with each other. They observed that team members who developed close relationships exchanged significantly more task-related messages than personal messages. Their findings support Jarvenpaa et al.'s (1998) findings that focusing on shared objectives and tasks is related to closer personal relationships in virtual teams. Hart and McLeod further found that team members with weak relationships to each other exchanged significantly fewer messages compared to team members with strong relationships. In addition, the communications between team members with strong relationships were "simple and direct, largely limited to unequivocal exchange of information" (p. 356). Hart and McLeod concluded that strong relationships between team members resulted in more frequent, clearer and more direct communication.

Proposition 2. Level of trust between members of virtual teams will partially mediate the relationship between shared leadership and knowledge sharing.

In the model presented in Fig. 1, the relationship between trust and knowledge sharing is predicted to be reciprocal. Gibson and Manuel (2003) explain the relationship between knowledge sharing and trust in virtual teams through three mechanisms. First, knowledge sharing involves interaction, and continued interaction is critical for relationship building. Second, sharing information provides evidence of a team member's credibility and trustworthiness. When team members provide unsolicited information this is a demonstration of goodwill and causes other team members to reciprocate, leading to sustained information flow which in turn creates a trusting environment. Third, open and timely communication allows team members to air and discuss differences, hence potentially avoiding conflict that can derail team process and harm team relationships.

THE MODERATING ROLE OF RELIANCE ON TECHNOLOGY-MEDIATED COMMUNICATION

Virtual teams differ in the extent to which they rely on technology-mediated communication (Gibson & Cohen, 2003; Griffith et al., 2003). For example, a team that works together exclusively via e-mail, phone, etc., and never meets face-to-face is a highly virtual team; by contrast, a virtual team that has periodic face-to-face meetings is less virtual. Virtual team researchers point out that it is important to look at the impact of different degrees of virtualness when developing models related to virtual teams (Griffith et al., 2003; Kirkman, Rosen, Tesluk, & Gibson, 2004; Lipnack & Stamps, 2000). For example, Kirkman et al. (2004) examined the relationship between virtual team empowerment and team performance and found that reliance on technology-mediated communication, which they operationalized as the number of face-to-face meetings between team members, moderated this relationship. Empowerment was more important for teams that were more virtual (i.e. fewer face-to-face meetings). Similarly, as shown in Fig. 1, a virtual team's degree of reliance on technology-mediated communication, as opposed to face-to-face communications, is predicted to moderate the shared leadership relationships developed so far in this chapter.

Reliance on Technology-Mediated Communication as a Moderator of the Shared Leadership-Knowledge Sharing Relationship

Proposition 1 argues that shared leadership will increase knowledge sharing within a virtual team because it (1) promotes interaction between team members, leading to greater opportunity to share knowledge (Pearce & Conger, 2003), and (2) increases team members' intrinsic motivation for the task (Avolio et al., 1996; Fisher & Fisher, 1998; Pearce, 1997) leading to greater willingness to share knowledge. As noted earlier, when team members spend time together face-to-face there is more opportunity for interaction that could result in knowledge sharing (Conrath, 1973; Fisher & Fisher, 1998; Monge & Kirste, 1980). Hence, more face-to-face interaction reduces the reliance on shared leadership as a mechanism for team interaction.

Similarly, in a virtual team setting, shared leadership will also be a more important factor for team member motivation, which encourages knowledge sharing. Kirkman et al. (2004) argued that virtual teams rely more on intrinsic motivation for virtual team performance than face-to-face teams. Extrinsic motivation factors, such as rewards and recognition, peer pressure, feedback from organizational stakeholders and customers (Deci & Ryan, 1980; Hackman, 1987), are more easily applied in teams that are face-to-face than in teams who are less connected to each other. Factors, such as shared leadership, that promote intrinsic motivation are likely to be more important for teams that have fewer face-to-face meetings. Consistent with this argument, Kirkman et al. (2004) found that the number of face-to-face meetings between members of a virtual team moderated the relationship between team empowerment (which they argued is a source of intrinsic motivation within the team) and team performance.

In summary, shared leadership is predicted to have a greater impact on knowledge sharing in a virtual team that has fewer opportunities to meet face-to-face than one in which team members have regular face-to-face interaction.

Proposition 3(a). A virtual team's reliance on technology-mediated communication will moderate the relationship between shared leadership and knowledge sharing in the team, such that the greater the use of technology-mediated communication, the stronger the relationship between shared leadership and knowledge sharing.

Reliance on Technology-Mediated Communication as a Moderator of the Shared Leadership-Trust Relationship

Reliance on technology-mediated communication is also predicted to moderate the relationship between shared leadership and trust. As discussed earlier, virtualness can negatively impact the formation of trust between team members, and virtual team researchers have argued that face-to-face encounters can play a critical role in building and repairing trust (Alge et al., 2003; Gibson & Manuel, 2003; Jarvenpaa et al., 1998; Maznevski & Chudoba, 2000; Mortensen & Hinds, 2001). Given this, virtual teams that have fewer face-to-face interactions will rely more heavily on other mechanisms, such as shared leadership to overcome the negative impact of virtualness on trust within the team.

Proposition 3(b). A virtual team's reliance on technology-mediated communication will moderate the relationship between shared leadership and trust in the team, such that the greater the use of technology-mediated communication, the stronger the relationship between shared leadership and trust.

IMPLICATIONS FOR RESEARCH AND PRACTICE

This chapter examined factors that increase collaborative capital in virtual teams as manifested by increased knowledge sharing between team members. Specifically, the model developed in this chapter proposes that shared leadership will be positively related to knowledge sharing in virtual teams, both directly, and through the mediating role of trust in the team. Further, a team's reliance on technology-mediated communication (or, frequency of face-to-face interaction) is predicted to moderate the shared leadership-knowledge sharing and shared leadership-trust relationships shown in the model. This model is a starting point for understanding factors that influence the development of collaborative capital in virtual teams, and more specifically the role of leadership. The message to practitioners is that it is possible to improve the way in which virtual team members work together by developing certain types of leadership behaviors within the team. In order to better guide practitioners who wish to promote shared leadership as a way of building collaborative capital in virtual teams, future research should (1) build on the model in this chapter to gain additional insights into the nature of the shared leadership-collaborative capital relationship, (2) identify other moderators of the shared leadership-collaborative capital relationship, and (3) identify limitations for the model.

The Shared Leadership and Collaborative Capital Relationship

Leadership of teams operating in a virtual environment has been termed "e-leadership" by leadership researchers (Avolio et al., 2001; Cascio & Shurygailo, 2003; Zaccaro & Bader, 2003), and there is a need to better understand this phenomenon, and the role of leadership in facilitating the development of collaborative capital within virtual teams (Avolio et al., 2001; Bell & Kozlowski, 2002; Yukl, 2002). "The trend toward physically dispersed work groups has necessitated a fresh inquiry into the role and nature of team leadership in virtual settings" (Kayworth & Leidner, 2001, p. 7). This chapter suggests that one form of leadership, shared leadership, plays an important role in building collaborative capital.

Virtual team researchers have suggested that shared leadership is particularly important in virtual teams where coordination of team interaction and task is more challenging due to the geographic dispersion of team members (Avolio et al., 2001; Lipnack & Stamps, 1997; Pearce & Conger,

2003; Pearce & Sims, 2000). Similarly, Avolio et al. (2001) questioned whether, in the context of e-leadership, it is better to examine the behaviors of an individual or the collective. Although this chapter has focused on the relationship between shared leadership and knowledge sharing, researchers should also examine other forms of collaborative capital that result from shared leadership. In addition to knowledge sharing, collaborative capital is also manifested in outcomes such as increased innovation and creativity, commitment and involvement, flexibility and adaptability, and enhanced learning. Shared leadership, through its positive influence on interpersonal relationships and cooperative behaviors within the team, is likely to influence other forms of collaborative capital in addition to knowledge sharing.

Research should also focus on understanding which aspects of shared leadership behaviors are more important for building collaborative capital. The model in this chapter treats shared leadership as a one-dimensional construct; however, the leadership literature distinguishes between different types of leadership (Avolio, Bass, & Jung, 1999; Pearce et al., 2003), such as transformational, transactional, and directive. Empirical work to test the model should also consider whether certain types of shared leadership behaviors are more or less influential in building collaborative capital, and under what conditions.

Moderators of the Shared Leadership-Collaborative Capital Relationship

Although, the focus in this chapter has been on the moderating role of reliance on technology-mediated communication, it is likely that other factors, that have been shown to play a role in virtual team functioning might also moderate the relationship between shared leadership and collaborative capital. For example, research has shown that temporal scope is a predictor of virtual team performance, and that virtual teams who have a past history of working together (compared to virtual teams who have no history of working together) develop the same level of trust and knowledge sharing as face-to-face teams (Alge et al., 2003). It is possible, that temporal scope could moderate the relationship between shared leadership and trust, such that shared leadership has less of an impact in developing trust for teams that already have a history of working together. Future research should draw on the virtual teams literature in order to identify other potential moderators of the shared leadership-collaborative capital relationship.

Limitations of the Shared Leadership-Collaborative Model

It is important to identify situations in which the model developed in this chapter may not apply. Pearce and Conger (2003) describe a number of limitations of shared leadership that are applicable here. They suggest that shared leadership will not be effective when team members lack the knowledge, skills and abilities to take on a leadership role, teams do not have sufficient time for shared leadership to develop, and team members are not receptive to other team members exerting influence within the team.

Task interdependence has also been identified as an important factor in determining the relevance of shared leadership in a team. Task interdependence is the degree to which accomplishing the goal of the team requires completing interconnected or dependent subtasks. Van de Ven, Delbecq and Koenig (1976) proposed four basic workflow patterns in teams, that range from low to high interdependence: (1) pooled/additive, in which work is completed separately by each team member and then assembled into a finished product, (2) sequential, in which work is passed in a serial fashion from one team member to another, (3) reciprocal, in which work flows back and forth between team members, and (4) intensive, in which team members must work on tasks simultaneously. More interdependent tasks require higher levels of collaboration and information sharing among team members (Bell & Kozlowski, 2002). In teams with less interdependent tasks, there is less of a need for collaboration and information sharing; hence shared leadership may be less applicable to these types of teams (Cox, Pearce, & Perry, 2003).

The model presented in this chapter provides a basis for several promising areas of future research in the area of collaborative capital in virtual teams. The traditional leadership wisdom is that a team can have only one leader. In fact, the opposite may be true; furthermore, team members that share leadership may in fact develop greater levels of collaborative capital.

REFERENCES

Alge, B. J., Wiethoff, C., & Klein, H. J. (2003). When does the medium matter? Knowledge-building experiences and opportunities in decision-making teams. *Organizational Behavior and Human Decision Processes, 91*(1), 26.

Argote, L., Ingram, P., Levine, J. M., & Moreland, R. L. (2000). Knowledge transfer in organizations: Learning from the experience of others. *Organizational Behavior and Human Decision Processes, 82*(1), 1–8.

Argote, L., McEvily, B., & Reagans, R. (2003). Managing knowledge in organizations: An integrative framework and review of emerging themes. *Management Science, 49*(4), 571.

Athanasiou, R., & Yoshioka, G. A. (1973). The spatial character of friendship formation. *Environment and Behavior, 5*(1), 43–65.

Avolio, B. J., Bass, B. M., & Jung, D. I. (1999). Re-examining the components of transformational and transactional leadership using the Multifactor Leadership Questionnaire. *Journal of Occupational and Organizational Psychology, 72*(4), 441–462.

Avolio, B. J., Jung, D. I., Murry, W., & Sivasubramaniam, N. (1996). Building highly developed teams: Focusing on shared leadership process, efficacy, trust, and performance. In: M. M. Beyerlein, D. A. Johnson & S. T. Beyerlein (Eds), *Advances in interdisciplinary studies of work teams: Team leadership*, (Vol. 3, pp. 173–209). Greenwich, CT: JAI Press, Inc.

Avolio, B. J., Kahai, S., Dumdum, R., & Sivasubramaniam, N. (2001). Virtual teams: Implications for e-leadership and team development. In: M. London (Ed.), *How people evaluate others in organizations* (pp. 337–358). Mahwah, NJ: Lawrence Erlbaum Associates, Publishers.

Bartol, K. M., & Srivastava, A. (2002). Encouraging knowledge sharing: The role of organizational reward systems. *Journal of Leadership and Organizational Studies, 9*(1), 64–76.

Bass, B. M. (1990). *Bass & Stogdill's handbook of leadership: Theory, research, and managerial applications*, Vol. 3. New York: Free Press.

Bell, B. S., & Kozlowski, S. W. J. (2002). A typology of virtual teams: Implications for effective leadership. *Group and Organization Management, 27*(1), 14.

Biggs, M. (2000). Assessing risks today will leave corporate leaders well-prepared for the future of work. *InfoWorld, 22*(39), 100.

Cascio, W. F., & Shurygailo, S. (2003). E-leadership and virtual teams. *Organizational Dynamics, 31*(4), 362–376.

Cohen, W. M., & Levinthal, D. A. (1990). Absorptive capacity: A new perspective on learning and innovation. *Administrative Science Quarterly, 35*(1), 128.

Conrath, D. W. (1973). Communications environment and its relationship to organizational structure. *Management Science, 20*(4), 586.

Cox, J. F., Pearce, C. L., & Perry, M. L. (2003). Toward a model of shared leadership and distributed influence in the innovation process: How shared leadership can enhance new product development team dynamics and effectiveness. In: C. L. Pearce & J. A. Conger (Eds), *Shared leadership: Reframing the hows and whys of leadership* (pp. 48–76). Thousand Oaks, CA: Sage Publications.

Cramton, C. D. (2001). The mutual knowledge problem and its consequences for dispersed collaboration. *Organization Science, 12*(3), 346.

Cramton, C. D., & Orvis, K. L. (2003). Overcoming barriers to information sharing in virtual teams. In: C. B. Gibson & S. G. Cohen (Eds), *Virtual teams that work: Creating conditions for virtual team effectiveness* (pp. 21–36). San Francisco: Jossey-Bass.

Cruz, M. G., Henningsen, D. D., & Smith, B. A. (1999). The impact of directive leadership on group information sampling, decisions, and perceptions of the leader. *Communication Research, 26*(3), 349.

Cummings, L. L., & Bromiley, P. (1996). The organizational trust inventory (OTI): Development and validation. In: R. M. Kramer & T. R. Tyler (Eds), *Trust in organizations: Frontiers of theory and research* (pp. 429–436). Thousand Oaks, CA: Sage Publications, Inc.

Dawes, R. M., Van de Kragt, A. J., & Orbell, J. M. (1988). Not me or thee but we: The importance of group identity in eliciting cooperation in dilemma situations: Experimental manipulations. *Acta Psychologica, 68*(1), 83–97.

Deci, E. L. (1975). *Intrinsic motivation.* New York: Plenum Press.

Deci, E. L., & Flaste, R. (1995). *Why we do what we do: The dynamics of personal autonomy.* New York: Putnam.

Deci, E. L., & Ryan, R. M. (1980). The empirical exploration of intrinsic motivational processes. In: L. Berkowitz (Ed.), *Advances in experimental social psychology* (Vol. 13, pp. 39–80). New York: Academic Press.

Drolet, A. L., & Morris, M. W. (2000). Rapport in conflict resolution. *Journal of Experimental Social Psychology, 36*(1), 26.

Fisher, K., & Fisher, D. F. (1998). *The distributed mind.* New York, NY: American Management Association.

Furst, S., Blackburn, R., & Rosen, B. (1999). Virtual team effectiveness: A proposed research agenda. *Information Systems Journal, 9*(4), 249.

Gibson, C. B. (1997). Do you hear what I hear? A framework for reconciling intercultural communication difficulties arising from cognitive styles and cultural values. In: M. Erez & P. C. Earley (Eds), *New perspectives on international industrial organizational psychology.* San Francisco, CA: Jossey-Bass.

Gibson, C. B., & Manuel, J. A. (2003). Building trust: Effective multicultural communication processes in virtual teams. In: C. B. Gibson & S. G. Cohen (Eds), *Virtual teams that work: Creating conditions for virtual team effectiveness.* San Francisco, CA: Jossey-Bass.

Gibson, C. B., & Cohen, S. G. (Eds) (2003). *Virtual teams that work: Creating conditions for virtual team effectiveness.* San Francisco, CA: Jossey-Bass.

Griffith, T. L., Sawyer, J. E., & Neale, M. A. (2003). Virtualness and knowledge in teams: Managing the love triangle of organizations, individuals, and information technology. *MIS Quarterly, 27*(2), 265–287.

Hackman, J. R. (1987). The design of work teams. In: J. Lorsch (Ed.), *Handbook of organizational behavior* (pp. 315–342). Englewood Cliffs, NJ: Prentice-Hall.

Hart, R. K., & McLeod, P. L. (2003). Rethinking team building in geographically dispersed teams: One message at a time. *Organizational Dynamics, 31*(4), 352–361.

Henningsen, D., Henningsen, M. L., Jakobsen, L., & Borton, I. (2004). It's good to be leader: The influence of randomly and systematically selected leaders on decision-making groups. *Group Dynamics, 8*(1), 62–76.

Hinds, P. J., & Bailey, D. E. (2003). Out of sight, out of sync: Understanding conflict in distributed teams. *Organization Science, 14*(6), 615–632.

Hinds, P. J., & Weisband, S. P. (2003). Knowledge sharing and shared understanding. In: C. B. Gibson & S. G. Cohen (Eds), *Virtual teams that work: Creating conditions for virtual team effectiveness* (pp. 21–36). San Francisco, CA: Jossey-Bass.

Jarvenpaa, S. L., Knoll, K., & Leidner, D. E. (1998). Is anybody out there? Antecedents of trust in global virtual teams. *Journal of Management Information Systems, 14*(4), 29.

Kahn, A., & McGaughey, T. A. (1977). Distance and liking: When moving close produces increased liking. *Social Psychology Quarterly, 40*(2), 138–144.

Kayworth, T. R., & Leidner., D. E. (2001). Leadership effectiveness in global virtual teams. *Journal of Management Information Systems, 18*(3), 7.

Keller, R. T., & Holland, W. E. (1983). Communicators and innovators in research and development organizations. *Academy of Management Journal, 26*(4), 742.

Kirkman, B. L., Rosen, B., Tesluk, P. E., & Gibson, C. B. (2004). The impact of team empowerment on virtual team performance: The moderating role of face-to-face interaction. *Academy of Management Journal, 47*(2), 175–192.

Kraut, R. E., Fussell, S. R., Brennan, S. E., & Siegel, J. (2002). Understanding effects of proximity on collaboration: Implications for technologies to support remote collaborative work. In: P. Hinds & S. Kiesler (Eds), *Distributed work* (pp. 137–162). MIT Press.

Larson, J. R., Christensen, C., Franz, T. M., & Abbott, A. S. (1998). Diagnosing groups: The pooling, management, and impact of shared and unshared case information in team-based medical decision making. *Journal of Personality and Social Psychology, 75*(1), 93–108.

Leonard, D., & Sensiper, S. (1998). The role of tacit knowledge in group innovation. *California Management Review, 40*(3), 112.

Levin, D. Z., & Cross, R. (2004). The strength of weak ties you can trust: The mediating role of trust in effective knowledge transfer. *Management Science, 50*, 1477–1490.

Lipnack, J., & Stamps, J. (2000). *Virtual teams: People working across boundaries with technology*, (2nd ed.). New York: Wiley.

Locke, E. A. (2003). Leadership: Starting at the top. In: C. Pearce & J. A. Conger (Eds), *Shared leadership: Reframing the hows and whys of leadership* (pp. 271–284). Thousand Oaks, CA: Sage Publications.

Mayer, R. C., Davis, J. H., & Schoorman, F. D. (1995). An integrative model of organizational trust. *Academy of Management Review, 20*(3), 709–734.

Maznevski, M. L., & Chudoba, K. (2000). Bridging space over time: Global virtual team dynamics and effectiveness. *Organization Science, 11*(5), 473.

McAllister, D. J. (1995). Affect- and cognition-based trust as foundations for interpersonal cooperation in organizations. *Academy of Management Journal, 38*(1), 24.

McEvily, B., Perrone, V., & Zaheer, A. (2003). Trust as an organizing principle. *Organization Science, 14*(1), 91.

McEvily, B., & Zaheer, A. (1999). Bridging ties: A source of firm heterogeneity in competitive capabilities. *Strategic Management Journal, 20*(12), 1133–1157.

McGinn, K. L., & Croson, R. (2004). What do communication media mean for negotiators? A question of social awareness. In: M. J. Gelfand & J. M. Brett (Eds), *The Handbook of Negotiation and Culture* (pp. 334–349). Palo Alto, CA: Stanford University Press.

Miranda, S. M., & Saunders, C. S. (2003). The social construction of meaning: An alternative perspective on information sharing. *Information Systems Research, 14*(1), 87–107.

Monge, P. R., & Kirste, K. K. (1980). Measuring proximity in human organization. *Social Psychology Quarterly, 43*(1), 110–115.

Mortensen, M., & Hinds, P. J. (2001). Conflict and shared identity in geographically distributed teams. *International Journal of Conflict Management, 12*(3), 212.

Nadler, J., Thompson, L., & Van Boven, L. (2003). Learning negotiation skills: Fours models of knowledge creation and transfer. *Management Science, 49*(4), 529–540.

Nahapiet, J., & Ghoshal, S. (1998). Social capital, intellectual capital, and the organizational advantage. *Academy of Management Review, 23*(2), 242–266.

Nonaka, I. (1994). A dynamic theory of organizational knowledge creation. *Organization Science, 5*, 14–37.

Olson, G. M., & Olson, J. S. (2000). Distance matters. *Human-Computer Interaction, 15*(2/3), 139–178.

Osterloh, M., & Frey, B. S. (2000). Motivation, knowledge transfer, and organizational forms. *Organization Science, 11*(5), 538.

Pearce, C. L. (1997). *The determinants of change management team effectiveness: A longitudinal investigation.* Unpublished doctoral dissertation. University of Maryland, College Park.

Pearce, C. L., & Sims, H. P. (2000). Shared leadership: Toward a multi-level theory of leadership. In: M. M. Beyerlein, D. A. Johnson & S. T. Beyerlein (Eds), *Advances in interdisciplinary studies of work teams: Team development,* (Vol. 7, pp. 115–139). New York: Elsevier Science Inc.

Pearce, C. L., & Sims, H. P. (2002). Vertical versus shared leadership as predictors of the effectiveness of change management teams: An examination of aversive, directive, transactional, transformational, and empowering leader behaviors. *Group Dynamics, 6*(2), 172–197.

Pearce, C. L., & Conger, J. A. (2003). *Shared leadership: Reframing the hows and whys of leadership.* Thousand Oaks, CA: Sage Publications.

Pearce, C. L., Sims, H. P., Cox, J. F., Ball, G., Schnell, E., & Smith, K. (2003). Transactors, transformers and beyond: A multi-method development of a theoretical typology of leadership. *Journal of Management Development, 22*(4), 273–307.

Pearce, C. L., Yoo, Y., & Alavi, M. (2004). Leadership, social work, and virtual teams: The relative influence of vertical vs. shared leadership in the nonprofit section. In: R. E. Riggio & S. Smith Orr (Eds), *Improving leadership in nonprofit organizations.* San Francisco: Jossey-Bass.

Polanyi, M. (1966). *The tacit dimension.* New York: Doubleday.

Reagans, R., & McEvily, B. (2003). Network structure and knowledge transfer: The effects of cohesion and range. *Administrative Science Quarterly, 48*(2), 240–267.

Reagans, R., & Zuckerman, E. (2001). Networks, diversity, and productivity: The social capital of corporate R&D teams. *Organization Science, 12*(4), 502–518.

Rousseau, D. M., Sitkin, S. B., Burt, R. S., & Camerer, C. (1998). Not so different after all: A cross-discipline view of trust. *Academy of Management Review, 23*(3), 393.

Scott, J. E. (2000). Facilitating interorganizational learning with information technology. *Journal of Management Information Systems, 17*(2), 81.

Siegel, J., Dubrovsky, V., Kiesler, S., & McGuire, T. W. (1986). Group processes in computer-mediated communication. *Organizational Behavior and Human Decision Processes, 37*(2), 157.

Stasser, G., & Titus, W. (1985). Pooling of unshared information in group decision making: Biased information sampling during discussion. *Journal of Personality and Social Psychology, 48*(6), 1467–1478.

Straus, S. G. (1997). Technology, group process, and group outcomes: Testing the connections in computer-mediated and face-to-face groups. *Human-Computer Interaction, 12*(3), 227.

Straus, S. G., & McGrath, J. E. (1994). Does the medium matter? The interaction of task type and technology on group performance and member reactions. *Journal of Applied Psychology, 79*(1), 87–97.

Szulanski, G. (2000). The process of knowledge transfer: A diachronic analysis of stickiness. *Organizational Behavior and Human Decision Processes, 82*(1), 9–27.

Taggar, S., & Hackett, R. (1999). Leadership emergence in autonomous work teams: Antecedents and outcomes. *Personnel Psychology, 52*(4), 899.

Townsend, A. M., & DeMarie, S. M. (1998). Virtual teams: Technology and the workplace of the future. *Academy of Management Executive, 12*(3), 17.

Tsai, W., & Ghoshal, S. (1998). Social capital and value creation: The role of intrafirm networks. *Academy of Management Journal, 41*(4), 464.

Von Hippel, E. (1994). "Sticky information" and the locus of problem solving: Implications for innovation. *Management Science, 40*(4), 429.

Van de Ven, A. H., Delbecq, A. L., & Koenig, R. (1976). Determinants of coordination modes within organizations. *American Sociological Review, 41*, 322–328.

Walther, J. B., & Burgoon, J. K. (1992). Relational communication in computer-mediated interaction. *Human Communication Research, 19*(1), 50–88.

Weber, R., & Camerer, C. (2003). Cultural conflict and merger failure: An experimental approach. *Management Science, 49*(4), 400.

Wofford, J. C., Calabro, P. J., & Sims, A. (1975). The relationship of information sharing norms and leader behavior. *Journal of Management, 1*(1), 15.

Yoo, Y., & Alavi, M. (2004). Emergent leadership in virtual teams: What do emergent leaders do? *Information and Organization, 14*(1), 27.

Yukl, G. (2002). *Leadership in organizations* (5th ed.). Englewood Cliffs, NJ: Prentice-Hall.

Zaccaro, S. J., & Bader, P. (2003). E-leadership and the challenges of leading e-teams: Minimizing the bad and maximizing the good. *Organizational Dynamics, 31*(4), 377–387.

LEADERSHIP, COLLABORATIVE CAPITAL, AND INNOVATION

Xiaomeng Zhang and Henry P. Sims, Jr.

ABSTRACT

Based on a four-factor leadership typology, this theoretical chapter proposes four alternative models to investigate how collaborative capital moderates the relationships between leadership and innovation. Beyerlein, Beyerlein, and Kennedy (2004) define collaborative capital as "how well people work together toward shared goals and outcomes." In this chapter, we focus on empowerment as an important manifestation of collaborative capital. That is, first, empowerment enhances collaboration across vertical hierarchical lines through sharing of decision-making authority. Also, since empowerment is typically implemented as a team form of organizational structure, empowered teams enhance collaboration through the process of decentralized team decision-making. Thus, the accumulation of successful empowerment and the qualities of empowered team member represent the collaborative capital. Specifically, the models suggest that empowerment may function as a partial mediator, or as a moderator, or as both, in the basic relationship between transformational leadership and innovation. In addition, although transformational leadership and empowering leadership elicit different attitudes and behaviors of team members that may facilitate innovation, the interactions between these outcomes will maximize the effects of leadership on innovation.

Collaborative Capital: Creating Intangible Value
Advances in Interdisciplinary Studies of Work Teams, Volume 11, 211–236
ISSN: 1572-0977/doi:10.1016/S1572-0977(05)11008-5

The implications of these observations and the possible directions for future research are discussed.

In today's complex, knowledge-rich, and hypercompetitive global environment, innovation has become a key strategy for organizations, especially for organizations attempting to attain a sustainable competitive advantage over a growing group of efficient and professional competitors (Devanna & Tichy, 1990; Halbesleben, Novicevic, Harvey, & Buckley, 2003). Consistent with increasing pressure for innovation as a key strategy, the exploitation and utilization of human capital as a source of innovation has gained importance. The role of team members' innovative behaviors as building blocks for organizational innovation highlights the need for such exploration (Amabile, 1988; Tierney, Farmer, & Graen, 1999). Among the variety of factors that influence team members' creative behaviors and performance, many researchers have identified leadership and empowerment as being the most powerful influences (e.g., Amabile, 1998; Conger & Kanungo, 1988; Jung, 2001; Jung, Chow, & Wu, 2003; Kark, Shamir, & Chen, 2003; Mumford, Scott, Gaddis, & Strange, 2002; Shin & Zhou, 2003; Tierney et al., 1999).

In this chapter, we view empowerment as an important manifestation of collaborative capital. Beyerlein, Beyerlein, and Kennedy (2004) have defined collaborative capital as "… *how well people work together toward shared goals and outcomes.*" To us, empowerment is one form of collaborative capital (not the only form) because the essence of empowerment entails people working together. First, empowerment requires people at different levels in a hierarchy to cooperate. To empower, managers must delegate, facilitate, and, most of all, trust those lower in a hierarchy. In turn, to be empowered, employees must trust leaders who make the decision to share power. Thus, the mutual trust enhances collaboration between leaders and followers to work together toward the common goal. That is, empowerment across hierarchical levels is a form of collaborative capital.

In addition, empowerment is, more often than not, a team or group phenomenon. While individuals can be empowered, the most common form of empowerment in organizations is through some sort of group effort, usually a team. For example, self-managing teams are a common manifestation of collaborative capital in U.S. organizations because the qualities of empowered team members and their accumulated empowerment represent collaborative capital. In self-managing teams, collaboration and trust are necessary elements of the successful function of the team. Effective teams have learned that trust and ability work together, and this represents another manifestation of collaborative capital. In summary, we use the term "empowerment" as a special manifestation of collaborative capital to investigate its influence in leadership–innovation relationship.

Although the extant literature has done much to inform our understanding of leadership's influence on organizational innovative processes (e.g., Fuller, Morrison, Jones, Bridger, & Brown, 1999; Jung & Sosik, 2002), conceptual efforts aiming at open up the black box, or the mechanisms through which leadership influences innovation remains sparse (Jaussi & Dionne, 2003; Jung, 2001; Mumford et al., 2002). Furthermore, prior research has focused on Bass and colleagues' transactional–transformational leadership typology and the impact of transformational leadership on innovation (Bass, 1981, 1998; Bass & Avolio, 1990). A recent chapter by Pearce et al. (2003) clearly indicated that the two-factor theory of leadership did not adequately account for the underlying nature of leadership and proposed a four-factor leadership typology (directive, transactional, transformational, and empowering leadership). Hence, Pearce et al. (2003) is one of the first articles to separate empowering leadership from transformational leadership, thus moving the dynamic leadership typology paradigm ahead and providing an impetus for further exploration of the leadership style–innovation relationship that had been called for by many researchers in the field.

The main purpose of this chapter is to explore how transformational leadership, empowering leadership, and empowerment influence team member innovation. As a beginning model, for example, Jung et al. (2003) proposed a simple intervening model indicating the potential mediating role of empowerment in transformational leadership–innovation relationship. However, we believe the mechanisms of empowerment in leadership–innovation links are more complex because leaders can affect team members' innovative behaviors in both direct and indirect way. Following this logic, we argue that empowerment may function as a mediator, or a moderator, or both theoretically. Thus, multiple configurations are necessary to specify the complexity among leadership, empowerment, and innovation.

The remainder of this chapter is organized as follows. The next three sections provide an overview of the relevant literature about leadership typology, empowerment, and innovation, respectively, as the basis for the generation of propositions. The following section then provides the construction of four models (a mediating model, a moderating model, and two integrative models) that investigate the relationships between leadership, empowerment, and team members' innovative behaviors. The chapter concludes with future research implications.

In summary, our models will begin with leadership as a prominent driving variable, which, in turn, creates empowerment (a manifestation of collaborative capital), which finally enhances team member innovation. We will propose and discuss several alternative models of these three classes of variables: (1) leadership, (2) empowerment, and (3) innovation.

LEADERSHIP

We define leadership similar to Yukl's (2002) treatment of leadership as influence. That is, leadership consists of patterns of behavior of a person that influence other entities such as individuals and teams. It is common to conceptualize leadership as a typology, which defines patterns or clusters of leader behaviors (Yukl, 2002). Leadership typologies have changed and evolved over the past few decades. From the very beginning of the Ohio State leadership behaviors (e.g., consideration and initiating structure), articulated by a group of Ohio State researchers (Fleishman, 1973; Judge, Piccolo, & Illies, 2004), to the currently dominant transactional–transformational paradigm identified by Bass and his colleagues (Bass, 1981; 1998; Bass, & Avolio, 1990), researchers have explored and articulated typologies that could clearly delineate classes or patterns of leader behavior. Although there is no "one best" typology, the more we can capture the conceptual representations of leadership, the more effectively real leaders can behave in practice (Pearce et al., 2003).

Numerous empirical studies of the relationships between leadership and individual, team, and organizational outcomes have been conducted based on the transactional–transformational paradigm. Clearly, this typology of leadership is the dominant conceptualization of leadership today. However, despite its popularity, the two-factor theory of leadership has been criticized for oversimplifying a complicated phenomenon (Yukl, 1989) and cannot adequately account for many other aspects of the leadership phenomenon (Pearce et al., 2003; Sims Jr. & Manz, 1996; Yukl, 2002). For example, Judge et al. (2004) objected to the omission of earlier stages of leadership theory by deploring the fact that initiating structure (directiveness) had become a "forgotten" aspect of leadership theory. Moreover, Pearce et al. (2003) extended the transactional–transformational model of leadership by deductively developing four theoretical behavioral types of leadership based on a historical analysis of the leadership literature: directive leadership, transactional leadership, transformational leadership, and empowering leadership. In this chapter, we will mainly depend on the Pearce et al. (2003) typology, which is an extended version of the more dominant transactional–transformational typology.

Directive leadership describes leader behaviors that primarily rely on position or coercive power. Directive leaders define and organize the roles of followers and emphasize direction, command, assigned goals, and punishments (Sims Jr. & Manz, 1996). Followers rarely exert control over their jobs and have almost no chance to participate in decision-making processes.

Transactional leadership refers to the behaviors that establish the conditions of the exchange relationship between leaders and followers. In line with expectancy theory and reinforcing theory, transactional leaders exert influence in terms of specifying expectation, clarifying responsibilities, negotiating contracts, providing feedback, and exchanging rewards and recognitions for accomplishments (Bass, Avolio, Jung, & Berson, 2003).

In contrast, transformational leadership goes beyond the exchange of inducements for desired performance (Bass, 1985) and involves developing, intellectually stimulating, and inspiring followers to transcend their own self-interests for a higher collective purpose, mission, or vision (Howell & Avolio, 1993). In addition, transformational leaders exhibit charismatic behaviors that provide a sense of vision, encourage followers to view problems from new perspectives to challenge the status quo, and help them to reach their potential and generate the highest level of performance (Dvir, Eden, Avolio, & Shamir, 2002; Pearce et al., 2003).

Finally, empowering leadership emphasizes the development of followers' self-management or self-leadership skills, encourages opportunity thinking, self-rewards, participative goal setting, and teamwork. Consequently, empowering leadership builds subordinates into effective self-leaders who are capable of creativity, initiative, and the ability to act on their own volitions (Pearce et al., 2003).

Earlier formulations of transformational leadership did not include empowerment as an important aspect. However, some more recent views have extended the concept of transformational leadership to include empowering behaviors (Bass, 1997; Dvir et al., 2002; Kark et al., 2003). In contrast, Pearce et al. (2003), and Manz and Sims Jr. (2001) have maintained that empowering leadership is conceptually and empirically distinct from transformational leadership. Therefore, in this study, we do not treat empowering leadership as a subset of transformational leadership, but view it as a conceptually and behaviorally distinct type of leadership.

In sum, Pearce et al. (2003) indicated that these four types of leadership are conceptually and empirically different from each other and that they represent distinctively separate constructs. Table 1 (adapted from Pearce &

Table 1. Theoretical Bases and Representative Behaviors of Four Types of Leader Behavior.

Leader Type	Theoretical Bases	Representative Behaviors
Directive leadership	Theory X management (McGregor, 1960) Initiating structure behavior from Ohio State studies (e.g. Fleishman, 1953) Task-oriented behavior from Michigan studies (e.g., Bass, 1967)	Issuing instructions and commands Assigning goals
Transactional leadership	Expectancy theory (e.g., Vroom, 1964) Equity theory (e.g., Adams, 1963) Path goal theory (e.g., House, 1971) Exchange theory (e.g., Homans, 1958)	Providing personal rewards Providing material rewards Managing by exception (active) Managing by exception (passive)
Transformational leadership	Sociology of charisma (e.g., Weber, 1946, 1947) Charismatic leadership (e.g., House, 1977) Transforming leadership (e.g., Burns, 1978) Transformational leadership (e.g., Bass, 1985)	Providing vision Expressing idealism Using inspirational communication Having high-performance expectations
Empowering leadership	Behavioral self-management (e.g. Thorenson & Mahoney, 1974) Social cognitive theory (e.g., Bandura, 1986) Cognitive behavior modification (e.g., Meichenbaum, 1977) Participative goal setting (e.g., Locke & Latham, 1990)	Encouraging independent action Encouraging opportunity thinking Encouraging teamwork Encouraging self-development Participative goal setting Encouraging self-reward

Source: From Pearce and Sims Jr. (2002).

Sims Jr., 2002) represents the historical analysis and behaviors that underlie each of the four main types of leadership.

The interest of this study is to explore the relationships among leadership, empowerment, and innovation. For purposes of further theoretical development in this chapter, we will focus only on transformational and empowering leadership. These two types of leaderships promote subordinates' potential development and creative thinking and emphasize empowerment. Directive and transactional leaderships, on the other hand, lack such innovation inducements due to their up–down coercion, exchange-based agreement, and rule enforcement nature.

EMPOWERMENT

There has been a growing interest in the study of empowerment and related management practices among both management researchers and practitioners (Conger & Kanungo, 1988; Kirkman & Rosen, 1999; Liden, Wayne, & Sparrowe, 2000; Manz & Sims Jr., 1993; Seibert, Silver, & Randolph, 2004; Spreitzer, 1995). Widespread interest in empowerment comes at a time when global competition and profound change require employee initiative and innovation (Drucker, 1988). In response to increasing global competition, many companies have undergone dramatic structural changes, transforming from traditional hierarchical management to empowered work team structure, to improve the overall flexibility and the efficiency of the organization (Arnold, Arad, Rhoades, & Drasgow, 2000). From a cognitive perspective, empowerment has been defined as the increased self-efficacy and the intrinsic task motivation manifested in cognitions that reflect a team member's active orientation to his or her work role (Conger & Kanungo, 1987; Spreitzer, 1995). From a management practices perspective, vertically, empowerment strengthens collaboration across vertical hierarchical lines in organizations through sharing of decision-making authority; horizontally, empowered teams enhance collaboration through the process of decentralized team decision-making. Such delegation and increase autonomy boost team members' self-efficacy and intrinsic motivation. Combining both perspectives represents a comprehensive view of empowerment.

Studies on leadership suggest that the practice of empowering followers is an important component of team and organizational effectiveness (Bass, 1997; Bennis & Nanus, 1985; Conger & Kanungo, 1988; Dvir et al., 2002; Kark et al., 2003; Manz & Sims Jr., 1993). For example, Bass (1997) indicated that the impact of transformational leadership on follower's performance stemmed from followers' empowerment and development, which increased followers' motivation and ability. Conger and Kanungo (1988), and Kark et al. (2003) also implied that transformational leadership had clear empowering effects on followers, in terms of raising their self-efficacy. This results in higher-performance ratings.

In addition, the relationship between transformational leadership and empowerment is now well founded in the literature. In a longitudinal, randomized field experiment, Dvir et al. (2002) indicated that transformational leadership has a positive impact on the development of followers' empowerment. Specifically, transformational leadership influenced subordinates' self-efficacy and critical-independent approach. The critical-independent approach is an essential empowerment-related process that places an emphasis on the development of followers' self-management and self-development. The empowerment of followers is often recognized as one of the most important features that distinguish transformational leadership from transactional leadership (which does not aim to empower followers but merely to influence their behaviors). To achieve these ends, transformational leadership includes empowering behaviors such as delegation of responsibility to followers, enhancing followers' capacity to think on their own, and encouraging them to generate new and creative ideas. Furthermore, both Jung et al. (2003) and Jung and Sosik (2002) revealed a positive relationship between transformational leadership and empowerment.

Compared to transformational leadership, empowering leadership has received considerably less attention. Although, by definition, empowering leaders influence their followers through empowerment, no theoretical or empirical research, to the authors' knowledge, has conceptualized or tested the relationship between empowering leadership and follower empowerment. Note carefully that, conceptually, we regard empowering leadership as actions and behaviors by the leader, while empowerment is an attribute of the follower. In essence, the leader acts to empower, while the follower is (or is not) empowered.

Two perspectives underlie the link between empowering leadership and empowerment. First, empowering leadership emphasizes followers' self-influence and self-management by encouraging them to act on their own instead of telling them what to do. Such an emphasis increases intrinsic task motivation because followers play an active role in processes, such as participative goal setting and decision-making. Further, the ultimate goal of empowering leadership is to help followers establish self-leadership, broadly conceptualized as the influence that people exert over themselves and the intention to control their own behaviors (Manz & Sims Jr., 1990; Sims Jr. &

Manz, 1996). Indeed, self-leadership is a form of empowerment. In other words, empowering leaders intend to develop the actions and thoughts followers use to motivate themselves from within. The primary mechanism through which such influence occurs is self-efficacy, which is the belief in his or her ability to successfully perform tasks (Bandura, 1986). It is only when people believe that they have the ability to lead themselves that they can become real self-leaders. Therefore, empowering leadership influences followers' self-control by increasing their self-efficacy and intrinsic motivation. It is reasonable to say that the impact of empowering leadership on followers could be explained by empowerment. In addition, since previous research indicated a positive relationship between transformational leadership and empowerment, and Pearce et al. (2003) also showed that four types of leadership were highly and positively correlated, we expect a positive relationship between empowering leadership and empowerment.

Second, although both transformational and empowering leaderships seem to be related to empowerment, these two leadership types are distinct with different foci. Besides empowering followers to make them partners in a quest to achieve important objectives, transformational leaders also provide a sense of vision, which prompts followers to transcend their self-interest to a higher collective level. Such transcendence is sometimes accompanied by sacrifice. Clearly, this transformation is less likely to relate to empowerment. In addition, charismatic leadership (which we regard here as a subset of transformational leadership) emphasizes the need for radical change that can only be accomplished if followers put their trust in the leaders' unique expertise (Yukl, 1999). This is the bottom–up process opposite to the top–down empowerment process. However, the core of empowering leadership is empowerment, with which empowering leaders can develop followers' self-management and self-leadership skills and eventually mold them into self-leaders. Therefore, we expect that the positive correlation between empowering leadership and empowerment would be stronger than the correlation between transformational leadership and empowerment. In sum, we propose the following proposition with Fig. 1. By doing so, we establish the foundation premise for the subsequent four alternative models investigating the role of empowerment in leadership–innovation links:

Proposition 1. Both transformational leadership and empowering leadership are positively related to empowerment, but empowerment is more strongly related to empowering leadership than transformational leadership; that is, the positive partial correlation between empowering leadership and empowerment is higher than the positive partial correlation between

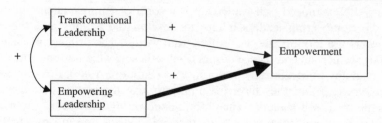

Fig. 1. Relationship between transformational leadership, empowering leadership, and empowerment.

transformational leadership and empowerment. (Note that the partial correlation controls for the effect of the other leadership type.)

INNOVATION

Nowadays, the rapid pace of change, increasingly turbulent environments, and unpredictability of technological change force most firms to face serious competitive challenges (Dess & Pickens, 2000; Mumford, Connelly, & Gaddis, 2003). The central role of innovation in the long-term survival of organizations provokes continuing interest among both social scientists and practitioners (Scott & Bruce, 1994). Innovation is a multi-stage process that includes generation, development, and implementation of novel and useful ideas or behaviors. Different individual, team, and organizational activities and behaviors are necessary at each stage of the innovation process. An innovation can be a new product or service, a new production process technology, a new structure or administrative system, or a new plan or program pertaining to organizational members (Damanpour, 1991; Kanter, 1988; Scott & Bruce, 1994).

Since the foundation of innovation is ideas, the study of what motivates or enables innovative behavior is critical (Scott & Bruce, 1994). In regard to the research on the effectiveness and innovation of teams, creative performance of team members is potentially relevant. Research indicates that ability, self-efficacy, intrinsic motivation, and other needs of team members are important for the functioning of the entire team (Stoker, Looise, Fisscher & Jong, 2001). This is because innovation begins with problem recognition, and the generation of novel and useful ideas or solutions, which often occurs at the team member level. It is this initial step that provides a team and an organization with important raw materials for subsequent development and possible implementation (Oldham & Cummings, 1996; Woodman, Sawyer & Griffin, 1993).

Numerous studies have investigated the determinants of innovative behaviors of team members such as employees' creativity-relevant personal characteristics, and supportive supervision (Oldham & Cummings, 1996), individual problem-solving style, work group relations, task characteristics, leader–member exchange, leader role expectation (Scott & Bruce, 1994), managerial attitudes, technical knowledge resources, administrative intensity, external and internal communication, and professionalism (Damanpour, 1991). Among the variety of factors that affect innovative behaviors, leadership acts as one of the most important roles in the innovation process (Anderson & West, 1998; Damanpour, 1987, 1991; Mumford et al., 2003; Oldham & Cummings, 1996; Scott & Bruce, 1994; Sosik, Kahai, & Avolio, 1998, 1999).

In a meta-analysis of the relationships between innovation and its determinants, Damanpour (1991) indicated managerial attitude toward change and administrative intensity were important determinants and positively related to innovation. Managers' favorable attitude toward change leads to an internal climate conducive to innovation. Managerial support for innovation is especially required in the implementation stage, when coordination and conflict resolution among team members and units are essential. Administrative intensity refers to a higher proportion of managers who facilitate innovation because the successful adoption of an innovation depends largely on the leadership, support, and coordination mangers provide (Damanpour, 1987). In addition, Scott and Bruce (1994) found leadership, support for innovation, and managerial role expectation to be significantly related to innovation. Their study also indicated that innovative behavior was related to the quality of the supervisor–subordinate relationship. High-quality dyadic relationships may give subordinates the levels of autonomy and discretion necessary for innovation to emerge (Grane & Scandura, 1987). What's more, their findings implied that individuals generalized their supervisor–subordinate relationships to their teams and organizations. This was because of the fact that subordinates who reported having relationships with their supervisors characterized by high levels of support, trust, and autonomy also reported the team and organization to be supportive of innovation and judged the resource supply to be high.

The above empirical studies unanimously indicate that leader's attitudes of support for innovation significantly facilitate followers' innovative behaviors. Actually, supervisory style (supportive or controlling) is often considered a potent determinant of employee innovations at work (Deci & Ryan, 1987; Oldham & Cummings, 1996). In particular, supportive supervision is expected to facilitate innovation because supportive supervisors' concerns for employees' feelings and needs encourage followers to voice their own concerns and actively participate, provide them with timely feedback, and emphasize the development of personal skills. All of these are expected to promote employees' self-determination and their intrinsic motivation. Consequently, intrinsic motivation and self-determination are expected to increase work-related interests and enhance creative achievement. In contrast, controlling supervision is expected to diminish creative performance (Deci, Connell, & Ryan, 1989), because controlling supervisors closely monitor employee behaviors, make decisions on their own, and do not encourage creative thinking but pressure employees to think and behave in certain ways. Such supervisory control behaviors undermine intrinsic motivation and distract employees from focusing on job-related activities and toward external pressures (Deci et al., 1989; Oldham & Cummings, 1996). Since intrinsic motivation is considered as an essential determinant of innovation (Deci & Ryan, 1987), the reduced intrinsic motivation that results from controlling supervision will impede creative performance.

As a matter of fact, the characteristics of supportive supervisory style are quite consistent with that of empowerment discussed above. Both viewpoints emphasize employees' self-determination and intrinsic motivation, which are the core determinants of innovation behaviors. In the next section, we explore the relationships between leadership, empowerment, and innovation, with special focus on both transformational and empowering leadership.

LEADERSHIP, EMPOWERMENT, AND INNOVATION

Although previous studies support the notion that leadership plays a fundamental role in the innovation process, the leadership typologies discussed in section Leadership suggest that not all types of leadership facilitate innovation (e.g., directive leadership and transactional leadership). Therefore, a particularly promising direction for studying the relationship between leadership and innovation is to specify the unique or distinctive role of particular types of leadership such as transformational and empowering leadership on innovation. In this section we construct four different models: a mediating model, a moderating model, and two integrative models, in order to explore the role of empowerment in the relationships between leadership and innovation.

The Mediating Model

Transformational leadership can affect team members' innovative behaviors in both direct and indirect ways (Jung et al., 2003). Directly, transformational leaders go beyond providing extrinsic motivation for desired performance specified in the leader–follower exchange contract by being actively involved in followers' personal values (Bass, 1985; Shamir, House, & Arthur, 1993). They encourage followers to challenge the status quo and think about old problems in new ways. In addition, transformational leaders promote innovation by emphasizing long-term and vision-based motivational processes (Bass & Avolio, 1997). This emphasis increases followers' intrinsic motivation and higher-level needs (Tierney et al., 1999). Several studies have examined the direct relationship between transformational leadership and innovation and found positive results (e.g., Howell & Avolio, 1993; Jung et al., 2003; Keller, 1992; Sosik, Kahai, & Avolio, 1998).

Indirectly, leaders establish a welcoming group environment where team members are encouraged to explore all kinds of innovative approaches without the threat of punishment in the event of negative outcomes (Amabile, Conti, Coon, Lazenby, & Herron, 1996). In this environment, transformational leaders seek followers' participation by emphasizing the importance of cooperation and shared experience, and meanwhile followers are empowered to seek innovative approaches to perform their job (Jung et al., 2003). People who are empowered are more likely to be intrinsically motivated because they feel self-efficacious and less constrained, thus facilitating innovative performance (Jung & Sosik, 2002; Redmond, Mumford, & Teach, 1993). Therefore, according to this viewpoint, transformational leadership works through empowerment to influence followers' innovation behaviors.

A few empirical studies investigated the mediating role of empowerment in the relationship between transformational leadership and innovation. This work was particularly inspiring for the theoretical development of our chapter. For example, Jung (2001) argued that transformational leaders' encouragement of innovative ideas and a participative decision-making process through empowerment was an important reason for creativity among followers. Janssen, Schoonebeek, and Van Looy (1997) concluded from a study of information technology (IT) organizations that considerate

and consultative leadership correlates with the empowerment of the followers, and that, in turn, empowerment correlates with innovative behavior,
which further correlates with effectiveness and innovativeness (Stoker et al.,
2001). In addition, Jung et al. (2003) found that transformational leadership
was positively related to both empowerment and innovation. However, they
unexpectedly found a significant but negative relationship between empowerment and innovation, which seems to obscure the mediation effect of
empowerment. They pointed out that their sample of Taiwanese subjects
was relatively high in power control, which would weaken the empowerment
effect on followers' innovation. Another plausible reason is that the high
correlation between empowerment and the support for innovation simultaneously occurred in the model, confounding the positive relationship between empowerment and innovation. Therefore, empowerment's role as a
mediator between transformational leadership and innovation is still worthy
of future exploration. Based on the discussion above, we propose that empowerment functions as a mediator between transformational leadership
and innovation. Since many empirical studies found a direct and positive
relationship between transformational leadership and innovation, there
should be a partial mediation effect. Accordingly:

Proposition 2. Transformational leadership is positively related to empowerment, which, in turn, is positively related to innovation behaviors.
In sum, empowerment partially mediates the relationship between transformational leadership and innovation.

Similar to the relationship between empowering leadership and empowerment, the links between empowering leadership, empowerment, and innovation is almost a virgin land. Theoretically, empowering leaders develop
followers' self-management and self-leadership skills by delegating authority
or autonomy to them to make decisions and implement actions without
direct supervision or intervention (Bass, 1985; Jung et al., 2003). Autonomy
is an important determinant of innovative behaviors because the increased
control over tasks boosts followers' intrinsic motivation, thus significantly
inspiring creativity (Amabile et al., 1996). In addition, autonomy provides
team members with flexibility; Thomas and Velthouse (1990) posited a link
between empowerment and flexibility, which may contribute to innovative
behaviors. Zhou (1998) found that employees who worked in high-task
autonomy environments generated the most creative ideas. Damanpour
(1991) also indicated that centralization (lack of empowerment) was negatively related to innovation. In sum, empowering leadership influences
team members' self-control by increasing their self-efficacy and intrinsic

motivation, in other words, by empowerment. Therefore, we expect that empowerment also functions as a mediator between empowering leadership and innovation. Although there are no empirical results verifying the direct positive relationship between empowering leadership and innovation, we would still anticipate a direct and positive relationship due to (1) the important role of leadership in innovation process discussed in section Innovation, and (2) the positive correlation between transformational and empowering leadership. In addition, based on the possible higher correlation between empowering leadership and empowerment proposed in Proposition 1, we expect a stronger mediating effect of empowerment for empowering leadership. Therefore, we propose the following propositions illustrated in Fig. 2:

Proposition 3. Empowering leadership is positively related to empowerment, which in turn is positively related to innovation. In sum, empowerment partially mediates the relationship between empowering leadership and innovation.

Proposition 4. On the basis of Proposition 1, the mediating effect of empowerment on innovation is stronger for empowering leadership than for transformational leadership.

The Moderating Model

Mediation is not the only way that empowerment exerts its influence in the leadership–innovation relationship. It is reasonable to assume that transformational leaders encourage followers to challenge the status quo and stimulate change without empowerment, and followers who are stimulated or inspired are more likely to become involved in innovative behaviors.

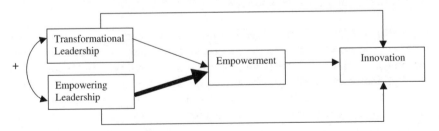

Fig. 2. Mediation relationship between transformational leadership, empowering leadership, empowerment, and innovation.

However, the presence of empowerment would significantly enhance the positive effects of transformational leadership behaviors on followers' performance, because empowerment increases employees' self-efficacy and intrinsic motivation, both of which are critical to the employees' commitment to and involvement in the job (Conger & Kanungo, 1988; Dvir et al., 2002; Spreitzer, 1995). Therefore, empowerment could interact with leadership to affect team members' performance. In essence, this interaction suggests that empowerment would function as a moderator.

Fuller et al. (1999) examined the effect of psychological empowerment on transformational leadership and job satisfaction based on the transactional–transformational leadership paradigm. They found that psychological empowerment moderated the relationship between three of the four dimensions of transformational leadership (idealized influence, inspiration, and individualized consideration) and followers' job satisfaction. Until now, no empirical research has investigated the moderating role of empowerment in a transformational leadership–innovation relationship except Jung et al. (2003), who conducted the research at the organizational level. They hypothesized that empowerment moderated the relationship between transformational leadership and organizational innovation, and further, that the relationship would be stronger when empowerment was higher rather than lower. Results indicated that although the path coefficient was higher in the high-empowerment group than in the low-empowerment group, the difference was not statistically significant. Therefore, the lack of empirical investigations and the lack of results make it unclear whether the interaction between transformational leadership and empowerment would significantly increase innovation behaviors. This leaves a rich space for future research:

Proposition 5. Empowerment moderates the relationship between transformational leadership and innovation; more specifically, a higher level of empowerment strengthens this relationship.

Similar to transformational leadership, empowerment could also interact with empowering leadership to enhance team members' innovation behaviors such that higher levels of empowerment strengthen the relationship through increased perceptions of autonomy and control. In addition, based on the possibility of a higher correlation between empowering leadership and empowerment proposed in Proposition 1, we would expect a stronger interaction effect between empowerment and empowering leadership compared to transformational leadership. Therefore, we propose the following propositions with Fig. 3:

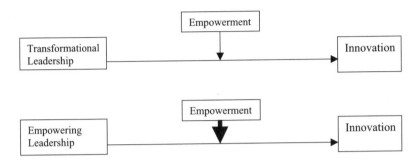

Fig. 3. Moderation relationship between transformational leadership, empowering leadership, empowerment, and innovation.

Proposition 6. Empowerment moderates the relationship between empowering leadership and innovation behavior; more specifically, a higher level of empowerment strengthens this relationship.

Proposition 7. On the basis of Proposition 1, the moderating effect of empowerment on innovation is stronger for empowering leadership than for transformational leadership (or the interaction effect between empowerment and empowering leadership on innovation is stronger than that between empowerment and transformational leadership on innovation).

The Integrative Models

Theoretically, empowerment could work as a mediator, moderator, or as *both* in the relationship between leadership and innovation. Based on the above discussion about the mediating and moderating model, we propose two integrative models indicating a combined role of empowerment.

In Fig. 4, empowerment works as both a partial mediator and a moderator between transformational and empowering leaderships and team member innovative behaviors. This model indicates that empowerment is a very essential, although not indispensable, mechanism through which both transformational and empowering leaders work to stimulate and inspire innovation behaviors of team members. First, empowerment functions as a partial mediator, demonstrating that some behaviors of transformational and empowering leaders first directly enhance followers' empowerment as a way to increase their innovative behaviors. For transformational leadership, leaders inspire followers, emphasize shared experience, and create a group

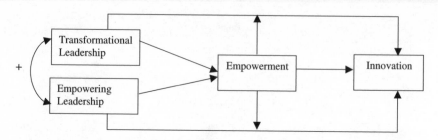

Fig. 4. Integrative model 1.

environment where followers feel empowered to seek an innovative approach to performing their job without fear of being punished. Through these efforts, leaders endeavor to increase team members' self-efficacy and intrinsic motivation by giving them a chance to participate without hesitation. For empowering leadership, leaders delegate autonomy and authority to followers to develop their self-management and self-leadership skills. Autonomy increases team members' intrinsic motivation and flexibility, thus inspiring creativity.

Second, empowerment functions as a moderator. As we discussed in the moderating model, not every behavior of transformational and empowering leadership aims to increase followers' self-efficacy and intrinsic motivation. Some leader behaviors that are not related to empowerment are also conductive to innovative behaviors. These include charismatic behaviors in transformational leadership or encouragement of opportunistic thinking in empowering leadership. However, the presence of empowerment mechanisms will significantly increase the positive effects of these leader behaviors on followers' innovative behaviors. For example, one charismatic leader who is personally very creative and innovative establishes a vision or model for followers to follow. But only when followers are empowered to a certain degree, can they really implement that vision by engaging in innovative behaviors themselves. In this mechanism, empowerment acts as a catalyst in facilitating the effect of leadership on innovation.

In sum, this model integrates both the mediating model and moderating model by indicating that different leadership behaviors work with empowerment through specific mechanisms to affect innovative behaviors:

Proposition 8. Empowerment can act as both a moderator and a partial mediator simultaneously in the relationship between transformational leadership, empowering leadership, and innovation.

However, in both the mediation and moderation model, empowering leadership would have a stronger effect on innovation through or interacting with empowerment. This view is not reflected in the above model. Therefore, we propose a second integrative model to address this issue. Basically, we expect empowering leadership to have a stronger effect than transformational leadership.

As we already know from the above discussion, transformational and empowering leadership are both important for encouraging and stimulating innovative behaviors, although the two work in different ways. Thus, it is necessary for organizations to have both types of leadership in order to maximize innovation. However, this does not necessarily mean that one organization should have different leaders, each possessing different types of leadership, respectively. Pearce et al. (2003) indicated that various types of leadership are conceptually and empirically distinct, yet highly related. Therefore, within a single leader, those forms of leadership are not mutually exclusive, and leaders need not choose between being one type vs. another type. Indeed, a specific leader may actually use behaviors from more than one type, which is the essence of the integrative model shown in Fig. 5.

Fig. 5 indicates that when leaders aim at stimulating team members' innovative behaviors, they should use empowering leadership behaviors to increase followers' self-efficacy and intrinsic motivation through empowerment. At the same time, they should also use transformational leadership behaviors to encourage followers to challenge the status quo and think about old problems in new ways, provide a sense of vision, elicit inspiration from followers, and stimulate change intellectually. All of these attitudinal and behavioral outcomes elicited by empowering and transformational leadership would facilitate innovative behaviors of team members. However, when these behaviors interact, they will produce the optimal effect on innovation.

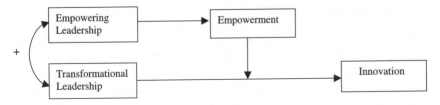

Fig. 5. Integrative model 2.

In sum, based on Proposition 1, that empowerment is more directly related to empowering leadership than transformational leadership, this model suggests that for organizations seeking to stimulate innovation, empowerment from empowering leadership will strengthen the positive effect of transformational leadership on innovative behaviors. Therefore, both types of leadership, which can exist within the same leader, are necessary and empowerment is an important mechanism through which transformational and empowering leadership are related to each other in their influence on innovative behaviors:

> **Proposition 9.** Empowerment elicited from empowering leadership moderates the relationship between transformational leadership and innovation; more specifically, such interaction maximizes the effect of leadership on innovation.

CONCLUSION

As we move into the 21st century, the globalization of the competitive environment, the increasing complexity of work processes, and the rapid pace of technological advancement accentuates the need for innovation in order to achieve sustained competitive advantage (Halbesleben et al., 2003; Mumford et al., 2002). A key catalyst of innovation facilitation is leadership with appropriate characteristics for influencing creativity in the workplace (Halbesleben et al., 2003). Although the past decade has witnessed a burgeoning of interest in creativity and innovation research (Zhou & George, 2003; Zhou & Shalley, 2003), little has been done to integrate innovation research with leadership theory. In addition, the leadership typology is, per se, a dynamic paradigm. Hence, we are still not clear about which leader behaviors are appropriate for promoting innovation, and through which mechanisms. The purpose of this chapter is to explore how transformational leadership and empowering leadership influence innovation through the creation of collaborative capital that is manifested as empowerment within the team.

In this chapter, we propose four models, including a mediation model, a moderation model, and two integrative models to investigate the possible role of collaborative capital in leadership–innovation relationships. These models suggest that both transformational leadership and empowering leadership are positively related to empowerment, with the positive correlation between empowering leadership and empowerment expected to be higher due to its special focus on empowerment. Based on this proposition, four different models indicate that empowerment, a form of collaborative capital, may function as a partial mediator, or a moderator, or both in the leadership–innovation relationship. In each model, empowering leadership has a stronger effect on empowerment directed at team members' innovative behaviors. In addition, although transformational and empowering leadership elicit different attitudes and behaviors of team members, the use of both of these leadership types maximizes the effect of leadership on innovation.

Like any research, this one is not without limitations. First, this chapter only investigated the effect of leadership and empowerment on team members' innovative behaviors. However, more attention should be devoted to innovation at the organizational level, because this is the final stage at which those novel and useful ideas generated at the team level become mass-produced and implemented. If leadership only stimulates individuals or team members to generate innovative ideas irrespective of the pragmatic implications, the effects of leadership on innovation will be discounted. Therefore, future research should devote more efforts to the exploration of the different effects of transformational leadership, empowering leadership, and empowerment on organizational level innovation.

Second, this study does not consider the possible curvilinear relationship between autonomy and innovation. Pelz and Andrews (1976) found that both overly loose and overly tight control tended to inhibit innovation with productivity and motivation peaking at moderate levels of control (Mumford et al., 2002). Therefore, even for empowering leaders who aim to mold followers into self-leaders, certain guidance and control seems to be necessary when a leader attempts to stimulate followers' innovative behaviors. Future research may look into this issue more deeply to see whether a curvilinear relationship would confound the tentative models when autonomy is high.

Empirical investigation of the above alternative models will help us more comprehensively and thoroughly understand the potential functions of empowerment. Future studies may use appropriate measures for the concepts articulated in this study in a longitudinal setting, which is conducive to the examination of the direction of causality. The work of Pearce and Sims Jr. (2002), for example, demonstrates the measurement of both transformational and empowering leadership. In addition, structural equation modeling methods can be employed to effectively compare the total variance between the different models proposed here to indicate which model provides the best fit.

Despite the limitations, this view of leadership and innovation contributes to the literature and practice in two important ways. First, it extends the leadership research from the currently dominant transactional–transformational leadership typology to a broader and dynamic four-factor leadership typology by articulating the different roles and effects of transformational and empowering leadership on innovation. Previous studies have not differentiated beyond these two types of leadership. In addition, the four different models also point out future research orientations. Second, the chapter contributes to practice by articulating that both transformational and empowering leadership styles, with different foci, are important facilitators of innovative behaviors. Further, the alternative models suggest alternative configuration by which empowerment, as a manifestation of collaborative capital, mediates and moderates the relationship between leadership and innovation. Most of all, the theoretical analysis reported here suggests that organizations should emphasize and utilize both transformational and empowering leadership as a means to enhance collaborative capital and subsequent innovation.

REFERENCES

Adams, J. S. (1963). Wage inequities, productivity, and work quality. *Industrial Relations, 3,* 9–16.
Amabile, T. M. (1988). A model of creativity and innovation in organizations. In: B. M. Staw & L. L. Cummings (Eds), *Research in organizational behavior*, Vol. 10 (pp. 123–167). Greenwich, CT: JAI Press.
Amabile, T. M., Conti, R., Coon, H., Lazenby, J., & Herron, M. (1996). Assessing the work environment for creativity. *Academy of Management Journal, 39,* 1154–1184.
Anderson, N. R., & West, M. D. (1998). Measuring climate for workgroup innovation: Development and validation of a team climate inventory. *Journal of Organizational Behavior, 19,* 235–258.
Arnold, J. A., Arad, S., Rhoades, J. A., & Drasgow, F. (2000). The empowering leadership questionnaire: The construction and validation of a new scale for measuring leader behaviors. *Journal of Organizational Behavior, 21,* 249–269.
Bandura, A. (1986). *Social foundations of thought and action: A social cognitive theory.* Englewood Cliffs, NJ: Prentice-Hall.
Bass, B. M. (1967). Some effects on a group of whether and when the head reveals his opinion. *Organizational Behavior and Human Performance, 2,* 375–382.
Bass, B. M. (1981). *Handbook of leadership: A survey of theory and research.* New York: Free Press.
Bass, B. M. (1985). *Leadership and performance beyond expectation.* New York: Free Press.
Bass, B. M. (1997). Does the transactional–transformational leadership paradigm transcend organizational and national boundaries? *American Psychologist, 52,* 130–139.
Bass, B. M. (1998). *Transformational leadership: Industry, military, and educational impact.* Mahwah, NJ: Erlbaum.

Bass, B. M., & Avolio, B. J. (1990). The implication of transactional and transformational leadership for individual, team, and organizational development. In: R. W. Woodman & W. A. Pasmore (Eds), *Research in organizational change and development*, (Vol. 4, pp. 231–272). Greenwich, CT: JAI Press.

Bass, B. M., & Avolio, B. J. (1997). *Full-range of leadership development: Manual for the multifactor leadership questionnaire*. Palo Alto, CA: Mind Garden.

Bass, B. M., Avolio, B. J., Jung, D. I., & Berson, Y. (2003). Predicting unit performance by assessing transformational and transactional leadership. *Journal of Applied Psychology*, *88*, 207–218.

Bennis, W., & Nanus, B. (1985). *Leaders*. New York: Harper & Row.

Burns, J. M. (1978). *Leadership*. New York: Harper & Row.

Conger, J. A., & Kanungo, R. N. (1987). Towards a behavioral theory of charismatic leadership in organizational settings. *Academy of Management Review*, *12*, 637–647.

Conger, J. A., & Kanungo, R. N. (1988). The empowerment process: Integrating theory and practice. *Academy of Management Review*, *3*, 471–482.

Damanpour, F. (1987). The adoption of technological, administrative, and ancillary innovations: Impact of organizational factors. *Journal of Management*, *13*, 675–688.

Damanpour, F. (1991). Organizational innovation: A meta-analysis of effects of determinants and moderators. *Academy of Management Journal*, *34*, 555–590.

Dess, G. G., & Pickens, J. C. (2000). Changing roles: Leadership in the 21st century. *Organizational Dynamics*, *28*, 18–34.

Devanna, M. A., & Tichy, N. (1990). Creating the competitive organization of the 21st century: The boundaryless corporation. *Human Resource Management*, *29*, 445–471.

Deci, E. L., & Ryan, R. M. (1987). The support of autonomy and the control of behavior. *Journal of Personality and Social Psychology*, *53*, 1024–1037.

Deci, E. L., Connell, J. P., & Ryan, R. M. (1989). Self-determination in a work organization. *Journal of Applied Psychology*, *74*, 580–590.

Drucker, P. F. (1988). The coming of the new organization. *Harvard Business Review*, *66*, 45–53.

Dvir, T., Eden, D., Avolio, B. J., & Shamir, B. (2002). Impact of transformational leadership on follower development and performance: A field experiment. *Academy of Management Journal*, *45*, 735–744.

Fleishman, E. A. (1953). The description of supervisory behavior. *Personnel Psychology*, *37*, 1–6.

Fleishman, E. A. (1973). Twenty years of consideration and structure. In: E. A. Fleishman & J. G. Hunt (Eds), *Current developments in the study of leadership* (pp. 1–37). Carbondale, IL: Southern Illinois University Press.

Fuller, J. B., Morrison, R., Jones, L., Bridger, D., & Brown, V. (1999). The effects of psychological empowerment on transformational leadership and job satisfaction. *The Journal of Social Psychology*, *139*, 389–391.

Grane, G. B., & Scandura, T. A. (1987). Toward a psychology of dynamic organizing. In: L. L. Cummings & B. M. Staw (Eds), *Research in organizational behavior*, (Vol. 9, pp. 175–208). Greenwich, CT: JAI Press.

Halbesleben, J. R. B., Novicevic, M. M., Harvey, M. G., & Buckley, M. R. (2003). Awareness of temporal complexity in leadership of creativity and innovation: A competency-based model. *Leadership Quarterly*, *14*, 433–454.

Homans, G. C. (1958). Social behavior as exchange. *American Journal of Sociology*, 597–606.

House, R. J. (1971). A path-goal theory of leadership effectiveness. *Administrative Science Quarterly*, *16*, 321–338.

234   XIAOMENG ZHANG AND HENRY P. SIMS, JR.

House, R. J. (1977). A 1976 theory of charismatic leadership. In: J. G. Hunt & L. L. Larson
   (Eds), *Leadership: The cutting edge* (pp. 189–207). Carbondale, IL: Southern Illinois
   University Press.
Howell, J. M., & Avolio, B. J. (1993). Transformational leadership, transactional leadership.
   Locus of control, and support for innovation: Key predictors of consolidate-business-
   unit performance. *Journal of Applied Psychology, 78*, 891–902.
Janssen, O., Schoonebeek, G., & Van Looy, B. (1997). Cognitions of empowerment: The link
   between participative management and employees' innovative behavior. *Gedrag en
   Organisatie, 10*, 175–194.
Jaussi, K. S., & Dionne, S. D. (2003). Leading for creativity: The role of unconventional leader
   behavior. *Leadership Quarterly, 14*, 475–498.
Judge, T. A., Piccolo, R. F., & Illies, R. (2004). The forgotten ones? The validity of
   consideration and initiating structure in leadership research. *Journal of Applied
   Psychology, 89*, 36–51.
Jung, D. (2001). Transformational leadership and transactional leadership and their effects on
   creativity in groups. *Creativity Research Journal, 13*, 185–195.
Jung, D. I., & Sosik, J. J. (2002). Transformational leadership in work groups: The role of
   empowerment, cohesiveness, collective-efficacy on perceived group performance. *Small
   Group Research, 33*, 313–336.
Jung, D. I., Chow, C., & Wu, A. (2003). The role of transformational leadership in enhancing
   organizational innovation: Hypotheses and some preliminary findings. *Leadership
   Quarterly, 14*, 525–544.
Kanter, R. M. (1988). When a thousand flowers bloom: Structural, collective, and social con-
   ditions for innovation in organizations. In: B. M. Staw & L. L. Cummings (Eds),
   Research in organizational behavior, (Vol. 10, pp. 169–211). Greenwich, CT: JAI Press.
Kark, R., Shamir, B., & Chen, G. (2003). The two faces of transformational leadership:
   Empowerment and dependency. *Journal of Applied Psychology, 88*, 246–255.
Keller, R. T. (1992). Transformational leadership and the performance of research and devel-
   opment project groups. *Journal of Management, 18*, 489–504.
Kirkman, B. L., & Rosen, B. (1999). Beyond self-management: Antecedents and consequences
   of team empowerment. *Academy of Management Journal, 42*, 58–74.
Liden, R. C., Wayne, S. I., & Sparrowe, R. T. (2000). An examination of the mediating role of
   psychological empowerment on the relations between the job, interpersonal relation-
   ships, and work outcomes. *Journal of Applied Psychology, 85*, 407–416.
Locke, E. A., & Latham, G. P. (1990). *A theory of goal setting and task performance*. Englewood
   Cliffs, NJ: Prentice-Hall.
Manz, C. C., & Sims, H. P., Jr. (1990). *Super leadership: Leading others to lead themselves*.
   New York: Berkeley Books.
Manz, C. C., & Sims, H. P., Jr. (1993). *Business without bosses: How self-managing teams are
   building high-performing companies*. New York: Wiley.
Manz, C. C., & Sims, H. P., Jr. (2001). *The new super leadership: Leading others to lead
   themselves*. San Francisco: Barrett-Kohler.
McGregor, D. (1960). *The human side of enterprise*. New York: McGraw-Hill.
Meichenbaum, D. (1977). *Cognitive-behavior modification: An integrative approach*. New York:
   Plenum.
Mumford, M. D., Scott, G. M., Gaddis, B., & Strange, J. M. (2002). Leading creative people:
   Orchestrating expertise and relationships. *Leadership Quarterly, 13*, 705–750.

Mumford, M. D., Connelly, S., & Gaddis, B. (2003). How creative leaders think: Experimental findings and cases. *Leadership Quarterly, 14*, 411–432.

Oldham, G. R., & Cummings, A. (1996). Employee creativity: Personal and contextual factors at work. *Academy of Management Journal, 39*, 607–634.

Pearce, C. L., & Sims, H. P., Jr. (2002). Vertical versus shared leadership as predictors of the effectiveness of changed management teams: An examination of aversive, directive, transactional, transformational, and empowering leader behaviors. *Group Dynamics: Theory, Research, and Practice, 6*, 172–197.

Pearce, C. L., Sims, H. P., Jr., Cox, J. F., Ball, G., Schnell, E., Smith, K. A., & Trevino, L. (2003). Transactors, transformers and beyond: A multi-method development of a theoretical typology of leadership. *Journal of Management Development, 22*, 273–307.

Pelz, D. C., & Andrews, F. M. (1976). *Scientists in organizations.* Ann Arbor, MI: Institute for Social Research.

Redmond, M. R., Mumford, M. D., & Teach, R. (1993). Putting creativity to work: Effects of leader behavior on subordinate creativity. *Organizational Behavior & Human Decision Processes, 55*, 120–151.

Scott, S. G., & Bruce, R. A. (1994). Determinants of innovative behavior: A path model of individual innovation in the workplace. *Academy of Management Journal, 37*, 580–607.

Seibert, S. E., Silver, S. R., & Randolph, W. A. (2004). Taking empowerment to the next level: A multiple-level model of empowerment, performance, and satisfaction. *Academy of Management Journal, 47*, 332–349.

Shamir, B., House, R. J., & Arthur, M. B. (1993). The motivational effects of charismatic leadership: A self-concept based theory. *Organization Science, 4*, 577–593.

Shin, S. J., & Zhou, J. (2003). Transformational leadership, conservation, and creativity: Evidence from Korea. *Academy of Management Journal, 46*, 703–714.

Sims, H. P., Jr., & Manz, C. C. (1996). *Company of heroes: Unleashing the power of self-leadership.* New York: Wiley.

Sosik, J. M., Kahai, S. S., & Avolio, B. J. (1998). Transformational leadership and dimensions of creativity: Motivating idea generation in computer-mediated groups. *Creativity Research Journal, 11*, 111–122.

Sosik, J. M., Kahai, S. S., & Avolio, B. J. (1999). Leadership style, anonymity, and creativity in group decision support systems. *Journal of Creative Behavior, 33*, 227–257.

Spreitzer, G. M. (1995). Individual empowerment in the workplace: Dimensions, measurement, validation. *Academy of Management Journal, 38*, 1442–1465.

Stoker, J. I., Looise, J. C., Fisscher, O. A. M., & Jong, R. D. (2001). Leadership and innovation: Relations between leadership, individual characteristics and the functioning of R&D teams. *The International Journal of Human Resource Management, 12*, 1141–1151.

Thomas, K. W., & Velthouse, B. A. (1990). Cognitive elements of empowerment: An "interpretive" model of intrinsic task motivation. *Academy of Management Review, 15*, 666–681.

Thorenson, E. E., & Mahoney, M. J. (1974). *Behavioral self-control.* Austin, TX: Holt, Rinehart and Winston.

Tierney, P., Farmer, S. M., & Graen, G. (1999). An examination of leadership and employee creativity: The relevance of traits and relationships. *Personnel Psychology, 52*, 591–620.

Vroom, V. H. (1964). *Work and motivation.* New York: Wiley.

Weber, M. (1946). The sociology of charismatic authority. In: H. H. Mills & C. W. Mills (Eds), *From Max Weber: Essays in sociology.* New York: Oxford University Press.

Weber, M. (1947). *The theory of social and economic organization* [*T. Parsons, Trans.*]. New York: Free Press (Original work published 1924.).

Woodman, R. W., Sawyer, J. E., & Griffin, R. W. (1993). Toward a theory of organizational creativity. *Academy of Management Review, 18*, 292–321.

Yukl, G. (1989). *Leadership in organizations* (2nd ed.). Englewood Cliffs, NJ: Prentice-Hall.

Yukl, G. (1999). An evaluation of conceptual weaknesses in transformational and charismatic leadership theories. *Leadership Quarterly, 10*, 285–305.

Yukl, G. (2002). *Leadership in organizations* (5th ed.). Englewood Cliffs, NJ: Prentice-Hall.

Zhou, J. (1998). Feedback valence, feedback style, task autonomy, and achievement orientation: Interactive effects on creative performance. *Journal of Applied Psychology, 83*, 261–276.

Zhou, J., & George, J. M. (2003). Awakening employee creativity: The role of leader emotional intelligence. *Leadership Quarterly, 14*, 545–568.

Zhou, J., & Shalley, C. E. (2003). Research on employee creativity: A critical review and proposal for future research directions. In: J. J. Martocchio & G. R. Ferris (Eds), *Research in personnel and human resource management*. Oxford, England: Elsevier.

MINIMIZING THE IMPACT OF ORGANIZATIONAL DISTRESS ON INTELLECTUAL AND SOCIAL CAPITAL THROUGH DEVELOPMENT OF COLLABORATIVE CAPITAL

Michael F. Kennedy and Michael M. Beyerlein

ABSTRACT

Intellectual capital (IC) and social capital (SC), as forms of intangible value in organizations, are crucial assets in today's volatile business environment. Efforts to retain and develop these intangibles are becoming more deliberate and disciplined. However, organizations fail to recognize the relationship between organizational distress and the loss and/or reduction of intangible value. The loss of intangible value may potentially impact an organization with equal or greater damage than the loss of more tangible value. IC and SC generate many outcomes beneficial to the individual and the organization. These benefits are reduced when stress of employees becomes excessive and damaging. The relationship between the health of an organization and the degree of impact of distress serves as a lingering threat to organizational financial resources. Managers must

Collaborative Capital: Creating Intangible Value
Advances in Interdisciplinary Studies of Work Teams, Volume 11, 237–284
Copyright © 2005 by Elsevier Ltd.
ISSN: 1572-0977/doi:10.1016/S1572-0977(05)11009-7

build upon the growing knowledge from research and practice to help
organizations account for the costs of organizational distress, translate
the importance of intangible value into tangible terms, and garner support
for developing IC and SC to obtain business objectives. Deliberate and
disciplined effort to build collaborative capital can facilitate the growth of
IC and SC which minimize the damage of organizational distress.

INTRODUCTION

Capital represents resources: either tangible or intangible; organizations rely
on both, but traditionally and formally have focused on the tangible, i.e.,
financial and physical assets. Although intangible resources have clearly
been recognized and manipulated informally throughout history, deliberate
attention to their role in the organization has only emerged in the past
decade. Intellectual capital (IC) has been the primary focus, perhaps because
of the transformation of the economy from a predominantly production-
based to a knowledge-based system. However, a large number of other types
of intangible capital have been described in research journals since then,
including: social, relationship, political, customer, organizational, human,
structural, process, knowledge market, innovation, and collaborative. The
complexity of this set of asset concepts and the recency of their emergence in
the literature makes an integrated presentation problematic. In this chapter,
we will focus on three aspects (intellectual, social, and collaborative), their
interrelationship, their relationship to organizational effectiveness, and the
impact of employee distress on their value.

Job stress pervades the daily work lives of individuals around the world.
Stress experienced by employees at work is more strongly associated with
health complaints than any other life stressor (National Institute of Organizational Safety and Health (NIOSH), 2000). The notion that work may
cause stress is widely recognized by the current research (e.g., Hesselbein,
Goldsmith, & Beckhard, 1997; Quick, Quick, Nelson, & Hurrell Jr., 1997;
Hurrell, Murphy, & Sauter, 1988; Cooper & Quick, 1999; Levi, Sauter, &
Shimomitsu, 1999; Quick, Nelson, & Quick, 2001; Weaver, Bowers, & Salas,
2001) in the field of job stress.

For instance, a survey conducted by Northwestern National Life in the
late 1990s reports that one-fourth of employees consider their jobs to be the
most significant source of stress in their lives. Additionally, 40% of workers
report their job is very or extremely stressful, while 26% of workers report

they are burned out or stressed by their work (NIOSH, 2000). A growing number of European workers attribute increasing workplace stress to the changing nature of work. In response, the social partners of the European Union (EU) indicate rising concern regarding the effects of workplace stress based on a survey of 1451 companies from seven EU members (Geurts & Grundemann, 1999). Clearly, across the world, job stress has an impact on individual employees and in turn, a systemic effect on their organizations.

Over the years, excessive job stress has grown to become a common occurrence in the workplace and an evasive, damaging, and costly problem to organizations (Cooper & Quick, 1999; NIOSH, 2000). Past and present stress research identifies the following aspects surrounding the preventative nature of job stress: what could and should be done, when, how, by whom, to whom, and why. Regardless of this body of knowledge, the current trend by the majority of organizations is to regard current conditions of job stress as inevitable and curtail any action. However, the misguided and minimal attention given by organizations toward the impact of organizational stress is comparable to chipping off the rust while the boat sinks (Levi et al., 1999). The link between stress and health is both real and extensive, and there is an imperative for organizations to come to this realization now in terms of the health of the employee and the organization (Hesselbein et al., 1997).

Organizations need to recognize that stress is inevitable, while excessive stress, or distress, is not (Hurrell et al., 1988; Cooper & Quick, 1999). There are various costs for distress at both the individual and organizational levels. When an employee experiences distress, these potential personal costs extend beyond individual consequences (e.g., symptoms of illness) to organizational consequences (e.g., high-absenteeism rates) (Quick et al., 2001). For example, tardiness, absenteeism, poor decision-making, peptic ulcers, insomnia, and migraine headaches are just a few of the consequences of job stress that translate into organizational costs over time (Cooper, 1996). A wakeup call is sounding and those organizations that react appropriately to this warning will outperform their competitors (Amidon, 2000; Barney, 2001a; Adler & Kwon, 2002; Chabrow & Colkin, 2002). Therefore, the current role of researchers and practitioners is to build upon growing knowledge in attempts to help these organizations relate the costs of organizational distress to their organization, translate the widespread individual and organizational impact, and garner support for the assessment and prevention of organizational distress across organizational practices.

The following discussion uncovers what many organizations are either unaware of or are unwilling to investigate, the loss of and failure to enhance IC and social capital (SC) due to organizational distress (Nelson, 2000).

While both IC and SC share common conceptual boundaries, the discussion recognizes the unique elements and costs of each. Building on previous research (e.g., Quick et al., 1997), the relationship between the health of an organization and the degree of impact of distress outcomes are examined as real and threatening organizational financial costs in the form of organizational intangible value loss. Thus, the following discussion investigates the relationship between organizational distress, the reduction of intangible value in the form of IC and SC (Lesser, 2000; Quick et al., 2001; Adler & Kwon, 2002), and the possible mitigating impact of collaborative capital.

What Is Distress?

The heightened interest coupled with concern regarding the multiple costs of organizational stress affecting the organizational finances has increased the debate over the correct conceptualization of stress. Stress means different things to many people, described as one of the most imprecise terms in the dictionary. Moreover, stress research lacks a unifying theory because of the varied perspectives and disciplines of study (Scharbracq, Winnubst & Cooper, 1996). Stress is a focus of research in at least seven distinct disciplines (Burke, 1986).

At the individual level, distress is defined as "the harmful physical and emotional responses that occur when the requirements of the job do not match the capabilities, resources, or needs of the worker" (NIOSH, 2000, p. 6). Individuals encounter distress when unable to satisfy important needs or having no way of changing the job (Peterson, 1999). Distress occurs when stress levels exceed an individual's ability to cope long-term, enduring unhealthy consequences as a result. As economic forces shape an increasingly competitive business landscape, these forces challenge each and every employee to adapt to the responsibilities of work (Quick et al., 2001).

Human distress involves three categories: medical (i.e., physical), psychologic, and behavioral. Medical distress includes such stress-related ailments as cardiovascular disease and cancer. Psychologic distress represents individuals suffering from depression and anxiety, the two most common stress-related complaints made to medical physicians. For instance, anxiety disorders affect one in every six Americans and one in every five workers in the United Kingdom (Cooper, 1996; Cooper & Quick, 1999). Industrial and heavy manufacturing work entails a wide range of physical distress risks due to injury or accidents, while more service and information-based knowledge work relates to increased worker vulnerability to psychologic distress, such as anxiety, depression, burnout, cardiovascular disease, and carpal tunnel syndrome (Quick et al., 2001).

Behavioral distress results in substance abuse, violence, and industrial accidents, the leading cause of death for men working in the United States. Conversely, homicide is the leading cause of death of women at work (Quick et al., 1997). Non-fatal forms of human suffering such as substance abuse in the form of tobacco products may be the most preventable cause of human ailment and death. Additionally, the Federal Bureau of Investigation suggests 90% of workplace violence stems from a preventable stressful event (Mack, Shannon, & Quick, 1998).

There is a new call for research to examine the impact of distress on individuals' health and well-being in addition to impacts at the group or organizational level (Quick et al., 2001). Traditional distress research has focused on the individual and only recently has the field started studying groups and team level outcomes (Weaver et al., 2001). The effects of distress are in different forms for the individual and for the organization. For example, a cardiovascular disease due to distress can affect an employee physiologically, psychologically (in the form of depression), and behaviorally (in the form of displaced aggression or violence). Each of these effects impacts the organization in various forms, such as increased health care costs, absenteeism, turnover, and weakened working relationships. These outcomes of individual distress contribute to organizational distress, defined as "the degree of deviation an organization experiences from a healthy, productive level of functioning" (Quick et al., 1997, p. 6). While the job of an individual and the job environment are not the only sources of distress for an employee, they are major sources deserving the attention of the organization (Briner & Reynolds, 1999). The outcomes of distress are manifested as a variety of detrimental consequences to individuals, families, organizations, and society.

In order to fully understand employee distress, there is a need for organizations to recognize that stress has a positive role to play in employee satisfaction, health, effectiveness, commitment, and performance when managed at an optimal level. Stress places special demands on employees, harmful, or beneficial. Many stressors result in distress; however, there are many stressors that also produce eustress, or stress that produces positive outcomes (Matteson & Ivancevich, 1987; Quick et al., 1997). For instance, eustress can be a response to a stressor that an employee finds challenging or satisfying. Challenge in turn energizes employees both physically and psychological, and motivates employees to learn new skills and improve individual performance. Challenge is an important ingredient for healthy and productive work; the importance of challenge in the workplace is comparable to what people are referring to when they say "a little of stress is good for you" (NIOSH, 2000). This type of stress is needed for motivation and creativity; thus, organizations must recognize the benefits of managing organizational distress at an optimal level.

In order for organizations to interpret the costs of employee distress, an understanding of distress at the individual and organizational level must be developed (Cooper & Quick, 1999). With this understanding, organizations may begin to minimize the costs of excessive stress, while communicating the awareness of these costs to the entire organization. When stress is excessive, organizations run into damaging problems and varied costs in terms of the loss and/or reduction of intangible organizational value, such as IC and SC which are discussed later in the chapter.

Why Focus on Organizational Distress Now?

In today's world, the nature of work is changing at whirlwind speed. This is attributed to the globalization of the developing world of work. Perhaps, now more than at any other time, job stress poses a threat to the health of the individual, and in turn, to the health of the organization in the form of organizational distress ("Tokyo Declaration," 1999). Today, workers face many more stressors and are working at a faster pace than workers of the past (Scharbracq & Winnubst, 1996). Evidence is provided by the Princeton Survey Research Associates who report that three-fourths of employees believe that the worker has more on-the-job stress than a generation ago (NIOSH, 2000).

"Occupational stress was a major industrial concern of the 1990s because the 1990s have proved to be a time of dramatic global change in the world's industrial and economic systems" (Quick et al., 2001, p. 19). Rising demands in employee workloads and deadlines, coupled with massive technologic changes, have directed attention to the health of employees (Scharbracq & Winnubst, 1996). Economic, technologic, and competitive forces extend beyond international boundaries, and influence political and social changes; thus, this is a period of tremendous economic change around the world (Beckhard, 1997; Gowing, Kraft, & Quick, 1998; Quick et al., 2001).

The incidence of mergers and acquisitions (M&As) has also increased significantly. M&As, which are large scale, organizational change events, strongly affect organizational members unequipped with effective coping strategies to deal with the resulting distress (Dunham, 2001). Even though the incidence of M&As has increased, less than 50% of M&As are successful in achieving anticipated financial expectations over the long term (Cartwright & Panchal, 2001). The attributed cause of this lack of success stems from employee relationship problems: failure to integrate organizational workforces smoothly or maintain employee morale, poor communication, and insensitive management (Walsh, 1999). The unexpected and non-routine nature of M&As represents a unique type of organizational change event, increasing employees' distress (Cartwright & Panchal, 2001).

Traditionally, employers have assumed that stressful working conditions are a necessary evil of the means and methods of an organization. These employers feel that organizations must turn up the pressure on employees, setting aside health concerns to remain productive and profitable in today's economy (NIOSH, 2000). Very few organizations assume responsibility for employee distress, and most refuse to account for their part in producing employee distress. The most common organizational approach is for organizations to push the responsibility for managing employee stress to the family of the employee (Wojcik, 2001). In addition, individuals feel increasingly isolated with mounting loneliness and seclusion from colleagues due to the changing work environments, such as the use of virtual teams and telecommuting activities (Winnubst & Schabracq, 1996).

Furthermore, many top executives label distress a health-related issue oblivious to the invasive consequences to the organization. Stress-related issues are generally delegated to human resources (HR) departments (Wojcik, 2001). These executives fail to recognize the process of identifying and managing distress as a form of organizational risk management. Executives should be asking what their organizations' exposure is to distress and what is it costing the organization to deal with this exposure. Organizational distress is a multi-level phenomenon that affects employees at all levels of the organization and across departments. When approaching the issue of organizational distress, organizations should be concerned about how employees are responding to distress physically, psychologically, and behaviorally: all three impact performance in both the short and long term.

Organizational Health. Distress is steadily becoming a topic of concern to organizations (NIOSH, 2000). Executives are beginning to ask the question, "Why should my organization be concerned about organizational distress?" The answer is the notion that those organizations that advance beyond their competitors are those that make certain realizations before they become permanent organizational setbacks. These setbacks are in the form of organizational costs that begin and end with the treatment and care of employees. "Informed and progressive companies are realizing that count-ing the cost of human resources has tremendous potential benefit" (Hurrell et al., 1988, p. 3).

Progressive organizations have begun to engage in extensive organiza-tional distress assessments based on the premise that distress is the main threat to work (Hurrell et al., 1988). This group of developing organizations is spending money to invest in becoming healthier organizations. What is a healthy organization and why should organizations strive to be healthier? A "healthy" organization is defined as an organization "that has low rates of illness, injury, and disability in its workforce and is also competitive in the marketplace" (NIOSH, 2000, p. 12). A healthier workforce would be ex-pected to produce a more effective organization. Healthy organizations have higher morale and greater effectiveness (Koslowsky, 1998).

While there is no consensus on how to define healthy organizations, NI-OSH has identified several organizational characteristics associated with healthy organizations, exhibiting low levels of distress and high levels of productivity (Beckhard, 1997; NIOSH, 2000). These characteristics include the recognition of employees for good work performance, opportunities for career development, an organizational culture that values the individual worker, and management actions that are consistent with organizational values (NIOSH, 2000). Recognizing the relationship between the health and effectiveness of an organization, organizational leaders must pay attention to the needs of their employees by facilitating the understanding of the costs of distress to the individual and the organization (Koslowsky, 1998).

Even with the advantages of developing a healthier organization, there is a growing concern that distress should be prevented and remedied at the collective level as a basic obligation of the employer. This obligation in-volves analyzing current working conditions, detecting possible stressors, evaluating risks, and taking appropriate measures to alleviate employee distress (Levi et al., 1999). Organizations that make these financial and resource investments in health generate gain in such forms as increased productivity, decreased workers' compensation costs, decreased health costs, and improved morale (Lennart, 2001). However, the majority of or-ganizations are slow to move in this direction, oblivious to the underlying array of consequences of individual and organizational distress (Levi et al., 1999).

The slow movement of organizations to address work distress is generated by the challenging task of establishing the cost relationship between dis-tress and organizational financial viability, resulting from the lack of integrated measurement (Liukkonen & Cartwright, 1999). For instance, the multiplicative and diverse impact of distress on organizations remains undetected, as organizations tend to rely on outdated traditional HR measurement methods (i.e., health and personnel data). In order to gain the attention of organizational leaders, the focus must be on the relationship of organizational distress to the financial vitality of the organization in the marketplace. This is both important and difficult when one recognizes that workplace "injuries and illnesses have become increasingly subjective, invisible, chronic, and multi-causal" (Polanyi & Tompa, 2004, p. 17).

Financial Impact. One of the most influential factors in gaining support for the recognition of organizational distress outcomes is the recent body of research uncovering the diverse effects of excessive stress on the bottom line (e.g., Quick, 1997; Marks, 1999; DeVoge & Shiraki, 2000). Most companies fail to realize how much distress costs them, both directly and indirectly. According to the U.S. Bureau of Labor Statistics, distress costs employers an estimated $10,000 per worker per year (Wojcik, 2001). Working conditions creating distress are associated with increased absenteeism, tardiness, and intentions by workers to quit their jobs – all of which have a negative effect on the financial resources of the organization.

Furthermore, recent research of organizations exhibiting healthy characteristics suggests that policies benefiting employee health also benefit the organization's financial vitality (NIOSH, 2000). Consequently, unhealthy organizations encounter enormous financial and human costs. For instance, U.S. industry suffers the loss of 550 million working days each year as a result of sickness absences, 54% of which are stress related. Costs to organizations of individuals distressed by the work environment result in these individuals contributing decreased or limited service (Scharbracq & Winnubst, 1996).

Distress takes a toll on the health of both the employee and the organization (Scharbracq & Winnubst, 1996; Levi et al., 1999). For example, the personnel director for a large New York company reported that 2400 employees a month were using the company's medical services. After further analysis, the director found that the equivalent of the entire employee population was going through the medical department every 2 months, causing the company's medical cost coverage to climb steadily (Matteson & Ivancevich, 1987). Consequently, when additional medical costs, as well as lost productivity and absenteeism, are added to this equation, employers spend from $1 to $1.50 in indirect costs for every $1 spent on disability payments (Wojcik, 2001). Intangible costs may greatly exceed this amount.

Employee Value. The fundamental question underlying the financial impact of organizational distress is "What are the reasons for valuing employees today?" Employees are the most important resource of an organization (Hurrel et al., 1988). Organizations must retain their top talent to remain competitive and to ensure the survival in the marketplace; thus, most organizations make a large investment of resources in recruiting and hiring processes (Bowen, Ledford, & Nathan, 1991; Bartlett & Ghoshal, 2002). For example, a major car manufacturing company in Michigan spent about $13,000 per employee to staff its plant over 10 years ago (Bowen et al., 1991).

Another reason for concern involves the retention of corporate bench strength. There is an extensive loss of HR when those devoted employees that have climbed the organizational hierarchy become mentally or physically impaired and retire early or even die. These valuable employees leave the organization before they are able to make their most significant contributions based on their experience (Wojcik, 2001). A substantial amount of investment expense is lost in terms of development time and money, as well as the loss of skills, abilities, experience, and knowledge, discussed later in this chapter in the terms of SC and IC.

All of these elements designed to acquire and retain the right talent need to be considered in combination with the extensive costs for insurance coverage and court-ordered compensation for distress when discussing the financial impact of stress. Organizations are putting substantial investments into increasing retention rates, lowering insurance costs, and cutting down the number of court-ordered compensation claims, among other initiatives. This handful of cost-incentive initiatives begins and ends with the accountability and understanding of the financial impact of employee distress on the entire organization (Levi et al., 1999; NIOSH, 2000).

In addition to these more well-known and previously recognized costs of distress, such as the decrease in quantity and quality of production, there are a number of typically unforeseen, long-term consequences that are related to the costs of employee stress to the organization. For example, a highly stressed employee is not able to be as creative, as interpersonally effective, or as team-oriented as one who is not stressed (Waldo, 2001). The numerous problems resulting from distress in terms of lost opportunities, poorer decision-making, and the improper management of people are impossible to calculate. While these are only a few examples of outcomes, one purpose of this chapter is to identify additional outcomes or costs of distress to the organization. This includes moving future investigations beyond traditional, direct outcomes, such as absenteeism and turnover, by expanding upon the current body of knowledge regarding the costs of organizational distress.

This importance of valuing employees is most notable due to the frequent workforce reductions in the slowing economy of recent times. There is an impetus to "get to the decision-makers in our companies and share with them the importance of considering the human impact of a recession and its most immediate consequence, downsizing" (Waldo, 2001, p. 51). The effects of the recent recession will determine whether organizations learned from the experiences of the recession of the early 1990s. Widespread layoffs and the anticipation of staff reductions dramatically influence individual and organizational productivity. Practitioners in the field of dealing with employees should lead the effort to address the impact of layoffs on employee motivation. Realistically, layoffs are inevitable; however, the resounding message lies in downsizing wisely and rarely to avoid substantial costs related to distress.

The understanding of distress is progressing with the compilation of research drawn from multiple organizations, professions, and positions. Based on this growing body of knowledge, the purpose of the following discussion is to investigate that which is not widely known – the exhaustive impact of direct and indirect costs of distress in the form of the reduction or loss of intangible value (Levi et al., 1999; Waldo, 2001; Wojcik, 2001). There are convincing reasons for organizations to understand how work demands exert a negative toll on organizational health and to devise effective prevention and intervention strategies for reducing these potentially costly problems.

Progressive Action. A limited number of organizations connect overall organizational distress to consequences affecting the financial health and future of the organization. These companies are pioneers of new organizational perspectives on distress ("Tokyo Declaration," 1999). What is the impact of these types of programs and perspectives? Researchers are beginning to look to these companies for lessons learned, areas of focus, and methods used to further organizational support for these efforts. There is much to be learned from pioneering, progressive organizations that are attempting to account for the costs of distress and communicating these costs to gain organizational support. Employers of today are being forced to adapt to changing economic conditions, thus, those organizations addressing employee distress at the individual and organizational level gain a competitive edge in the industry (Kompier & Cooper, 1999; Wojcik, 2001).

The Johnson & Johnson company is a unique example of a company using stress-related programs to help recruit as well as retain the top organizational talent (Johnson & Johnson, 2000a, b). The company's work and family programs reflect the commitment of the company to help employees manage the stress of balancing work and family matters. The devotion of the company to its employees is exemplified by the following statement found on the companys' web site (http://www.johnsonandjohnson.com), "By recognizing and supporting the needs of our working mothers, fathers, and all our employees, we are investing in our own future." In addition to touting the benefits of the work and family programs, Johnson & Johnson offers a comprehensive health appraisal assessment to all of their employees working in the United States. Ulrich captures this sentiment writing, "The impact of HR practices on business results can and must be measured. HR professionals must learn how to translate their work into financial performance" (Barney, 2001b, p. 18).

Another example of a company at the forefront of this movement to address the risk of organizational stress is BellSouth. The top management of BellSouth decided to use an organizational stress assessment on employees after a consultant demonstrated the effects of stress using a biofeedback device at an executive retreat. As a result of this experience, many executives were surprised to see how their bodies responded to stress (Wojcik, 2001). The company received group data identifying company-wide trends. The analysis of the data was used to make changes to reduce stress levels; for example, the organization implemented split shifts for night-shift workers to allow employees to help children off to school. In addition, a number of parenting workshops were held to help cut down on psychiatric costs for adolescent hospitalizations. Researchers and practitioners are eager to learn and build upon the ideas and perspectives of these kinds of programs that are currently being used by these progressive organizations.

ORGANIZATIONAL INTANGIBLE VALUE

Organizational intangible value has received considerable attention in current research (e.g., Ulrich, 1997; Brown & Lauder, 2001; Cariner, 2000; Becker, Huselid, & Ulrich, 2001; Cohen & Prusak, 2001; Kaplan & Norton, 2001; Lev, 2001, 2004; Chabrow & Colkin, 2002; Ulrich & Smallwood, 2004; Boudreau & Ramstad, 2005). Organizational intangible assets, such as knowledge and employee morale, contribute indirect value to the organization. These assets seldom have direct, traceable impact on organizational revenue and profit; instead, intangible assets make indirect contributions to organizational financial vitality (Kaplan & Norton, 2001). Intangible assets seldom have individual value; these assets, bundled with additional intangible and tangible assets, create value arising from the multiplicative properties of each entity. Conversely, tangible assets appear to have a strong cause-and-effect relationship to the organization. For instance, the value contribution of tangible assets is detected directly, such as the value of financial or physical assets (Lev, 2001). James O'Shaughnessy, chief intellectual property counsel at Rockwell International, say, "The more intangible capital you have, the less financial capital you need" (Osterland, 2001, http://www.cfo.com/printable/article.cfm/2992885?f = options).

The costs of employee distress reduce intangible value in organizations. Typically, the reduction or loss of intangible value due to distress has not received enough attention by researchers or practitioners. This is attributed to the fact that the decrease in value is harder to measure, yet the loss of intangible value may impact an organization with equal or greater damage than the loss of more tangible value (Lev, 2001). For instance, during the period after a company announces downsizing and layoffs, employees are simultaneously exposed to high levels of distress. The result of this type of continuous exposure to distress creates a workplace in which employees revert to less sophisticated ways of dealing with work and with colleagues, competence suffers, morale declines, and performance deteriorates (Allcorn & Diamond, 1997; Koslowsky, 1998). Moreover, there are indirect psychologic outcomes, such as a loss of vitality, lowered morale, and apathy. The following discussion is provided to demonstrate the relationship between organizational distress and the loss of intangible value (Quick et al., 1997; Cooper & Quick, 1999).

Intangible assets are becoming increasingly important in today's economy. The most representative proof lies in studying the ratio of an organization's market value (i.e., the shareholders' assessment of the firm's full, perceived value) to the organization's book value (i.e., the shareholders' initial investment). This ratio has doubled over the past 10 years (Becker et al., 2001; Lev, 2001, 2004). Therefore, organizational leaders must internally develop these intangible assets, including the recognition and prevention of the reduction of this value by organizational distress. Many organizations are either unaware or unwilling to investigate the loss of intangible value in the forms of IC and SC due to organizational distress (Nelson, 2000; Ittner & Larcker, 2003). While both IC and SC share common conceptual boundaries, this discussion recognizes the unique elements and organizational value of each. These unique elements include competitive advantages related to adaptability, innovation, and technology (Brown & Lauder, 2001; Lev, 2001).

A number of types of intangible value have been identified in the study of organizations. Over the past decade, the general concept of intangible value has been increasingly articulated into a number of specific categories. The growing list includes: intellectual, social, relationship, human, political, organizational, structural, innovative, process, and collaborative. The type receiving the most attention in both research and practice has been IC.

Intellectual Capital

Many organizations realized that an enormous amount of organizational intellectual information and unique knowledge was leaving with exiting employees after a number of the highly publicized downsizings during the late 1980s and early 1990s (Erickson & Rothberg, 2000). The concept of IC embodies this unique set of organizational knowledge, intellectual property, and experience of an organization's workforce (Stewart, 1997). As a result of organizational distress organizations are reducing or limiting organizational IC, failing to take advantage of a competitive resource that has remained devalued until recently (Quick et al., 1997). There is a strong business case to control organizational distress in order to sustain and enhance a competitive advantage in the market by leveraging IC.

A broad definition of IC is "the knowledge and knowing capability of a social collectivity, such as an organization, intellectual community, or professional practice" (Nahapiet & Sumantra, 1998, p. 245). Organizational IC consists of "the sum of everything everybody in a company knows that gives it a competitive edge" (Stewart, 1997, p. IX). Therefore, the concept of IC encompasses the organizational knowledge, information, intellectual property, and experience used to generate organizational wealth (Stewart, 1997). IC is a nebulous and expansive concept, composed of relationships between customers and partners, innovation efforts, company infrastructure, and the knowledge and skills of employees (Roos, Roos, Edvinsson, & Dragonetti, 1998). For example, the training and intuition of a group of chemists who uncover a billion-dollar new drug or a group of workers who discover a series of critical ways to improve the efficiency of a factory represent organizational value outcomes gained by leveraging IC (Stewart, 1997).

The definitions range from explicit knowledge (www.seeport.com/usda/GLOSSARY.htm) to comprehensive statements of capability and infrastructure (e.g., www.bcinow.com/demo/workforce/Glossary.htm). Such a range of definitions seem to exist for each of the types of intangible capital, so further articulation seems warranted. SC is similar to IC in the proliferation of definitions and consequent confusion, ranging from the degree to which a community collaborates through networks, shared trust, norms, and values (www.hc-sc.gc.ca/hppb/voluntarysector/glossary.html) to a broad definition of capital that includes everything the economy can invest in – physical capital to produce goods and services, education, infrastructure, and renewable and non-renewable natural resources including environmental resources (highered.mcgraw-hill.com/sites/0070880506/student_view0/chapter1/key_terms.html). This definition is so inclusive that it is not useful for our purposes.

Defining IC is an ongoing process. IC has been used synonymously with intellectual property, intellectual assets, and knowledge assets. IC is "the total stock of capital or knowledge-based equity that the company possesses ... In balance sheet terms, intellectual assets are those knowledge-based items, which the company owns which will produce a future stream of benefits for the company" (Dzinkowski, 2000, p. 32). Ulrich (1998) defined IC as competence X Commitment. Due to the concern that this was too rational and limited, Burr and Girardi (2002) added control to the definition, where competence refers to rationalist measures of capacity (knowledge, skills, and abilities – KSAs), interpretative measures (skill utilization) and cognitions of capability (efficacy beliefs); commitment refers to affective, continuance and normative commitment; and control refers to work autonomy. Although work stress was not mentioned by Burr and Girardi, it is widely recognized in the stress literature that control is a critical condition for coping.

During the 1990s, IC has gained increasing attention as numerous organizations, with few assets besides the collective brainpower of the organization's workforce, have experienced tremendous growth (Stewart, 1997; Erickson & Rothberg, 2000; Sullivan, 2000; Lev, 2001). This is due in part to the fundamental changes in the business world during the past 10 years, culminating in the current business environment's value creation stemming from IC. Knowledge is now the most important organizational resource. The organizational value creation gained through leveraging IC is insurmountable. The novel concept of IC brings a new attention to the forefront of the business scene for the assets of the organization, deserving just as much attention as traditional labor assets, if not more (Department of Trade and Industry, 1998; Sullivan, 2000).

For example, the Google search engine whose stock was recently offered to the public represents a case where physical assets are worth a small fraction of intellectual property. For most companies, an average market to book value ratio of three supports the trend of the appreciation and significance of knowledge value. This average ratio figure indicates that while an organization's physical and financial assets are valued at $100 million, according to the market, the value of the whole organization (tangible plus intangible assets) is three times that or $300 million in the eyes of investors (Roos et al., 1998).

IC is a relatively new way to think about the value of organizations. The topic debuted on the business scene in the 1990s, launched by Tom Stewart's article "Brainpower" published in 1991 by *Fortune* magazine (Roos et al., 1998; Sullivan, 2000). By 1999, a number of conferences devoted to the discussion of IC followed numerous articles discussing the concept and implications.

Conceptual Framework. The strongest general agreement regarding the conceptualization of IC is the nebulous and amorphous nature of this all-embracing concept (Sullivan, 2000). Depending on the perspective and discipline of the researcher or practitioner, IC has a different shape and form. A survey administered to a random sample of people results in many definitions to the concept of IC, characteristic of a concept with such broad terms and lacking a clear focus.

For the purposes of this study, the following outline distinguishes the individual components of IC as defined by the leading pioneer in the field of IC research and practice, Leif Edvinsson and his work at the Swedish firm, Skandia (Roos et al., 1998; Sullivan, 2000). Leading the IC movement, Skandia publishes annual reports evaluating the organization's IC holdings led by Edvinsson, serving as the Director of IC (Erickson & Rothberg, 2000). "Skandia practically single-handedly started the IC movement, in 1994, through the publication of an IC Report as a supplement to its Annual Reports" (Roos et al., 1998, p. 30).

Following the organizational model of IC, Skandia divides market value into financial capital and IC. Physical and monetary assets compose financial capital, while all of the invisible processes and organizational assets compose IC. IC is defined as "the unique combination of our customers, employees, and processes that drive Skandia's future value creation" (http://www.skandia.com/en/sustainability/intellectualcapital.shtml). Together, financial and IC make up the total value of the company. The Skandia model then separates IC into divisions of structural capital and human capital – separating the invisible or intangible assets and processes of structural capital from the employee knowledge of human capital (Roos et al., 1998).

Structural Capital. Typically, IC is mistakenly viewed as the limited value of the employees and human capital in the organization, failing to identify the expansive area of structural capital. The value of organizational assets that remain in the company when the employees go home construct structural capital, such as brands, trademarks, written procedures for processes, daily tasks and routines, systems, etc. (Cariner, 2000). The value of structural capital draws from the combined value of relationships and organizational value, representative of the internal and external focus of the organization.

At Skandia, structural capital includes customer capital (also referred to as relationship capital) which is externally focused and organizational capital which is internally focused. In the context of IC, the term organizational capital refers to all physical and non-physical extensions of IC, such as all databases, organization charts, intellectual property, day-to-day operations, and anything whose value to the organization is higher than the material value of the asset (Skandia, 2001). However, Tomer (1987) defines organizational capital reporting structures, planning processes, administrative and management systems, and informal relationships among groups within the firm, and between the firm and its environment. At Skandia, organizational systems fall under the scope of organizational capital, especially those systems creating more efficient labor and resources (Erickson & Rothberg, 2000). Organizational value, a result of organizational effort to turn human capital into proprietary information, also includes internal networks that facilitate the sharing of information among all employees.

In deliberately attempting to nurture organizational value, some organizations develop knowledge management programs (Roos et al., 1998). Knowledge management falls under the realm of structural capital, represented by the storage, transfer, and migration of knowledge (Cariner, 2000). The type of knowledge involved in structural capital consists of both tacit and explicit knowledge (Nonaka & Takeuchi, 1995). Tacit or personal knowledge possessed by employees is difficult to communicate to others in the organization. Explicit or identified knowledge is knowledge accessible to all employees throughout the organization (Erickson & Rothberg, 2000). It is easily captured, stored, and shared.

Furthermore, the Skandia model divides organizational capital into process and innovation capital. Manuals, best practices, Intranet resources, and project libraries are examples of process capital assets that formalize the know-how inside the organization (Roos et al., 1998). Innovation capital includes intellectual assets and intellectual property, creating future success for the organization.

Customer capital represents the current value of customer relationships. All relationships with other individuals in the organizational environment, external to the organization, such as customers, suppliers, and alliance partners create customer capital value (Sullivan, 2000). Inside customer capital category resides the customer preferences held by employees, thus enhancing relationships with organizational partners (suppliers, vendors, etc.) who hold intimate knowledge of the organization or industry (Erickson & Rothberg, 2000). Moreover, there is much more expense incurred gaining a sale from a new customer as opposed to gaining the same sale with a current customer. The interaction of human capital and organizational capital refines and transforms customer capital into financial value (Skandia, 2001).

For example, the more mutual value created with organizational suppliers, vendors, and customers, the closer the attachments and mutual loyalties that enhance the company's profits and performance (Sullivan, 2000). The value of customer capital increases when facing reliance on external assistance for daily operations, such as outsourcing. Cost-cutting measures in the form of downsizing and the increased interconnectedness of industries and markets has led to organizations relying on these external resources (Roos et al., 1998).

Skandia set an important precedent in using the value of intangible forms of assets in accounting processes and continues to serve as an example for other companies. However, lumping all forms of intangible values under IC and its subcategories no longer seems sufficiently discriminating. With new categories for intangible capital emerging in the literature, more refined ways of conceptualizing and accounting for value are emerging.

Human Capital. Human capital, defined as anything that thinks, consists of the brains, skills, insights, and potentials of the organization's individual members (Roos et al., 1998). Human capital embraces the acquired knowledge, skills, and capabilities that enable employees to work in new and innovative ways, thus contributing to the overall success of the organization (Nahapiet & Sumantra, 1998; Erickson & Rothberg, 2000). A recent report by Price Waterhouse identifies that many chief executive officers (CEOs) consider a shortage of qualified workers to be the most impending barrier to the future growth of their companies. Herein lies the potential value of identifying and supporting critical human capital as organizations wrestle to attract, hire, and sustain employment of the top talent with high levels of individual IC. Moreover, regardless of the employment rate, organizational leaders work in the best interest of the organization to make better use of the current human capital in the organization to sustain organizational competitiveness, countering the effects of organizational distress (Nelson, 2000).

Human capital embodies the collective experience, skills, and basic know-how of the organization's workforce (Sullivan, 2000). Employee abilities or competence generate value for the organization, representing the innermost potential of the organization (Roos et al., 1998). The critical elements of employee knowledge and skill drive organizational potential that determines what the organization will and will not accomplish successfully in the future (Becker et al., 2001). Organizations developing employee knowledge and skill improve the overall competence of the organization's workforce. For example, organizations seek to develop an employee possessing the ability to use a computer (good skill) in addition to the ability to explain how the computer works (good knowledge) (Roos et al., 1998). Furthermore, organizations rely on employee attitude and behavior through the use of employee skills and abilities to further the advancement of the organization.

Every employee participates in the organization of his or her free will; therefore, not all of the organization's value is under organizational direct control. Stories concerning the drop in stock price upon the announcement of an important employee leaving a company represent examples of this lack of organizational control over organizational value (Ulrich, 1997; Roos et al., 1998). The realization of a lack of organizational ownership for human capital sheds new light on developing and retaining employees, such as training and HR management policies. If companies minimize turnover, a substantial investment in employee training and development contributes to organization's competitive advantage by retaining the value of human capital (Kenneth, 2000).

Innovation. In a constantly evolving business landscape, organizations thrive on the ability of employees to apply knowledge in different situations and the ability to innovate and transform ideas into products (Roos et al., 1998; Kalimo & Toppinen, 1999; Hamel, 2000, 2003). Human capital encompasses the ability of employees to transform knowledge from one context to another through innovation, building on previous knowledge and generating new knowledge. These innovative abilities, such as detecting common factors in two pieces of information and creating a new link, drive company performance through adaptation. Innovation capital consists of the individual ability to increase an existing body of knowledge based on additional insights or rethinking of the situation, resulting in a paradigm shift. Organizations sustain competitiveness through the application of knowledge and skills in practical contexts and building this knowledge through learning (Lev, 2001).

Innovation is not limited to R&D; beliefs concerning the market and competition increase know-how as well. Tucker (2002) identifies four categories of innovation in organizations: strategies, processes, products, and services. While innovation involves the ability to increase new knowledge, imitation involves the ability to survey other industries and companies to apply this knowledge to the situation at hand. Imitation is a valuable resource wrapped into human capital, as organizations must rethink the current approach to innovation, apply the approach to the organization and create something new.

The rules of competition and the evolving criterion of organizational success, such as changes in technology, new government regulations, shift in customer tastes, etc., dictate the value and profitability of organizational adaptation (Kalimo & Toppinen, 1999). Through adaptation, an organization applies solutions in different contexts (Dove, 1994). If the organization anticipates future changes, adaptation serves as proactive efforts in the strategic financial forecasting, scenario planning, or other planning techniques for the advancement of the organization. Understandably, the organizational abilities characteristic of adaptation rely heavily on the strong motivation and attitude of the organizational workforce to create a shift in the whole market (Amidon, 2000). Human capital determines the degree of success of such a shift in market.

Generalized Conceptualization. While a lack of common definitions confuses the discussion of IC, managers use terms based on different models or perspectives, each model describing IC in a different way. These models have foundations in both a knowledge-based and economic-based view; therefore, the terms of these models have different meanings (Sullivan, 2000). The IC model determines the different categories and flows of IC (Roos et al., 1998).

In spite of these imperfections, IC models share a common three-way distinction between external structure, internal structure, and employees composing the over-arching concept of IC (Erickson & Rothberg, 2000). Researchers group the components of these three categories using slightly different terminology.

IC harbors significant levels of knowledge, contextually and socially embedded in the organization. The complex and rich value of IC far surpasses the simple aggregation of knowledge gained from a set of employees (Nahapiet & Sumantra, 1998). IC feeds the future earnings potential of the organization by transforming organizational knowledge and intangible assets into organizational successes (Lev, 2001). These successes stem from the significant interaction of human capital and structural capital (Nahapiet & Sumantra, 1998; Cariner, 2000).

Competitive Edge. Across industries, those organizations that have the best information and employ this information most effectively are more competitive than those companies strictly relying on the size of organizational financial capital (Stewart, 1997). However, the process of identifying and leveraging IC for organizational success is challenging. Once an organization identifies and develops IC, the organization finds added strength and competitiveness due to the changing landscape of the economy.

IC helps provide a language for thinking, talking, and addressing the drivers of the future earnings of the company. For example, "in a world where a slight advantage easily turns into a leading position, think about the profits a company correctly utilizing all its assets might gain over a company that uses only 20–30% of its assets, that is only the financial ones" (Roos et al., 1998, p. 14). In the economy of today, wealth is the product of knowledge. "IC has become so vital that it's fair to say that an organization that is not managing knowledge is not paying attention to business" (Stewart, 1997, p. 56). A growing number of executives are beginning to understand the value of knowledge as a resource facilitating organizational performance and economic activity. "Knowledge is the most powerful engine of production...the economic and producing power of the firm lies more in its intellectual and service capabilities than its hard assets – land, plant, and equipment" (Nahapiet & Sumantra, 1998, p. 245). "In the modern business world, the business imperative is to manage IC or die" (Roos et al., 1998, p. 5). Progressively, knowledge obtains incremental value over previously held organizational treasures of natural resources, expansive factories, or exorbitant bankrolls (Stewart, 1997). Regardless of this change in the business landscape and the increased potential for financial gain, organizations commonly struggle with the intangibility of managing IC (Cariner, 2000). Although growing evidence provides support for a strong link between IC and organizational value, it is difficult to identify and quantify.

Intangible Investment. Currently, intangible investments in R&D, education and competencies, information technologies software, and the Internet dominate intangible investments. These investments in the intangibles drive the economies of the world, estimated at 10% of the gross domestic product of OECD countries. The depth of organizational IC, the value-added IC capital, and the new wealth of organizations appears to overshadow the meager financial capital (Cariner, 2000). The old accounting system for costing physical material and labor is no longer appropriate with the increase in the value of intangible assets such as IC (Stewart, 1997; Osterland, 2001). Failing to accommodate the current shift in capital value, these financial accounting processes provide information for only 20% of the real organizational value. Intangible value composes the remaining 80% of value overlooked by currently outdated accounting systems. Up to 90% of some organizations' market capitalization value, such as America Online and Microsoft, are composed of intangible assets (Cariner, 2000; Lev, 2001).

By identifying future financial indicators, IC supplements traditional accounting systems. Forward-looking IC reporting moves beyond the historically focused perspective of financial accounting. Traditional accounting procedures fail to identify critical intangible value, such as the effect of the resignation of a vital employee, unless the employee is the CEO of the organization (Cariner, 2000; Lev, 2001; Chabrow & Colkin, 2002; 2004). With one or a thousand employees walking out the door, the organization decreases this knowledge and organizational value. Thus, as organizational distress increases, turnover increases, resulting in the substantial loss of IC (Quick et al., 2001).

If IC is such a valuable asset to organizations, why do organizations manage IC so haphazardly? Furthermore, why do organizations fail to consider the ramifications of organizational distress on IC? Typically, organizational leaders hold a degree of skepticism concerning the notion of IC, failing to distinguish between the costs of simply paying individuals and investing in them. Many executives fail to grasp the wide-reaching value of IC, represented by all of the employees of an organization. For example, AT&T announced a workforce reduction of 40,000 employees in 1996. A consultant estimated the massive downsizing cost $4 to $8 billion in IC loss or the equivalent of destroying one third of the organization's resources of property, plant, and equipment. In addition, the value of investing in IC for an organization triples the value of simply investing in machinery (Stewart, 1997).

Several organizations, including IBM, Motorola, APQC, and GE show signs of investing in employees, capitalizing on the value of IC. Skandia stands at the forefront of this field of research publishing annual reports with evaluations of the organization's IC holdings (Erickson & Rothberg, 2000). However, not many companies realize the severity and costs associated with loss or reduction of IC attributed to organizational distress.

Summary. Organizational leaders investing more attention on issues of IC by focusing on the competence of current employees as well as the talent of new employees increase the attractiveness and value of the company. Focused attention at both the organizational and individual level addresses the challenge of fostering IC as a personal and health-oriented concept, caring about individual employees – nurturing the organization's talent potential (Cariner, 2000). By working with employees to uncover the tacit knowledge embedded in the organization, this tacit knowledge becomes explicit knowledge, available to others in the organization (Erickson & Rothberg, 2000). This is the process by which organizations gain a competitive advantage through the retention and development of IC, countering the reduction of this organizational value by recognizing the influence of organizational distress.

Social Capital

Organizations have unique avenues for creating and sharing knowledge that provide them with a competitive advantage over competing organizations. Knowledge processes provide a significant foundation for organizational advantage (Nahapiet & Sumantra, 1998; Kenneth, 2000; Turner, 2000). SC embodies the notion of creating and sharing knowledge, including the fundamental elements of this organizational flow of information and myriad of relationships. Progressively, the concept of SC has gained the attention of sociologists, economists, anthropologists, as well as organizational researchers, and practitioners investigating the value of SC in organizations (Snell, 1999).

The texture of SC is constructed of "the actual and potential resources embedded within, available through, and derived from the network or relationships possessed by an individual or social unit" (Snell, 1999, p. 62). SC includes the relationship connections between people, such as trust, mutual understanding, and the common values and behaviors binding individual networks and communities that make improved coordination and cooperation possible (Snell, 1999; Cohen & Prusak, 2001).

"Unlike the traditional factors of production – land, labor, and capital – knowledge is a resource locked in the human mind... creating and sharing knowledge are intangible activities that can neither be supervised nor forced out of people... they happen only when people cooperate voluntarily" (Ehin, 2000, p. 10), therefore, the psycho-social environment influences the development and use of SC.

SC is not a new concept; however, the majority of attention on the subject has focused on individuals, nations, cultures, or regions, rather than organizations (Cohen & Prusak, 2001). Furthermore, little attention has been given to the costs of organizational distress in the form of reduced SC. A fundamental principle for forming an organization lies in the competitive advantage of combing networks of individuals with varying knowledge and abilities to contribute to the success of the aggregate (Snell, 1999; Lesser, 2000). Organizational SC involves the trust-based connections between individuals, in addition to the networks and communities used for cooperative action (Cohen & Prusak, 2001). Thus, as a critical rule of organizations, individuals do not work alone; individuals combine talents and energies to accomplish unified goals (Snell, 1999).

Typically, when addressing a problem, individuals access the organization's network of colleagues, friends, associates, neighbors, and subordinates harboring credibility, trust, and expertise in the area (Lesser, 2000).

For instance, the ability of an individual to leverage his or her intelligence, education, and experience relies heavily on how well, to whom, and from whom the individual exchanges information and knowledge (Snell, 1999). A key competitive element lies in the recognition of the shifting trend from the historically dominant approach of determining current organizational value to the creation of organizational value (Nahapiet & Sumantra, 1998). Therefore, coupled with the attention needed to address organizational distress, efforts to develop and enhance SC are significantly advantageous in today's business environment.

Relationship Between SC and IC

Although IC and SC are strongly integrated concepts, the framework of IC excludes the unique aspects of SC (Snell, 1999). IC and SC share common elements of an organization; yet, SC has been shown to facilitate the development of IC in the organization (Leana & Van Buren, 1999). For instance, the direct, voluntary collaboration among all members of an organization results in high levels of IC. This voluntary collaborative behavior (i.e., SC) facilitates the unleashing of inherent creative potential (i.e., IC) of individuals. Organizations are living systems, continuously changing; however, organizational leaders repeatedly treat these living systems like machines, failing to recognize the damaging influence of organizational distress on SC (Ehin, 2000).

Conceptual Framework. Prior research (see Adler & Kwon, 2002, for critique of previous SC research) has sought to clarify the conceptualization of SC, establishing a framework consisting of three dimensions: structural, relational, and cognitive dimensions. Structural elements of SC include the expansive networks of relationships and the various assets that may be activated through each network. The conceptual umbrella of structural SC covers the overall pattern of connections between individuals in a network, such as whom an individual reaches and how that individual reaches others. The presence or absence of network ties between individuals determines the degree of structural SC. Appropriate organization inside structural SC determines the existence of networks created for a specific purpose that may be used for other objectives (Nahapiet & Sumantra, 1998).

Relational SC includes the type of personal relationship, such as respect and friendship, individuals develop with others through a series of interactions in the organization. The type of relationship within relational SC determines the behavior of individuals. For example, two individuals occupying the same position in a similar network may choose different critical actions if the personal and emotional attachments to other network members vary between the two (Nahapiet & Sumantra, 1998).

The cognitive dimension of SC refers to the resources used for sharing representations, interpretations, and systems of meaning among different groups in the organization. Knowledge and experience are shared through the existence of shared language and vocabulary as well as through the sharing of collective narratives, such as myths, stories, and metaphors. These vehicles of communication comprise the basic elements of shared cognition that facilitates the exchange of information and facilitates the combination of different forms of knowledge (Nahapiet & Sumantra, 1998).

Unlike other forms of capital, the parties involved in each relationship jointly own the value of that relationship; thus, no individual has exclusive ownership of value. Another commonality lies in the inability to easily trade SC; e.g., exclusive friendships and obligations do not transition from one person to another without intensive development and trust. Additionally, SC mechanisms facilitate individual actions to the extent that the achievements of particular objectives would be unattainable without the presence of these mechanisms (Nahapiet & Sumantra, 1998).

Multiple Levels. SC operates at the level of an individual, a team, an organization, an industry, a community, nation or entire economy; therefore, organizational distress affects the loss or reduction of SC on multiple levels of the organization (Snell, 1999). Organizational SC benefits both the organizational members (e.g., enhancing employee skills) and the organization (e.g., creating value for shareholders) (Leana & Van Buren, 1999).

At the individual level, SC represents an attribute of an individual who recognizes the advantages of his or her status or position in a group (Leana & Van Buren, 1999). The value of SC to the individual comes from the individual's ability to negotiate opportunities. For example, one manner in which a manager contributes to an organization is his or her ability to co-ordinate people, discovering opportunities that will add value to an organization and gathering the right individuals to develop these opportunities. The value of SC increases or decreases in relation to an individual's position in the framework of organizational relationships. Those individuals filling "structural holes," (Burt, 1992) or locations in networks where individuals are not generally linked, have privileged access to organizational information and resources. Therefore, these individuals have a potential advantage over others when competing for promotions, jobs, and pay (Snell, 1999).

At the organizational level, SC represents an attribute of groups, departments, and organizational networks, reflecting the character of social relations within an organization. Levels of collective goal orientation and shared trust through individual organizational members create the value of SC by facilitating successful collective action (Leana & Van Buren, 1999). Previously, more attention given to organizational SC research has investigated the returns to the individual and focused less on the returns to the organization. The degree of value of SC depends on the organizational level under analysis. For instance, human capital (e.g., education and experience) is more important for promotions at a lower level in the organization while SC has more importance for positions at the executive level. Moving up the levels of the organization, the underlying elements of SC (i.e., network ties, interpersonal trust, and shared knowledge) become more complex and more difficult to manage (Snell, 1999).

The ultimate value of SC benefits the organization if organizational distress levels remain low, allowing both the individual and organizational levels of SC to increase. The benefits of increasing SC at multiple levels in the organization result in tangible as well as intangible outcomes. For example, Xerox copier repair technicians shared tips for solving difficult problems using an online system; yet, the technicians refused financial rewards for providing these tips. The technicians rejected these rewards because the intrinsic rewards of reputation and gratitude by peers was more important. The personal satisfaction and reputation of the technicians represent individual value that complemented the competitive effectiveness of the organization (Cohen & Prusak, 2001). The effects of organizational distress derail these benefits of SC in the form of deflated job satisfaction and reduced morale (Quick et al., 2001).

Competitive Edge. By facilitating the growth of SC and minimizing the limiting effect of organizational distress, SC generates many outcomes beneficial to the individual and the organization in various ways (Leana & Van Buren, 1999; Cohen & Prusak, 2001). SC leads to better sharing of knowledge due to established relationships of trust, common frames of reference, and shared goals. SC lowers transaction costs with an increased cooperative spirit developed within the organization, as well as the relationships between the organization and customers, and partners of the organization (Cohen & Prusak, 2001).

Lower turnover rates, associated with organizations with high levels of SC, reduce severance costs, hiring and training expenses, help to avoid disruptions resulting from frequent personnel changes, and help maintain valuable organizational knowledge (Adler & Kwon, 2002). SC also helps facilitate the execution of joint problem-solving and decision-making by providing easier access to explicit and tacit organizational knowledge. SC provides a mechanism for vicariously learning from the insight and experiences of their peers, thus establishing an organizational context for exchange (Snell, 1999). UPS, Aventis, 3M, Hewlett-Packard, Russell Reynolds Associates, SAS Institute, Viant, and other organizations have made investments in SC that enables these organizations to attract and retain talented and skilled employees (Cohen & Prusak, 2001).

A primary way that SC benefits the organization is the justification of individual commitment to the collective interest of the organization. For example, if an individual feels his or her efforts contribute in a vital way to the collective, he or she is more likely to engage in extra-role behavior, striving to coordinate more effectively with others in the organization, among other pro-social behaviors. This recognition decreases the time spent by individuals in pursuits beneficial only to themselves, such as social loafing, self-promotion, and unwillingness to cooperate (Leana & Van Buren, 1999). Russell Reynolds' President and CEO Hobson Brown Jr., says, "everything in this firm works because of SC," believing that the firm's trust-based collaboration is instrumental to the organization's success (Cohen & Prusak, 2001, p. 41).

SC allows the organization to react quickly and operate in a flexible manner, providing support for the organization to survive in a turbulent business environment. SC facilitates the ability for organizations to become more flexible and decreases rigidity in the way individuals conduct and organize work. SC increases the efficiency of action, such as networks of social relations, particularly those characterized by weak ties or structural holes. Investments into programs emphasizing employee involvement, training, flexible deployment, and labor-management cooperation are associated with improvements in productivity, cost savings, and product quality enhancements (Leana & Van Buren, 1999). Organizational distress effects (i.e., lowered morale, reduced productivity, and poor communication for instance) limit the organizational flexibility gained by high levels of SC.

Era of Volatility. While facing exorbitant external and internal volatility, organizations today must attract, employ, and retain workers whose specialization of skill is in high demand, sought by competitors striving to persuade these individuals to consider other employment options in the "war for talent." The waves of volatility arrive in new technologies, mergers and acquisitions, and an unmapped global marketplace rich with developing opportunities and competition. Based on threats of survival and effectiveness, organizations typically undertake enormous internal changes in response or anticipation of a developing business environment (Bartlett & Ghoshal, 2002).

Partnerships, mergers and acquisitions, product changes, or redirection of organizational focus influence how individuals work and modify the values and goals of the organization. The most obvious example of disruptive change is downsizing, or the laying off of workers, which increases organizational distress, destroying networks, communities, and trust. Increased volatility leads to heightened organizational distress, resulting in organizational costs. These costs are associated with the disruptions of stable connections and work relationships that bind networks of individuals to one another and the organization as a whole (Cohen & Prusak, 2001).

These disruptions, uncertainties, and outlook toward a volatile age make SC more important than ever before. Cyclically, mergers and acquisitions, shifting partnerships, and downsizings continue to tear down and rebuild the boundaries of organizations again and again. With this pattern of regeneration, organizations continually search and rely on the discovery of novel ideas, the formation and exploitation of established trust relationships, the foundation and enhancement of mutual understanding, and other elements associated with of high levels of SC (Adler & Kwon, 2002). High levels of SC provide the stability and relationships that allow members of organizations to work together facing the additive consequences of organizational distress at the hands of a volatile environment (Ganster & Murphy, 2000). In the software industry, where turnover typically exceeds 20% per year, SAS has achieved a high level of employee commitment by developing a culture rich in trust, respect, and recognition for employees' personal lives, personified by day-care services, recreational facilities, and flexible work schedules. This long-term investment and commitment to building this culture generated savings of $70 million a year due to reduced turnover rates (Cohen & Prusak, 2001). In addition, the stable workforce ensures a 98% customer retention rate, resulting in strengthened customer relationships (i.e., customer capital).

Those organizations on the cutting edge work hard to reduce the consequences and potentially destructive effects of organizational distress on SC due to these aforementioned aspects of volatility. By consciously and deliberately investing in SC, organizations help to preserve organizational values, connections, and employee skills during time of distress and disruptive situations (Lesser, 2000; Morphew, 2001). Longevity builds SC by strengthening relationships and trust over time; the longer people stay in an organization, the more they will know and understand one another, deepening extensive networks and relationships. The challenge in improving organizational strength lies in convincing organizational leaders to invest in SC, thus reducing the loss of value due to organizational distress.

Downsizing Reduction. For effectiveness and survival, organizations frequently undertake internal changes in response or anticipation of a change in the business environment (Marks, 1999; Adler & Kwon, 2002). This type of internal volatility erodes SC that lives or dies by the strength and stability of connections within the organization. Additionally, the degree to which SC thrives in the organization depends on the adherence of the workforce to explicit and tacit agreements that bind employees to the organization and to one another. The most obvious example of organizational disruptive change is downsizing, a strong impetus for increased organizational distress. Downsizing activities degrade networks and communities while reducing trust among the "survivors," or those employees left in the organization to fill in the gaps of those missing by increasing workloads and performance expectations. These downsizing effects are worsened exponentially as those leaders making the decision to cut costs grant themselves enormous amounts of bonuses, breeding resentment, and cynicism in the workforce.

If organizational distress attacks the organization, mismanagement and neglect of SC factors damages the individual and the organization (NIOSH, 2000). For example, the absence or reduction of SC makes the effort of collective action less profitable and generates more self-seeking behavior (Leana & Van Buren, 1999). Ramifications of individual self-interests include lowered morale, lowered productivity, and loss of vitality, all affecting the bottom line. Moreover, if unmanaged, an individual's SC increases while the overall SC at organizational level decreases (Snell, 1999). This type of behavior is rampant during downsizings, mergers and acquisitions, and periods of uncertainty (Burt, 2000).

Typically, organizations react to the crisis of lower sales or stock market valuation by cutting the very things that build SC, from training to travel budgets for internal meetings. These organizations fail to recognize the threat these actions pose to the SC drivers of trust and collaboration (Cohen & Prusak, 2001; Quick et al., 2001).

Today, disruptions, uncertainties, and the opportunities of the business climate draw attention to the value of SC more than ever. Mergers, acquisitions, shifting partnerships, and the constant banding and disbanding of companies cause organizations to seek and retain new ideas, stability, and connections that allow employees to work together, all characteristics of favorable SC (Marks, 1999).

Investment in Stability. Decreased job security, a common result of organizational distress, leads to potential costs for organizations as a result of failing to maintain or develop organizational SC (NIOSH, 2000). For example, an unfortunate byproduct of organizational efforts to downsize is the endorsement of individualistic behavior on the part of organizations, thus decreasing collective action and trust in the organization. In the absence of organizational SC, individuals invest less effort in learning organizational-specific knowledge and more in learning knowledge valued by the external labor market, thus improving personal marketability for a potential up-coming job search (Leana & Van Buren, 1999).

The following example clearly illustrates the value of SC by investing directly in the organizational workforce (Cohen & Prusak, 2001). In 1995, a fire destroyed the Malden Mills Factory in Lawrence, Massachusetts. Aaron Feurestein, CEO, provided his 3000 employees with full salaries after the fire, opting not to take the insurance money and retire. Conversely, Feu-restein drew attention from the business community calling his actions "very unbusinesslike," suggesting that the majority of the business community does not understand the competitive value of organizational SC (Gewirtz & Gumpert, 2003).

With the benefits of SC close in mind, Feurestein's decision to keep his entire workforce on the payroll throughout the rebuilding of the plant makes very good business sense. The money spent on the payroll was a direct investment in the future of his business, along with the humane wel-fare of his workforce. By continuing to pay salaries and recognizing he had been investing in these individuals for years, Feurestein retained a workforce that had previously proven to be reliable and skillful. One of the more outstanding benefits of this type of investment results in the organization's employee retention rate of 95%. Clearly, Feurestein made an investment in SC and continues to reap the rewards in low turnover rates (Gewirtz & Gumpert, 2003).

The hearing-aid firm, Oticon, represents another example of a company investing in SC for organizational competitiveness (Cohen & Prusak, 2001). The CEO at Oticon recognized the value of social space to facilitate social interaction; therefore, he built more social space for employees to talk in areas where employees walk or already gathered. For example, he noticed that employees meeting on the stairwells typically stopped to converse; thus, he built broader stairwell landings with coffee machines and chairs to sit down, encouraging employees to extend conversations in areas where they naturally occurred. These changes increased opportunities for employees to exchange ideas and build relationships of trust.

Trust. SC depends on trust. Trust, an essential element in developing and retaining SC, and collective identity facilitate the effectiveness of more flex-ible, high-performance work practices, compared to traditional economic incentives (e.g., increased compensation, etc.). Stable employment practices and reciprocal labor-management relations develop SC. Characteristics of organizations with high levels of SC, such as longer job tenure and higher trust, affect the adoption of flexible work practices. For example, the job stability of a research management team in an organization within the automobile industry was associated with the incidence of flexible work practices, such as employee involvement teams and job rotation (Leana & Van Buren, 1999). The more an organization depends on the creativity and collaboration of employees, the more instrumental levels of trust are to achieving organizational success (Adler & Kwon, 2002).

SC helps to manage the collective action of an organization (Leana & Van Buren, 1999). SC, in the form of high levels of trust, diminishes the probability of opportunism and reduces the need for costly monitoring processes, thus reducing the cost of transactions (Nahapiet & Sumantra, 1998). With stable employment relationships, individuals recognize the rationale for developing firm-specific knowledge and skills, thus increasing the collective IC and SC of the organization. Organizations benefit from this development, realizing the efficiency of lower turnover and resistance to change on account of the heightened job security (Leana & Van Buren, 1999). Together, organizational stability and shared understanding provide a greater coherence of organizational action (Adler & Kwon, 2002). SC levels fail to respond to imitation or enticement using monetary rewards, as evidenced by the Xerox repair technicians refusal to receive pay for sharing problem-solving tips (Ehin, 2000; Cohen & Prusak, 2001). Genuine relationships comprising SC are only found in the social context of trust, a rarity in this age of competitiveness (Glaeser, Laibson, Scheinkman, & Soutter, 1999).

Innovative Rewards. Another way that SC provides organizations with a competitive edge lies in the resulting creativity and learning generated by the increased collective efficiency. By encouraging cooperative action and increasing the efficiency of information, SC facilitates the development of innovative ideas, processes, relationships, and products (Nahapiet & Sumantra, 1998). SC provides the foundation for risk taking through the development of new ways of conducting daily work and through the new outcomes of these innovative processes. The inherent trust associated with organizations developing and retaining high levels of SC helps employees feel secure in taking risks while representing the organization's best interest (Leana & Van Buren, 1999).

For 3M, the trust in supervisors and colleagues formed the critical collaboration and entrepreneurial spirit characteristic of the company. The relationship between trust and innovation at 3M is best explained as, "on the organizational trapeze, individuals will take the entrepreneurial leap only if they believe that there will be a strong and supportive pair of hands at the other end to catch them" (Cohen & Prusak, 2001, p. 40). Developed SC supplies this strength, support, and approval needed for new organizational ideas needed for gaining market share and organizational viability (Dove, 1994; Shafer, 1999).

Conversely, organizational SC may adversely affect the adoption and diffusion of innovation in organizations. SC can be an impetus or impediment to innovation, depending on the culture of the organization (Leana & Van Buren, 1999). The more an organization depends on the ingenuity and collaboration of organizational members, the more the level of trust becomes increasingly valued (Cohen & Prusak, 2001). This last realization of mismanaged SC generally stems from organizational distress, allowing the organization to negatively impact the positive value of SC. Organizational distress taxes individuals' resources (e.g., physical and mental strength) better used for innovative, creative thinking, yet these resources focus on potential threats to job security or confrontational coworker relationships (Ganster & Murphy, 2000). Thus, organizational distress counteracts the organizational innovative process.

Technologic Value. Just as trust and stability are critical to harnessing innovation, so to is SC a driver of harnessing the value of technology. Through social networks, even the most sophisticated technology relies on the ability of employees to produce value (Moran, 2001; Morphew, 2001). An organization needs to have a strong information-sharing culture; that is why SC is so critical. For example, *Fortune* magazine Editorial Director Geoffry Colvin (1997) identifies the significant link between technology and employees stating "bottom line: the more that information-technology revolutionizes business, the more economically valuable are the exclusively human qualities of the people who work in companies" (Ehin, 2000, p. 9).

Unlike the duplication of new technologies and software, collaborative relationships require longer periods of time to foster and develop SC value, impossible to duplicate by other organizations. In organizations, the explicit knowledge generated by internal employees, suppliers, competitors, and customers is constantly gathered and made accessible to all organizational members. Thus, organizations rely heavily on investments in information technology and providing maintenance for these systems (Bettis & Hitt, 1995; Hamburg & Greif, 1996; Moran, 2001). Organizations generally overlook the similar need to invest in the social aspects that accompany technology. For example, in a time when innovation is progressively accelerating, "the soft trumps the hard, the most powerful technologies are those that enhance, amplify, extend, augment, distill, recall, expand, and develop soft relationships of all types" (Ehin, 2000, p. 166). These soft relationships involve the SC structure of employee value.

The future of organizations will increasingly rely on the competitive use of technology and information; therefore, work focusing on the human context of the use of technology is extremely useful for gaining organizational support for the enhancement of SC. Organizational informatics is a growing area of research involving the use of technology and information dispersal, referred to as social informatics (Amidon, 2000; Sawyer & Rosenbaum, 2000).

The transfer of technology, or "the process by which ideas are translated into new products," is an invaluable strength for increasing organizational advantage over competitors (Jassawalla & Sashittal, 1996, p. 25). However, typically the complexity of human interactions hinders the efficient management of this process. Many technologic endeavors require high levels of cooperation involving a variety of organizational participants. A study of 10 high-tech organizations identified interpersonal difficulties as the most significant challenge to the transfer of technology, as opposed to technologic issues. Facilitating the development and retention of SC helps to integrate diverse organizational skills, capturing the creative potential resulting from the network and interactions inside the organizational dimensions of SC (Moran, 2001; Morphew, 2001).

Summary. A minimum level of organizational SC ensures an organization's short-term activity as a shared enterprise; however, this low level of SC does not ensure the organization's survival over the long term (Leana & Van Buren, 1999). All organizations have some level of SC, yet only those taking advantage of the value from leveraging SC outperform the competition. Just as IC has become an increasingly important intangible element of organizational capability, so too has SC. Basically, organizations in a highly competitive, global economy must invest in the value of intangible assets (e.g., IC and SC), maximizing the value of all organizational attributes (Cohen & Prusak, 2001).

Organizations seeking to maintain and enhance SC need to take a long-term perspective when viewing employee relations, investing in employees as assets to be developed rather than damaging costs to be minimized. The construction of strong and stable relationships helps to build and to maintain organizational SC by increasing trust. In order to enhance SC, organizations should develop employment practices that provide stability among organizational members and how employees are deployed into these stable relationships. Organizations allocating investments into training, job security, and collaborative work and learning build strong models of SC. These investments strengthen the relationships between employees, employers, and among coworkers within an organization (Leana & Van Buren, 1999).

Downsizings and layoffs, quickly destroy slowly developed SC by damaging employment relationships. Downsizing and the regular use of temporary employees erode the ability of individuals to form meaningful relationships at work and therefore reduce organizational SC. The importance of organizational SC helps facilitate the shifting emphasis on the short-term, individual contributions in organizations to the integrated, long-term contributions of the collective to organizational success. The overarching organizational culture developing shared commitment, teamwork, shared learning, and collective high-performance work helps the organization offset the costs of organizational distress (Leana & Van Buren, 1999).

Organizational distress leads to a common caveat of SC, the caveat that SC is not a universally beneficial resource (Leana & Van Buren, 1999). The damage SC inflicts if unmanaged occurs when the same cohesive organizational characteristics that pull employees together to conduct business, cause groups to become clannish, narrow-minded, and suspicious of outsiders (Adler & Kwon, 2002). For example, simultaneously, the strong mutual identification that exerts a positive effect on group performance may periodically reduce the openness to information, creating a collective blindness that results in negative consequences for the organization (Nahapiet & Sumantra, 1998). Organizational distress limits and reduces the level of organizational SC. Actions taken by organizational leaders to recognize and limit the costs of distress to SC, increase the overall competitive advantage for the organization.

Collaborative Capital

IC and SC are valuable and interrelated assets in the organization. Many companies have invested significant financial capital to develop IC, particularly the hard infrastructure, such as computers and software, that provides part of the context for knowledge development, storage, and sharing. However, even leading companies have invested less in the soft infrastructure, including the development of SC. The question then becomes: How does one create the conditions for growing IC and SC? One disciplined approach to developing an organizational context that supports the development of intangible capital in a variety of forms can be found within collaborative capital (Beyerlein, Freedman, McGee & Moran, 2002). Creating the culture, processes, and tools for developing a collaborative organization (Beyerlein & Harris, 2003) is a major step toward building enabling conditions for the development of IC and SC. The enabling context can be created within and across systems at all levels.

Collaboration is working together. Collaboration enables members of an organization to work together toward common goals using the resources, talents, tools, and assets they can access (Morse, 2004). It involves attitudes, practices, processes, routines, social networks, shared mental models and goals, and a supportive environment. Collaborative capital is an asset in the organization that enables development of other valued assets. It depends on a context that supports working together well.

In many organizations, a wide variety of barriers to collaboration reduce the opportunities for building IC and SC. Barriers may consist of policies, organizational boundaries, cultural assumptions and expectations, distress, lack of collaborative competencies, and events like downsizing. In the 1990s, the relationship of organizational change initiatives and SC to downsizing was seldom recognized, and subsequent damage to intangible capital from loss of employees was ignored. Today, there is more awareness, but many organizations continue to downsize in a destructive manner. In general, the knowledge about distress and intangible capital is seldom utilized by strategic decision-makers.

The work context has a number of facets and so a number of options for investing that can reduce barriers. The context includes the cultures (micro and macro) and the support systems, including: leadership, rewards, information systems, training, empowerment, change, work design, etc. (see Beyerlein & Harris, 2003, for complete listing). Every organization depends on collaboration and most have some supportive context. One ideal is the collaborative organization (Beyerlein et al., 2002).

The shared goals, practices, and mental models of employees at all levels define the collaborative organization and include such core principles as:

(1) align support systems with collaboration;
(2) raise the level of discussion, dialog and sharing;
(3) foster personal accountability;
(4) align authority, information, and decision-making;
(5) treat collaboration as a disciplined process (see Beyerlein et al., 2002, for detailed list).

Disciplined process refers to systematic and systemic development of collaborative capital. It implies cultural change, so collaboration and the means of supporting it become automatic. All of these principles contribute to reducing distress. For example, raising the level of discussion and dialog produces more open channels for problem-solving and dispute resolution. Quick and innovative solutions emerge when the people involved communicate freely. This reduces the number of causes of distress and the intensity of the distress that does occur.

Collaborative capital can be built at any level of organization to contribute to the quality of communication, joint effort, and creative knowledge generation that makes high levels of performance possible. For example, in this volume, chapters focus on collaboration within teams, across teams, across companies and agencies, and across national cultures. For example, Powell, Koput, Smith-Doerr, and Owen-Smith (2005) discuss the collaboration of companies, quoting from their own earlier work: "Collaborative capital builds over time as a firm participates in research, gains experience, develops capacity, and assembles a diverse profile of activities that moves it toward the center of the network and makes it privy to knowledge spillovers. Once centrally placed, then, collaborative capital enables an organization to create opportunities with the greatest potential for timely impact and payoff" (http://www.stanford.edu/~woodyp/Rso1.pdf). This pattern seems to apply to industries where knowledge is changing rapidly and distributed across many people and sites. Collaborative capital provides opportunities for bringing these people and their ideas together in new and innovative ways.

The changing nature of work demands improved collaboration. The development of IC is at the center of this need as work becomes more complex and knowledge based. Effective sharing of expertise promotes both creativity and learning for the participants which enables exchanges of knowledge and information, participative decision-making, and co-created solutions to emerging problems. Effective sharing occurs across the links of social networks which may look like spider webs when mapped but which represent constant and possibly delicate channels for information flow. Disruption of a social network can be sudden and extreme. For example, when a question of trust arises, flow is immediately impeded.

Effective collaboration is rather difficult and rather rare. Most attempts at collaboration achieve mediocre levels of performance. People settle for communication and coordination (Morse, 2004) and do not reach the level of sharing that creates conditions for discovery and innovation. Collaboration across boundaries is even more difficult. Enabling conditions become more important and distress becomes potentially more destructive.

The ability to produce IC depends on the density of the social network that provides the context for the effort (Nahapiet & Ghoshal, 1998). That density is diffused when distress enters the environment. Distress drives people apart or leads to withdrawal. The investment in collaborative capital reduces the causes and effects of distress. For example, in a team where trust is well established and the members are committed to each other's success, social support emerges for a member who must deal with significant distress, such as a family or health crisis. The development of that trust can be enhanced through investments in the collaborative context, such as team chartering, facilitated team meetings, team-based rewards, etc.

Collaborative capital has been defined as including both the process of collaboration and the context that enables effective work interaction (Beyerlein et al., 2002) – process and environmental assets that can be developed over time. However, in this chapter, we prefer to emphasize the enabling context that collaborative capital represents. The context is difficult to create and represents a form of competitive advantage, because it is difficult to copy but provides benefits for multiple stakeholders. For example, the customer base of a company is a significant asset based on established relationships. The capability for collaboration across boundaries, whether functional, geographic, or line of business, allows the firms to find broader solutions for client problems (Liedtka & Haskins, 1997).

Effective collaborative practices require development of individual and organizational competencies that include: the ability to recognize when to collaborate (and when not to), the ability to determine who needs to be involved in the collaboration, the group processes that enable effective collaboration, etc. Mankin and Cohen (2004) refer to this as lateral skills, i.e., competencies that enable people to build bridges with others.

The collaborative capital concept helps both explain and encourage the view of collaboration as a process that adds value, and that can be managed and improved with intervention points at all levels of the organization. Collaboration as an organizational capability or core competence (Hamel & Prahalad, 1994) is a related set of skills, processes, and social structures that enable the organization to produce something else with inherent value, such as IC or SC, and so generate collaborative advantage.

The collaborative network of relationships within an organization or across its boundaries with customers, suppliers, and partners cannot be bought, copied, or stolen; it must be created from scratch in competing organizations. For example, most mergers fail (Marks & Mirvis, 1997) to achieve their expected financial goals. Although some mergers are intended as a way to buy the intellectual and customer capital of the other company, other intangibles are usually ignored. There is a failure to recognize the existence and value of those intangibles and of their holistic interdependence. So, when an acquisition occurs that results in downsizing and even elimination of the acquired company.

Managers expect their workers to work together, often with changing collections of colleagues, to accomplish complex and demanding work. They expect their members to accomplish tasks that require sophisticated understanding of the tradeoff decisions inherent in their businesses; tasks that require almost constant learning of new skills; and work that requires the trust, respect, and commonality of purpose necessary for cooperative effort. This expectation assumes peak performance is easy and common rather than difficult and rare.

Knowledge work is divided into exploration and exploitation. Exploration involves creative and breakthrough work, and a safe environment (West, 2002). Exploitation represents incremental change, and focuses on finding new uses and markets for products and services, which requires a different environment. Both exploration and exploitation can occur across boundaries of teams, projects, disciplines, functions, companies, and cultures. Collaborative knowledge generation depends on collaborative learning, as well as collaborative creativity. The shared learning may be incremental but can become profound with changes in basic assumptions that lead to significant shifts in perspectives (Liedtka & Haskins, 1997). New ways of seeing provide opportunities for breakthrough work. External demands, perceived threat, and psychologic safety hinder creative work (West, 2002).

Collaborative capital represents the assets the organization has for generating such collaborative output as synergies of ideas and perspectives, joint decision-making, and mutual support. Collaborative assets in the organization may include video conferencing hardware and software for virtual meetings, a climate of trust and experimentation to support sharing and idea generation, and the availability of meeting facilitators or team coaches to aid the process of meeting. Contrast two imaginary companies where one is managed through fear and top-down control so collaboration is stifled in exchange for a perceived sense of control and predictability by those with formal authority and the other is based on open communication, shared learning, egalitarianism, and joint effort, the latter will have significantly more collaborative capital to apply to problems and opportunities. Employees in the fear and control-based organization will experience significantly more distress for several reasons, including: lack of control over their work environments (Karasek & Theorell, 1990), low self-efficacy, demands and pressure from supervisors and managers, psychologically unsafe environment, fear of punishment for collaborating across boundaries, etc. The theory of attention and performance (Eysenck, 1982) suggests that fear of failure lowers performance because it distracts attention from the primary task to be performed. Loss of concentration results in poorer performance. Downsizing provides a similar example: when employees see others in their work area being fired, they begin to think about job hunts rather than work performance.

A wide array of collaborative organizational forms have been developed in recent years. They include the work team, cross-disciplinary work team, virtual team, team-based organization, collaborative organization, partnership, and alliance (Beyerlein & Harris, 2003). The types of collaborative form in this array are similar in that they depend on some key processes and practices as shared leadership, shared mental models, common goals, and joint decision-making. The types differ in scope and complexity. For example, the more boundaries that have to be crossed (disciplinary, organizational, cultural, etc.), the more hurdles there are to successful collaboration (Mankin & Cohen, 2004; Beyerlein, Johnson, & Beyerlein, 2004). Knowledge transfer becomes more difficult as the number of boundaries increases (Dixon, 2000). Complex systems are more vulnerable (Wheatley, 1998), so distress is a greater concern; its impact may have more wide spread consequences. Without an enabling context for collaboration, human and organizational resources remain underutilized and opportunities for sharing, networking, and partnering are missed.

Mankin, Cohen, and Fitzgerald (2004) identify a meta-principle for linking collaborative processes and structures that may be similar to our idea of collaborative capital: two threads interweave to create the context: structure and relationships. Collaboration leverages individual competencies and expertise into enhanced creativity and problem-solving (Liedtka & Haskins, 1997) through relationship. Relationships and the skills that make them sustainable are clearly the cornerstone of collaboration in settings where knowledge work is complex and dynamic. This seems somewhat like social and human capital. Structure represents tools, processes, roles, and links across social networks that reduce uncertainty and increase predictability in the collaborative context. This seems similar to our concept of collaborative capital; i.e., the context that enables effective relating which is the cornerstone for successful knowledge work.

CONCLUSION

Stress is inevitable, whereas distress is not (Hurrell et al., 1988; Cooper & Quick, 1999). Organizations that react appropriately to address distress will be expected to outperform their competitors by retaining and developing organizational intangible value (e.g., IC and SC). Therefore, researchers and practitioners must build upon growing knowledge to help organizations relate the costs of organizational distress, translate the importance of intangible value, and garner support for developing IC and SC to obtain business objectives. The relationship between the health of an organization and the degree of impact of distress serves as a lingering threat to organizational financial costs in the form of organizational intangible value loss (Lesser, 2000; Quick et al., 2001; Adler & Kwon, 2002). Consequently, in order to gain the attention of organizational leaders, there is a tremendous benefit in presenting a more holistic perspective when discussing the relationship of organizational distress to the financial vitality of the organization in the marketplace (Liukkonen & Cartwright, 1999).

No longer may organizations remain unaware or unwilling to address the loss of and failure to enhance IC and SC due to organizational distress (Nelson, 2000; Sullivan, 2000). In order for organizations to interpret the costs of organizational distress, organizations need to develop an understanding of distress at the individual and organizational level (Cooper & Quick, 1999). With this understanding, organizations may begin to minimize the costs of distress, while communicating the awareness of these costs to the entire organization. Failing to address organizational distress leads organizations to run into damaging problems and varied costs in terms of the loss and/or reduction of intangible organizational value.

Bundled with additional intangible and tangible assets, IC and SC create value arising from the multiplicative properties of each entity, contributing indirectly to organizational financial vitality (Kaplan & Norton, 2001; Lev, 2001). Thus, organizational leaders capitalize on this multiplicative value by understanding the key element of this chapter, the interaction of all three concepts: IC, SC, and organizational distress. Each of these three concepts encompasses a series of complex variables that compromise each of these expansive constructs. Although IC and SC possess unique elements, these concepts are strongly integrated, relying on the other to maximize added value to the company in a symbiotic existence. SC has been shown to facilitate the development of IC in the organization (Leana & Van Buren, 1999; Snell, 1999). Therefore, organization distress has a devastatingly influential impact on both IC and SC due to the shared, conceptual boundaries.

The intersection between these three concepts becomes the critical area of focus for organizations striving to harness the competitive gain of maximizing intangible value. The careful handling of this intersection of organizational distress and organizational intangible value determines the degree to which organizations take advantage of this competitive edge. The current volatile business environment exacerbates the dynamics of these concepts. The waves of volatility arrive in new technologies, mergers and acquisitions, and an unmapped global marketplace rich with developing opportunities and challenges organizations to address organizational distress. Based on threats of survival and effectiveness, organizations typically undertake enormous internal changes in response to a continuously developing business environment (Bartlett & Ghoshal, 2002). This reactionary response by organizations generates enormous distress at both the individual and organizational level. Unfortunately, these organizations fail to realize the consequences, resulting in the reduction or loss of intangible value.

The loss of intangible value may potentially impact an organization with equal or greater damage than the loss of more tangible value (Lev, 2001). Moreover, organizations fail to recognize the relationship between organizational distress and intangible organizational value. For example, during the period after a company announces downsizing and layoffs, employees are simultaneously exposed to high levels of distress, facing possible job loss, increased workloads, and physical symptoms of distress. These physical illnesses lead to heightened health care costs for the organization. Consequently, employees lose trust in the organizational leadership, becoming less willing to offer new ideas to spur creativity and innovation. This devastates the development of new products and restricts research and development progress (Allcorn & Diamond, 1997; Koslowsky, 1998).

Mergers and acquisitions, shifting partnerships, and downsizings tear down and rebuild the boundaries of organizations repeatedly. The result of this type of continuous exposure to distress creates a workplace in which employees revert to less sophisticated ways of dealing with work and with colleagues, competence suffers, morale declines, and performance deteriorates (Allcorn & Diamond, 1997; Koslowsky, 1998). However, organizations fail to protect investment in the discovery of novel ideas, the formation and exploitation of established trust relationships, the foundation and enhancement of mutual understanding, and other elements associated with of high levels of intangible value from the damaging impact of organizational distress (Adler & Kwon, 2002).

The effects of organizational distress, such as indirect psychologic outcomes in the form of a loss of vitality, lowered morale, and apathy, restrict employees from accessing key organizational members due to the impact of impending layoffs or lack of organizational support. Typically, when addressing a problem, individuals access the organization's network of colleagues, friends, associates, neighbors, and subordinates harboring credibility, trust, and expertise in the area (Lesser, 2000). For instance, the ability of an individual to leverage his or her intelligence, education, and experience relies heavily on how well, to whom, and from whom the individual exchanges information and knowledge (Snell, 1999). Individuals facing organizational distress restrict the exchange of information, allowing IC and SC value to diminish.

Working conditions creating high levels of distress are associated with increased absenteeism, tardiness, and intentions by workers to quit their jobs, limiting intangible value (Quick et al., 1997). Loss of vitality reduces the production of IC due to poor communication in addition to diminishing SC by disengaging networks of employee relationships used for transferring knowledge needed to achieve business objectives. Absenteeism reduces SC as absent employees disrupt communication channels with coworkers and restricts IC due to employees failing to absorb new information or exchange expertise. Furthermore, limited interaction disrupts the network of department or group members communicating knowledge, resulting in slowed business and lowered productivity. The direct, voluntary collaboration among all members of an organization results in high levels of IC. This voluntary collaborative behavior (i.e., SC) facilitates the unleashing of inherent creative potential (i.e., IC) of individuals. However, disruptive actions producing distress antagonize the stability and relationships characteristic of high SC levels, limiting the ability of the organizational members to work together, facing the additive consequences of organizational distress at the hands of a volatile environment (Ganster & Murphy, 2000).

Moreover, while facing exorbitant external and internal volatility, organizations today must retain top talent to remain competitive and to ensure the survival in the marketplace; thus, most organizations make a large investment of resources in recruiting and hiring processes (Bowen et al., 1991; Bartlett & Ghoshal, 2002). However, organizations do not recognize organizational actions relating to an increase in organizational distress; thereby reducing IC by spurring top talent to separate from the company. An enormous amount of organizational intellectual information and unique knowledge leaves organizations with exiting employees, common during layoffs and downsizings (Erickson & Rothberg, 2000). Top talent not only takes valuable IC (i.e., implicit knowledge) out the door with them, they also take valuable SC in the form of key relationships, the foundation for trust, and transference of knowledge (Department of Trade and Industry, 1998; Sullivan, 2000). The flow of critical information is disrupted restricting the efficiency in providing internal and external customer service due to the destruction of trust-based connections held between organizational members, decreased coordinated activity, and poor communication (Snell, 1999; Cohen & Prusak, 2001).

A key competitive element lies in the recognition of the shifting trend from the historically dominant approach of determining current organizational value to the creation of organizational value (Nahapiet & Sumantra, 1998). Therefore, coupled with the attention needed to address organizational distress, efforts to develop and enhance IC and SC are significantly advantageous in today's business environment. There is a strong business case to control organizational distress in order to sustain and enhance a competitive advantage in the market by leveraging IC and SC. These disruptions, uncertainties, and outlook toward a volatile age make IC and SC more important than ever before.

By facilitating the growth of IC and SC and minimizing the limiting effect of organizational distress, IC and SC generate many outcomes beneficial to the individual and the organization in various ways (Leana & Van Buren, 1999; Cohen & Prusak, 2001). Knowledge processes provide a significant foundation for organizational advantage (Nahapiet & Sumantra, 1998; Kenneth, 2000; Turner, 2000). Further research into the relationship between organizational distress and the reduction of intangible value in the form of intellectual and SC will assist organizational leaders in navigating through an increasingly volatile business environment (Lesser, 2000; Quick et al., 2001; Adler & Kwon, 2002).

Concluding Paragraph

IC is the cornerstone for creating sustainable competitive advantage in industry. Development and effective use of IC depends on the quality of the social network that surrounds it. The processes in that network can be enhanced by disciplined, systematic, and systemic investment in collaborative capital; i.e., creating enabling conditions for relationships that effectively generate new ways to explore and exploit IC. Stress can benefit the processes involved, but distress interrupts them. Collaborative capital can be spent to offset the effects of distress and even prevent some it. Spending money, time, and energy to build collaborative context will generate returns in IC and SC that add value for all stakeholders.

REFERENCES

Adler, P. S., & Kwon, S. (2002). Social capital: Prospects for a new concept. *Academy of Management Review, 27,* 17–40.

Allcorn, S., & Diamond, M. A. (1997). *Managing people during stressful times: The psychologically defensive workplace.* London, England: Quorum Books.
Amidon, D. M. (2000). Power of innovation capital: Leveraging collaborative advantage. *Entovation International News.* Retrieved October 7, 2001, from http://www.skyrme.com/updates/u43_F3.htm
Barney, M. (2001a). Macro, meso, micro: Human capital. *The Industrial-Organizational Psychologist, 39,* 58–63.
Barney, M. (2001b). Macro, meso, micro: McDonald's. *The Industrial-Organizational Psychologist, 39,* 95–97.
Bartlett, C., & Ghoshal, S. (2002). Building competitive advantage through people. *MIT Sloan Management Review, Winter,* 34–42.
Becker, B. E., Huselid, M. A., & Ulrich, D. (2001). *The HR scorecard: Linking people, strategy, and performance.* Boston, MA: Harvard Business School Press.
Beckhard, R. (1997). The healthy organization: A profile. In: F. Hesselbein, M. Goldsmith & R. Beckhard (Eds), *The organization of the future* (pp. 325–328). San Francisco, CA: Jossey-Bass.
Bettis, R. A., & Hitt, M. A. (1995). Technological transformation and the new competitive landscape. *Strategic Management Journal, 16,* 7–200.
Beyerlein, M., Freedman, S., McGee, C., & Moran, L. (2002). *Beyond teams: Building the collobrative organization.* San Francisco, CA: Jossey-Bass/Pfeiffer.
Beyerlein, M., & Harris, C. L. (2003). *Guiding the journey to collobrative work systems: A strategic design workbook.* San Francisco, CA: Jossey-Bass/Pfeiffer.
Beyerlein, M., Johnson, D., & Beyerlein, S. (Eds) (2004). *Advances in interdisciplinary studies of work teams (Vol. 10). Complex collaboration.* Oxford, UK: Elsevier Ltd.
Boudreau, J. W., & Ramstad, P. M. (2005). Where's your pivotal talent? *Harvard Business Review, 83*(4), 23–25.
Bowen, D. E., Ledford, G. E., & Nathan, B. R. (1991). Hiring for the organization, not the job. *Academy of Management Executive, 5,* 35–51.
Briner, R. B., & Reynolds, S. (1999). The cost, benefits, and limitations of organizational level stress interventions. *Journal of Organizational Behavior, 20,* 647–664.
Brown, P., & Lauder, H. (2001). *Capitalism and social progress.* Basingstoke: Macmillan.
Burr, R., & Girardi, A. (2002). Intellectual capital: More than the interaction of competence × commitment. *Australian Journal of Management, 27,* 77–89.
Burt, R. S. (1992). *Structural holes: The social structure of competition.* Cambridge: Harvard University Press.
Burt, R. S. (2000). The contingent value of social capital. In: E. L. Lesser (Ed.), *Knowledge and social capital: Foundations and applications* (pp. 255–286). Boston, MA: Butterworth Heinemann.
Cariner, S. (2000). 1 + 1 = 11. *Across the Board, 37*(10), 29–34.
Cartwright, S., & Panchal, S. (2001). The stressful effects of mergers and acquisitions. In: J. Dunham (Ed.), *Stress in the workplace: Past, present and future* (pp. 67–89). Philadelphia, PA: Whurr Publishers.
Chabrow, E., & Colkin, E. (2002). Hidden value. *Information Week.* Retrieved May 21, 2002, from http://www.informationweek.com/story/IWK20020421S0025
Cohen, D., & Prusak, L. (2001). *In good company: How social capital makes organizations work.* Boston, MA: Harvard Business School Press.
Cooper, C. L. (1996). *Handbook of stress, medicine, and health.* Boca Raton, FL: CRC Press.

Cooper, C. L., & Quick, J. C. (1999). *Fast facts: Stress and strain.* Oxford, England: Health Press.

Department of Trade and Industry. (1998). *Our competitive future: Building the knowledge driven economy.* London, England: Department of Trade and Industry.

DeVoge, S., & Shiraki, J. (2000). People factors: The missing link in merger success. *Compensation and Benefits Management, 16,* 26–32.

Dixon, N. (2000). *Common knowledge: How companies thrive by sharing what they know.* Cambridge: Harvard Business School Press.

Dove, R. (1994). The meaning of life and the meaning of agile. *Production, 106,* 14–15.

Dunham, J. (Ed.) (2001). *Stress in the workplace: Past, present and future.* Philadelphia, PA: Whurr Publishers.

Dzinkowski, R. (2000). The measurement and management of intellectual capital: An introduction. *Management Accounting: Magazine for Chartered Management Accountants, 78*(2), 32–36.

Ehin, C. (2000). *Unleashing intellectual capital.* Boston, MA: Butterworth Heinemann.

Erickson, G. S., & Rothberg, H. N. (2000). Intellectual capital and competitiveness: Guidelines for policy. *Competitiveness Review, 10,* 192–198.

Eysenck, M. W. (1982). *Attention and arousal: Cognition and performance.* New York: Springer Verlag.

Ganster, D. C., & Murphy, L. (2000). Workplace interventions to prevent stress-related illness: Lessons from research and practice. In: C. L. Cooper & E. A. Locke (Eds), *Industrial and organizational psychology: Linking theory with practice* (pp. 34–51). Malden, MA: Oxford.

Geurts, S., & Grundemann, R. (1999). Workplace stress and prevention in Europe. In: M. Kompier & C. Cooper (Eds), *Preventing stress, improving productivity: European case studies in the workplace* (pp. 9–32). London, England: Routledge.

Gewirtz, M., & Gumpert, P. (2003). Sustaining leadership teams at the top: The promise and the pitfall. In: M. Beyerlein, C. McGee, G. Klein, J. Nemiro & L. Broedling (Eds), *The collaborative work systems fieldbook* (p. 170). San Francisco, CA: Jossey-Bass.

Glaeser, E. L., Laibson, C. L., Scheinkman, J. A., & Soutter, C. L. (1999). *What is social capital? The determinants of trust and trustworthiness.* Working Paper no. 7216. Cambridge, MA: NBER.

Gowing, M. K., Kraft, J. D., & Quick, J. C. (1998). *The new organizational reality: Downsizing, restructuring, and revitalization.* Washington, DC: American Psychological Association.

Hamburg, K., & Greif, S. (1996). New technologies and stress. In: M. J. Schabracq, J. A. M. Winnubst & C. L. Cooper (Eds), *Handbook of work and health psychology* (pp. 161–181). New York, NY: Wiley.

Hamel, G. (2000). *Leading the revolution.* Boston, MA: Harvard Business School Press.

Hamel, G. (2003). Innovation as a deep capability. *Leader to Leader, 27,* Winter.

Hamel, G., & Prahalad, C. K. (1994). *Competing for the future.* Cambridge: Harvard Business School Press.

Hesselbein, F., Goldsmith, M., & Beckhard, R. (Eds) (1997). *The organization of the future.* San Francisco, CA: Jossey-Bass.

Hurrell, J. J., Jr., Murphy, L. R., & Sauter, S. L. (1988). *Occupational stress: Issues and developments in research.* London: Taylor & Francis.

Ittner, Christopher, D., Larcker, & David, F. (2003). Coming up short on nonfinancial performance measurement. *Harvard Business Review, 81*(11), 88.

Jassawalla, A., & Sashittal, H. C. (1996). Practical issues of technology transfer in high-tech industrial organizations. *Industrial Management, 38*, 25–31.

Johnson & Johnson (2000a). *Balancing work and family.* Retrieved October 27, 2000, from http://www.johnsonandjohnson.com/job_postings/prog/famwork_index.html

Johnson & Johnson (2000b). *Johnson & Johnson – Environmental, Health and Safety Report 1998 – Health & Wellness.* Retrieved October 27, 2000, from http://www.johnsonand-johnson.com//who_is_jnj/1998_enviro/health_and_wellness.html

Kalimo, R., & Toppinen, S. (1999). Finland: A forest industry corporation. In: M. Kompier & C. Cooper (Eds), *Preventing stress, improving productivity: European case studies in the workplace* (pp. 52–85). London, England: Routledge.

Kaplan, R. S., & Norton, D. P. (2001). Transforming the balanced scorecard from performance measurement to strategic management: Part I. *Accounting Horizons, 15*, 87–104.

Karasek, R. A., & Theorell, T. (1990). *Healthy work: Stress, productivity, and the reconstruction of working life.* New York: Basic Books.

Kenneth, K. J. (2000). Observations on social capital. In: P. Dasgupta & I. Serageldin (Eds), *Social capital: A multifaceted perspective* (pp. 3–5). Washington, DC: The World Bank.

Kompier, M., & Cooper, C. (Eds) (1999). *Preventing stress, improving productivity: European case studies in the workplace.* London, England: Routledge.

Koslowsky, M. (1998). *Modeling the stress–strain relationship in work settings.* London, England: Routledge.

Leana, C. R., & Van Buren III, H. J. (1999). Organizational social capital and employment practices. *Academy Management Review, 24*, 538–555.

Lesser, E. L. (2000). Leveraging social capital in organizations. In: E. L. Lesser (Ed.), *Knowledge and social capital: Foundations and applications* (pp. 3–16). Boston, MA: Butterworth Heinemann.

Lev, B. (2001). *Intangibles: Management, measurement, and reporting.* Washington, DC: Brookings Institute Press.

Lev, B. (2004). Sharpening the intangibles' edge. *Harvard Business Review, 82*(6), 109.

Levi, L., Sauter, S. L., & Shimomitsu, T. (1999). Work-related stress – It's time to act. *Journal of Occupational Health Psychology, 4*, 394–396.

Liedtka, J. M., & Haskins, M. E. (1997). The generative cycle: Linking knowledge and relationships. *Sloan Management Review, 39*, 47–59.

Liukkonen, P., Cartwright, S., & Cooper, C. (1999). Costs and benefits of stress prevention. In: M. Kompier & C. Cooper (Eds), *Preventing stress, improving productivity: European case studies in the workplace* (pp. 33–51). London, England: Routledge.

Mack, D. A., Shannon, C., & Quick, J. C. (1998). Stress and the preventive management of workplace violence. In: R. W. Griffin, A. O'Leary-Kelly & J. Collins (Eds), *Dysfunctional behavior in organizations: Violent and deviant behavior* (pp. 119–141). Greenwich, CT: JAI press, Inc.

Mankin, D., & Cohen, S. G. (2004). *Business without boundaries: An action framework for collobrating across time, distance, organization, and culture.* San Francisco, CA: Jossey-Bass.

Mankin, D., Cohen, S. G., & Fitzgerald, S. P. (2004). Complex collobrations: Basic principles to guide design and implementation. In: M. M. Beyerlein, D. A. Johnson & S. T. Beyerlein (Eds), *Advances in interdisciplinary studies of work team (Vol. 10). Complex collobration.* San Diego, CA: Elsevier.

Marks, M. L., & Mirvis, P. H. (1997). *Joining forces: Making one plus one equal three in mergers, acquisitions, and alliances.* San Francisco, CA: Jossey-Bass.

Marks, M. L. (1999). Surviving a merger. *Electric Perspectives, 24,* 26–35.

Matteson, M. T., & Ivancevich, J. M. (1987). *Controlling work stress: Effective human resource and management strategies.* San Francisco, CA: Jossey-Bass.

Moran, G. (2001). Come together. *Small Business Computing, 6,* 43–46.

Morphew, M. E. (2001). The future of human performance and stress research: A new challenge. In: P. A. Hancock & P. A. Desmond (Eds), *Stress, workload, and fatigue* (pp. 249–262). London, England: Lawrence Erlbaum Associates.

Morse, S. W. (2004). *Smart communities: How citizens and local leaders can use strategic thinking to build a brighter future.* San Francisco, CA: Jossey-Bass.

Nahapiet, J., & Ghoshal, S. (1998). Social capital, intellectual capital, and the organizational advantage. *Academy of Management Review, 23,* 242–267.

Nahapiet, J., & Sumantra, G. (1998). Social capital, intellectual capital, and the organizational advantage. *Academy of Management Review, 23,* 242–266.

National Institute for Occupational Health and Safety (NIOSH) (2000). *Stress.* Cincinnati, OH: NIOSH. Retrieved October 27, 2000, from http://www.cdc.gov/niosh

Nelson, M. C. (2000). Facing the future: Intellectual capital of our workforce. *Vital Speeches of the Day, 67,* 138–143.

Nonaka, I., & Takeuchi, H. (1995). *The knowledge-creating company: How Japanese companies create the dynamics of innovation.* New York, NY: Oxford University Press.

Osterland, A. (2001). Decoding intangibles. *CFO, 17*(4), 56–62. http://www.cfo.com/printable/article.cfm/2992885?f = options

Peterson, C. L. (1999). *Stress at work: A sociological perspective.* New York, NY: Baywood Publishing.

Powell W. W., Koput, K., Smith-Doerr, L., & Owen-Smith, J. *Network position and firm performance: Organizational returns to collaboration in the biotechnology industry.* http://www.stanford.edu/~woodyp/Rso1.pdf, downloaded 1/15/05.

Polanyi, M., & Tompa, E. (2004). Rethinking work-health models for the new global economy: A qualitative analysis of emerging dimensions of work. *Work, 23,* 3–19.

Quick, J. C., Quick, J. D., Nelson, D. L., & Hurrell, J. J., Jr. (1997). *Preventive stress management in organizations.* Washington, DC: American Psychological Association.

Quick, J. C., Nelson, D. L., & Quick, J. D. (2001). Occupational stress and self-reliance: Developmental and research issues. In: J. Dunham (Ed.), *Stress in the workplace: Past, present and future* (pp. 19–33). Philadelphia, PA: Whurr Publishers.

Roos, J., Roos, G., Edvinsson, L., & Dragonetti, N. C. (1998). *Intellectual capital: Navigating in the new business landscape.* New York, NY: New York University Press.

Sawyer, S., & Rosenbaum, H. (2000). Social informatics in the information sciences: Current activities and emerging directions. *Informing Science, 3,* 89–95.

Schabracq, M. J., Winnubst, J. A. M., & Cooper, C. L. (Eds) (1996). *Handbook of work and health psychology.* New York, NY: Wiley.

Shafer, R. A. (1999). Only the agile will survive. *HR Magazine, 44,* 50–51.

Skandia (2001). Retrieved November 1, 2001, from http://www.skandia.com

Snell, S. A. (1999). Social capital and strategic HRM: It's who you know. *Human Resource Planning, 22,* 62–65.

Stewart, & Thomas, A. (1997). *Intellectual capital: The new wealth of organizations.* New York, NY: Doubleday.

Sullivan, P. H. (2000). *Value-driven intellectual capital: How to convert intangible corporate assets into market value.* New York, NY: Wiley.

Tokyo declaration. (1999). On work-related stress and health in three postindustrial settings —
     The European Union, Japan and the United States of America (1999). *Journal of Oc-
     cupational Health Psychology, 4*, 397–399.
Tomer, J. F. (1987). *Organizational capital: The path to higher productivity and well-being.* New
     York: Praeger.
Tucker, R. B. (2002). *Driving growth through innovation: How leading firms are transforming
     their futures.* San Francisco: Berrett-Koehler.
Turner, J. H. (2000). The formation of social capital. In: P. Dasgupta & I. Serageldin (Eds),
     Social capital: A multifaceted perspective (pp. 94–146). Washington, DC: The World
     Bank.
Ulrich, D. (1997). *Human resource champions: The next agenda for adding value and delivering
     results.* Boston, MA: Harvard Business School Press.
Ulrich, D. (1998). Intellectual capital equals competence × commitment. *Solan Mangement
     Review, 39*, 15–26.
Ulrich, D., & Smallwood, N. (2004). Capitalizing on capabilities. *Harvard Business Review,
     82*(6), 119–128.
Waldo, D. (2001). Lessons for employers in a slowing economy. *The Industrial-Organizational
     Psychologist, 39*, 50–51.
Walsh, J. (1999). Merged steel giants aim to sidestep HR policy pitfalls. *People Management, 12*
     June 17.
Weaver, J. L., Bowers, C. A., & Salas, E. (2001). Stress and teams: Performance effects and
     interventions. In: P. A. Hancock & P. A. Desmond (Eds), *Stress, workload, and fatigue*
     (pp. 83–106). London, England: Lawrence Erlbaum Associates.
West, M. A. (2002). Sparkling fountains or stagnant ponds: An integrative model of creativity
     and innovation implementation in work groups. *Applied Psychology, 51*, 355–388.
Wheatley, M. J. (1998). Leading through the unknowns of Y2K. *Strategy and Leadership,
     26*(5), 10–15.
Winnubst, J. A. M., & Schabracq, M. J. (1996). Social support, stress and organizations:
     Towards optimal matching. In: M. J. Schabracq, J. A. M. Winnubst & C. Cooper (Eds),
     Handbook of work and health psychology (pp. 87–102). New York, NY: Wiley.
Wojcik, J. (2001). Cutting costs of stress. *Business Insurance, 35*, 1–2.

MANAGING SOCIAL ENTROPY IN THE URBAN DEVELOPMENT OF A CITY AND THE ROLE OF SOCIO-ENGINEERING

Claudia Bettiol

ABSTRACT

This chapter examines the fourth kind of intangible capital, which is the capability to transform a heterogeneous aggregate of people, first into a group and then into a team. This is useful both on a macro- and micro-scale. This is shown through the case of people involved in an urban transformation with its endogenous and exogenous complexities. Following the definition of sustainability, people can be divided into three different kinds that use language differently to be understood. Communication happens only on each personal boundary line, which is dynamic, and acts on two levels: the technical and the relational. The presence of a connector, mediator, translator, and negotiator, who has both human and technical training, is essential.

Collaborative Capital: Creating Intangible Value
Advances in Interdisciplinary Studies of Work Teams, Volume 11, 285–305
Copyright © 2005 by Elsevier Ltd.
ISSN: 1572-0977/doi:10.1016/S1572-0977(05)11010-3

INTANGIBLE CAPITAL

The definition of intangible capital is not unique because it involves different sciences and the study of actual social behavior. The perception and the consciousness of how people feel cannot be isolated from the definition of a work group. The passage from the management of human resources to improving the skills of each single individual (i.e., the transition from worker to collaborator) involves new perspectives and it is a consequence of social evolution. The traditional scientific and mechanical disciplines of re-engineering have left room to human disciplines, such as sociology, philosophy, and cognitive science, to address this need.

More generally, in modern countries every relationship based on power is arriving at a breaking point that corresponds to a form of failure. The philosopher Habermas (1998) affirmed that in the modern age, forms of life which progressively stiffen become victims of entropy. And we have to consider entropy as an uncontrolled state or a breaking point. In this way work organization theories in the past, which tried to define everything, have created a system which no longer connects with reality. The over-rigid rules that drove the procedures in the first place end up in counter position with the growing complexity of social relationships. If communication involves two levels: technical and relationship, these overly rigid systems address only one of them: lose efficiency and create disease among people.

At the middle of last century, Ortega and Gasset (1962) described the Rebellion of the Mass and more recently Lasch (1995) has described the Revolt of the Elite. This passage corresponds exactly to the passage from general to particular, from the consideration of a worker without a face to the perfect knowledge of his or her face. It means also that there is a self-consciousness. Each "brain-worker" feels him- or herself as an individual company with its intangible capital that is represented by him- or herself. People know that their power is invisible and it is inside their mind and their heart and that their intangible capital is a center of attraction. So they consider their knowledge as a power that needs special attention to grow continuously. Since they are alert to maintain the value of their capital, they follow a learning program and creativity developing courses all their life. They take care of their investments (Ciuffoli, 2004; Castagna, 2001).

These aspects are evident in different circumstances, and if we look at the nature of commerce, we understand why the marketing strategies are not concentrated on the product anymore but on the single consumer. It is the birth of one-to-one marketing (Pepper & Rogers, 2002) which means that sellers have to concentrate on each buyer and on his or her unique facets. With respect to the single individual, it is also the birth of cause-related marketing (Pitteri, Picucci, & Villani, 2002). It means that any factory has to be harmonically inserted in the context in which they reside. In the 1930s, industry tycoons created a social backup to their factories (hospitals, schools, roads, lodgings); this originated bilateral goodwill (Sennet, 1999). We can call this the beginning of collaborative capital, which has been eliminated during 1970s and 1980s. During this period of re-engineering programs, the value of collaboration has been lost. Nowadays, industries should recuperate in part the old time links with local communities to build up new collaborative capital (e.g., my birthplace, Colleferro, a small town near Rome, built round a bomb industry in the 1930s). Now it is evident that such attention will multiply the number of relationships that everyone has to cope with.

After accepting these premises, we can define the essence of intangible capital. If we follow the development of knowledge management (Steward, 2002), we will find four kinds of intangible capital that are emerging with the growth of modern economy. The first two kinds of intangible capitals are related to the internal work in the organization while the others are connected with the managing of external relationships.

The first form of intangible capital is individual knowledge which includes preparation and background. The individual is responsible for increasing it by courses and up-dating studies. The second form is the capability of working in a team without egoism and personal prevarications and the organization of work groups. The importance of this second form of intangible capital can be easily understood if we think of the differences between a soccer team and a rugby team. A soccer team is based more on individual capacity, whereas a rugby team is forced to rely on the teamwork of friends. Soccer champions cover headlines and front pages: single rugby champions simply do not exist.

These two forms of intangible capital belong to the internal context of a single company. On the other hand, there are two more intangible forms of capital that are connected with factors external to the organization and with the ability to cope with external complexity. The third kind of intangible capital is directly related to management of personal relationships or the external network. We can understand its importance if we think of the differences between junior and senior professionals. One of the most important differences is the kind of individual contacts that have become deeper and evolved into a relationship for the senior professional. This is one of the reasons why senior experts are natural problem solvers.

The fourth form of intangible capital is collaborative. This can be described as the capacity of transforming work groups into teams, perhaps with very different people who do not belong to the same organization. Single people in an internal organization can form a team by integrating and collaborating with resources from outside the group: independent but connected. Going back to interacting structures of the 1930s where big factories comprised all production efforts, we see that now this large factory has been decentralized to include a head office and several external detached branches. These new branches need to learn how to collaborate again, obviously in modern terms, shifting from work group to work team. It is the re-creation of a sense of belonging to a group that is important; this means, no more individual flexibility but group flexibility (Sennet, 1999). By this process of humanization, industrial companies are trying to overcome the troubles of de-humanization of the past. We chose the prefix "de-", considering the ancient Latin. It means that there is de-segregation or de-construction while the prefix "in-" means an evolution in a negative way.

For example, in commercial matters, considering the single buyer, we can imagine that the work of organizations has enlarged to include buyers as well. But those people cannot be directed and organized, and they do not want to be a part of a constrictive program. These people do not want to be a part of a tangible work team, so every single seller has to gain the confidence of the buyer in order to let him feel being a part of a team. Therefore, the sellers need to acquire a new capability to connect with their costumers in order to get to a non-prejudicial opening toward others. It is an inter-cultural matter.

This fourth type of intangible capital means that people have to work with heterogeneity, without any leadership *a priori*, and they have to be able to create very flexible teams that can adapt themselves to all circumstances. We will show how this is evident in the managing of environmental and urban transformations.

MACRO- AND MICRO-ASPECTS OF COLLABORATION

Analyzing more profoundly the meaning of collaborative capital in different situations, scholars have arrived at describing the importance of collaboration starting from a variety of perspectives. All arguments that we have described can be observed in macro- and in micro-settings and there is a perfect parallel between the two levels. When we think on micro- and macro-scales, we can find also Eastern and Western situations which correspond in many ways to our current and past situations. And this corresponds also to our language structures including those of our sons or daughters and those of our parents.

Generally every single industry or company follows two roads that are crossing or diverging at different times. Apart from a single-market policy, there is a common-market strategy for the same aims of groups of manufacturers of similar products. Cartels matter. It is the work of the lobbies which is the only way to focus the attention on a particular aspect. If this is common in the Anglo-Saxon world, and especially in the U.S.A. as described in 1835 by Alexis de Tocqueville (1971), this is not usual in a small Latin country like Italy. In Italy there are also other questions connected with the size of its industries and the global competition on the world market. The growth of Eastern industries has forced government policy to encourage new forms of collaboration between small industries in two ways: same localization and intangible cooperation for homogeneous manufacture of similar products. There is a law for the district of a particular product specialization and a law for a new form of partnership between industries for lobby actions. It is an Italian strategy, as the Japanese have done with their keiretzus (Milgron & Roberts, 1992), and this new collaboration is the natural evolution of Italian middle-size factories during this growth of economic globalization.

Therefore, examining the macro-scale, there is worldwide competition in manufacturing and the de-localization of production factories to emerging countries, the struggle for respect of the environment and the growth of social movements, the old trade organization (World Trade Organization, WTO) and the new trade organizations of third-world country cooperatives. It is the beginning of sustainable and jointly liable commerce, with its spokesperson, Arundhati Roy (2003), and with new commercial spaces. A city like Rome has designated 4 hectares for this kind of trade in opposition to the great malls.

Also, on a macro-level, we find the new webs created by the Internet. We can refer to very different situations and each one has its own experiences. Without the Internet, the anti-globalization movements would not be able to connect and exchange their opinions on the environment. With the Internet, each day they are becoming more important and now they are involved practically in all the policies of the third world. For example, when the WTO or other international organizations have a meeting, suddenly there are people from all parts of the world that arrive with a parallel net organization. Non-government organizations (NGOs) are the natural supporters of the governments of poor emerging countries.

If we examine the definition of sustainability by Nobel Laureate Robert Solow (1970), we can find the seeds of a new form of collaboration in conscious negotiation. In 1992, the United Nations Conference on Environment and Development (UNCED) in Rio de Janeiro, called The Earth Summit, focused on environment and sustainable development. People from all parts of the world, 2,400 representatives of NGOs and 17,000 other people, attended the parallel NGO Forum to understand the meaning of sustainability. During this conference the Brundtland Repor (1987) was presented. It states that sustainable development has to be based on a multi-negotiation of three different spheres: environmental, social, and economic. Looking into these three aspects we can find inter-generational negotiation represented by the contraposition of long- and short-term advantages. The German philosopher Dahrendorf (1988) has already suggested that every revolution has a generational revolution within it. Dahrendorf's statement captures the connection between the macro- and the micro-scale. The generational conflict means that a revolution generally involves substitution of main characters with younger people both in central and in peripheral governments where the latter mirrors the former. This is exactly the relationship between macro- and micro-scale and how the former tends to hide the latter.

Looking at the micro-scale, we find the questions of the organization of the new work team. The macro- and the micro-scale have other degrees of complexity, and we can say that the presence of several actors in every situation creates two kinds of difficulties: endogenous and exogenous. The former is related to the management of this group of individuals and to its transformation into a real work team. The latter is the relationship that this new unit has with the external world. We will examine this situation in detail in the urban negotiation.

URBAN PLANNING AND INSTITUTIONAL ARCHITECTURE

The philosopher, Daniel Elazar (Elster, 1989), affirmed that in urbanism there are experimentations of new Institutional Architecture. The future development of the relationship between citizens and governments is built on the results of city planning. The growth of a new city, or a part of it, involves the entire community with its social and political aspects (Pizziolo & Micarelli, 2003).

Politicians have known, since the beginning of the social life, that there is a strict connection between the form of the city and the kind of social construction of the rules of its inhabitants. As examples, we can point out the foulness of Emperor Nero who burned the suburbs of Rome in his dream of social renaissance, and the Italian Nobel Laureate, Italo Calvino (1997), who wrote *The Invisible Cities* where there is a perfect correspondence between his improbable cities and each different social character of their inhabitants.

During the 18th century, a group of social utopian philosophers tried to build, at the same time, both societies and cities (Pombeni, 1997). Robert Owen created New Lamark and Charles Fourier created the Phalanstery. These were both failures. Every process of society creation which proceeds from top to bottom is a failure. The birth of a society comes only from an inverse process, a bottom-up one, especially in a democratic and non-totalitarian system.

In this framework, if someone wants to understand which will be the evolution of a community – or more generally, of a state – he or she must look at the kind of relationship and expectation that is evident during a territorial transformation. Following these steps we find that the process of a territorial transformation has a parallel with the evolution of our democracies as in a mirrored play.

This is a social matter (Kroll, 2001). Kroll is a Belgian architect who restores large public buildings erected during the 1970s around big factories in many European countries. He also works in Eastern European cities such as East Berlin where the scene was culturally dominated by Soviet architecture. There are big concrete agglomerations with more than a thousand inhabitants who live in a frustrating condition. Kroll works together with the people who benefit from the transformation with very interesting results. For the first time the inhabitants are happy and proud to live in their houses and in their neighborhood.

STAKEHOLDERS INVOLVED IN URBAN TRANSFORMATION

Before we examine these differences, we will describe the dynamics of a process of urban territorial transformation. This process is a complex endeavor and its management requires the presence of multi-sector specialists called on to resolve any particular problem on the spot. In this process there are also different well-defined interests that are interconnected. For example, an urban transformation plan involves a big part of a city; for example, apart from landowners, there are also company owners, shopkeepers, and the entire social economic structure which must be considered. It often happens that every landowner or investor has his or her own architect. At the same time, different stakeholders who belong to this community have differentiated needs and they ask for different public investments. The final project represents a balance between these varied interests, a series of compromises, and is the result of a concerted negotiation process.

Public administrations usually have no ready money to invest in their projects. Civil engineers and architects know it. Every transformation is composed of public and private elements. In Europe, if you build a private agglomeration, you have to build public roads, with light, water, electricity and perhaps a school, or a church that generally for public use. Public administrations need to collaborate with private companies in order to keep taxes from increasing. Over time, the decision-making process has changed its dynamics – from a pyramidal one, with the public administration at the top, to a star-shaped one – where different players negotiate their desires, with the project in the center of the star. Fundamentally, there tends to be three kinds of individuals who correspond to the three aspects of any major change process: the social, the economic and the environmental aspects of community life. These three points of view correspond to the three elements of Solow's (1970) definition of sustainability outlined above. The final project ultimately represents the compromise of mediated interests and emerges when all players converge on a mutually agreed upon workable plan.

The social, environmental, and economic aspects outlined above are represented by several different groups of people. This illustrates the fourth type of intangible capital where individuals who belong to different organizations work together on the same project theme. Analyzing the dynamics of this heterogeneous aggregate, we try to understand when and how they become a group, following the theories of group dynamics, how they communicate, and how they create their own symbols.

First of all, it is important to name these groups of people. As Confucius (Collis, 1970) affirmed, the essence of life is to give the exact name to things. If it is clear who the representatives are from the economic point of view, their dynamics and their way of thinking, it is easier to comprehend other groups. Therefore, from a financial perspective, the most important person is the entrepreneur who is the initiator of this urban territorial transformation, and is often accompanied by bankers, finance companies, and risk insurance operators.

The other two aspects are practically connected to all the players, thus everyone has the right to explain his or her thoughts. In either a politically strong or ideologic society this is fairly easy to obtain but in complex Western society this is increasingly difficult. The social and the environmental aspects are controlled at the same time by public administrations and stakeholders. The consequence is that they are both projected on a medium- or long-term horizon while contractors tend to concentrate on the short-term advantages applicable to their own interests.

Acknowledging the presence of public administrations is very important because under the same name they represent very different organizational situations. We can recognize four decisional levels inside a single administration: different departments, the overall bureaucracy, political majority (executive power), and political minority (legislative power). Each level corresponds to a group of people that has to find both its own equilibrium and a multi-level equilibrium.

We can say that a project of urban territorial transformation draws its own boundary only from a mediation of several solutions (Bettiol, 2005). The entire process consists of two very different phases: the intangible and the tangible. The authorization and planning phase is open to a great and heterogeneous number of players while the realization phase is dominated by technical specialists; that is, the construction companies and the project teams.

The number of individuals involved in the first phase grows moment by moment; for example, in recent years there has been an increase in the length of this phase (which can be twice that of the second) depending on the different local laws, the importance of the project, and its symbolic social value. The extension of the process is due to the greater power of the stakeholders (Cardinali, Fedeli, Gelli, & Milanesi, 2002).

We will focus on the role of heterogeneity in the first phase, as illustrated in the Map of Transformation (Fig. 1). If we want to reduce the duration of the first phase, we have to act in two ways; that is, be sure that everyone is understood and comprehended by the others, and transform this aggregate of people with different interests into a team. These important requirements set a complex process of inter-cultural communication in motion. In the spider chart in Fig. 1, different levels of action are represented, each one with its specific complexity. We can say that there is an endogenous complexity inside each oval space and an exogenous complexity represented by the two-way arrows. The project is in the center and represents the contact element of all those oval spaces, and it is also the means of communication between the parts.

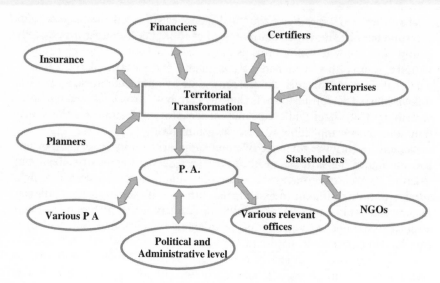

Fig. 1. Map of Transformation.

ENDOGENOUS AND EXOGENOUS COMPLEXITY

The endogenous and exogenous complexity in urban transformation is parallel to the macro- and the micro-scale in industrial organization, but it is more sophisticated. In fact, some of the actors are affiliated with the public administrations and thus inhabit very different roles from private company workers. In Italy, as in many others countries, civic servants have special work contracts which are not very flexible. They have been formed following the Latin Law with the oriental influence of the Byzantine Empire and are very far from the usual pragmatic way of thinking of contractors and entrepreneurs. Generally those people who are represented in the Map of Transformation are experts and they are middle aged or older. Age is one of the main differences between people who have different backgrounds, culture and expectations, and perceptions of the future. On the other hand, stakeholders are indefinable *a priori*. If we imagine the participants of an environmental association, there is not a uniform profile, but generally they tend to be young people. They tend to be students, unemployed, and thus exist in a different realm part from professionals and teachers. These individuals are also very different in their social frameworks or in their origins. The one thing they have in common with the others is the project. But this is not the same project as that of the public administrators or of the contractors; it is the symbolization of the project itself.

In the group of participants represented in the Map of Transformation, only a few persons, the planners and the designers, are able to comprehend the drawings of a city transformation. The contractors may understand only something of the lines and the totality of the business plan. The stakeholders only comprehend something of the technical relations, so they need a technical mediation. In this way, they judge only the kind of connections that they can feel and that link the future town to their present social city (Hall, 1966).

From this description of heterogeneity in urban transformation, it is evident that it is difficult to transform all these individuals into an effective group. But what is a group? If we use the definition from the field of sociology, we can say that an assembly of people becomes a group when they have a common scope, when they choose a leadership, when they have cohesion, and when each member recognizes his or her role inside the group (Bertani, Manetti, & Venini, 2002; Voci, 2003).

Some of these ideas have been well analyzed by those in engineering management, but we will focus our attention on the scope that will become first of all the object and then the symbol of the group, because it is the common reason for all members to participate. Normally, the scope has to be well defined, measurable, and achieved by different steps. In an urban transformation, this is impossible to obtain. The project often involves a large area of a city, and represents the tangible (the construction) and the intangible (the relationship between the project and the local community).

If a project is not completely understood, then aspects of the project may become a focal point for symbolically representing the whole project. The parts may become either negative or positive symbols. The negotiation of the boundary means the creation of positive symbols. There are several steps involved in creating positive symbols. First of all, a negotiator has to analyze the local community engaged in forming focus groups or other mechanisms for quality analysis. Then he or she needs to divide the projects in several parts and select the one that the people can immediately recognize as being familiar. When someone who is not an expert reads a project, he or she tends to have partial understanding rather than a holistic vision. The first step in this process is recognizing the capacity of the group to accept the heterogeneity of the group's membership and gain mutual comprehension. Establishing a common language is the means of communication to this end. A language, with its grammar and syntactic rules, represents the way to create and to share new, common symbols. This is a managerial application of the dynamics described by Berger and Luckman (1966) in *The Social Construction of Reality*, on the need to create reference systems, understood as common languages, social anchorages, and symbols, shared together in relation to the objective being aimed at.

Public administrations are directly responsible for the relationship with their citizens, who are also the stakeholders, and experimenting with different kinds of contact. There are four steps for building effective relationships that begin with a simple consultation when public administrations inform their community of their decisions through the media (Caudo & Palazzo, 2000). Then there is the sharing of decisions derived from public consultations and meetings. The third step involves the participation process (Venti, Baruzzi, Capelli, Ginocchioni, & Morello, 2003) when local people are directly involved in the planning phase. The management of this local participation process is complex, yielding positive results for small sized projects, such as schools or public gardens. The last step is the negotiation of the project with all the main players in the Map of Transformation, which includes those directly involved in the realization of the project and users of the realization, the local community.

The shift from the narrow scale of a single building being constructed to the wide scale of urban transformation changes the nature of contact between the actors in this process. In city planning and in environmental projects the relationship between players is a multi-negotiation of differing interests. Measurement of the value of collaboration becomes immediately evident (Elazar, 1998) and parallels exist between the form of institutional architecture (i.e., the order of a state) and territorial policies. In the case of a territorial transformation, quantification of the collaborative capital is expressed in two ways: by the success of the initiative itself and by the time of approval.

INTER-CULTURAL DIFFERENCES AND DIFFERENT USES OF LANGUAGE

The three different types of actors involved in a territorial transformation (everyone with his or her different education) –use language in different ways. For example, public administrators use words in a very different way from designers, to the extent that they could have the same degree of difficulty in inter-cultural communication similar to two people from different countries. These problems emerge from the different use of the rules of the language, even if the words are the same.

Philosophers divide the study of these situations into three disciplines: syntax, semantics, and pragmatics (Bianchi, 2003). The discipline of syntax concerns how linguistic expressions can be put together from a grammatical point of view, analyzing which ones lend importance to their meaning. It involves the sequence of symbols. Semantics deals with the meaning of linguistic expression, words or sentences apart from the situation they are used in. Semantics involves a focus on the relationships between linguistic expression and subjects of the words. Pragmatics is the study of the relationship between symbols and idiom, between linguistic expression and who uses them to communicate their thoughts. It is the study of ways to use the sentence in an actual social situation.

Starting from these considerations, sociologists are divided into three schools of thought at well. There is the school of language as a means of representing an external reality, the school which constitutes language as a reality, and the school of social constructivism. Communication happens when someone crosses the pre-fixed boundaries and understands the rules and symbols of others. Once across the boundaries, there is the potential for the development of creativity. When De Bono (1991) suggests changing "the hat on the head" to understand the other points of view, he is changing our understanding of the structure of language as well.

We are going to illustrate this phenomenon among three particular groups; that is, by looking at the language of designers, that of public administrators, and the language of stakeholders. The different schools of sociology find their mirrored representations in those different experts and this fact can be further underscored in analyzing the dynamics of work teams.

Normally, individuals who use language as means of representing an external reality are designers, such as engineers or architects. From a study of their inner nature and background, these experts tend to be multilingual and use several languages at the same time. In a planning team, people can communicate both with words or graphics and designs, but they are experts in information technology (IT) as well.

These observations suggest that communication acts on different levels. Different senses are involved in this context and individuals can use their preferred communication channels. In this way, individuals who prefer visual language can use drawings while others use oral language. A complete communication happens when there is a mixture of all languages (i.e., visual as well as written), as a drawing with written explanation and with virtual representation. It is impossible to give priority to one specific language, and we term this is a multilingual communication (Pinneri, Ruiu, & Verona, 1988).

The indifferent use of different means of communication underscores again that technicians belong to the school of thought that supposes that language is only a means necessary to represent reality and that this is external to its representation, reality is object and not subject. This is different from the works of experts that assume the social construction of reality.

Professional specialists (e.g., architects, engineers, geologists) are typically concentrated on objective reality and tend to focus their attention on tangible matter. This is a consequence of a cartesian representation of reality that does not leave room for different representations. In this way of thinking, the world has only three dimensions within which everything can be understood. This cartesian perspective has been superseded with the development of non-euclidean mathematics and most recently quantum physics with their study of untouchable reality (Popper, 1970; Sklar, 1992).

The case of public administrators, including also bankers and insurance operators, is very different. Since the beginning of human life there are individuals who have spent their time identifying the borders of human freedom and who have tried to create a boundary around human actions. They have tried to create a reality that would suit everybody. Legislative work is concentrating on including all people with respect to their own particular characteristics.

For these reasons, public administrators tend to instinctively follow the school of thought which constitutes language as a reality, and they spend most of their time choosing their words carefully. Their concern with words absorbs all of their energy and attention, and they lose contact with the larger reality. This is the reason why some norms and laws sound incomprehensible to ordinary people.

THE SOCIAL CREATION OF REALITY

The last school of thought is the social constructionist perspective whose stakeholders generally use language following this strategy, recognizing that social interaction creates our reality. As each one of us is a stakeholder, in both the local community and in larger environmental matters; we are motivated in contributing to those constructions.

Each territorial transformation creates stakeholders' movements that are generally opposed to its construction. A project will create a new future reality, and every change carries uncertainties that can produce cultural shocks in people. The magnitude of these shocks depends on the perception of externality of the future order. Linguistic schools have an answer also for the definition of this critical point.

As people move through different realities, they give order and priority to them. The dominating reality is the daily one which has its own language; for example, in Latin: Hic et Nunc. Some individuals experience this reality as ordinary, clear, and bright while the others find themselves inside an obscure framework. For this reason, if a project is anchored within the daily reality, and individuals can bring it back to the present from its future realization, a project will really start to live after its construction, and people will experience it as friendly.

The daily language is dominated by pragmatism and creates objective meanings. The sharing of these meanings gives a measure of familiarity and creates an aggregate of people. When these meanings become symbols, the aggregate becomes a group, which follows from theories of group dynamics. We can say that this transition could be the same as the birth of an ideology. An external observer may recognize this moment as a crucial one, in fact, this is the passage from chaos to order not in a figurative way, of course, but different facts that have occurred can finally be read in their exact meanings, thus completing the puzzle. In this moment, there exists the solution of the urban transformation, or a frontal encounter, a crash. This contact finishes only with a winner and a loser, and in each case the project loses its value and cannot be the same. If the aggregate of people who oppose the project becomes a group, it will be very difficult, and sometimes impossible, to transform these individuals into the work team we have described above.

Merton (2002), considered the Father of the Theoretical Foundations of Functional Sociology, in his theory of reference group behavior has defined this moment as the beginning of a self-fulfilling prophecy. This is a prediction that, in being made, actually causes itself to become true. For example, if it is widely believed that when people think that a crash is imminent, this may reduce confidence and actually cause such a crash.

Just after the creation of social symbols, when a part of the project has taken an objective meaning, people start to belong to a group which gives common sense to their actions from the part of the project itself. The future becomes present and part of the daily language.

If an individual wants to build something, he or she needs to contact the stakeholders and have experience with emerging symbols and with the social construction of reality. The passage from future to present could mean both the passage from idealism to a sense of danger; that is, we can say from a dream to a nightmare. Griswold (1997) has described the cultural shocks that could occur when something unknown arrives well. So this unknown object which lives in the future, the project, needs to become familiar to be approved by stakeholders. Before its presentation, the project has to be seen as present and people have to feel its absence.

CONNECTOR, MEDIATOR, TRANSLATOR, AND NEGOTIATOR

After these considerations, it is time to analyze the modern work team of an urban transformation where a temporary work group – composed of designers, public administrators, lawyers, financial companies' managers, contractors, and stakeholders – must communicate and work together. As stated above, each member of this work group belongs to and is a representative of a different organization which has different aims.

But due to the three fundamental categories of different language use, teamwork, an ostensibly simple situation, can become like climbing walls. In many cases, it is very difficult to communicate, and the presence of someone external to the situation who can translate the growth of social symbols into a mediation of the project boundaries is necessary.

It is interesting to note that the anthropologist, Anzalduà (1987), has defined "borderlands" as the place where there is communication, and where it is possible to exchange experiences. We can imagine that someone has his or her own field of experience and that this overlaps other fields only in a restricted way. Communication could occur only in this zone (borderlands) where there are shared interpretations of words and action and the same symbols are used. Generally, when two people give a different meaning to the same word, they are not able to recognize this situation immediately. For this reason, the discussion could easily arrive at a complex point, and a conflict arise. This is typical of technical conflicts but can also degenerate into relationship conflicts depending on the importance of the word. A third person, a negotiator, would understand the situation better and help the individuals arrive at a convergence of the two meanings. Considering the variety of language use and of individuals involved in work groups, this situation is very common.

The main role of the mediator is to enlarge the boundary areas that the aggregate of people has in common. When these borderlands are sufficiently wide, then the aggregate can be transformed initially into a group, and eventually into a work team.

In different work teams, in urban transformation endeavors as in all the other industrial situations that we have already described, the managing of relationships has become one of the most important matters. This has created a need for new professionals that cannot be defined in traditional ways. They are inter-professional mediators who are able to cross over the boundaries of different disciplines of study to enlarge the borderlands of the aggregate of individuals in groups. We can define them as managers of variety and diversity. They have to be able to constitute work teams around common symbols and need both human and technical preparation, such as in the social sciences and engineering management. In particular, the new expert needs to be familiar with linguistic theories, and knowledge of practical applications, such as how individuals use language and group dynamics.

The life of a group is often viewed as a cyclic one from the perspective of Tuckman's (1965) classic four-phase model, forming, storming, norming, and performing. We suggest that the second phase is most important because relations can quickly degenerate into conflict or conversely yield common symbols. During this phase people may not have found what they were looking for and need to share new common rules and to define new common aims. This is typically an opportunity for negotiation, and not only an economic mediation but also potentially a cultural mediation. We have already said that the approval phase of an urban project could last 2 or 3 years (or more, depending on the importance of the transformation), so all these individuals must learn to work and to live together for an extended period.

The variety of the members of the initial aggregate in the Map of Transformation, their different uses of language, and their differing scopes of interest (economical, environmental, or social) are obstacles to the transformation of the group into a team. Also, if these differences are overcome, they may inadvertently create an un-synchronized process resulting in an increase in the length of the first phase of the project of an urban transformation and an increase of internal conflicts due to misunderstandings.

A mediator has to re-synchronize communication and teach each of the participants how to decode the non-verbal communication; that is, the silent language (Hall, 1966). The largest part of the communication (80–93%) is non-verbal, but each culture and even each individual attaches different meanings to the same symbols. This is exactly the reason for the importance of a mediator (or facilitator) who has to be also a translator of meanings. The negotiator must be able to recognize and to coordinate important aspects of the personalities, abilities, and skills of each and every member of the group. This is a very difficult process, and this is the reason for the enormous length of the decisional phase in every environmental transformation. He or she must be able to help individuals find their own roles as well as develop empathy among the members. This can be done in two ways: by addressing each personal attitude that seems to be impacting the transformation of a group into a team, and by using the technique of altercasting. This is a technique for persuading people by gently forcing them into a designated social role so that they will be inclined to behave according to that role. Group life is based on single work but also on collective work, as shown in Mandeville's (2003) "The Fable of the Bees." In this tale, the author emphasizes the role of the private interests of the individual action that can begin to promote collective growth.

Defining a personal role for each member of the group, according to his or her characteristics, means that everyone experiences him- or herself in harmony with an increasingly cohesive group. In this way the transformation of the work group into team occurs as well as growth of collaborative capital. This also becomes a means of overcoming the embarrassing situation described by Arendt (1951) where everyone has the need to distinguish his or her single identity inside a collective identity. Arendt states that this is the transformation, or evolution, from I to we, and that this process is a continuous negotiation. It means that while we are engaged in action, including in work, we are also engaged in the construction of a collective identity where we can identify ourselves and our actions.

CONCLUSION

Complexity of work life is related to the complexity of society, thus if an individual wants to manage complexity he or she must understand the behavior of society, groups, and also individuals. This fact means that he or she must comprehend heterogeneity (or diversity) and the variety of relationships that develop between different individuals. This suggests that everyone needs to be well prepared in both the technical and the relational side of life. However, it is clear that sometimes individuals need help in building awareness and skills in one or another of these areas, thus the need for individuals who can assume the connector, translator, mediator, and negotiator roles and provide such assistance.

People need a connector to create links with external society. Sometimes this action can be achieved by technical means, as with computers and the Internet, but it is not always possible with the same efficiency. Hall (1966) affirmed that human beings have lost their ability to improve their senses and instead they are increasingly relying on artificial senses. Mazlish (1993), in *The Fourth Discontinuity*, affirmed that humans and machines are growing together converging toward a symbiosis, a state of affairs which has growing implications for both.

However, individuals also need a translator in order to understand different daily and social and technical languages. There are some invisible experts who work for us. For example, when we buy a book written in a foreign language which is translated into our language, there is a hidden mediation between the author and us (Eco, 2003). Also, when we go to an information point or to a call center in order to understand imprecise guidelines and cryptic instructions, we are using another kind of cultural mediation.

In addition, people need a mediator to sort out problems such as the encounters of two different cultures. When there is direct contact, not simply in a written form, we need to share the meaning of body language, behavior, and symbols. The public administrations in many large cities have cultural mediation departments. In commercial circumstances, the mediator represents a key figure and he or she is essential. We have shown that cultural differences can be found also in individuals who speak the same language but use it in different ways.

Individuals also need a negotiator, especially when they live in a work group and each member belongs to a different organization with different aims. Realization of the common aim can be only obtained through the negotiation of social, environmental, and economic aspects of the project.

In this third millennium, we observe the end of micro-specialization and the birth of inter-disciplinary and inter-cultural work groups. It is imperative that individuals continue to work toward collaborating in ways outlined above, as well as continue to improve their understanding of what can be accomplished with a broadened perspective on the potential of the effective encounter between the human and technical aspects of collaborative work. This is the role of socio-engineering.

ACKNOWLEDGMENTS

A special thanks to my personal English teacher, Mrs. Margot van de Graaf, who connects me with other parts of the world (the non-Italian speakers), who translates my words, who sometimes mediates the structure of my thoughts in English, and who converses with me about particular meanings I wish to convey.

REFERENCES

Anzalduà, G. (1987). *Borderlands/la frontera. The new mestiza.* San Francisco: Aunt Lute Books.

Arendt, H. (1951). *Le origini del totalitalismo.* Torino: Einaudi.

Berger, P. L., & Luckman, T. (1966). *The social construction of reality.* New York: Doubleday.

Bertani, B., Manetti, M., & Venini, L. (2005). *Psicologia dei gruppi. Teoria, contesti e metodologie di intervento.* Milano: Franco Angeli.

Bettiol, C. (2005). *Negoziare l'urbanistica.* Firenze: Alinea.

Bianchi, C. (2003). *Pragmatica del linguaggio.* Bari: Editori Laterza.

Brundtland, G.H. (1987) *Our common future.*Brundtland Report. World Commission on Environment Development Oxford University Press Oxford.

Calvino, I. (1997). *Le città invisibili.* Milano: Mondatori.

Cardinali, D., Fedeli, V., Gelli, F., & Milanesi, E. (2002). *Esperienze di governo locale. Quattro casi internazionali.* Milano: Franco Angeli.

Castagna, M. (2001). *Role playing, autocasi ed esercitazioni psicosociali.* Milano: Franco Angeli.

Caudo, G., & Palazzo, A. L. (2000). *Comunicare l'urbanistica.* Firenze: Alinea.

Ciuffoli, F. (2004). *Giochi, esercizi e test di creatività.* Milano: Franco Angeli.

Collis, M. (1970). *Confucio.* Milano: Longanesi.

Dahrendorf, R. (1988). *The modern social conflict. An essay on the politics of liberty.* New York: Weidenfeld & Nicolson.

De Bono, E. (1991). *Sei cappelli per pensare.* Milano: Rizzoli.

Eco, U. (2003). *Dire quasi la stessa cosa. Esperienze di traduzione.* Milano: Bompiani.

Elster, J. (1989). *Nuts and bolts for the social sciences.* Cambridge: University Press.

Elazar, D. (1998). *Idee e forme del federalismo.* Milano: Mondadori.

Griswold, W. (1997). *Sociologia della cultura.* Bologna: Il Mulino.

Habermas, J., & Taylor, C. (1998). *Multiculturalismo.* Milano: Feltrinelli.

Hall, E. T. (1966). *The hidden dimension.* Milano: RCS.

Kroll, L. (2001). *Ecologie urbane.* Milano: Franco Angeli.

Lasch, C. (1995). *The revolt of the elite and the betrayal of democracy.* New York, London: W.W. Norton & Co.

Mandeville, B. de (2003). *La favola delle api.* Bari: Laterza.

Mazlish, B. (1993). *The fourth discontinuity: The co-evolution of humans and machines.* London: Yale University Press.

Merton, R. K., & Fallocco, S. (2002). *La "serendipity" nella ricerca sociale e politica: cercare una cosa e trovarne un'altra.* Roma: Luiss Edizioni.

Milgron, P., & Roberts, J. (1992). *Economics, organization and management.* Upper Saddle River, NJ: Prentice Hall.

Ortega, & Gasset, J. (1962). *La ribellione delle masse.* Bologna: Il Mulino.

Pepper, D., & Rogers, M. (2002). *Enterprise one to one. Tolls for competition in the interactive age.* New York: Random House.

Pinneri, R., Ruiu, M., & Verona, S. (1988). *La programmazione neurolinguistica.* Milano: Xenia.

Pitteri, D., Picucci, S., & Villani, R. M. (2002). *Cause related marketing.* Milano: Franco Angeli.

Pizziolo, G., & Micarelli, R. (2003). *L'arte delle relazioni.* Firenze: Alinea.

Pombeni, P. (1997). *Introduzione alla storia contemporanea.* Bologna: Il Mulino.

Popper, K. (1970). *The logic of scientific discovery.* Einaudi: Torino.

Roy, A. (2003). *An ordinary person's guide to empire.* Parma: Guanda Editore.

Sennet, R. (1999). *The corrosion of character.* New York, London: W.W. Norton & Co.

Sklar, L. (1992). *Philosophy of physics.* San Francisco: Westview Press.

Solow, R. (1970). *La teoria della crescita.* Milano: Edizioni di comunità.

Steward, T. A. (2002). *La ricchezza del sapere.* Milano: Ponte alle Grazie.

Tocqueville, A. de (1971). *La democrazia in America.* Bologna: Cappelli Editore.

Tuckman, B. (1965). Developmental sequence in small groups. *Psychological Bulletin, 63,* 384–399.

Venti, D., Baruzzi, V., Capelli, M., Ginocchioni, G., & Morello, M. R. (2003). *Esperienze di progettazione partecipata negli USA.* Bologna: La Mandragora.

Voci, A. (2003). *Processi psicosociali nei gruppi.* Bari: Laterza.

KNOTWORKING TO CREATE COLLABORATIVE INTENTIONALITY CAPITAL IN FLUID ORGANIZATIONAL FIELDS

Yrjö Engeström

ABSTRACT

The chapter makes an attempt at hybridization between three relatively separate fields of inquiry: (a) theories and studies of collective intentionality and distributed agency, (b) theories and studies of social capital in organizations, and (c) cultural–historical activity theory. Employees' collective capacity to create organizational transformations and innovations is becoming a crucially important asset that gives a new, dynamic content to notions of social and collaborative capital. In philosophy, sociology, anthropology and cognitive science, such capacity is conceptualized as distributed agency or collective intentionality. The task of the chapter is to examine the possibility that current changes in work organizations may bring about historically new features of collective intentionality and distributed agency. The understanding of these new features is important if we are to give viable content to the emerging notion of collaborative capital. After a conceptual overview, the chapter will first analyze a fictional example of distributed agency, then findings from the author's fieldwork in health care settings. In conclusion, the chapter will

Collaborative Capital: Creating Intangible Value
Advances in Interdisciplinary Studies of Work Teams, Volume 11, 307–336
Copyright © 2005 by Elsevier Ltd.
All rights of reproduction in any form reserved
ISSN: 1572-0977/doi:10.1016/S1572-0977(05)11011-5

propose the notions of 'object-oriented interagency' and 'collaborative intentionality capital' as characterizations of important aspects of agency and intentionality currently taking shape in work organizations.

INTRODUCTION

In this chapter, I make an attempt at hybridization between three relatively separate fields of inquiry. These fields are (a) theories and studies of collective intentionality and distributed agency,[1] (b) theories and studies of social capital in organizations, and (c) cultural–historical activity theory.

I will argue that employees' collective capacity to create organizational transformations and innovations is becoming a crucially important asset that gives a new, dynamic content to notions of social and collaborative capital. In philosophy, sociology, anthropology, and cognitive science, such capacity is conceptualized as distributed agency or collective intentionality (e.g., Barnes, 2000; Meggle, 2002). The problem with theories of intentionality and agency is that they are seldom grounded in empirical observations or interventions in people's daily realities and practices at work.

Theories and studies of social capital in organizations, on the other hand, have largely focused on the value-generating potential of social ties, network relations, and trust (e.g., Lesser, 2000; Lin, Cook, & Burt, 2001). Issues of agency and intentionality have remained marginal in this literature. Furthermore, this literature has also been quite separate from issues of transformations in work and emergence of new organizational forms. On the other hand, there are indications of emerging interest in issues of volition, intentionality, and energy as organizational assets, evidenced for example in the recent articles by Ghoshal and Bruch (2003), and Cross, Baker, and Parker (2003).

I will suggest that cultural–historical activity theory (e.g., Engeström, Miettinen, & Punamäki, 1999b; Leont'ev, 1978; Vygotsky, 1978) can serve as a challenging mediator between agency and intentionality on the one hand and social capital on the other hand. Intentionality and agency were central concerns already in the founding texts of the cultural–historical approach in the 1920s. For Vygotsky (1999, pp. 64–65), voluntary action "probably distinguishes man from the animals which stand closest to him to a greater extent than his more developed intellect." A number of recent studies inspired by activity theory have focused on problems of agency in organizational transformations (e.g., Blackler, McDonald, & Crump, 1999; Blackler, Crump, & McDonald, 2000; Engeström, 2000, 2004;

Uden & Engeström, 2004), as well as on the forms and formation of social capital (Engeström, 2001).

There is a good reason to bring together and hybridize the three fields. The task of this chapter is to examine the possibility that current changes in work organizations may bring about historically new features of collective intentionality and distributed agency. The understanding of these new features is important if we are to give viable content to the emerging notion of collaborative capital, or as I will suggest, *collaborative intentionality capital*.

I will build my argument in six steps. Firstly, I will briefly introduce the notions of emergent interactive intentionality and distributed agency, as they have been recently put forward by a number of scholars. Secondly, I will present five principles of cultural–historical activity theory as potential enrichments, or perhaps challenges, to the existing literature. Thirdly, I will take up the historicity of agency, focusing in particular on historical changes currently visible in work organizations and asking what might be the contours of agency in new network- and amoeba-like organizational forms. Fourthly, I will analyze a fictional example of distributed agency, namely a recent detective novel by Tony Hillerman. Fifthly, I will analyze some data and findings from my own fieldwork in health care settings. And finally, I will sum up the outcomes of the analyses, proposing the notions of "object-oriented interagency" and "collaborative intentionality capital" as tentative characterizations of certain important aspects of agency and intentionality currently taking shape in work organizations.

EMERGENT INTERACTIVE INTENTIONALITY AND DISTRIBUTED AGENCY

Searle's (1990) notion of "we-intentions" has served as a springboard for interesting attempts to conceptualize collective intentionality. The recent philosophical arguments of Bratman (1999) and Tuomela (2002) are two prominent examples. The two also exemplify the difficulties of overcoming cognitivism and individualism. Bratman practically equates intentions with plans, while Tuomela prefers to see intentions in terms of goals.

In contrast to these views, Gibbs (2001) argues that intentions are emergent products of social interaction. The interaction may take place between multiple humans or between a human actor and his/her tools and material environment. People assign meanings, intentions, goals, and plans to their ongoing interactions as they occur. Thus, actions are not primarily results of privately held, internalized mental representations. In a similar vein, Fogel (1993, pp. 124–125) discusses the development of intentionality in terms of "participatory future" and "anticipatory directionality": "Direction is not a static initial condition, not an executive giving orders that guide action, it is a fluid part of a dynamic perception–action system."

In sociological studies of agency, a similar move may be observed. Barnes (2000, p. 55) points out that the successful execution of routine collective practices always involves the continual overriding of routine practices at the individual level. An orchestra playing a familiar work serves as an example: "Any description of these activities as so many agents each following the internal guidance of habit or rule would merely describe a fiasco." What is needed is constant mutual adjustment and alignment, agreement out of difference.

Pickering (1995, pp. 21–22) characterizes intentionality in human practice as "dance of agency," or "dialectic of resistance and accommodation." As active, intentional beings, scientists tentatively construct some new machine. They then adopt a passive role, monitoring the performance of the machine to see whatever capture of material agency it might effect. "Symmetrically, this period of human passivity is the period in which material agency actively manifests itself. Does the machine perform as intended? Has an intended capture of agency been effected? Typically the answer is no, in which case the response is another reversal of roles (…)."

Gell (1998, p. 21) pushes this argument further:

> Anti-personnel mines are not (primary) agents who initiate happenings through acts of will for which they are morally responsible, granted, but they are objective embodiments of the *power or capacity to will their use*, and hence moral entities in themselves. I describe artefacts as "social agents" not because I wish to promulgate a form of material-culture mysticism, but only in view of the fact that objectification in artefact-form is how social agency manifests and realizes itself, via the proliferation of fragments of "primary" intentional agents in their "secondary" artefactual forms.

Gell (1998, p. 23) adds the important observation that the concept of agency implies "the overcoming of resistance, difficulty, inertia, etc." However, that should not be confused with control.

Ciborra (2000) points out that in organizations, agency is typically framed in terms of control. But we live in a runaway world (Giddens, 1991) in which the technologies and organizations we create keep drifting, generating unintended, sometimes monstrous consequences. This calls for a notion of distributed agency not obsessed with control: "What if our power to bring to life sophisticated and evolving infrastructures must be associated with the acceptance of the idea that we are bound to lose control? And that any attempt to regain top-down control will backfire, lead to further centrifugal drifts, and eventually impede our making sense and learning about how to effectively take care of the infrastructure?" (Ciborra, 2000, pp. 39–40). Ciborra suggests a reframing of agency in terms of drift, care, hospitality, and cultivation.

Perhaps the most radical accounts of distributed or "fractured" agency are to be found in the works of Deleuze and Guattari' (1977, 1987) and Latour (1993, 1996, 2004). Schatzki (2002, p. 205) provides an eloquent summary of these "posthumanist" views:

> Consider the practice-order bundle that is the day trading branch office. This complex of traders, managers, technicians, rooms, computers, computer network, power system, potted plants, and day trading, managerial, repair, and other practices converts electricity, computer graphics, trader savvy, and money into (1) commissions that subsidize expansion of the firm, (2) greater visibility or notoriety for the branch office in the firm, and (3) waste products such as used paper, burnt-out wiring, and carbon dioxide. If such actions as making commissions, projecting an image, and producing waste are grouped together, the actor that performs them, that is to say, the substance to which they are attached, is the practice-order bundle (the branch office). More precisely, the actor that performs these actions is this bundle treated as a unit. If, by contrast, such actions as scanning a computer screen and keeping a diary, or such doings as straining a trader's eyes and crashing, are grouped together, the actors involved are the traders or computers, respectively. These agents, too, are networks taken as units. For Latour and Callon, consequently, an ascription of agency, as in Deleuze and Guattari, is an instantaneous apprehension of multiplicity. By considering different congeries of action, moreover, agency can be seated in any component of a network, as well as in the network as a whole.

While I endorse the general thrust expressed in these multiple strands of theorizing, I also feel that they are often relatively vague and partial. For instance, talk about "practice-order bundles" seems more metaphorical than analytically rigorous. Above all, as a student of real work practices and organizations, I wonder how one might use such conceptualizations in detailed empirical field studies and interventions.

Thus, I will try and spell out a few key principles of cultural–historical activity theory as a potential contribution toward increased systematicity, and also as a challenge to some possible limitations or gaps in the approaches mentioned above.

The Contribution of Activity Theory

If intentions are emergent and not reducible to individually held mental representations of goals and plans, how do we explain the persistence and durable guiding power often associated with collective intentions? Shweder (1991, pp. 74–76) attempts to explain this with the notions of "intentional worlds" and "intentional things." However, the explanation is somewhat circular: "Intentional things are causally active, but only by virtue of our mental representations of them. Intentional things have no 'natural' reality or identity separate from human understandings and activities. Intentional worlds do not exist independently of the intentional states (beliefs, desires, emotions) directed at them and by them, by the persons who live in them" (pp. 74–75). This leads Shweder to maintain that there is no logical requirement that the identity of things remain fixed across intentional worlds. Shweder seems to conceive of intentional worlds and intentional things mainly as situated achievements without much historical inertia and dynamics of their own.

Understanding the durability of collective intentions seems to require a historical concept of object. Vedeler (1991) points out that infant intentionality may be best explained as striving after external objects, as object-directedness. In a larger scale, Knorr-Cetina (2001) discusses the tremendous motivating power of incomplete but durable epistemic objects (such as markets-on-the screen) for entire professional groups. In these views, objects do have historical dynamics and trajectories of their own. These trajectories and dynamics stem from the fact that objects are constructed by much more multi-layered, temporally and spatially distributed actors and forces than just the human participants observably present in a given situation.

In cultural–historical activity theory, Leont'ev (1978) distinguished between goal-oriented individual or group actions and object-oriented collective activity. The latter is a product of division of labor. Leont'ev's classic example is a tribal hunt in which some individuals chase the animals while others wait in ambush and kill them. The action of chasing the game away makes no sense if separated from the overall activity and its object. Leont'ev argues that there is no activity without an object. The object carries or embodies the true motive of the activity. Activities are systemic formations which gain durability by becoming institutionalized. But activities only take shape and manifest themselves through actions performed by individuals and groups.

In complex activity systems such as today's work organizations, it is difficult for practitioners to construct a connection between the goals of their ongoing actions and the more durable object/motive of the collective activity system. Objects resist and bite back, they seem to have lives of their own. But objects and motives are hard to articulate, they appear to be vague, fuzzy, multi-faceted, amoeba-like, and often fragmented or contested. The paradox is that objects/motives give directionality, purpose, and meaning to the collective activity, yet they are frustratingly elusive. The activity of health care is a case in point. Without the object of illness there would be no hospitals and health professionals. But despite its pervasive presence, illness is very hard to define, it does not obey the mental representations of professionals and patients, and it certainly does not disappear no matter how well one does one's work (Engeström, 1995; Engeström, Puonti, & Seppänen, 2003b).

In practical actions, objects, and motives are stabilized, temporarily "closed," by means of auxiliary artifacts – tools and signs. Vygotsky described this artifact-mediated nature of intentional action as follows:

> The person, using the power of things or stimuli, controls his own behavior through them, grouping them, putting them together, sorting them. In other words, the great uniqueness of the will consists of man having no power over his own behavior other than the power that things have over his behavior. But man subjects to himself the power of things over behavior, makes them serve his own purposes and controls that power as he wants. He changes the environment with the external activity and in this way affects his own behavior, subjecting it to his own authority (Vygotsky, 1997, p. 212).

Vygotsky (1997) pointed out that voluntary action has two phases: a *design phase* in which the mediating artifact is (often painstakingly) constructed and an *execution phase* which typically looks quite easy and almost automatic. Classic examples of mediated intentionality include the use of an alarm clock to wake up early in the morning, to master the conflict between motives of work and rest. Vygotsky's examples of voluntary action are focused on individual actors. This must not be interpreted as neglect of collective intentionality. According to Vygotsky's famous principle, higher psychological functions appear twice, first interpsychologically, in collaborative action, and later intrapsychologically, internalized by the individual. The interpsychological origins of voluntary action – and collective intentionality – would be found in rudimentary uses of socially shared external prompts, reminders, plans, maps, etc.

Mediating artifacts such as an alarm clock typically serve as signs which trigger a consequential action. They are mediators of action-level decisions. But humans also need and use mediating artifacts to stabilize future-oriented images or visions of their collective activity systems. Language and various semiotic representations are needed to construct and use such "tertiary artifacts," as Wartofsky (1979) called them. Human agency gains unusual powers when the two, future-oriented activity-level envisioning and consequential action-level decision-making, come together in close interplay

(Engeström, Engeström, & Kerosuo, 2003a). Ghoshal and Bruch (2003, p. 53) provide a nice example from organizational practice:

> Thomas Hill was a midlevel manager in a U.S.-based pharmaceuticals company. Comfortable in his job as head of Central European sales, Hill suddenly faced the possibility of becoming the Indian subsidiary's general manager.
> After days of internal battles, Hill asked two colleagues to debate the pros and cons in his presence. "I was distanced because the struggle took place outside of me," he recalls. "And yet it made the facts and my inner situation crystal clear." The colleagues continued the discussion until Hill was sure what he wanted. Impressed, he now uses the process regularly for tough decisions.

In activity theory, contradictions play a central role as sources of change and development. Contradictions are not the same as problems or conflicts. Contradictions are historically accumulating structural tensions within and between activity systems. The activity system is constantly working through tensions and contradictions within and between its elements. Contradictions manifest themselves in disturbances and innovative solutions. In this sense, an activity system is a virtual disturbance- and innovation-producing machine.

The primary contradiction of activities in capitalism is that between the use value and exchange value of commodities. This primary contradiction pervades all elements of our activity systems. The work activity of general practitioners (GP) in primary medical care may serve as an illustration. The primary contradiction, the dual nature of use value and exchange value, can be found by focusing on any of the elements of the doctor's work activity. For example, instruments of this work include a tremendous variety of medicaments and drugs. But they are not just useful preparations for healing – they are above all commodities with prices, manufactured for a market, advertised, and sold for profit. Every doctor faces this contradiction in his/her daily decision-making, in one form or another.

Activities are open systems. When an activity system adopts a new element from the outside (e.g., a new technology or a new object), it often leads to an aggravated secondary contradiction where some old element (e.g., the rules or the division of labor) collides with the new one. Such contradictions generate disturbances and conflicts, but also innovative attempts to change the activity. The stiff hierarchical division of labor lagging behind and preventing the possibilities opened by advanced instruments is a typical example. A typical secondary contradiction in the working activity of GPs would be the tension between the traditional biomedical *conceptual instruments* concerning the classification of diseases and correct diagnosis on the one hand *and* the changing nature of the *objects*, namely the increasingly ambivalent and complex problems and symptoms of the patients. These problems more and more often do not comply with the standards of classical diagnosis and nomenclature. They require an integrated social, psychological, and biomedical approach which may not yet exist.

Contradictions are not just inevitable features of activity. They are "the principle of its self-movement and (...) the form in which the development is cast" (Ilyenkov, 1977, p. 330). This means that new qualitative stages and forms of activity emerge as solutions to the contradictions of the preceding stage or form. This in turn takes place in the form of "invisible breakthroughs," innovations from below:

> In reality it always happens that a phenomenon which later becomes universal originally emerges as an individual, particular, specific phenomenon, as an exception from the rule. It cannot actually emerge in any other way. Otherwise history would have a rather mysterious form.
>
> Thus, any new improvement of labour, every new mode of man's action in production, before becoming generally accepted and recognised, first emerge as a certain deviation from previously accepted and codified norms. Having emerged as an *individual exception* from the rule in the labour of one or several men, the new form is then taken over by others, becoming in time a new *universal norm*. If the new norm did not originally appear in this exact manner, it would never become a really universal form, but would exist merely in fantasy, in wishful thinking (Ilyenkov, 1982, pp. 83–84).

Activity systems take shape and get transformed over lengthy periods of time. Their problems and potentials can only be understood against their own history. History itself needs to be studied as local history of the activity and its objects, and as history of the theoretical ideas and tools that have shaped the activity. Thus, medical work needs to be analyzed against the history of its local organization and against the more global history of the medical concepts, procedures, and tools employed and accumulated in the local activity.

To sum up, five principles of cultural–historical activity theory seem relevant for the study of collective intentionality and distributed agency. These may be called (1) the principle of object-orientation, (2) the principle of mediation by tools and signs, (3) the principle of mutual constitution of actions and activity, (4) the principle of contradictions and deviations as source of change, and (5) the principle of historicity. The last one, historicity, requires that I now turn briefly to the changing landscape of agency in work organizations.

Agency in Hierarchies, Markets, Networks, and Beyond

Many recent attempts to analyze historical change in work organizations (e.g., Powell, 1990) have condensed the current landscape into three major

forms: hierarchy, market, and network. In this view, organizations in cap-
italist society have been built either along the principles of centralized
hierarchy (e.g., large vertically integrated corporations and big bureaucra-
cies) or along the principles of the market (typically more agile companies
seeking to exploit new opportunities). Hierarchies are strong in securing
standardization needed in traditional mass production, but they are limited
by their rigidity. Market organizations are strong in their flexibility, but they
are limited by their excessive competitiveness which tends to exclude collaboration and reciprocity.

In a simplified form, we might characterize the nature of agency in
hierarchies with the imperative "control and command" for the management, and with the imperative "resist and defend" for the workers. In an
ideal market organization, this dualism melts into one overriding imperative: "Take advantage and maximize gain."

Powell and many others point out that these two classic forms of organizing work in capitalism are increasingly being challenged or even replaced
by various forms of networks in which different organizations or organizational units seek new innovations by means of collaboration across traditional boundaries. In network organizations, the imperative would be
"connect and reciprocate."

The rate of alliance and partnership formation in work organizations has
exploded in recent years. Firms no longer compete as individual companies,
they compete as rapidly changing constellations of companies that cooperate to succeed. Across virtually all sectors of the economy, alliances have
reshaped the interactions of companies. While partnerships and alliances are
clearly spearheads toward the future, they are also full of tensions, and thus
extremely difficult to sustain and manage (Spekman, Isabella, & MacAvoy,
2000).

Partnership and alliance formation typically takes place in multiorgan-
izational fields (Scott, Ruef, Mendel, & Caronna, 2000). In activity–theoretical terms, these may be called distributed multi-activity fields or terrains,
bound together by partially shared large-scale objects. The mastery and/or
cultivation of such "runaway objects" urgently requires new forms of distributed and coordinated agency.

In a series of recent studies (Engeström, Engeström, & Kärkkäinen, 1995;
Engeström, Engeström, & Vähäaho, 1999a; Hasu & Engeström, 2000),
we have encountered numerous examples of work organization in which
collaboration between the partners is of vital importance, yet takes shape
without strong predetermined rules or central authority. I call such forms
of collaborative work *knotworking.* The notion of knot refers to rapidly

pulsating, distributed, and partially improvised orchestration of collaborative performance between otherwise loosely connected actors and organizational units. Knotworking is characterized by a movement of tying, untying, and retying together seemingly separate threads of activity. The tying and dissolution of a knot of collaborative work is not reducible to any specific individual or fixed organizational entity as the center of control. The locus of initiative changes from moment to moment within a knotworking sequence. Thus, knotworking cannot be adequately analyzed from the point of view of an assumed center of coordination and control, or as an additive sum of the separate perspectives of individuals or institutions contributing to it. The unstable knots themselves need to be made the focus of analysis.

The concept of network is somewhat problematic as a framework for understanding knotworking. A network is commonly understood as a relatively stable web of links or connections between organizational units, often materially anchored in shared information systems. Knotworking, on the other hand, is a much more elusive and improvised phenomenon. Knotworking is similar to the "latent organizations" described by Starkey, Barnatt, and Tempest (2000, p. 300) in that it "persists through time as a form of organization that is periodically made manifest in particular projects," remaining dormant until market or user demand presents an opportunity or necessity for the organization to reanimate itself as an active production system. However, Starkey, Barnatt, and Tempest (2000, p. 300) argue that latent organizations "come to exist when a central broker reconstitutes the same creatively unique set of agent partners on a recurring project basis." This is clearly not the case in the knotworking settings we have analyzed. As pointed out above, in these settings the center just does not hold.

Authors like Howard Rheingold (2002) have began to prophesize "smart mobs" as radically new forms of organization made possible by mobile technologies. Initial conditions of such "swarm" or "amoeba" organizations were nicely captured by Rafael in an essay where he discusses the overthrowing of President Estrada in the Philippines in 2001:

> Bypassing the complex of broadcasting media, cell phone users themselves became broadcasters, receiving, and transmitting both news and gossip and often confounding the two. Indeed, one could imagine each user becoming a broadcasting station unto him- or herself, a node in a wider network of communication that the state could not possibly even begin to monitor, much less control. Hence, once the call was made for people to mass at Edsa, cell phone users readily forwarded messages they received, even as they followed what was asked of them.
>
> Cell phones then were invested not only with the power to surpass crowded conditions and congested surroundings brought about by the state's inability to order everyday life.

They were also seen to bring a new kind of crowd about, one that was thoroughly
conscious of itself as a movement headed towards a common goal (Rafael, 2003).

Clearly such a "smart mob" has no single, permanent center. Mobile technologies make it possible that each participant is potentially a momentary
center. Rafael's example underlines the importance of a shared goal. But the
emphasis on goal also implies the problem. Since goals are relatively short-
lived, also "smart mobs" seem to be very temporary organizational forms.

However, there are amoeba-like organizations which are not limited to
the pursuit of short-term goals. Two quite resilient examples are the activities of birding (e.g., Obmascik, 2004) and skateboarding (e.g., Borden,
2001). These might be also called "wildfire activities" as they have the peculiar capacity to disappear or die in a given location and suddenly reappear
and develop vigorously in a quite different location, or in the same location
after a lengthy dormant period. While participants in these activities commonly use mobile technologies to communicate with one another and to
broadcast information about their objects (rare birds, good skating spots),
these activities are much older than mobile phones and the Internet. Birding
has a history of several hundred years, and skateboarding dates back at least
to the early 1970s. Two additional features need to be mentioned. Both
birding and skateboarding are peculiar combinations of leisure, work, sport,
and art. And they both have consistently defied attempts at full commercialization, offering ample opportunities for entrepreneurship but not
becoming themselves dominated by commercial motives.

What might be the nature of collective intentionality, or distributed
agency, in knotworking and amoeba-like organizations? I will now turn to
cases, first a fictional one, to examine this question.

A Fictional Case: Hillerman's The Sinister Pig

The classic mystery novel concentrates intentionality and agency into the
individual master detective (e.g., Poirot, Maigret), often supported by a
slightly shadow-like sidekick (e.g., Holmes and Watson), and working on an
equally individual master criminal or crime. The historical evolution of the
genre has led to increasingly complex configurations and plots, yet the focus
on an individual or dyadic central agent has stubbornly remained.

Tony Hillerman's mystery novels, located in the Navajo Reservation of
New Mexico, demonstrate the evolution of detective mysteries in a nice way.
Hillerman's first three books had a senior Navajo tribal police officer, Joe
Leaphorn, as their central hero. The next three books lifted a junior officer,

Jim Chee, into the position of central agent. In the subsequent books, Leaphorn and Chee worked together, in an often uneasy alliance. In his memoir, Hillerman (2001) muses on this as follows:

> Luck, for example, caused me to put Chee and Leaphorn in the same book. I was on a book tour promoting the third of the books in which Jim works alone. A lady I'm signing a book for thanks me and says:
> "Why did you change Leaphorn's name to Chee?"
> It took a split second for the significance to sink in. A dagger to the heart. I stutter. I search around for an answer, and finally just say they're totally different characters. "Oh," says she, "I can't tell them apart."
> I am sure there are writers self-confident enough to forget this. What does this old babe know? But that was not to be for me. Like what St. Paul called his "thorn in the flesh," it wouldn't go away. I decided to put both characters in the same book to settle the issue myself. I tried it in Skinwalkers. It worked so well I tried it again in A Thief of Time. Hurrah! It was the breakout book! (Hillerman, 2001, pp. 298–299).

An author's encounter with a reader, such as the one described by Hillerman, does not have to be characterized as luck. It may also be thought of as a relatively probable and common opportunity for knotworking – a point Hillerman himself seems to imply when he writes that he is sure that "there are writers self-confident enough to forget this." In terms of distributed agency, we might say that this step in Hillerman's writing resulted from knotworking between the fictional subjects of Joe Leaphorn and Jim Chee, and the real (?) subjects of the lady and Tony Hillerman.

The latest book, *The Sinister Pig* (2003), steps radically beyond this dyad. The field of actors developed in the book may be diagrammatically depicted as in Fig. 1. In the diagram, the unbroken two-headed arrows indicate relatively strong relationships of collaboration, while the broken two-headed arrow implies a weak collaborative relationship. Lightning-shaped two-headed arrows indicate hostile relationships. Letters A, B, and C signify that the actors represent three different law enforcement agencies,[2] namely the Navajo tribal police, the Border Patrol, and the Bureau of Land Management, respectively. Gray triangles signify "unofficial" actors who represent no institutional agencies.

A few interesting features are immediately evident in Fig. 1. First, the good guys are not a group in which everyone collaborates with everyone else. There are two very different hubs among the good guys: one frontline-oriented around Bernie Manuelito, the other more distant-from-action around Jim Chee and Joe Leaphorn. These two hubs are connected through a strong relationship between Chee and Manuelito, a weak relationship between Manuelito and Leaphorn, and weak mediation by Captain Largo. Secondly, there are three relationships which are both collaborative and

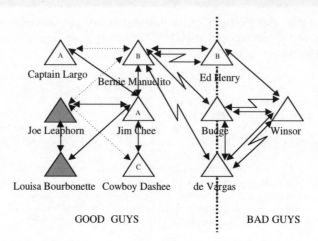

Fig. 1. Network of distributed agency in *The Sinister Pig.*

hostile, indicating a radical switch in the nature of the interaction at some point. Thirdly, three actors are placed on the boundary between the good and the bad, indicating serious ambiguity and uncertainty. Fourthly, three different law enforcement agencies are involved. And finally, along with official representatives of different agencies, also individuals without an official status are involved in the work.

From the point of view of activity theory, what kind of agency and intentionality is involved in the Hillerman book? To answer this, I will examine *The Sinister Pig* with the help of the five principles of activity theory presented earlier.

The first principle, *object-orientation*, calls attention to the object of the activities under scrutiny. In criminal investigation, the object is a suspected crime. In *The Sinister Pig*, the crime is highly distributed in time and space. Initially the focus is on a murder case. But it gradually drifts to suspected smuggling of narcotics over long distances across the Mexico–U.S. border through abandoned oil pipelines. This widely distributed and highly ambiguous nature of crime as object is not at all unrealistic. My student Anne Puonti recently published her dissertation on collaboration between authorities in the investigation of economic crimes. She points out that whereas a "traditional" crime always takes place at a certain time and place, economic, or white-collar crime is typically committed over an extended period of time, and nobody can point to an exact time at which the boundary between legal and illegal was crossed. Nor can an exact place for economic crime be determined: the perpetrator may have a permanent residence in one location, the company domicile may reside somewhere else, and company property may even be located in other countries (Puonti, 2004).

The second principle, *mediation by tools and signs*, asks us to look into the artifacts involved in the activities under scrutiny. *The Sinister Pig* itself turns out to be a crucial artifact, a mobile module originally used to clean oil pipelines, now converted into a container for the illegal drugs. The pig is a tool for the bad guys, but it also serves as a boundary object, an emblematic semiotic mediator by means of which Leaphorn begins to formulate a theory of the crime:

> (…) Chee shook his head. "I'm way behind you on that connection."
> Louisa had poured their coffee, a mug for herself, had joined them at the table, but had politely refrained from getting into this discussion. Now she cleared her throat.
> "Of course he's behind, Joe. Who wouldn't be? Tell him about your pig theory." She smiled at Chee. "As Joe sees this situation these are very sinister pigs."
> Leaphorn looked slightly embarrassed.
> Pig is the name pipeline maintenance people use for a device they push through the pipes to clean them out (…) (Hillerman, 2003, p. 153).

For both the bad guys and the good guys, the functioning of the central artifact of the pig is dependent on a constellation of supporting artifacts, primarily mobile phones and maps (on tool constellations, see Keller & Keller, 1996):

> "When we get about an hour from El Paso, I'm making some calls," Winsor said. "You take care of dealing with getting my plane parked. I'll meet a man I need to talk to at the administration building. You brought your cell phone?"
> "Always. And the pager" (Hillerman, 2003, p. 146).
> "There's more I want to explain," Leaphorn said. "I want you to take a look at an old map I dug up."
> Now Chee snorted. "A map! Have I ever discussed anything with you when you didn't pull a map on me?" (Hillerman, 2003, p. 150).

The third principle, the *mutual constitution of actions and activity*, prompts us to inquire into the relationship between situated consequential decisions and future-oriented visions. In *The Sinister Pig*, the coming together of activity-level envisioning and action-level decision-making is vividly described in two subsets of encounters. The first one is that between two bad guys, Budge de Baca and Diego de Vargas:

> "I don't know what he thinks. But I think that if we kill her, he has it figured so he'll get away with it. But if he has it figured right, she is a federal cop. The federals will catch us, wherever we go. Not give up until they do. And then they either kill us or we die in a federal prison somewhere. And, of course, that's exactly the way he hopes it will work out. He wouldn't want us around anymore."

Diego sighed. "Yes," he said. "It would be true also among those where I've always worked."

"The way it happens in Washington, my patron is rich and powerful, and his roomful of lawyers and very important friends let the police know that our rich and powerful boss is innocent. He just came out here to shoot an African antelope for his trophy room. And he had me put his special trophy hunting rifle back there in the storage place to show them evidence that that's the truth. And then he says he was betrayed by two low-class scoundrels who already are wanted by the police."

"Yes," he said. "That sounds like it would be in Mexico too."

"I think there is a way out of this for us," Budge said.

"Tell me," Diego said (Hillerman, 2003, pp. 187–188).

"What's the trouble?" he asked. "Worried, or is it love sick?"

"Worried," Chee said. "How am I going to get Bernie to quite this damned Border Patrol job and come on home?"

"That's easy," Cowboy said.

"Like hell," Chee said. "You just don't understand how stubborn she is."

(...)

"If you want her to come home, you just say, 'Bernie, my sweet, I love you dearly. Come home and marry me and we will live happily ever after."

"Yeah," Chee said (Hillerman, 2003, pp. 191–192).

These two exchanges of future-oriented envisioning move at the level of activity systems. In the first one, Budge and de Vargas, anticipating the critical action assigned to them, envision their future fate as members of the criminal activity system led by Winsor. The envisioning leads toward a preliminary commitment to new action – but due to interruption an action plan is never formulated and the new action is subsequently improvised. In the second example, Chee and Dashee, also anticipating critical actions ahead of them, envision Chee's future life activity. In this case, the very actions of seeking out officer Manuelito are driven by the activity-level envisioning – which itself is articulated only as the critical actions unfold.

The fourth principle, *contradictions and deviations as source of change*, invites us to examine systemic tensions in the activities under scrutiny. The two excerpts just sited also exemplify the key contradictions operating in Hillerman's novel. The first contradiction is embedded in the criminal activity system which depends on unquestioning obedience from subordinates but at the same time puts the subordinates at unacceptable risk in demanding violent actions from them. This is of course the classic contradiction that has made it possible for law enforcement to use lower-level members of organized crime as informants. The tension pushes Budge and de Vargas to take actions that radically deviate from the script devised by their boss.

The second contradiction is embedded in the professional activity systems of officers Chee and Manuelito. This is the equally classic tension between crime as invasive object and the pursuit of personal happiness. Much of today's crime drama and fiction is built around this tension between the official and the personal in police work. In Hillerman's story, the contradiction pushes Jim Chee to deviate radically from the rules of his institutional agency. In effect, his quest to solve the crime melts together with his personal quest to find Bernie Manuelito. This drives him to move far beyond his jurisdiction, with the help of a friend, Cowboy Dashee.

The fifth principle, *historicity*, tells us to explore the successive and intersecting developmental layers, including the emergent new ones, in the activities under scrutiny. Hillerman provides a lot of material for this, and his previous books set a historical stage for viewing changes at work in law enforcement. Joe Leaphorn, the legendary individual, is retired and stays in the background. Jim Chee is not in the center of frontline action, either. The focus drifts to the female officer Bernadette Manuelito, and eventually the climax takes place without a clear individual or dyadic hero, largely facilitated by unanticipated actions of the two bad guys, Budge and de Vargas. All in all, the center does not hold. Different actors put their spoons in the soup, none of them having the whole picture or complete information about what the other actors are doing. Historically, this is amplified in the image of the multiple institutional agencies involved.

> (...) and she missed the arrival of an SUV occupied by Drug Enforcement Agents, and the resulting dispute over which of the agencies had jurisdiction, which was eventually resolved by the arrival of someone representing Homeland Security, who declared himself in charge of the FBI, the DEA, the Border Patrol, the Department of Land Management, and the Najavo Tribal Police (Hillerman, 2003, pp. 220–221).

So what do we learn about distributed agency and collective intentionality from these five exercises?

In Hillerman's story, there is no fixed and stable center of control and command, individual or collective: the center does not hold. Yet the job gets done, and various individuals and subgroups contribute to the achievement in an intentional and deliberate manner. Moreover, it does not seem satisfactory to characterize the process simply as an accidental aggregation or combination of individual and subgroup efforts. There is a strong attempt among all participants to grasp and resolve the complex whole, even though it seems hopelessly beyond the limits of each participant's own horizon of understanding and capability.

In the story, the job gets done by means of numerous seemingly separate or quite weakly connected strings of actions that take place over an extended period of time and far apart from one another in geographical space. But again, they are not completely disconnected either. Partial connecting information, or hints and clues, do circulate and connect the various actions. Although often inefficiently, partially and belatedly, the different actors do seek interconnections and they do reciprocate.

The intention, or the goal, or the idea of what is actually being accomplished, emerges in bits and pieces spread among the dispersed actors over the course of the events, to become fully and jointly articulated only after it is all over. This after-the-fact articulation and stabilization applies also to control and command, as is made evident in the last excerpt above.

But why bother about a mere fictional detective story? I submit that fiction is often more sensitive to the changing landscape of societal life than are our everyday descriptive accounts or scientific analyses. The change in Hillerman's fiction provides one window into thinking of change more generally. Let me now try and open another window, this time grounded in longitudinal and interventionist field research in health care organizations.

An Empirical Case: Knotworking in the Care of Chronically Ill Patients in Helsinki

Can distributed, networked agency be purposefully cultivated? What kinds of tools and collaborative arrangements are needed to facilitate it? How does it manifest itself in situations of collaborative decision-making and problem solving? I will devote this section of my chapter to these questions, using examples from a series of longitudinal intervention studies we have conducted in the multi-activity field of health care in the city of Helsinki in Finland (see Engeström, Engeström, & Kerosuo, 2003a).

Scott and his co-authors (2000, p. 355) conclude that "much of the interest and complexity of today's healthcare arena, compared with its condition at mid-century, is due not simply to the numbers of new types of social actors now active but also to the multiple ways in which these actors have become interpenetrated and richly connected." Medical work is not anymore only about treating patients and finding cures. It is increasingly about re-organizing and re-conceptualizing care across professional specialties and institutional boundaries. This challenge of "clinical integration" is not easily accomplished. As Shortell, Gillies, Anderson, Erickson, and Mitchell (2000, p. 69) state, "overall, clinical integration for the management of people with chronic illness is still largely a promise in search of performance."

In other words, the shape and implications of spatio-temporally distributed work and expertise are still fragile and open, literally under construction. When professionals perform such work and discourse, they also give shape to it. Thus, a methodology is needed that allows us, in an anticipatory manner, to explore and make visible the potentials and problems of constructing and performing this emerging type of work.

To meet this challenge, we recently arranged a series of joint "laboratory sessions" for medical professionals involved in the care of chronic patients with multiple illnesses in the city of Helsinki. For such a session, one of the participating physicians was asked to select a patient and prepare a presentation of the patient's care trajectory. The patient attended the session, along with physicians and nurses representing different specialties and clinics involved in the patient's care. The session was aimed at improving coordination and collaboration among the parties. The physician presenting the case was asked to prepare drafts for (a) a care calendar summarizing the important events in the patient's care trajectory, (b) a care map depicting the key parties involved in the care, and (c) a care agreement summarizing the division of responsibilities among the caregivers involved. We gave the physician simple one-page templates for each one of these representations, but the participants were invited to modify and redesign them according to their preferences.

This procedure generated two kinds of data. First, the physician preparing the case usually invited the patient to a consultation where they discussed the patient's care to prepare for the presentation. Sometimes the physician invited a key colleague from another clinic to join in this consultation, or arranged a separate meeting with one or more relevant colleagues. A researcher from our group videotaped the preparatory consultation and collected copies of the documents used or prepared in it. The researcher was also available if the practitioners or the patient wanted to discuss the arrangements of the forthcoming laboratory session. Secondly, we videotaped the laboratory session itself, and collected copies of the documents presented or produced in the course of the session. Here are three examples from discussions in three different laboratory sessions, each attached with a short analysis.

Example 1.

Heart specialist	Who in your opinion should from the point of view of the care of the heart deficiency take the initiative with regard to producing the care plan? Who is responsible, who makes it or sees to it that it is made?
Administrator physician	As I see it, it is still the expertise of the cardiology clinic to make the plan.

Heart specialist	Yes, it should be, but there must be a specified person in the cardiology clinic...
Administrator physician	Yes.
Heart specialist	...a man or a woman who does it. The clinic as such doesn't do anything.
Administrator physician	No, it doesn't. I'm getting there, I am of course looking at the only one who is present here, with burning eyes...
[laughter]	
Researcher	You've been put in charge of quite a lot, you know.
Administrator physician	And then it's Mary, too, in that this is kind of pressure, if Mary is indeed the personal physician...
Administrator physician	Yes, it is so that the personal physician is here under the pressure that the plan will be made....

The first example illustrates the importance of *contradictions*. It contains an attempt to assign initiative and responsibility to identifiable participants. The patient has a serious heart deficiency and the discussion has led to a point where the participants realize that this condition is not properly under anyone's care responsibility. The heart specialist represents Cardiology Clinic, but he has not treated this particular patient and due to the constant rotation of physicians at his clinic, he is uncertain if he will ever have a chance to deal with this patient. So the first contradiction surfaces: Cardiology Clinic has the needed expertise, but as the heart specialist says, they need "a man or a woman who does it. The clinic as such doesn't do anything." The specialist can offer no continuity of care.

To answer the patient's need for continuity of care, the focus shifts to the patient's personal physician, a GP in the local primary care health center: "The personal physician is here under the pressure that the plan will be made." This brings up the second contradiction: the personal GP has the required continuity of care, but little authority and often limited competence in matters of specialized medicine.

Example 2.

Chief physician	So, will you be first, as the physician responsible for her at the primary care health center, and then we will add...

Consulting physician	Here we are kind of documenting what is already in place, but *if we had a similar case* where these contacts had not yet been created, *this would serve as sort of a model* from which other patients could benefit.
Chief physician	It would be very important *if we had a situation* where the patient's personal physician is changed, the previous doctor would go on a leave, and the next doctor would come for half a year. *In such cases this has great importance*, so that the doctor knows...

[the patient's primary care GP signs the care agreement and starts to hand it back to the chief physician]

Chief physician	Please let the patient also sign it, while you are at it. ...From the signatures one sees that there are several people involved...

The second example illustrates the importance of *mediating artifacts* as well as the *coming together of activity-level visions and action-level decisions*. It contains a situation in which the laboratory session has led to drafting of a shared care agreement for a patient. The different professionals involved in the care of this patient, and the patient herself, are now ready to sign the care agreement – they are controlling their own behavior with the help of an external tool they have created. While signing the crucial artifact, the professionals discuss it. In the excerpt, I have identified segments of future-oriented activity-level envisioning by using italics. These envisioning segments are formulated by means of hypothetical language: "If we had a similar case", "if we had a situation." At the same time, the participants are making consequential action-level decisions: "So, will you be first", "Please let the patient also sign it." The last decision, realizing that the patient also needs to sign the agreement, illustrates the importance of *object-orientation*. This small but extraordinary realization was possible because the patient, the embodiment of the object of medical work, sat in as a knotworking partner with the medical professionals.

Example 3.

Researcher 2	What are we going to do with this agreement, what will be done with it now?
Researcher 1	Isn't it so that O [the GP] will follow the situation at this point...
Researcher 2	...Yes but this...
Researcher 1	...because there aren't clearly identified partners yet, before these are cleared up, these ongoing examinations and tests and their results.
GP	Yes, we still miss the signatures, so...
Researcher 2	Well.
Researcher 1	Or what do you have in mind?
Researcher 2	Well, I just asked, what do you think, now that such a document has been prepared, so...
Researcher 1	Or all this groundwork, yes.
Researcher 2	Groundwork, what will be done with it. And now that O [the GP] refers R [the patient] to different places, would it be good if those different places to which she sends her for a specific problem, if they got to know about this whole picture in which this specific is...?
GP	Well, do I understand correctly, that I'd attach to it [the referral] this whole bundle, if someone there wants to quickly glance through it. How much would it then...? If I'm completely honest, having worked as a replacement for a specialist at one time, I sense that the less extra [paperwork] one got beyond one's own specialty the happier most colleagues were. So what is the standpoint of the seniors here...?
Researcher 1	This is an interesting question when there is so much material coming from the personal physician.
GP	Does it make a difference for how the process gets started in that end [in specialized hospital care]? Because if one learns this [...], so that one just learns to use this tool, then one just does it. Surely at some point this will be

	moved from paper-and-pencil over to the other type...
Researcher 1	...Soon, over to Pegasos... [computerized medical records system currently being implemented in the primary health care system of Helsinki]
GP	...yes, so surely it will be much easier in there...or somehow to pick it up from there. Or maybe some aid might do it there, or something like that...
Nephrologist	But in my opinion, when someone has done this work, this will be useful for all.
Researcher 1	There is no reason not to send it all with a small statement, telling that "here is background information which may be helpful, and I am ready to discuss if needed," something like this.
Researcher 3	I think H [researcher 2] was thinking "why not attach this care agreement to the next referral."
GP	Yes, but in my opinion it would also require these care calendars.
Researcher 3	Aha, those should be added to it, yes.
Researcher 1	Those calendars were clearly very important tools for you when you sorted through all of this.
GP	Yes, that's how I started to make sense of the reality in which the lady had lived the years before returning to Finland and after it.
Researcher 1	Yes.
GP	It was not easy in the first consultation. I kind of thought when I was writing down those calendars that if I only had had this kind of a tool then. So that I would have been able to arrange these issues at once according to some jointly agreed-upon model. I experienced this as very good.
Researcher 1	Right, yes.
GP	I mean, the first contact is heavy because there are so many things, and they have to be sorted, and that takes time. But it pays off in the longer run.
Researcher 1	Excellent, well, let's quickly sum this up. Surely it is like you [nephrologist] said, when such a work

	has been done, there is no sense in keeping it to one's self. [...] And it will be nice to hear what kind of feedback you'll get on your referrals. [...]
GP	I could include an attachment, or an attachment to a referral I already sent.
Nephrologist	May I say something?
Researcher 1	Yes.
Nephrologist	Now before this work is completed, it may be that somebody kind of, not gets aggravated but wonders, if these care agreements begin to come in, before this practice has been officially fixed and its implementation announced.
Researcher 1	Right, so in this case...
Nephrologist	...So this is at an early stage. So I think that if we now send it, surely the physician who receives the referral is glad to get as much information as possible. But it may require a small explanation.
Researcher 1	Just so.
GP	Yes.

This lengthy excerpt may be used to demonstrate the utility of all the five principles of activity theory in the analysis of emerging forms of distributed agency at work. First of all, the principle of *object-orientation* guides us to ask: What is actually the object here? What are they talking about and trying to accomplish? In the excerpt, the talk is focused on the use and development of tools. This is triggered by the initial question of Researcher 2: "What are we going to do with this agreement, what will be done with it now?" In effect, the tools seem to have become the object here. We have analyzed such object-tool shifts in other contexts (Engeström & Escalante, 1995; Hasu & Engeström, 2000) and found them very problematic. Often the tool actually replaces the original object and becomes a substitute object, creating a hermetic bubble of design for the sake of design. The object (the client, the patient, the illness) is excluded from the discourse. Is this what is happening in the excerpt?

Early on in the excerpt, Researcher 2 specifies her initial question by bringing in the patient: "And now that O [the GP] refers R [the patient] to different places ..." A little later the GP brings in the patient with an identity situated in time and place: "Yes, that's how I started to make sense of the reality in which the lady had lived the years before returning to

Finland and after it." And shortly after that, the GP takes up the object of patients with multiple simultaneous illnesses in a more general sense: "I mean, the first contact is heavy because there are so many things, and they have to be sorted, and that takes time. But it pays off in the longer run." These references to the object indicate that the object-tool shift in this case may not lead to the formation of a self-sufficient substitute object.

The second principle, *mediation by tools and signs*, asks us to look into the potentials of artifacts as means of eliciting or triggering voluntary action. As I mentioned earlier in this chapter, rudimentary prompts may be regarded as early forms of mediated collective intentionality. The discussion in the excerpt focuses on the creation and implementation of such a rudimentary prompt. Researcher 1 states that: "There is no reason not to send it all with a small statement, telling that "here is background information which may be helpful, and I am ready to discuss if needed," something like this." The GP agrees and suggests that "I could include an attachment, or an attachment to a referral I already sent." Finally the experienced nephrologist refines the idea: "But it may require a small explanation." This is an example of the design phase of mediated collective intentionality.

The third principle of *mutual constitution of actions and activity* calls attention to the relationship between decision-making and envisioning. The excerpt shows how activity-level envisioning began to approach and resemble action-level decision-making. The participants were working on a future-oriented model: "This is at an early stage." Yet they were also working out a here-and-now decision: "I could include an attachment." What was particularly future-oriented about this decision was that the participants agreed that not only would the new mediating artifacts (care agreement, care map, care calendar) be attached to the referrals of this patient – they would also be introduced by a short note that explains to the receiving specialist what these new documents are all about. Such an introductory note was to have a standard text, prepared by the researchers and signed by the respective managing physicians of the primary care and the Central University Hospital. Yet, this general note was to be prepared quickly, so that this particular physician would use it in the particular referrals for this particular patient. In other words, the particular decision was simultaneously a general vision.

The fourth principle directs our analysis to *contradictions and deviations as source of change*. In the excerpt, the initial questioning of Researcher 2 led to the surfacing of a contradiction between administrative efficiency and patient-oriented quality of care. This tension was crisply articulated by the GP: "How much would it then …? If I'm completely honest, having worked as a replacement for a specialist at one time, I sense that the less extra [paperwork] one got beyond one's own specialty the happier most colleagues were." The decisive push to resolve the dilemma in an expansive manner came from the nephrologist who in a succinct way pointed out that the work done by the GP should not go wasted. This statement was a significant deviating action in that it came as if from the other side of the fence, from a leading hospital specialist whose position would normally suggest a very different script of reasoning.

The fifth principle, *historicity*, prompts us to ask what historical type of work and collaboration is actually being performed in the excerpt. The excerpt, and more generally all the three examples from laboratory sessions presented above, represent an attempt to break out of the confines of medical care divided horizontally in strictly bounded functional specialties and vertically in separate levels of expertise. The conscious aim in those sessions was to achieve negotiated knotworking between practitioners and patients. It is not yet clear what it will take to make such knotworking sustainable, or indeed whether it will even be possible in the near future. These sessions may thus be regarded as spearheads, microcosms that anticipate possible future developments in health care.

CONCLUSION: TOWARD CONCEPTS OF OBJECT-ORIENTED INTERAGENCY AND COLLABORATIVE INTENTIONALITY CAPITAL

Various attempts have been made to categorize different dimensions of agency. For example, Patricia Mann (2002, p. 128) proposes a three-dimensional theory of agency which "involves inquiring not merely about one's desires, but also one's sense of responsibility, as well as one's expectations of recognition and reward in taking a particular action." Mustafa Emirbayer and Ann Mische (1998) also suggest that agency should be analyzed in terms of three dimensions or elements: the iterational element, the projective element, and the practical evaluative element. While interesting, these categorizations have some serious weaknesses from the point of view of activity theory. They explicitly or tacitly take the individual as the foundational agent, and they display little if any historicity, and thus little potential for understanding change.

The five principles of activity theory sketched and used above may offer a somewhat more differentiated framework for analyzing agency. Most importantly, these principles do not assume that the foundational agent is an individual. To the contrary, all the five principles, most obviously the principle of mutual constitution of actions and activity, the principle of contradictions as source of change, and the principle of historicity call for a serious examination of the social constitution and institutional embeddedness of agency.

The fictional case of Hillerman's *The Sinister Pig* and the empirical material from our fieldwork in medical settings point to the possibility that agency and collective intentionality may be taking on interesting new qualities in the context of network and post-network organizations. Earlier I suggested that the nature of agency in network organizations may be condensed in the imperative "connect and reciprocate." Now this does not seem sufficient anymore. First of all, both in the fictional and the empirical examples I have discussed above, the connecting and reciprocating are done *focused on and circling around a complex object.* Secondly, the connecting and reciprocating are done in fields of multiple, often severely divided activity systems. Reaching beyond and across the dividing boundaries and gaps between the activity systems needs to be acknowledged as a foundational feature of this type of agency – thus I prefer to talk about *inter*agency. These reasons seem sufficient to put forward a tentative concept of object-oriented interagency. This notion is above all a call for further studies of the formation and execution of collective intentionality in distributed activity fields. Tentatively, the imperative of this type of agency might be formulated as "Dwell in the object, connect and reciprocate across boundaries."[3]

Formations such as the agentic collaboration between actors in *The Sinister Pig* or the knotworking between practitioners and patients in the laboratory sessions are valuable assets for the organizations involved. They perform a dual job in that they solve very complex problems and also contribute to the reshaping of the entire way of working in their given fields. They are very cost efficient in that they do not require establishing new positions or new organizational centers. Indeed, these formations tend to reject such attempts. Rejection and deviation from standard procedures and scripted norms are foundational to the success of such amoeba-like formations. Their efficacy and value lie in their distributed agency, their collective intentionality. In this sense, I suggest the notion of *collaborative intentionality capital* as an emerging form of organizational assets.

Obviously object-oriented interagency and collaborative intentionality capital are not mature concepts or solutions that can be easily implemented. These concepts are meant to open up a field for further theoretical work and experimentation in organizational fields with complex runaway objects.

NOTES

1. The discussions on collective intentionality and distributed agency are two fairly separate though overlapping fields themselves, collective intentionality being mainly a topic for analytical philosophy and cognitive science, and distributed agency being mainly debated by sociologists, anthropologists, and social philosophers. Since a thorough review and comparison of these two fields is impossible within the scope of this chapter, I take the liberty of moving across their boundaries without much warning.

2. The term "agency" appears here interestingly in its formal institutional sense. One of the central points of Hillerman's novel is that such official agencies gain real agency only through the often deviating actions of flesh-and-blood people.

3. By "dwelling in the object" I refer to a longitudinal dialogical relationship with the object that goes beyond "focusing on" or "appropriating" the object.

REFERENCES

Barnes, B. (2000). *Understanding agency: Social theory and responsible action*. London: Sage.

Blackler, F., McDonald, S., & Crump, N. (1999). Managing experts and competing through innovation: An activity theoretical analysis. *Organization, 6*, 5–31.

Blackler, F., Crump, N., & McDonald, S. (2000). Organizing processes in complex activity networks. *Organization, 7*, 277–300.

Borden, I. (2001). *Skateboarding, space and the city: Architecture, the body and performative critique*. New York: Berg.

Bratman, M. E. (1999). *Faces of intention: Selected essays on intention and agency*. Cambridge: Cambridge University Press.

Ciborra, C. (2000). A critical review of the literature on the management of corporate information infrastructure. In: C. Ciborra, et al. (Eds), *From control to drift: The dynamics of corporate information infrastructures*. Oxford: Oxford University Press.

Cross, R., Baker, W., & Parker, A. (2003). What creates energy in organizations?, *Sloan Management Review*, Summer, *44*, 51–56.

Deleuze, G., & Guattari, F. (1977). *Anti-oedipus: Capitalism and schizophrenia*. New York: Viking.

Deleuze, G., & Guattari, F. (1987). *A thousand plateaus: Capitalism and schizophrenia*. Minneapolis: University of Minnesota Press.

Emirbayer, M., & Mische, A. (1998). What is agency? *The American Journal of Sociology, 103*, 962–1023.

Engeström, Y. (1995). Objects, contradictions and collaboration in medical cognition: An activity–theoretical perspective. *Artificial Intelligence in Medicine, 7*, 395–412.

Engeström, Y. (2000). Activity theory as a framework for analyzing and redesigning work. *Ergonomics, 43*, 960–974.

Engeström, Y. (Ed.) (2001). *Activity theory and social capital*. Technical Reports no. 5. Helsinki: Center for Activity Theory and Developmental Work Research, University of Helsinki.

Engeström, Y. (2004). The new generation of expertise: Seven theses. In: H. Rainbird, A. Fuller & A. Munro (Eds), *Workplace learning in context*. London: Routledge.

Engeström, Y., & Escalante, V. (1995). Mundane tool or object of affection? The rise and fall of the Postal Buddy. In: B. Nardi (Ed.), *Consciousness in context: Activity theory and human–computer interaction*. Cambridge: The MIT Press.

Engeström, Y., Engeström, R., & Kärkkäinen, M. (1995). Polycontextuality and boundary crossing in expert cognition: Learning and problem solving in complex work activities. *Learning and Instruction, 5*, 319–336.

Engeström, Y., Engeström, R., & Vähäaho, T. (1999a). When the center does not hold: The importance of knotworking. In: S. Chaiklin, M. Hedegaard & U. J. Jensen (Eds), *Activity theory and social practice: Cultural–historical approaches*. Aarhus: Aarhus University Press.

Engeström, Y., Miettinen, R., & Punamäki, R. -L. (Eds) (1999b). *Perspectives on activity theory*. Cambridge: Cambridge University Press.

Engeström, Y., Engeström, R., & Kerosuo, H. (2003a). The discursive construction of collaborative care. *Applied Linguistics, 24*, 286–315.

Engeström, Y., Puonti, A., & Seppänen, L. (2003b). Spatial and temporal expansion of the object as a challenge for reorganizing work. In: D. Nicolini, S. Gherardi & D. Yanow (Eds), *Knowing in organizations: A practice-based approach*. Armonk: Sharpe.

Fogel, A. (1993). *Developing through relationships: Origins of communication, self, and culture*. Chicago: The University of Chicago Press.

Gell, A. (1998). *Art and agency: An anthropological theory*. Oxford: Clarendon Press.

Ghoshal, S., Bruch, H. (2003). Going beyond motivation to the power of volition. *Sloan Management Review*, Spring, *44*, 51–57.

Gibbs, R. W., Jr. (2001). Intentions as emergent products of social interactions. In: B. F. Malle, L. J. Moses & D. A. Baldwin (Eds), *Intentions and intentionality: Foundations of social cognition*. Cambridge: The MIT Press.

Giddens, A. (1991). *Consequences of modernity*. Cambridge: Polity Press.

Hasu, M., & Engeström, Y. (2000). Measurement in action: An activity–theoretical perspective on producer–user interaction. *International Journal of Human–Computer Studies, 53*, 61–89.

Hillerman, T. (2001). *Seldom disappointed: A memoir*. New York: HarperCollins.

Hillerman, T. (2003). *The sinister pig*. New York: HarperCollins.

Ilyenkov, E. V. (1977). *Dialectical logic: Essays in its history and theory*. Moscow: Progress.

Ilyenkov, E. V. (1982). *The dialectics of the abstract and the concrete in Marx's "Capital"*. Moscow: Progress.

Keller, C. M., & Keller, J. D. (1996). *Cognition and tool use: The blacksmith at work*. Cambridge: Cambridge University Press.

Knorr-Cetina, K. (2001). Objectual practice. In: T. R. Schatzki, K. Knorr-Cetina & E. von Savigny (Eds), *The practice turn in contemporary theory*. London: Routledge.

Latour, B. (1993). *We have never been modern*. Cambridge: Harvard University Press.

Latour, B. (1996). On interobjectivity. *Mind, Culture and Activity, 3*, 228–245.

Latour, B. (2004). *Politics of nature: How to bring the sciences into democracy*. Cambridge: Harvard University Press.

Leont'ev, A. N. (1978). *Activity, consciousness, and personality*. Englewood Cliffs: Prentice-Hall.

Lesser, E. (Ed.) (2000). *Knowledge and social capital: Foundations and applications*. London: Butterworth-Heinemann.

Lin, N., Cook, K. S., & Burt, R. S. (Eds) (2001). *Social capital: Theory and research*. New York: Aldine de Gruyter.

Mann, P. S. (2002). Health-care justice and agency. In: R. Rhodes, M. S. Battin & A. Silvers (Eds), *Medicine and social justice: Essays on the distribution of health care*. New York: Oxford University Press.

Meggle, G. (Ed.) (2002). *Social facts and collective intentionality*. London: Fouque London Publishing.

Obmascik, M. (2004). *The big year: A tale of man, nature, and fowl obsession*. New York: The Free Press.

Pickering, A. (1995). *The mangle of practice: Time, agency, and science*. Chicago: The University of Chicago Press.

Powell, W. W. (1990). Neither market nor hierarchy: Network forms of organization. *Research in Organizational Behavior, 12*, 295–336.

Puonti, A. (2004). *Learning to work together: Collaboration between authorities in economic-crime investigation*. Vantaa: National Bureau of Investigation.

Rafael, V. L. (2003). The cell phone and the crowd: Messianic politics in the contemporary Philippines. *Public Culture, 15*(3), 399–425.

Rheingold, H. (2002). *Smart mobs: The next social revolution*. Cambridge: Perseus.

Schatzki, T. R. (2002). *The site of the social: A philosophical account of the constitution of social life and change*. University Park: The Pennsylvania State University Press.

Scott, W. R., Ruef, M., Mendel, P. J., & Caronna, C. A. (2000). *Institutional change and healthcare organizations: From professional dominance to managed care*. Chicago: The University of Chicago Press.

Searle, J. R. (1990). Collective intentions and actions. In: P. R. Cohen, J. Morgan & M. E. Pollack (Eds), *Intentions in communication*. Cambridge: The MIT Press.

Shortell, S. M., Gillies, R. R., Anderson, D. A., Erickson, K. M., & Mitchell, J. B. (2000) (2nd ed.). *Remaking health care in America: The evolution of organized delivery systems*. San Francisco: Jossey-Bass.

Shweder, R. A. (1991). *Thinking through cultures: Expeditions in cultural psychology*. Cambridge: Harvard University Press.

Spekman, R. E., Isabella, L. A., & MacAvoy, T. C. (2000). *Alliance competence: Maximizing the value of your partnerships*. New York: Wiley.

Starkey, K., Barnatt, C., & Tempest, S. (2000). Beyond networks and hierarchies: Latent organizations in the U.K. television industry. *Organization Science, 11*, 299–305.

Tuomela, R. (2002). *The philosophy of social practices: A collective acceptance view*. Cambridge: Cambridge University Press.

Uden, L., & Engeström, Y. (Eds). (2004). Activity theory for organisational development and management [Special Issue]. *International Journal of Human Resources Development and Management, 4*(1), 5–116 (Special Issue).

Vedeler, D. (1991). Infant intentionality as object directedness: An alternative to representationalism. *Journal for the Theory of Social Behaviour, 21*, 431–448.

Vygotsky, L. S. (1978). *Mind in society: The development of higher psychological processes*. Cambridge: Harvard University Press.

Vygotsky, L. S. (1997). *The collected works of L. S. Vygotsky. Vol. 4. The history of higher mental functions*. New York: Plenum.

Vygotsky, L. S. (1999). *The collected works of L. S. Vygotsky. Vol. 6. Scientific legacy*. New York: Kluwer/Plenum.

Wartofsky, M. (1979). *Models: Representation and scientific understanding*. Dordrecht: Reidel.

SET UP A CONTINUATION ORDER TODAY!

Did you know that you can set up a continuation order on all Elsevier-JAI series and have each new volume sent directly to you upon publication? For details on how to set up a **continuation order**, contact your nearest regional sales office listed below.

To view related series in Business & Management, please visit:

www.elsevier.com/businessandmanagement

30% Discount for Authors on All Books!

A 30% discount is available to Elsevier book and journal contributors on all books (*except multi-volume reference works*).

To claim your discount, full payment is required with your order, which must be sent directly to the publisher at the nearest regional sales office above.